Philosophy and the City

Philosophy and the City

Interdisciplinary and Transcultural Perspectives

Edited by Keith Jacobs and Jeff Malpas

ROWMAN & LITTLEFIELD
INTERNATIONAL

London • New York

Published by Rowman & Littlefield International Ltd.
6 Tinworth Street, London, UK, SE11 5AL
www.rowmaninternational.com

Rowman & Littlefield International Ltd.is an affiliate of Rowman & Littlefield
4501 Forbes Boulevard, Suite 200, Lanham, Maryland 20706, USA
With additional offices in Boulder, New York, Toronto (Canada), and Plymouth (UK)
www.rowman.com

British Library Cataloguing in Publication Data
A catalogue record for this book is available from the British Library

ISBN: HB 978-1-78660-459-0
        PB 978-1-78660-460-6

Library of Congress Cataloging-in-Publication Data Available

ISBN: 978-1-78660-459-0 (cloth : alk. paper)
ISBN: 978-1-78660-460-6 (pbk. : alk. paper)
ISBN: 978-1-78660-461-3 (electronic)

♾️™ The paper used in this publication meets the minimum requirements of
American National Standard for Information Sciences—Permanence of Paper
for Printed Library Materials, ANSI/NISO Z39.48-1992.

Printed in the United States of America

Contents

Acknowledgements

We would like to acknowledge the work of the contributors to this volume and thank them for their participation. We are also grateful to Sarah Campbell at Rowman & Littlefield International for suggesting the idea of this volume, and together with her colleague, Rebecca Anastasi, for the patience and continuing support without which the project would not have been brought to completion. Our thanks also go out to Adam Ousten for his invaluable assistance in preparing the manuscript for publication. The project benefitted from the assistance provided to Keith Jacobs by the Australian Research Council's Future Fellowship Award FT120100471 and to Jeff Malpas by the Australian Research Council's Discovery Grant Award DP160103644.

Introduction

On the Philosophy of the City

Keith Jacobs and Jeff Malpas

Historically, at least in the European tradition, philosophy and the city are inextricably linked. Philosophy begins in the city—in the city-states of Classical Greece. This is no accident, since philosophy also has its origins in discourse and conversation, in the free exchange of ideas between human beings.

Yet although philosophy begins in the city, the implications for philosophy, and for thinking, of this beginning are seldom explored. This is an especially important question for our own highly urbanized modes of living in which the city is the context in which most of us live and so in which most of our thinking takes place. The United Nations estimates that, by 2015, 68 percent of the world's population will live in cities, and already in 2018, the percentage stands at 55 (United Nations Department of Economic and Social Affairs 2018). Moreover, not only is the city increasingly the main locus for human habitation, but it is also the place that, even apart from the distribution of population, is determinative of much of the cultural, social, economic and political life of the contemporary world. The world's cities are the centres of the world's decision-making, of the world's economy, of its political, social and cultural development. It is also in the city that many of the challenges of the contemporary world come most forcefully to the fore.

If the city is demanding of philosophical attention, it is a direct consequence both of the centrality of the city to human life as a life lived with and among others, and of the way the collectivity of human life is now explicitly played out within and in relation to urban contexts. Consequently, the idea of some form of 'philosophy of the city' is not just the idea of a mode of thinking that aims to address a single phenomenon set off from others, but rather a mode of thinking that aims to address that which fundamentally conditions the phenomenon of human existence, both in general and in the historically specific context of modernity, the latter being essentially urban and urbanizing. The inquiry into the city thus follows from the character of human life and existence as inextricably tied to place and situation (see Malpas 2018; Benjamin 2010), not only because of its inevitable spatialization and materialization, but also because the being of the human *is political* (a point most famously made by Aristotle in his talk of the human as a 'political animal' [1984, 1253. a2]). To say that the being of the human is political is to say that it is *of* the *polis*—it is a being-with and together, a being 'in-commonality'—and so the city appears as *the place* of human being. The historical changes in the character of the city that are part of the development of modernity thus take on a special significance because they are changes in the underlying structures in and through which human life and existence is formed and shaped. On this basis, engaging with the city philosophically means the opening up of a mode of inquiry that asks both after the nature of the city itself and the modes of life and existence that the city enables. This involves not only what emerges within the physical bounds of the city, but also that which arises in the larger space—within the city or without, materially or conceptually—to which the city gives rise.

The philosophical engagement with the city is an engagement with the fundamental conditions of human life and existence. Moreover, such an engagement cannot result merely in a single philosophical account of the city. There can be no unique 'philosophy of the city' any more than there can be one city that is the model for all cities or for the modes of life the city enables. The exploration of any philosophy of the city must thus be an exploration of the multiple lines of thinking that the city opens up and that are opened within it. And at the same time as the city presents itself as an object of inquiry, although one whose faces and forms are many, it also appears as the domain within which the inquiry into modes of human life and existence, and their contemporary realization, are inevitably played out. The city is both object and field, both conditioned and conditioning, both product and producing. An important consequence of this is that the philosophical engagement with it cannot remain merely within the disciplinary bounds of contemporary academic philosophy (bounds that are, in any case, nowadays, increasingly under pressure).

On the one hand, the engagement with the city *must* be philosophical—that is, it must engage reflexively and critically with that which is fundamental to our situatedness, especially our contemporary situatedness, and to the very situatedness *of that engagement*—and yet on the other hand it *cannot only* be philosophical, which is to say that it must engage with the reality of the city as a social, political, economic, material, spatial, environmental and topological phenomenon. This has indeed been characteristic, we would argue, of almost all of those attempts at genuine philosophical engagement with the city that have occurred in the past—and especially so in the work of such as Georg Simmel, Walter Benjamin, Henri Lefebvre and even, perhaps, Iris Marion Young. Inasmuch as such engagement centres on the city, so it often appears as nevertheless situated not at the centre, but rather towards the edges of philosophy as a discipline, in, as it were, the philosophical 'suburbs' (see, for instance, the varied set of 'classic to contemporary' materials that constitute the basis for the philosophy of the city as envisaged in Meagher 2008). Perhaps this shows how awkward philosophy has often found the city, and sometimes too how awkward the city has found philosophy, but perhaps it also reflects the difficulty philosophy has had in engaging with place and situatedness as such (something partly explored in Casey 1997).

The philosophical engagement at work in the pages that follow is thus an engagement that moves in and through a range of disciplines and approaches, from a variety of perspectives and with regard to a diversity of questions. What draws this engagement together is the idea of the city as both object for and locus of a mode of critical and reflexive engagement with human situatedness and with our own contemporary situatedness.

This volume does not attempt, then, to provide any single definitive 'philosophy of the city' nor to set out the parameters within which such a philosophy might be erected. Such an attempt would already be doomed to failure by the city's own refusal of any such unique systematicity—its complexity, its indeterminacy, the multiplicity of its entanglements all operate against the idea that the city could be successfully subjected to any single definitive analysis. Neither does the volume aim to provide a comprehensive overview of that in which any philosophy of the city might consist—as is the case with any volume of this sort, there is much that the volume does not cover, and many ideas and approaches that are not included here. What the volume does do, in keeping with the ideas briefly set out above, is explore some parts of that larger territory across which the thinking of the city must range, to indicate directions and areas of significance, to give a sense of the breadth and challenge for thinking that the city presents—and to do it in a way that does not remain abstracted or merely 'formal', but connects with something of the reality and materiality of the city in its variety and complexity.

The essays/chapters contained here are thus quite diverse. Multiple trajectories of movements and lines of thought intersect within them, much as they do within the experience of the city itself. Yet multiple though these trajectories and lines may be, they do intersect and often overlap. Many of these chapters take up the issue of the connection between the city and contemporary capitalism—often seeing many of the problems of the city as arising out of this connection. But if capitalism is a recurring theme, so too is the emphasis on the city as always encompassing more than just capital alone, more than just the economic, more than any of the usual phenomena or structures with which it is associated and with which it often associates itself. Indeed, if there is one feature that stands out above all it is precisely the way the city encompasses its own 'other' within it. To the extent that almost all of these chapters do indeed respond to aspects of the city as the site in which contemporary thinking is situated, so too do they stand within similar horizons, responding to often similar problems and concerns. Not surprisingly, the immediate challenges that arise from demographic change, global warming and social inequality are important themes across many of these chapters, and so too are the broader political and social factors that themselves shape and constrain responses to these challenges as well as the forms in which they emerge. Despite differences of geography, topography, climate and history, almost every contemporary city is subject to similar such factors. No city, whether large or small, can immunize itself from processes such as financialization, neoliberalism and globalization. And while city governments have sought to mitigate some of the negative impacts that are constitutive of these processes, their success so far has been limited.

The failure of government policymaking to address social inequality and climate change, in particular, has led to a naïve faith in the capacity of technology to resolve what are political issues. So, for example, policymakers have espoused the smart city and as models for future governance and also fixes for issues such as congestion and climate change. As some of the contributors discuss, the embracing of technology as an alternative response to what are really political issues is a disturbing aspect of our contemporary era. Establishing that the problems of the modern city are inextricably linked to the logic and outcomes of late capitalism is essential if we are to return to the political challenges that have been put on hold. In short, cities and the life of the cities cannot be disconnected from the power structures that constitute the economy.

We cannot escape the political, and the city is inextricably bound to the political in a way that goes far beyond etymology alone. But neither can we afford to remain only within the political. The problems and challenges of the city are not solely political and cannot be approached only from the perspective of the political. This is a part of the reason for our explicit orientation of this volume towards the *philosophical*. Much of the argument, already presaged in the preceding discussion, is that the city demands a broader mode of engagement than is typical of much contemporary discourse, and especially of much contemporary discourse, and it also demands a mode of engagement that is more explicitly reflexive, critical, and that is also, therefore, aware of its own situatedness, and the demands of that situatedness, and capable of being responsive to it. This, we would argue, is just what is at issue in a genuinely *philosophical* engagement (there is a larger argument about the role of philosophical thinking in relation to situatedness as such, and so of situatedness in relation to reflection and critique, that must remain implicit here, but see Malpas 2012; 2018).

Two examples that serve to illustrate the point at issue here in a more concrete fashion are immigration and refugees. Currently, the UNHCR estimate that in 2015 over sixty million people were forced to move from their homes because of war or prosecution, and as many as 85 percent are from developing countries (UNHCR 2018). While most forty million are displaced internally, the movement of refugees to the United States and Europe has accentuated long-standing anxieties about national identity and belonging that have been exploited successfully by conservative populists such as Donald Trump and in the United Kingdom, Nigel Farage. Both Brexit and the 2016 US election hinged on issues such as immigration, border protection, employment and welfare. There are no easy responses that can address these issues—especially at a time when right-wing populists have managed to frame debates in ways that engender new fears and anxieties and inflame old ones. But whatever responses are to be made, they cannot operate simply at the level of existing political debate, but must instead engage with deeper issues about our understanding of the political, our understanding of ourselves and our understanding of the situation in which we find ourselves. This too is difficult, but it is also unavoidable. What these contemporary problems bring into view are questions—essentially philosophical questions—about the public realm, the nature of democracy, the nature and limits of speech, the character of identity and belonging, many of which have tended to remain dormant or that have, at least until the last couple of decades, often been ignored or their answers taken for granted. They also bring to the fore anxieties and fears, as well as hopes and desires, that are seldom made the object of direct critical interrogation or whose foundations are often left unexamined.

To engage philosophically here is to try to engage in ways that move beyond short-term media commentary or opportunistic political response. In concrete terms, and in relation to the issues of immigration and refugees, such engagement might lead us to inquire more closely into the anxieties that are often exploited by those opposing immigration (which also means acknowledging the reality of those anxieties even if remaining sometimes sceptical about the grounds for them), considering the cultural strategies that might ease social tensions in neighbourhoods that have been subject to large-scale development, identifying the reasons why rapid urban change so often appears to threaten our sense of who we are and trying to explore ways in which such threats can be addressed—and all of this against the background of a deeper understanding of the way self-identity is constituted, and also threatened, in relation to the materiality of situation, and of the ways human communities are shaped through notions of both identity and difference, belonging and separation, familiarity and strangeness.

If philosophy is bound to the city both inasmuch as the city is the pole (*polos* in the Greek) around which human life revolves, but also inasmuch as the city is the place (*polis* and *chora*) in which the real essence of human life as collective, and so as given over to conversation and exchange, is founded, then so too must the city be bound to philosophy—which is to say to philosophy as that mode of critical reflexive engagement that is directed towards our own situation, which must also mean, a mode of engagement directed *toward the city itself*. If we cannot escape politics any more than we can truly escape the city, neither can we escape the philosophical—and so we come to the idea of this volume as an exploration of philosophy *of* the city, of philosophy *in* the city, of the philosophical engagement *with* the city.

The structure of the volume is based around three areas of inquiry that correspond to three main divisions: Part I contains chapters that explore the idea of the city; Part II features chapters that consider the landscapes of the city—historical, topographical and experiential; Part III attends to the future of the city and its possibilities, especially in relation to questions of social justice and sustainability. What follows sketches out the contents of those three parts and the chapters that each contains.

PART I
CITY CONCEPTS:
Places, Processes, Structures

One starting point for an investigation of the city is with the *history* of the city; another is with the *concept* of the city—or, better, with the *concepts* with which the city is enmeshed. The latter is the starting point adopted here, and so the opening chapters of this volume take up a range of questions concerning the understanding of the city and the concepts appropriate to it.

Chapter 1, David Cunningham's 'Capitalism, Form and the Philosophy of the Urban', launches immediately into a set of questions about the relation between philosophy and the city, and about the nature of the city that is the focus of such inquiry. Taking up an idea from the work of the geographer Neil Brenner, and drawing on the thinking of Georg Simmel and Henri Lefebvre, Cunningham explores the way in which the transformation of the city in the face of modern capitalism appears to involve a shift in the mode of spatiality that the city exemplifies and embodies—a shift away from the self-enclosed and bounded toward the expansive and the boundless. Cunningham connects this transformation with the structures of contemporary capitalism, but also with Aristotle's concerns regarding the corrosive effects of money on the very character of common life that is given in the form of the city.

In chapter 2, 'The Discourse of the City', Kathleen Flanagan discusses how contemporary ideas of the 'city' have been inculcated by the insidious effects of commodification and profiteering. Among the claims made by Flanagan is that the city can be viewed as both an artefact and a consequence of predatory forms of capitalism. Flanagan points out that while governmental discourses of the city attend to its spatial form and the consumption practices within, there are also features which are neglected (what she calls silences). Her essay attends to these 'silences', for example 'exploitation' and 'the periphery', to highlight the impact on the dispossessed households who live or work in cities. In taking this approach, Flanagan's essay provides an important reminder of the problematic aspects of commodification and the exploitation that follows when governments prioritize profit over and above more collective concerns.

Wendy Steele's essay, 'The City as Wild' (chapter 3), lays bare the tensions between the ordered city and our desire for difference or what she terms 'wildness'. Like Flanagan, Steele seeks to provide an account of the city that more accurately accounts for the features that are absent in much of the contemporary discourse. The word 'wild', argues Steele, is an appropriate one to understand aspects of the city because it encapsulates its unmanaged, inhospitable and restless features. Steele develops her argument by making a contrast with a vision of 'the good city', which subscribes to the idea that cities offer the possibility for productive and successful forms of collective living. As she explains, the dimensions of the good city focus on cooperation and civic engagement. The concept of the good, in the context of the literature on cities, is aspirational; that is, something to strive towards. Steele's discussion makes use of Castells's (1979) essay 'The Wild City' and his focus on the underside that is an enduring feature of capitalist development. Like Castells, Steele suggests that the contemporary cities exhibit all the features good and wild that are intrinsic to capitalism. She also draws upon more recent work by Hinchliffe et al. (2005), which argues that a framing of the city that situates a binary of good and bad is not especially helpful. Instead, they suggest we should view the city as assemblages, some of which are hidden from view and so go unnoticed. Steele also makes the case for a conceptualization of the city as wild because of its incorporation of the wastelands and interstitial spaces that are a feature of rapid capitalist development. In short, her argument is that concepts such as wild have particular value for making sense of this particular stage of capitalism by prising open aspects of city life that are largely overlooked.

In chapter 4, 'Urban Time and the City as Event', Tony Fry argues for a view of the city as a complex metabolic process, one of 'continuous speeding, creation and destruction'. In developing this argument, he points out that our understanding of cities is subjectively formed and therefore dependent on one's own sociohistorical placement. He states therefore that an understanding of the city is challenging because of the unsettled and contingent aspects of life itself. Even what is termed the city cannot easily be answered. To address this complexity, Fry focuses on what he terms 'the city as a designing event' and the dislocation that is a feature of city life. Currently, there are contradictions between the fact that as cities get larger and larger, at some point they become metabolically unsustainable, causing catastrophic damage. Fry asks, can philosophy offer an entry point to engage with these issues? Drawing upon the writings of Whitehead, Heidegger, Deleuze and Badiou, he argues that 'to see the city as a designing event is to see it as a potential, consciously assembled composition'. Among Fry's conclusions are that if we frame the city as a design event, then 'a subterranean drama of appropriation, composition and decay' becomes clear. For Fry, this view opens up the possibility for a more productive engagement with the challenges that surround us.

Simon Sadler's essay (chapter 5) 'The Immanent City', critiques the notions of spontaneity and self-organization, both of which have been influential in urban studies. Central to his argument is that there are two idealizations that inform our understanding of the city, the planned city in which order is imposed and the spontaneous or immanent city in which serendipity, spontaneity and creativity are valorized. As Sadler points out, our vision of the city has oscillated between these two idealizations, and currently there has been a turning away from the planned city, partly in reaction to its association with bureaucracy and centralized control. Sadler questions whether, in a period of rising social inequality and fragmentation, there is value in privileging immanence as a city ideal. He concludes that the insidious imposts now being wrought on urban life require a response that attends to these in bold and incisive ways.

PART II
CITY LANDSCAPES:
Experience, History, Identity

Part II of the volume explores the landscape of the city experientially, historically and topographically, opening up questions of identity and belonging, but also of meaning and memory.

The opening essay by Allan Stoekl, 'Solar Le Corbusier' (chapter 6), considers the link between architecture, the city and philosophy. Stoekl argues that Le Corbusier's intent in his urban plan was to facilitate a rethinking of what constitutes selfhood. In pursuing this line of argument, Stoekl takes issue with the more common interpretation that Le Corbusier's architecture and writings are emblematic of some of the more problematic assumptions of postwar planning. As Stoekl argues, Le Corbusier viewed capitalism as destroying what we value as human. And his buildings have been intended to preserve the autonomy of the individual subject against the excesses of contemporary capitalism. Stoekl focusses on the importance of the sun's light and warmth for sustaining all forms of life. The project of architecture was, for Le Corbusier, to make it possible for humans to connect with the sun and in so doing generate opportunities for self-reflection. As Stoekl argues, the buildings designed by Le Corbusier, paradoxically, in privileging a form of self-reflection steer its residents away from sociality and human encounters.

Katie Campbell's essay (chapter 7), is explicitly historical. 'Escaping Mediocrity: Renaissance Florence and the Rejection of the City' traces the origins of the urban/rural divide through a discussion of early renaissance architecture and gardens in Florence. Using examples of villas built by the city's wealthy merchants, Campbell explores the enduring tension between the imperative of making money and fulfilling ambition with the desire to engage in intellectual pursuits and leisure. The heavy toll of commercial engagement led wealthy merchants to see their gardens and villas 'as places of liberty, in contrast to the city filled with traitors, murderers and gruesome torturers'. Cities represent aspects of our venal selves and guilt while the country is where we can enact a more idealized version of ourselves. And yet as Campbell shows, the view of the country is built on a fantasy. In reality, what takes place in the country 'is largely shaped by urban concerns, its survival depends on urban markets, and its depiction is largely shaped by urban intellectuals'.

Wendy Pullan's 'Justice as the Urban Everyday' (chapter 8) explores the discrepancy between everyday perceptions of justice within urban settings and the abstract legal codifications set up by nation-states. As she writes, 'the abstract nature of justice does not translate well into concrete city spaces and we have a poor sense of where to look for justice inside cities'. For Pullan, it is only through tangible practices and everyday experiences that a sense of justice can endure. In support of this claim, Pullan contrasts contemporary Hague as the location for trials concerning war and armed conflict with fourteenth-century Siena with its localized and small-scale approach to disputes. In showing the contrast between these two cities, Pullan is able to demonstrate that the remoteness of the twenty-first-century legal systems and their failings can be attributed to both bureaucracy and the virtual technologies that now undermine the tangible connection between justice and citizens.

As she explains, 'the replacement of de facto corporations rooted in praxis by the de jure corporation rooted in codes of law led to a greater universalization of urban practice and justice. It also meant that everyday life became less respected and less viable as an arbiter for urban justice'. To address these and similar problems is of course challenging, but one way to proceed is for governments to attend to the democratic values that are rooted in everyday experience so that they can be reconciled with the actual practices of the legal system. In addition, it is necessary to reduce the material inequalities that continue to undermine the lives of many of the city's poorest residents. Pullan's chapter, like others in this volume, makes the connection between the idea of a good city and economic and social justice.

Chapter 9, by Smriti Srinivas, considers the importance of gardens, utopias and radical experimentation in the life of the city, with examples from two south Indian cities, Bangalore and Chennai. As she argues, in the context of South Asia, gardens are viewed as a site to reconnect to the past and our place in the world. Using the concept of 'timescape', Srinivas evokes the ways in which 'we experience other or multiple times in the present by where and how we are positioned in or move through the city'. Srinivas shows that it is the creation of gardens that makes it physically possible for urban residents to contemplate and reflect. At the end of her chapter, Srinivas also considers the value of walking for city dwellers and how the very act of walking enables individuals to experience what she terms 'topographically layered time'.

Postwar system-built housing and tower blocks are the focus of Megan Nethercote's 'A Vertical Melbourne' (chapter 10). Drawing from the work of Stephen Graham's (2016) book *The City from Satellites to Bunkers*, Nethercote argues that social science disciplines have tended to focus on what she terms 'horizontalism', which portrays inequalities and other features of the city from a top-down cartography and horizontal frame of reference. Nethercote argues that it is helpful to see the city more volumetrically or vertically, and her discussion uses the example of the building of high-rise housing in inner-city Melbourne over the last thirty years or so. Nethercote notes these towers often marketed as luxury flats are a feature of shifts in capitalism. As she writes: 'since the 1980s/1990s there has been an historic shift in the underlying structural processes of capital accumulation itself, as the influence of financial capital has grown relative to production'. She uses the term 'asset price urbanism' (Byrne 2016) to show how real estate, banks and developers have become the primary influences shaping the skyline of cities such as Melbourne, London and Vancouver. As she explains in the conclusion, 'the crowding of towers across city skylines signals an important politics of verticality, whereby inequalities are accentuated, and the poor are pushed increasingly to suburban fringes'.

One of the most important figures in the philosophical urban discourse of the last century or so is Walter Benjamin, and it is Benjamin who figures centrally in the last chapter in the exploration of city landscapes. Emma Fraser's 'The City's Other Face: Modern Ruins and Urban Endings' (chapter 11) uses Benjamin's texts as the basis for an exploration of the ruin—both imagined and real—as it appears within the modern city. Presenting an image of forgetting and dereliction, of abandonment and loss, the ruin is present in every city, no matter its wealth or ambition. As the 'other face' of the city, the ruin is both imagined and a site for imagining, at the same time as it also opens up a space for critique. As a form of ending, the ruin enables us to explore what the city itself may be—every ending being a form of beginning.

PART III
CITY FUTURES:
Power, Risk, Value

The final part of the book contains chapters that attend to the future potentials, possibilities and challenges that the city presents—including its potentials and possibilities for social justice and for sustainability.

Saskia Sassen's essay (chapter 12), 'Beyond Differences of Race, Class: Making Urban Subjects', explores the potential for those living in the city to assuage wider global developments brought on by changes in capitalist production. As she writes, unlike nation-states that militarize conflict 'cities have distinctive capacities to transform conflicts into the civic'. Among the questions Sassen asks is whether cities have the capability to resist and transform long-standing conflicts such as racism and class antagonism. Sassen argues there is no turning back to some period that prefigures the current antagonisms and tensions. Nevertheless, she is optimistic that cities remain one of the key sites where 'new norms and new identities are made'. There are openings for actors who are currently without voice in participating in the struggles against gentrification, police brutality and homelessness. Cities are therefore strategic sites in which there are possibilities to resist the imposts that are features of financialized forms of capitalism. Sassen's grounds for optimism are based on her reading of the conditions of the modern city: the rescaling of strategic territories and the unbundling of the nation-state brought about by digitalization and globalization. Cities have for this reason become the key site for social change. The mix of these conditions, as she explains in her conclusion, can generate 'ironic turns of events; but this will require collective struggles. The city is a site that offers our best hope for renewal and hope'.

Janet Donohoe's essay (chapter 13), 'Cities Remade: On Deciding the Fate of Building in the City', identifies the enduring 'tension between the desire to tear down and the desire to preserve' that has been a feature of the modern city. In exploring these desires, Donohoe draws on Paul Ricoeur's ideas of narrative identity and concordant discordance. For Ricoeur, it is narrative that provides the basis for making sense of our place in the world, and Donohoe explores this idea by considering two neighbourhoods that have undergone change: Summerhill and Druid Hills in Atlanta, Georgia. In the contemporary city, Donohoe points out that while we see gentrification mainly in positive terms, in reality it necessitates the displacement of working-class residents. For Donohoe, there are no easy answers to resolve these processes or the tensions that arise. Instead, she suggests that we have to recognize the concordance of discordance or, in other words, negotiate the power struggles and tensions that are a feature of the city. Donohoe's essay concludes with the suggestion that if we can understand the city through the language of hermeneutic narrative, we have greater opportunities to 'give voice and place to much richer and more complex conceptions of who we are and what we value'.

Yosef Jabareen and Efrat Eizenberg's 'The City as a Construct of Risk and Security' (chapter 14) views the city as a site of discursive struggle in which competing political visions of the good life are played out. As they contend, these visions often take the form of political projects that are always incomplete, because policymakers work towards achieving an end point even though this can never be realized. In taking this approach, they explore the increasing risks that confront many of today's urban residents. One of their key arguments is that risk and ontological insecurity have always been features of urban life but technological change, spatial polarization and political uncertainty have accented the threats. As they point out, the city is a 'lacking subject' with deep sociopolitical and spatial implications for the way the city operates and the way we perceive it. So incompleteness is always a feature of our city, and we struggle to overcome this lack.

The focus of Michael Keith's essay (chapter 15) 'Philosophies of Commensuration, Value and Worth in the Future City: Rethinking the Interdisciplinary' establishes how knowledge not only makes claims about the world but also operates as a form of expertise that privileges certain understandings over and above others. In the modern era, it is economic and accounting knowledges that are valorised by policymakers and it is this tendency, argues Keith, that has important political ramifications. How we measure what is valuable and what is not shapes our understanding about the choices we make. In pointing out the limitations and territorializing features of a transactional view of cities, Keith makes the case for an interdisciplinary approach in preference to the market-based logics that remain ascendant. For Keith, debates about how we measure value are thus central to how we address problems that are a feature of modern cities. He draws upon forensic architectural investigations undertaken by Eyal Weizman and his colleagues at Goldsmiths College, London, as one of the approaches that show, in discernible ways, how knowledge practices and methods shape and inform politics.

Asma Mehan and Ugo Rossi's essay (chapter 16), 'Multiplying Resistance: The Power of the Urban in the Age of National Revanchism', explores the potential of street protests as a starting point for more emancipatory and collective forms of politics. They provide as examples women-led protests on the streets of Tehran against multiple forms of patriarchy and demonstrations in the cities of Italy opposing racism. Mehan and Rossi argue that these protests operate as a starting point for a larger project to transform social relations. As they write, 'in popular uprisings, resistance starts as a response to oppression and violence, setting in motion a larger process of insubordination that can lead to life emancipation'. Their chapter illustrates how the contemporary city establishes opportunities for acts of solidarity and empathy—both of which are necessary if new and progressive forms of politics are to take effect. Rather than frame acts of resistance in grandiose ways, Mehan and Rossi suggest it is best progressed through small-scale acts. As they conclude, 'the urban has the distinctive capacity to multiply the effects of resistance on politics and society, turning it into an active force of social and political change'.

Finally, Roger Burrows's essay (chapter 17), 'Urban Futures and the *The Dark Enlightenment*,' considers the influence of alternative right and neoreactionary thinking through a discussion of the writings of the former philosopher Nick Land. At the core of Land's thesis is that society is inevitably moving towards a singularity in which artificial intelligence and biotechnologies will eventually meld with the human form. For alternative right-wing ideologues, progress towards this singularity is being undermined by liberal elites and an adherence to democracy that fetters the workings of capitalism and the freedom of individuals. The project of the alt-right is therefore to attack existing governmental institutions such as the European Union or United Nations to reduce the influence of liberal elites (who occupy what is termed the cathedral or deep state) in obstructing free choice through the imposition of ideologies of equality, taxation and regulation. For Burrows, the significance of the alt-right has yet to be fully appreciated by urban theorists who take for granted the values placed on equality and collective forms of governance. As he shows, alt-right values tend towards neofascism and racism. Central to their notion of freedom is choice and right-to-exit governmental arrangements. In other words, primacy is accorded to individual choice over and above collective forms of organization. For Burrows, a better understanding is essential not least because artificial intelligence is informed by the biases and values of those who establish these technologies.

Neither this volume, nor the essays that make up the chapters within it, aim to provide simple or straightforward answers to the questions, problems and challenges that the city presents to us. Just as there is no single 'philosophy of the city' here, there is no unique or straightforward solution to any of the many problems that the city presents. But that is surely in the very nature of the philosophical: to open the space for questioning, rather than to bring such questioning to a close. In this regard, the character of the philosophical mirrors the character of the city—both open us up to the complex interrelatedness of the world as it occurs in and through the singularity of our situatedness. Yet if philosophy does not determine the answers to the problems that confront us, it also does not prevent such answers. Indeed, it acknowledges that answers—in the form of actions and decisions—are often demanded of us. Yet there can be no answer that is 'final'—that resolves an issue for all time, or that will forever preempt the need for reflection and critique. It is perhaps just this point that the philosophical engagement with the city ought to bring home to us above all else. The city is the primary site of human engagement in the world, it is that which is perhaps the site of our most pressing contemporary challenges, and yet it is also that which demands of us a constant responsiveness, a constant reflexivity and a constant criticality. And thus is made evident the essential and irreducible relatedness of philosophy with the city.

FURTHER READING

There is no well-defined canon of philosophical works on the city, and most of the works that are relevant to any such philosophy include works in architecture, geography, cultural and literary studies, political philosophy, urban planning and urban studies. For readers who wish to explore the philosophy of the city beyond the issues and approaches included in this volume, the following list includes some of the key texts and the most important anthologies.

Walter Benjamin, 2002. *The Arcades Project*. Translated by Howard Eiland and Kevin McLaughlin. Cambridge, MA: Harvard University Press.

Alan S. Berger, 1978. *The City: Urban Communities and Their Problems*. Dubuque, IA: William C. Brown.

Gary Bridge and Sophie Watson (eds.), 2010. *The New Blackwell Companion to the City*. Chichester, West Sussex: Wiley.

———. (eds.), 2010. *The Blackwell City Reader*. Chichester, West Sussex: Wiley.

Mary Ann Caws (ed.), 1991. *City Images. Perspectives from Literature, Philosophy and Film*. New York: Gordon and Breach.

Le Corbusier, 1987. *The City of Tomorrow and Its Planning*. Translated by Frederick Etchells. New York: Dover.

Ian Douglas, 2013. *Cities: An Environmental History*. New York: Palgrave-Macmillan.

Susan S. Fainstein and Scott Campbell (eds.), 2011. *Readings in Urban Theory*. Third Edition. Chichester, West Sussex: Wiley-Blackwell.

Günther Feuerstein, 2008. *Urban Fiction: Strolling through Ideal Cities from Antiquity to the Present Day*. Translated by Ilze Müller. Stuttgart: Axel Menges.

Susan S. Fainstein, 2010. *The Just City*. New York: Cornell University Press.

Hélène Frichot, Catharina Gabrielsson and Jonathan Metzger (eds.), 2016. *Deleuze and the City*. Edinburgh: Edinburgh University Press.

Jason Hackworth, 2007. *The Neoliberal City: Governance, Ideology, and Development in American Urbanism*. New York: Cornell University Press.

Peter Hall, 2014. *Cities of Tomorrow: An Intellectual History of Urban Planning and Design Since 1880*. Chichester, West Sussex: Wiley-Blackwell.

David Harvey, 2009. *Social Justice and the City*. Second edition. Athens: University of Georgia Press.

———. 2012. *Rebel Cities: From the Right to the City to the Urban Revolution*. London: Verso.

Jane Jacobs, 1961. *The Death and Life of Great American Cities*. New York: Random House.

———. 1969. *The Economy of Cities*. New York: Random House.

Roger Keil (ed.), 2006. *The Global Cities Reader*. Abingdon: Routledge.

Anthony D. King (ed.), 1995. *Re-Presenting the City: Ethnicity, Capital and Culture in the 21st Century Metropolis*. London: Macmillan.

Henri Lefebvre, 1996. *Writings on Cities*. Edited and translated by Eleonore Kofman and Elizabeth Lebas. Oxford: Blackwell.

Richard T. LeGates and Frederic Stout (eds.), 2011. *The City Reader*. Abingdon: Routledge.

Richard Lehan, 1998. *The City in Literature: An Intellectual and Cultural History*. Berkeley: University of California Press.

John R. Logan and Harvey Luskin Molotch, 1987. *Urban Fortunes: The Political Economy of Place*. Berkeley: University of California Press.

Kevin Lynch, 1960. *The Image of the City*. Cambridge, MA: MIT Press.

Tom McDonough (ed.), 2010. *The Situationists and the City: A Reader*. London: Verso.

Sharon M. Meagher (ed.), 2008. *Philosophy and the City: Classic to Contemporary Writings*. Albany: SUNY Press.

Don Mitchell, 2014. *The Right to the City: Social Justice and the Fight for Public Space*. New York: Guilford Press.

Lewis Mumford, 1938. *The Culture of Cities*. New York: Harcourt.

———, 1961. *The City in History: Its Origins, Its Transformations, and Its Prospects*. New York: Harcourt.

Frederick Law Olmstead, 1997. *Civilizing American Cities: Writings on City Landscapes*. New York: Dover.

Michael Pacione, 2001. *The City: Critical Concepts in the Social Sciences*. New York: Routledge.

Richard Sennett (ed.), 1969. *Classic Essays on the Culture of Cities*. Englewood Cliffs, NJ: Prentice-Hall.

Richard Sennett, 1973. *The Uses of Disorder: Personal Identity and City Life*. Harmondsworth: Penguin.

Georg Simmel, 1997. *Simmel on Culture: Selected Writings* (includes 'The Metropolis and Mental Life'). Edited by David Frisby and Mike Featherstone. London: Sage.

Neil Smith, 1996. *The New Urban Frontier: Gentrification and the Revanchist City*. London: Routledge.

Aidan Southall, 1998. *The City in Time and Space*. Cambridge: Cambridge University Press.

Henriette Steiner and Maximilian Sternberg (eds.), 2015. *Phenomenologies of the City: Studies in the History and Philosophy of Architecture*. Abingdon: Routledge.

Jeremy Tambling (ed.), 2016. *The Palgrave Handbook of Literature and the City*. London: Palgrave-Macmillan.

Max Weber, 1966. *The City*. Edited by Don Martindale. Translated by Gertud Neuwirth. Glencoe, IL: Free Press.

Part I

CITY CONCEPTS

Places, Processes, Structures

Chapter 1

Capitalism, Form and the Philosophy of the Urban

David Cunningham

In his recent introduction to the mammoth 2014 collection *Implosions/Explosions: Towards a Study of Planetary Urbanization*, geographer Neil Brenner argues that almost all major twentieth-century approaches to the 'urban question' have taken as their 'primary unit of analysis and site of investigation' what he terms an 'entity commonly labelled as *the city*' (2014, 14). If the work of the Chicago School and their influential 1925 'mission statement' *The City*, coauthored by Ernest Burgess and Robert Park, is identified by Brenner as perhaps particularly exemplary in this respect—certainly for urban sociology as a discipline—more generally, he argues, the epistemological frameworks dominant within urban studies have simply *assumed* as self-evident that their object of study should be 'primarily, if not exclusively, . . . "city-like" (nodal, relatively large, densely populated and self-enclosed) sociospatial units' (2014, 14). '[U]nderneath the tumult of disagreement and the relentless series of paradigm shifts that have animated urban theory and research during the last century, a basic consensus has persisted: the urban *problematique* is thought to be embodied, at core, in *cities*', understood as fundamentally and qualitatively distinct from 'a *non-city* social world . . . located "beyond" or "outside" them' (2014, 15).

Brenner's text is one of a series of recent accounts (see, for example, Brenner and Schmid 2013; Merrifield 2013) that—drawing, in particular, upon the writings of the French philosopher and social theorist Henri Lefebvre during the 1960s and 1970s, and upon his vision of an emergent *planetary* urbanization—have sought to argue that, in the face of an increasingly globalized capitalist modernity, the 'sociospatial relations of urbanism that were once apparently contained' within city-like 'units' have, as Brenner puts it in one evocative passage, 'now exploded haphazardly beyond them, via the ever-thickening commodity chains, infrastructural circuits, migration

3

streams and circulatory-logistical networks that today crisscross the planet'
(2014, 16). The consequence is that, as Edward W. Soja and J. Miguel Kanai
put it in their own contribution to the *Implosions/Explosions* collection, 'The
Urbanization of the World':

> More than ever before, it can be said that the Earth's entire surface is urban-
> ized to some degree, from the Siberian tundra to the Brazilian rainforest to the
> icecap of Antarctica, perhaps even to the world's oceans and the atmosphere we
> breathe. Of course, this does not mean there are dense agglomerations every-
> where, but the major features of urbanism as a way of life—from the play of
> market forces and the effects of administrative regulations, to popular cultural
> practices and practical geopolitics—are becoming ubiquitous. To a degree not
> seen before, no one on Earth is outside the sphere of influence of urban indus-
> trial capitalism. (2014, 150)

It is these 'new formations of a thickly urbanized landscape' that have therefore become 'extremely difficult, if not impossible, to theorize, much less to
map, on the basis of inherited approaches to urban studies' (Brenner 2014, 18).

Such accounts reflect a broader concern with dynamic *processes* of urbanization, as opposed to the apparently delimited object that is 'the "thing" we
call a "city"' in recent urban studies (Harvey 2014, 61). And, at a broadly empirical level, among the most obvious consequences of this reorientation has
been a shift of focus from the description of older city 'typologies'—centred
on those more or less 'constant' spatial forms that have been historically understood as characteristic of the 'city'—to a focus on various infrastructural
flows, logistics and networks as perhaps most constitutive of the ubiquity
of the urban today. At the same time, *conceptually*, however, what has been
principally at stake here are, I think, the ways in which, for Brenner and others, the 'city' has come to be constructed as an effectively *transhistorical*
and quasi-anthropological category in urban theory more generally. Projected
back from today into the ancient world of the *polis* or *urbs*, the essential *form*
of the city—'nodal, relatively large, densely populated and self-enclosed'—
has in this way been fixed in place as a means of continuing to conceptualize
the dominant social and spatial character of the urban present. Yet the consequence, Brenner argues, is an effective occlusion of the *history* of the 'urban'
or of 'urbanization' as distinctive socio-spatial logics that, far from being
reducible to or merely extending the form of the city, may in fact historically
supplant and displace it and so 'cast doubt upon established understandings of
the urban as [itself] a bounded, nodal and relatively self-enclosed sociospatial
condition' (2014, 15). As a call to reorient the 'discipline' of urban studies,
what Brenner terms the 'unit of analysis' thus shifts from 'methodological
cityism' (focused on a 'bounded' settlement type, in which 'the phenomenon

of cityness is increasingly universalized as a settlement type around the world') to a new conception or 'vision' of 'urban theory *without an outside*', focused on the 'urban as an unevenly developed yet *worldwide* condition and process of sociospatial transformation'; one that is, formally, 'open, variegated, multiscalar' (2014, 22; emphasis added).

While such an urban theory without an outside may build upon 'various concepts, methods and mappings' from the latter half of the last century, as Brenner makes clear, it is, first and foremost, the work of Lefebvre that constitutes the principal influence, both in Brenner's own work and that of others associated with his project including Andy Merrifield, Roberto Luis Monte-Mór and Christian Schmid (Brenner 2014, 15). Indeed, *Implosions/ Explosions* begins by situating the very foundations of 'the urbanization question' in an extract from Lefebvre's *The Urban Revolution*, published in 1970 but only translated into English in 2003, and closes, too, with one of Lefebvre's very final works, published in *Le Monde* in 1989, the essay 'Dissolving City, Planetary Metamorphosis'.

Famously, the 'theoretical hypothesis' at the heart of *The Urban Revolution*—pitched somewhere between speculation and emergent actuality, or what Lefebvre terms a 'virtual object'—is that 'society has been [or is becoming] *completely* urbanized' (Lefebvre 2003, 2; emphasis added; Brenner 2014, 17). The tendencies that Lefebvre observed in the late 1960s would, when 'actualized on a planetary scale', thus result in what Brenner describes as 'a relentless, if fragmentary, interweaving of an urban fabric—a "net of uneven mesh"—across the entire world' (Brenner 2014, 17; see also 36, 37–38). At its ultimate horizon lies a situation in which 'urban practices, institutions, infrastructures and built environments are projected aggressively into and across the erstwhile non-urban realm, annihilating any transparent differentiation between city and countryside, and linking local and regional economies more directly to transnational flows of raw material, commodities, labor and capital' (Brenner 2014, 17; Lefebvre 2003, 14). In Lefebvre's own words: if the '*urban fabric* grows, extends its borders', such a concept 'does not narrowly define the built world of cities but all manifestations of the dominance of the city over the country . . . a vacation home, a highway, a supermarket in the countryside are all part of the urban fabric' (Lefebvre 2003, 3–4).

In the essay that follows, I want to begin to consider what such an opposition between the 'bounded' or 'self-enclosed' city and the apparently limitless contemporary 'urban fabric'—as a question of the urban 'form(s)' at stake in recent urban studies—might mean, then, for an attempt to think the urban 'philosophically' today. But, before doing so, it is worth sketching out a little further Lefebvre's own appeal to the urban in this regard.

PHILOSOPHY, THE CITY AND THE URBAN

Although Brenner's concern is as much conceptual or theoretical as it is empirical—a large part of the argument of his work concerns, after all, the problems of defining the 'urban' itself and the problems entailed by its more or less exclusive association with an inherited notion of the bounded 'city'—perhaps understandably, he and the various contributors to *Implosions/Explosions* largely ignore, or steer clear of, Lefebvre's own pivotal claim that, in seeking to 'take up a radically critical analysis and to deepen the urban problematic', it is neither sociology nor geography but *philosophy* with which one has to begin. Yet, in fact, in both *The Urban Revolution* and his celebrated essay 'The Right to the City', published two years earlier in 1968, Lefebvre is remarkably clear that, as against the more or less specialized domains of economic, political or social science—the 'fragments of indigestible knowledge' characteristic of what he terms a 'fact-filled empiricism'—it is, above all, philosophers who have truly '*thought* the city', who 'have brought to language and concept urban life' (Lefebvre 1996, 86; emphasis added).

One answer to the question of 'why philosophy?' lies, in this context, in Lefebvre's own critique of a positivist 'urban sociology or urban economy' during the postwar period, which, as he notes, 'present[s] itself as a *counterweight* to classical philosophy' (Lefebvre 2003, 5, 16). Indeed, it was, from this perspective, the perceived need to *overcome* the fragmentation of such 'specialized work and compartmentalized specialisms in the sciences of human "reality"' (Lefebvre 2016a, 53) that largely explains Lefebvre's own vigorous assertion that it must be philosophy that remains the starting point for any urban theory worthy of the name:

> While it is true that the urban phenomenon, as a global reality, is in urgent need of people who can pool fragmentary bits of knowledge, the achievement of such a goal is difficult or impossible. Specialists can only comprehend such a synthesis from the point of view of their own field, using their data, their terminology, their concepts and assumptions. [. . .] The problem remains: How can we make the transition from fragmentary knowledge to complete understanding? How can we define this need for *totality*? (2003, 54, 56)

As he puts it elsewhere in *The Urban Revolution*, the 'urban phenomenon, taken as a whole, cannot be grasped by any *specialized* science' (53; emphasis added). As much to the point, as soon as it 'attempts to extend its properties', he argues, such positivism tends *itself* always to produce a covert and unreflective move from the specializations of 'science' to the more general terrain of 'philosophy', by virtue of its own necessary claim, 'consciously or not', upon this very 'need for totality', since it is, historically, philosophy which has 'totality as fundamental interest for its own sake' (Lefebvre 2003, 64). The result is that as 'soon as we insist on' totality, we cannot so much negate philosophy—as various positivisms might like to believe—as we must necessarily *extend* 'classical philosophy by detaching its concepts (totality, synthesis) from the contexts and philosophical architectures in which they arose and took shape' (63), given the necessity and unavoidability of general concepts as points of mediation between the different specific knowledges of the urban.[1]

Nonetheless, if it is philosophy, as Lefebvre writes, which, historically, 'supplies this scope and vision', this has to be read alongside his accompanying assertion in *The Urban Revolution* that 'whenever philosophy has tried to achieve or realise totality using its own resources, it has failed' (64). Consequently, philosophical thinking (or what Lefebvre sometimes terms a 'metaphilosophy') must be reconceived as a project of totality which nonetheless philosophy as such cannot accomplish. As Lefebvre puts it in the 1965 book *Metaphilosophy*, the 'difficulty' is that 'the notion of *totality* imposes itself. It is indispensable. Without it, knowledge is dispersed; it accepts the fragmented division of labor without challenging it'. Yet 'if we start from totality . . . reflection deduces or constructs arbitrarily instead of studying the facts. It systematizes. There is always a risk of passing from the partial to the total, concluding from the part to the ensemble' (2016a, 51). Philosophy cannot, in and of itself, 'resolve the split [between 'the real' and 'the ideal'] from which it starts' (46).

The obvious reference point here is Marx. Lefebvre begins the second chapter of *Metaphilosophy*, titled 'The Superseding of Philosophy', with a quote from the young Marx's notes for his doctoral thesis: '*The becoming-philosophy of the world is at the same time the becoming-world of philosophy. Its realization is at the same time its loss*' (Lefebvre 2016a, 13; Marx 1967, 62). To be something more than ideology, in other words, philosophy needs to actualize itself in the world, so negating its condition as mere thought or speculative 'abstraction'. This is what, following Marx's own recourse to Hegelian dialectics, Lefebvre describes as the demand for philosophy to *supersede* itself. (Lefebvre uses the French term *dépasser* here, as a translation of Hegel's *Aufhebung* [2016a, 22].) To think totality in relation to a contemporary *planetary* urbanization is a project 'issuing from philosophy but superseding it by definition' (38). What is meant by 'metaphilosophy' partly names then, for Lefebvre, this sense of a self-critical philosophical thought that, in reflection upon and reciprocal mediation with other modes of thinking, both retains its perspective of totality—in relation to a theoretical knowledge of urban form as an *immanently fragmented whole* (see Cunningham 2005; 2009)—and yet indicates and recognizes its own limits. As Lefebvre puts it: 'Totality, to the extent that there can be a question of such, reaches us only in fragmentary form' (2016a, 51).

Much more could be said of this conception of totality in Lefebvre, and of its relation to a wider Hegelian-Marxist tradition. Yet the important point to note—at least for my purposes here—is that such 'fragmentation' is not simply an intellectual, *disciplinary* question concerning philosophy and its necessary limits, but also concerns the (changing) character of the 'world' itself in capitalist modernity. That is to say: if, increasingly, the urban phenomenon itself is, in actuality, '*universal*', a 'global reality', as Lefebvre (like Brenner) claims, then one requires, more than ever, the 'scope and vision' provided by philosophy, even as one must recognize its radical lack of self-sufficiency to grasp this 'reality' fully in itself (2003, 54). As Lefebvre remarks, the question of the urban is one

> which is in itself neither economic, sociological nor political, but encompasses all these determinations and levels. The economic, the sociological, the political as such, as fragmented realities or fragments of reality, each make up a part of the works of social man in praxis. Investigation bears on a totality (broken, fragmentary, contradictory). Besides, it is neither external to the 'real', nor located above what the philosophical method contributes. It bears on the 'real'. (2016a, 39)

To the degree that the *actual* 'totality'—in this case, 'planetary urbanization'— to which 'investigation' is directed, is therefore itself contradictory and fragmentary, at the same time, since the urban has itself become a 'global reality', such totality 'bears on the "real"'. As Lefebvre puts it: 'By the process of growth, the city [and thus the form of 'totality' it has historically named] has itself shattered; it is perhaps in the process of disappearing' (111).

If nothing else, this indicates that (meta)philosophy's *own* relation to a specifically modern urban space must evidently be conceived in a quite different form from its classical relation to the ancient *polis*, which presumed a fundamental theoretical *unity* of knowledge(s) that would organize the city as a totality. Crucially, then, this is not merely a question of the changing disciplinary character of, say, post-Kantian or post-Hegelian 'philosophy' as such, but of the historically changing forms of the urban itself, in so far as 'what is at stake here, "objectively," is a [new] totality', requiring an 'emerging understanding of the overall process' (Lefebvre 2003, 18, 16).

Of course, as was already noted above, that philosophy might harbour some necessary relation to the city, and to our understanding of it, is, in one sense, historically self-evident (see Cunningham 2005; 2008). For, according to what are conventionally taken to be philosophy's classical origins in the work of Plato and Aristotle, if the 'object of politics is the unity of the city [*polis*]', then 'the knowledge that is suited to that object' *is* philosophy. The 'destiny of knowledge and that of communal [city] life' are inextricably linked (Pradeau 2002, 5). Hence, for Aristotle, while 'the association that takes the form of a *polis*', as the condition of the 'good life', is determined as 'that for the sake of which' man is designed by nature, it is, specifically, philosophical reflection that is required for the discovery of how this good life is actually to be attained (Aristotle 1992, 59, 54). As Lefebvre thus notes, for classical philosophy 'the city was much more than a secondary theme, an object among others' (1996, 86). Indeed, in its classical 'origins', philosophy is very precisely situated in the city. So, for example, in Socrates's dialogue with Adeimantus in Plato's *Republic*, an enquiry into the nature of 'justice' must be approached not only as a 'virtue of [or belonging to] an individual' but also, first of all, as 'the virtue of a city (*polis*)'. This is one crucial meaning, too, of Aristotle's famous definition of the human being as a *zoon politikon*—usually translated as 'political animal', but which can just as reasonably be translated as city or urban animal. (Dante translates it, significantly, as *companiable* animal.) To put it another way, philosophy's urbanity is here precisely the condition of its own connection with *social* life, or—in another register—of the 'reality' of a being-in-common and being-in-the-world. It is in this sense that, for the Greeks, the totality (of the *polis*) is 'neither external to the "real," nor located above what the philosophical method contributes', but 'bears on the "real"' (Lefebvre 2016a, 39).

The temptation, then, would be to see the contemporary conjuncture of the urban and philosophical thought as simply an (albeit massively expanded and extended) continuation of this history, as a thinking of contemporary 'globalized' social being as a kind of planetary or virtual *polis* or *agora*. Yet, as Lefebvre notes, for example, in one of his late texts:

> The citizen (*citoyen*) and the city-dweller (*citadin*) have been dissociated. Being a citizen used to mean remaining for a long period of time in a territory. But in the modern city, the city-dweller is in perpetual movement—constantly circulating and settling again, eventually being extricated from place entirely, or seeking to do so. Moreover, in the large modern city, social relations tend to become international, not only due to migration processes but also, and especially, due to the multiplicity of communication technologies, not to mention the becoming worldwide (*mondialisation*) of knowledge. Given such trends, isn't it necessary to reformulate the framework for citizenship (*le citoyenneté*)? (2014, 569–70)

What applies here to the social relations of citizenship goes too, more broadly, for the *form* of the urban itself, which is similarly defined, on someone like Brenner's account, by a certain 'perpetual movement' and by an 'extrication' from (fixed, material, delimited, 'city-like') 'place'. As such, if, as Lefebvre argues in classically dialectical fashion in the opening pages of *The Urban Revolution*, 'urban society cannot take shape conceptually until the end of a process during which the old urban [or 'city'] forms . . . burst apart', it is precisely the *difference*—historical and conceptual—between such urbanization and older 'city-like' forms that needs to be the central focus in considering the relationship between philosophy (as a necessarily incomplete project of totalization) and the urban as they bear upon the 'real' today (2003, 2). Conceptually, this means that—in a fashion analogous to Marx's account in the *Grundrisse* of 'how the concept of (social) labor could only be born and formulated in certain historical conditions' (Lefebvre 2016a, 43)—it is *only* 'in their current dissolution that we grasp what the town and the city were' (44). In other words, the urban presents itself from this perspective not as a simple synonym for the city, and for the ancient lineage it designates, but, on the contrary, as the manifestation of a distinctively modern spatial-productive form or logic which opposes and unsettles it, or explodes beyond its 'walls'.

CAPITALISM AND URBANIZATION

In the first chapter of *Metaphilosophy*, Lefebvre remarks the break between the 'political' character of the ancient *polis* and what he terms the '*medieval city and the project of accumulation* (of objects, goods, wealth, technologies and knowledge, a process of accumulation gradually extending into the constitution of capital)' (2016a, 9). Yet, while in the medieval city 'there is capital' (money, trade, markets), as well as the formation of a '"people" or rabble in the towns' that contains the 'germ' of a proletariat, we do not yet have here, he also argues, anything like either *capitalism* or an 'urban society' as such (2016b, 44). The social being of the 'city', in this sense, remains 'limited to direct, personal, immediate relationships. A certain threshold of social abstraction has not been crossed' (44). By contrast, modern urban form is profoundly linked to the 'generalization of the commodity and logical rationality' (2016a, 7), and hence is defined, in large part, by the question of its relation to '*abstract capital*, a realized abstraction, arising from a specific mode of production' (2016b, 44).

I want to return to this conception of a 'realized abstraction' in a moment, but the initial question raised by this is clearly one of how we can thus understand the historically specific relation between (planetary) urbanization and globalized capitalism as a whole. This is certainly an issue that is at stake, too, in Brenner's *Implosions/Explosions*, and underlies the argument in his introduction that, for example, 'zones of resource extraction, agro-industrial enclosure, logistics and communications infrastructure, tourism and waste disposal' should be properly considered as a part of 'the wide-ranging operations and impacts of urbanization processes beyond the large centres of agglomeration' (2014, 20). (Brenner draws special attention in his introduction to the book's use of the photographs of Garth Lenz, particularly the aerial image of Tar Sands that adorns the cover, as emblematic of this generalization, by contrast to what he describes as the 'strikingly conventional' covers of both the French and English editions of *The Urban Revolution* with their images of self-contained 'urban density' [26–27].) Following Andy Merrifield (2013) in this respect, it is such forms that thus speak, for Brenner, to what may be regarded as a specifically capitalist or neoliberal 'neo-Haussmannization' that increasingly takes places at a planetary level of 'evictions, enclosures and dispossessions' (Brenner 2014, 27). As he notes:

> Marx recognized in his classic analysis of original accumulation (*ursprüngliche Akkumulation*) in *Volume 1* of *Capital*, the enclosure, commodification and ongoing reorganization of such landscapes figured crucially throughout the history of capitalism in the dispossession, displacement and proletarianization of the very populations that so often cluster within large urban centres. The capitalist form of agglomeration thus presupposes the enclosure and operationalization of large-scale territories located well beyond the city to support its most basic socioeconomic activities, metabolic cycles and growth imperatives. (20)

Yet the danger here is that the identification of the urban with capitalist production *tout court*[2] risks an ultimately *empiricist* reduction of the urban to the self-evident proliferation of a built environment of infrastructural architecture per se, which is then taken, in turn, as the material expression or correlate of capitalist globalization as a whole—something perhaps reflected in the importance accorded in the work of Brenner and the Urban Theory Lab to *visual* manifestations (like satellite photography and GIS maps) of an exploded urbanism. It is striking, in this sense, that, by contrast to Marx's emphasis on capitalist *forms* elsewhere in *Volume 1* of *Capital*, what is lacking by and large in *Implosions/Explosions* is any real sustained attention to the historical production and conditions of the spatial logic of the urban or of its *social* form(s) 'in themselves', as a question, in this instance, of the relationship *between* urbanization and capitalist forms. It is this that I want to try to address in what follows. And it is here that the relation of planetary urbanization to '*abstract capital*, a realized abstraction, arising from a specific mode of production' assumes a position of central importance (Lefebvre 2016b, 44). My suggestion, as such, in the final part of this essay—albeit in necessarily programmatic fashion—will be that one key to this lies in thinking the form of the urban as both an abstract form *and* a form of abstraction itself.[3]

Among the signs of capitalist modernity observed by Marx and Engels in the nineteenth century, Lefebvre suggests, were 'the first indications of an immense transformation': the 'factitious, *practically abstract* character of the great modern cities' (2016a, 110). To the extent that this '*practically abstract* character' figures the development of capitalism as a culture of social (as much as narrowly 'economic') abstraction as a whole, it also recalls the work of a thinker who goes largely undiscussed by Lefebvre, despite his own focus upon 'the great modern cities': Georg Simmel, and in particular his seminal essay 'The Metropolis and Mental Life', first published in 1903 (Simmel 1997). Crucial here is less the rich typology of urban phenomena for which Simmel's essay is probably most famous, but rather the effectively *universalizing* forms of social and spatial relations that, for Simmel, the concept of the metropolis is understood to name—and which thereby gives it the apparent shape of a philosophical concept—as well as the underlying *social* logic that he identifies as driving forward such universalization itself: that of the money form (see Cunningham 2005). Suggesting, thus, in one of the essay's two footnotes that his account of the metropolis as a whole might well be understood as merely an addendum to his monumental 1900 book *The Philosophy of Money* (Simmel 1990), it is precisely *money*, Simmel writes, that 'becomes the common denominator of all values' within the social and spatial forms of modern urban capitalism.

Simmel echoes in this respect—or, rather, anticipates—Max Weber's arguments for the primarily economic character of the urban in his book *The City*, published posthumously some twenty years after Simmel's essay. 'In the meaning employed here', Weber writes, 'the "city" is a marketplace' (1958). However, while Weber tends towards an extension of urban man as *homo economicus* (as opposed to *homo politicus*) taken back to at least the Middle Ages, Simmel's use of the term 'metropolis' is considerably more historically specific. A crucial passage is worth quoting at length:

> The metropolis has always been the seat of the money economy. Here the multiplicity and concentration of economic exchange gives an importance to the *means* of exchange which the scantiness of rural commerce would not have allowed. Money economy and the dominance of the intellect are intimately connected. . . . Money is concerned only with what is common to all: it asks for the exchange value . . . All intimate emotional relations between people are founded in their particularity, whereas in rational relations man is reckoned with like a number, like an element which is itself indifferent. (1997, 176)

It is in this sense that, *experientially*, Simmel argues—as the flipside, so to speak, of its overwhelming onrush of images, goods, people, sensations or affects—things in the metropolis come, strangely, to be 'experienced as insubstantial'. Indeed, at its extreme, in the so-called blasé type, they appear 'in an evenly flat and grey tone: no one object deserves preference over any other'. This 'mood' is, Simmel writes, 'the faithful subjective reflection of the completely internalized money economy' (1997, 178).

Importantly, it is worth noting that the metropolis is conceptually elaborated by Simmel through a contrast not only, as one might expect, to rural life or the small town in this respect but also to the life of the *city* (or *polis*) in 'antiquity and in the Middle Ages' (1997, 180). ('The ancient *polis*', Simmel notoriously writes, 'seems to have had the very character of a small town' [181].) To the extent that the metropolis negates the social-spatial form of the *polis* or the medieval and Renaissance city, it does so, first and foremost, on this account, in its progressive replacement of existing social relations with relations of *exchange* exemplified by the abstractions of the money form. That is to say, as I have argued elsewhere (Cunningham 2005), if the metropolis is both 'the seat of', and is thus *dominated by*, the money economy, as Simmel argues, this is not only a question of the metropolis providing something like the necessary space 'in' which commodity and monetary exchange takes place. Rather, it indicates the degree to which a certain abstract form of social and spatial relationality characteristic of money would, from such a perspective, *be* the metropolis's real social 'form'. The metropolis, in other words, designates the universal processes by which both built and social spaces are themselves progressively *produced* by relations of exchange.

While abstraction in general cannot, on this account, be reduced therefore solely *to* the effects of money or the value form (cf. Sohn-Rethel 1978), it is nonetheless the case that, both conceptually and *socially*, abstraction's 'reign extends [specifically] with that of commodity production, with the domination of the privileged *form* that is exchange-value' in the urban as elsewhere (Lefebvre 2016a, 14; emphasis added). Consequently, for Lefebvre himself, as he articulates it in *The Production of Space*, this is 'embodied' by the fact that space itself 'has taken on, within the present mode of [capitalist] production . . . a sort of reality of its own, a reality clearly distinct from, yet much like, those assumed in the same global process by commodities, money and capital' (1991, 26). 'Is this space an abstract one?' Lefebvre asks. 'Yes, but it is also "real" in the sense in which concrete abstractions are real. Is it then concrete? Yes, though not in the sense that an object or product is concrete' (26–27). Capitalism has 'produced abstract space, which includes the "world of commodities", its logic and its worldwide strategies, as well as the power of money', and it is through this space that 'the town [or city]—once the forcing-house of accumulation, fountain-head of wealth and centre of historical space—has disintegrated' (Lefebvre 1991, 53). If the new 'public space' of globalization thus constitutes, as Peter Sloterdijk for example has argued more recently, the reduction of 'all local particularities to the common denominator: money and geometry' (2013, 30)—in which '[e]very place on the earth's surface becomes a po-tential address of capital' (31)—then one needs to understand the logic of this spatiality as it is realized, first of all, in urbanization. For it is precisely here, as Sloterdijk rightly observes, that 'the concerns of philosophy and historiography converge' (14).

THE UNLIMITED URBAN

Marx's *Capital*, as Lefebvre notes in his *Marxist Thought and the City*, 'starts explicitly from a *form*, completely purified (through reduction) of all content'—'a reduction that isolates the pure form of social relations: the form of exchange' (2016b, 109–10). Yet this is not a matter simply of a *theoretical* reduction. For as Chris Arthur has argued, in his own reading of Marx's *Capital*, in 'the "real abstraction" predicated on exchange rela-tions', there is an *actual* sense in which 'exchange [particularly monetary exchange] gives rise *immediately* to a world of pure form empty of content' (2001, 33). Such an abstraction is not simply an effect of consciousness but is 'objectively constituted in the real process of exchange'. Consequently, as Arthur continues, there is a strange 'void at the heart of capitalism', which 'arises because of the nature of commodity exchange, which abstracts from, or absents, the entire [material] substance of use value. What is constituted therewith is a form of unity of commodities that does not rest on any pre-given common content' (32).

One of the reasons why, then, the modern urban problematic as such arguably *requires* conceptualization is because, as itself a realized abstrac-tion, a 'form of unity' that has no 'pre-given common content', like 'value' or 'exchange', it must also be considered as, in crucial respects, essentially a question of '*pure form*: a space of encounter, assembly, simultaneity' (Lefebvre 2003, 118–19). Historically, no doubt, this conforms to the ways in which, as Lefebvre suggests, the city, 'to the extent that it is bound to productive forces and productive force itself, is the seat of the economic and its monstrous power. In it, during the course of history (its own), exchange value has slowly vanquished use value. This struggle was written on the walls of the cities, on their buildings, in their streets' (Lefebvre 2016b, 89).

While, however, in the medieval city this was mediated by and with 'the characteristic social relationships of medieval societies' in general, which 'were defined for Marx [like Simmel] as *personal* relationships, immediate and, therefore transparent' (Lefebvre 2016b, 90), the 'monstrous power' of money, and of *abstract capital*, progressively *de*personalizes these social relations, which thereby become themselves abstract. Historiographically, it is at this point that the urban comes to be dominated, both socially and spatially, by a new logic and form of what Alfred Sohn-Rethel (1978) most famously terms *real* abstractions; or, that is, what Lefebvre himself describes as the 'pivot' of Marx's account in *Capital* that resides in 'a quasi-void, a near-absence—namely the form of exchange, which governs social practice' (Lefebvre 1991, 101). (One should note that this is, of course, precisely how Simmel also describes the metropolis's dominance by the *money* economy as that which 'hollows out the core of things, their individuality, their specific value, and their incomparability' [1997, 178].) Practically speaking, it was via the ways in which, increasingly, 'land and even space itself were sold in parcels' that 'exchangeability becomes increasingly important in the transformation of cities', and in their transformation into 'urbanization' (Lefebvre 2016b, 136). Or, to put it more theoretically, it is the value form, in 'the shape of money' in particular, that constitutes, on this account, the dominant reality of contemporary social relationality at the heart of modern urbanization (Marx 1957, 107–8) and which is its 'primary determinant' rather than 'the content regulated by it' (Arthur 2001, 32; see also Arthur 2004; Postone 1993; Bellofiore and Riva 2015).

One specifically *urban* manifestation of this would be what, in his essay 'The Dialectics of the Negative and the Metropolis' published in 1973, Italian philosopher Massimo Cacciari identifies as the central 'image' of the metropolis that persists throughout the nineteenth and early twentieth centuries, not least in Simmel:

> . . . an uprooting *from the limits of the urbs*, from the social circles dominant within it, from its *form*—an uprooting from the place (as a place of dwelling) connected to dwelling. The city "departs" along the streets and axes that intersect with its structure. The exact opposite of Heidegger's *Holzwege*, they lead to no place. . . . The great urban sociologists of the early century perfectly understood the uprooting significance of the explosive *radiating* of the city. (1993, 199–200)

This of course is very much like what some forty years later Brenner will describe precisely as the 'form' of an exploding-imploding planetary urbanization. But we are now in a better position to see the ways in which this 'explosive *radiating* of the city', as Cacciari describes it, which ultimately displaces and dissolves the 'limits' of the *bounded* city itself, and of its specific 'form', is crucially determined by, above all, the real abstraction of the form of exchangeability as such. In antithesis to the forms of social relationality that governed what Lefebvre terms earlier forms of 'absolute' and 'historical' space, such abstraction apparently confronts no 'natural limit' as regards *what* can be exchanged; an absence of 'limit' with which space and spatial relations are as much imbricated as are, say, 'products' or 'goods' under commodification. As Lefebvre puts it:

> [The] entirety of space must be endowed with *exchange value*. And exchange implies interchangeability: the exchangeability of a good makes that good into a commodity . . . to be exchangeable, it must be comparable with other goods, and indeed with all goods of the same type. The "commodity world" and its characteristics, which formerly encompassed only goods and things produced in space, their circulation and flow, now govern space as a whole, which thus attains the autonomous (or seemingly autonomous) reality of things, of money. (1991, 336–37)

While then, in the *polis*, the 'incomparability' of the intrinsic 'use-values' of distinctive sites remains essential, in 'urbanization', by contrast, specific values of material place are no longer, in themselves, definitive of the urban's spatial organization. They are, instead, *abstracted*; rendered progressively, if never absolutely, *equivalent* in a system of universal circulation and exchange, in a way that extends far beyond the built environment as such. Indeed, we might say, this is one way in which abstraction comes precisely to have a social *reality*, in a form similar but not identical to that of the value form itself. In Lefebvre's words:

> [E]xchange value, the commodity, money and capital are concrete [or real] abstractions, forms having a social existence . . . but needing a content in order to exist socially. Capital inevitably subdivides and disperses as individual 'capitals', but this does not mean that it fails to retain its unity or ceases to constitute a whole—that being a necessary condition of its operation. The *form* persists, subsuming all such 'fractions'. (306)

It is in this sense, too, that, particularly as itself a 'medium of exchange', the abstract space of planetary urbanization also 'has a *social* existence, just as exchange value and the value form themselves have' (307).

What then does this mean for the *form* of the urban itself as opposed to the 'bounded' or 'self-enclosed' form of the city (Brenner 2014, 14)? At first sight, the answer would seem to lie in a paradoxical form of *formlessness*. Cities, Lefebvre writes, 'are being transformed into enormous human conglomerations that no longer have any form. They are called "cities" out of habit. The urban phenomenon is dislocated by its development' (Lefebvre 2016a, 111). Most obviously, 'the uprooting significance of the explosive *radiating* of the city' (Cacciari 1993, 200) produces, in this sense, what appears, first and foremost, as a kind of *endlessness*, whereby if every particular 'place' is rendered speculatively equivalent (and *produced* as such) in a universal interchangeability and exchange, there is thus no 'natural' or 'intrinsic' limit on what can be urbanized. Architecturally, it is this that would be implied, for example, in such speculative projects as Hilberheimer's modernist *Metropolitan Architecture*—with its endless, repetitive equality of the individual 'cell'—or, later, in Archigram's *Plug-In City* or Superstudio's *Continuous Metropolis*, with their visions of always incomplete, unlimited spatial accumulation. It is in relation to this tradition, too, that, for instance, in their influential 2007 *The Coming Insurrection*, the French 'ultra-leftist' Invisible Committee articulate what they call 'the metropolis' as 'one single urban cloth, without form or order, a bleak zone, *endless* and undefined', in which, under the sovereignty of exchange value and securitization, '[a]ll territory is subsumed . . . if not geographically then through the intermeshing of its networks' (Invisible Committee 2009, 52, 23; emphasis added).

How then are we to understand this apparent 'without form or order'? One answer is to note that such 'formlessness' is, again, governed by a specific 'form'. In his chapter on 'The General Formula of Capital', Marx writes that, as against 'the simple circulation of commodities', the 'circulation of money as capital is an end in itself, for the valorization of value takes place only within this constantly renewed movement. The movement of capital has therefore no limits [*masslos*]' (1957, 107). As Arthur observes, Marx's account of money as capital recalls here Hegel's famous conception of the 'bad' or 'spurious' infinite that is precisely defined by an endless accumulation or infinite 'progression', and which is thus not 'the genuine infinite, which consists rather than in remaining at home with itself in its other, or (when it is expressed as a progress) in coming to itself in its other' (Hegel, *The Encyclopaedia Logic*, cited in Arthur 2004, 138). (The appearance of formlessness that adheres in cities' transformation 'into enormous human conglomerations that no longer have any form', in Lefebvre's words, results, in turn, from the sense that, as Hegel writes, 'something only is what it is *within* its limit and by *virtue* of its limit' [cited in Arthur 2004, 138].) But, and particularly as regards the conception of the city, it also notably recalls a far more ancient account; that is, Aristotle's discussion of money and exchange (or *chrematistics*) in Book One of the *Politics*, and in particular, of the threat the latter poses, according to Aristotle, to the *order* of the *polis* and to the proper role within the city-state of *oikonomia* as subordinated to political life.

Famously, this 'threat' to the proper form of the *polis* concerns, for Aristotle, first and foremost, the potential for what Joseph Vogl terms a 'ruinous *escalation*', associated with 'money-making' in general and with the spatial expansion of trade in particular, whereby the *'natural'* limits of commonality constituted by the form of the *polis* are destructively and unnaturally breached. 'The "aberrant" use of money', as Vogl puts it, 'thus raises the spectre of the ruin of the *polis* and its communal form' (2015, 90). In 'the boundless proliferation of money and its offspring, a spectral double or travesty of the natural order is invoked; an erratic movement is unleashed that perverts the internal dynamic driving the growth and preservation of the political organism' (89–90; see also Sennett 2017[4]). In his fascinating book *Money and the Early Greek Mind*, the classicist Richard Seaford suggests that these *unsettling* effects of monetization—'both abstract and concrete, visible and invisible'—are located, in particular, in the 'collision between the unlimit of money and the limit inherent in ritual' (2004, 166). Displacing ritual forms of exchange, the money *form*—precisely as the form *of* the 'unlimited' (*apeiron*)—produces an abstract and impersonal exchange and circulation of things as a competing and seemingly inexhaustible mode of social being. It is this that it is taken up in Aristotle's *Politics*, where the unlimited or boundless wealth accumulated through monetary exchange thus poses a specific threat to the necessary limits of the city or *polis* through which the wealth that is properly adequate to the 'good life' of the political community is measured in its 'natural' end in domestic use. 'Stripped of all personal association, money is promiscuous, capable of being exchanged with anybody for anything, indifferent to all non-monetary interpersonal relationships' (155). The result is, as Seaford notes, a series of 'polarities' that inform the account of the city in Aristotle's *Politics* more generally: self-sufficiency versus trade, goods versus money, limit versus unlimit, natural bounds versus unnatural accumulation (168). Where Aristotle thus defines 'such boundlessness as manifestly unnatural, what he has in mind is, in the first place, a departure from the series of political goals, a rejection of communal involvements and a depoliticization of the political bond. The proportions of commonality grow indistinct' (Vogl 2015, 88).

From the perspective of capitalism proper, the consequence of this is, among other things, as Marx writes in the *Grundrisse*, that money 'directly and simultaneously becomes the *real community* . . . and at the same time the social product of all. . . . The community of antiquity presupposes a quite different relation to, and on the part of, the individual. The development of money . . . therefore smashes this community' (1973, 225–26). Or, as he puts it earlier on in the same text, 'in antithesis to those of personal dependence', the '*objective* dependency relations' of capitalism (as of the urban) appear 'in such a way that individuals are now ruled by *abstractions*, whereas earlier they depended on one another' (Marx 1973, 164). In contrast to the social forms and bonds of earlier, bounded communities, on this account, the 'real community' of money is both intrinsically abstract and formally *unlimited*, and thus threatens progressively in urbanization to dissolve all other forms of mediation or value, or at least to reconfigure them in its own image. As a real abstraction, Lefebvre writes, 'the urban *accumulates* all content' (2003, 119).

Politically, as well as philosophically, it is perhaps tempting then, in resistance to such (endless) accumulation, precisely to seek to re-erect the 'walls' of the city as *polis against* the 'formless' and 'unlimited' character of the 'urban' today. Certainly it is in something like this sense that the architectural theorist Pier Vittorio Aureli, for example, in a series of recent books, suggests that 'the concept of the formal and the concept of the political'—since each 'essentially involves an act of spatial determination, of (de)limitation'—'can be posited against [contemporary] notions such as urban space, urban landscape, and network' and an 'ever-expanding and all-encompassing' urbanization (2011, 31; see also 2013). Yet such calls on the part of Aureli or other thinkers like Sloterdijk for the restoration of 'polis-based immune forces and local civic spirits' can only ultimately seem anachronistic, severing both politics and philosophical thought, formalistically, from the historical realities of urbanization and capitalist development itself (Sloterdijk 2013, 262). Instead, if the very possibility of a 'philosophy' of the urban is not to drift into mere archaism or romanticism, it must also entail a coming to terms with the seeming ineliminability—and, indeed, necessity—of forms of *social* abstraction (and not merely narrowly 'economic' abstraction) to the modern urban problematic. It is in this sense that the problem of how to conceptualize a planetary urbanization raises a question of the forms of universality and totality at stake in thinking capitalist modernity today.

NOTES

1. It is worth noting, it seems to me, that, among other things, this matters if only because the sheer contemporary speed and scale of global urbanization today—of the kind that Brenner and others seek to theorize under the concept of the 'planetary'— has tended to generate what one might call a kind of statistical sublime in much recent writing on the metropolis, from which, indeed, various essays in *Implosions/Explosions* are not entirely free. Whether in the vein of infrastructural studies of the global networks necessary to logistics and financial capital, or of what Mike Davis (2005) terms a 'planet of slums', the tendency to accumulate *data* about contemporary

urbanization as something of an end in itself—starting with the obligatory mention of the fact that we have now reached the point of a 50 percent urbanized planetary population—risks reducing us to a kind of pacified awe in the face of these staggering figures. Yet it needs always to be accompanied by an attempt at a *conceptual* understanding of current forms and processes if we are to get beyond a merely positivist accounting of the contemporary conjuncture, which, in turn, necessitates some recourse to philosophical 'forms'.

2. This was on Lefebvre's own account a problem that posed itself to Marx also. As he observes in *Marxist Thought and the City* of Marx's work of the 1840s, 'the dissolution of the feudal mode of production and the transition to capitalism was attributed to and associated with a *subject* [of history]: the city. The city shattered (simultaneously superseding itself) the medieval (feudal) system by promoting the transition to capitalist *relations of production*' (Lefebvre 2016b, 60). However, by 1857, insofar as it is 'economic force that dominates social relationships in bourgeois society', Marx found it increasingly impossible 'to accept, as he had ten years earlier, the town and the countryside as autonomous concepts and categories' (65–66). Instead, such categories appear as 'subordinate to more general categories arising from features common to every society (production, consumption, and their internal connection, their unity) as well as from features specific to modern society', i.e. capitalism (66).

3. Part of what would be at stake here, today, would thus be the question of how exactly we are to understand the relationship between the universality and abstraction definitive of the capitalist value form and the developing planetary horizon of a contemporary urban theory today, not least as the latter is necessarily marked by those forms of universality and abstraction which have been historically associated with the philosophical concept itself (cf. Osborne 2004). From this perspective, what Peter Sloterdijk terms a general 'marginalization of philosophy' (as a 'quasi-science of totalizations and their metaphors') in discussions of globalization, and, in particular, what he describes as the 'most effective totalization, the unification of the world through money in all its transformations—as commodity, text, number, image and celebrity—[that] took place through its own momentum' is thus surprising, if only because, as he argues, 'the basic concepts of these debates are almost all unrecognized philosophical terms' (2013, 7).

4. As Richard Sennett argues, with some plausibility I think, from this perspective the rise of nationalism in the nineteenth century through to today—and the ideas of citizenship accompanying it—could be understood, in part, as a response to 'the onset of mercantile development after 1815' and the 'unsettling effects of industrialism and rapid urban migration' (2017, 90), since, in reality, the (European) cities themselves 'to which immigrants came were less and less places of a settled "native" population' (2017, 91). As he continues: 'It was under these conditions that the ideal of a national *being* appealed to those who were displaced. Urban migration and its attendant economics was one of the forces which created nationalism, an image of some fixed place necessary for those who were experiencing displacement' (91).

Chapter 2

The Discourse of the City

Kathleen Flanagan

Have we always lived in cities? Even if we have, they have not been the experience of the majority, and nor are they now. The proportion of the world's population living in urban areas may surpass that living in rural areas, but 'urban area' should not be conflated with 'city'. Moreover, the processes by which people who are 'rural' become 'urban', while normalized as inevitable and uniform, are in practice contingent and situated, and always have been, and the places in which they take place are plural, diverse and distinctive. The working title of this collection was *Towards a Philosophy of the City*, but perhaps because cities and the ideas associated with them are so multitudinous and contested, identifying a single philosophy that we might work towards is profoundly difficult, even if we could agree on a definition, experience or interpretation of 'the city', which we probably can't.

In response to this difficulty, I have chosen to examine just one aspect of 'the city': the city as a consequence of consumer capitalism, and to do so using a form of discourse analysis. Discourse, rather than, say, political economy or critical urbanism, might be an unusual way to approach this form of 'the city', but the value of a discourse approach is that it exposes not just complexity, but the systems of regulation and ordering of knowledge that, in the usual course of events, prevent us from easily seeing that complexity in the first place. My approach is derived from the work of Michel Foucault, particularly his book *The Archaeology of Knowledge* (2002). Most notably, within this approach 'discourse' is not another word for 'text', verbal or written. Rather, discourses, says Foucault (2002, 45–47, 54–61, 63), should be treated as 'practices that systematically form the objects of which they speak'. Such objects emerge from particular 'surfaces', are 'delimited, designated, named and established', and categorized and classified according to 'grids of specification'. Their emergence makes available positions, functions or statuses that can be occupied by discursive subjects. Brought together in regularized, specific relation to each other, they enable the existence of 'a set of rules for arranging statements in series, an obligatory schemata of dependence, of order, and of successions, in which the recurrent elements that may have value as concepts [are] distributed'. Compliance with these rules determines the truth or falsity of statements made with respect to them. Put simply: discourses form systems by which we order and make sense of the raw material of the world; discourses make available to us ways of thinking, being and acting in relation to these systems of order; discourse forms the conditions by which knowledge emerges as legitimate, credible and authoritative.

What all this means with respect to cities is spelled out below. My aim is to describe the city as a discursive object and the subjectivities that are available in relation to it, and then, from this, the knowledge that is thereby enabled, the ways it is operationalized into practice, and finally, and importantly, the discursive silences, the things that are not said or sayable about the city. Since a discursive object is 'what [a discourse] is talking about' (Foucault 2002, 46), in talking about the city as an object, I am also speaking about the discourse of which it is an object, and this brings me to consumer capitalism. This is a notion that all by itself could occupy several books—but instead, I adopt the approach of Ritzer and Jurgenson (2010, 15), who suggest that '[w]hether it is called consumer society, consumer culture, or even consumer capitalism is less significant than the fact that all of these ideas draw our attention to the increasing importance of consumption'. In most societies of the Global North, 'norms, values and meanings' have been reorganized around consumption, and increasingly exclusively so. Yet Ritzer and Jurgenson (2010) go on to argue, separating 'consumption' from its corollary, 'production', is problematic: they develop an argument for the importance of what they refer to as 'prosumption' (production and consumption), especially as it operates in digital space.

The particulars of their argument are less relevant here as I am not exclusively focused on the digital city. But their point—that practices of consumption and production are interdependent, even coconstituted—is important. Discursively, consumption and production remain separate—'prosumption' is an arcane academic contention rather than 'truth'—if related concepts. But more than this, within the discourse of the city I am describing, they are required to be separate, for reasons that will become evident below. The discourse of the modern city, the global city, the city brand, the consumer city, contains within it distinct discursive silences, and at a very crude level, production is one of these—the other is the silence of those discursively aligned with neither production nor consumption. It is through consideration of these silences that I seek to demonstrate some of the contradictions that underpin the edifice of 'the city' and to draw attention to the potential for other ways of seeing and doing urban life.

DESCRIBING THE CITY

As a discursive object, 'the city' contains particular elements and associations—the city is, in the words of the children's song, 'hustle and bustle / Living in the city is fun / Cars and buses rushing by, / buildings twenty storeys high / Living in the city is fun' (Donlan n.d.). Cities are 'magnificent and exciting places' (Franklin 2010, 10), more than the sum of their parts: 'the beginning of what is distinctively modern in our civilization is best signalized by the growth of great cities . . . gigantic aggregations around which cluster lesser centres and from which radiate the ideas and practices that we call civilization' (Wirth 1938, 1–2).

The magnificence of cities derives in part from the labour with which they have been produced. A city is 'built'—it is purposefully and artificially created and recreated over time, the tangible product of human ingenuity, of strength and effort and energy exerted, of matter extracted and processed, manipulated and reordered. Cities are frequently characterized using biological language: as 'organisms' or 'ecosystems', implying the integrated operation of multiple, interdependent components organized into scalable networks directed at sustaining life (Bettencourt et al. 2007, 7302). This metabolism is not purely biological: '[t]he urban world is a cyborg world, part natural part social, part technical part cultural' (Swyngedouw 2006, 118). A city's infrastructure regulates, directs and contains the movements of its contents, be they people, cars, things or information, human or nonhuman. Commuters, encased in their cars, are channelled into road networks, over which their movements are centrally controlled by the strategic use of traffic lights and speed limit signs, or collected into train stations from which they are disgorged at timed, regular intervals; random and unpredictable elements like pets or children are contained in designated spaces marked out for 'play'; information flows through sealed conduits below ground or through wires suspended on poles (see Filion and Keil 2017; O'Neill 2017). And increasingly, these complex configurations of the built and material are replicated in the digital domain as such 'hard' means of regulation become digitized and thereby both absent (unseeable, untouchable) and omnipresent (as mobile phone networks and Wi-Fi) (Steele, Hussey and Dovers 2017).

The complexity of cities means they are crowded with people, yet these crowds provoke not intimacy and involvement but anonymity (Simmel [1903]

2002). Such anonymity confers a sort of privacy, in that one's presence in the city can pass unremarked and one's activities, through the sheer duplication of them by multiple, proximate others, can become invisible. However, despite this, living in a city remains an inherently public experience. Cities of course contain private and semiprivate spaces. People live in homes and work in offices and institutions, and they frequent parks, gyms, cafés and shops, spaces to which entry is, if not entirely privatized, certainly contingent on behaving in certain legitimate ways and having certain legitimate purposes. However, in a city, life is inherently experienced and more importantly expressed as a public activity. Increasingly, it is also an activity involving, even mandating, consumption, a consumption that extends beyond the familiar idea of the accumulation of 'stuff' to encompass the consumption of experiences. City dwellers do not just drink coffee—they drink particular types of coffee in particular ways in particular locations (Laurier, Whyte and Buckner 2001), and their choices say something not just about who they are, but also about the nature of the urban place within which those choices are made.

In the city, urban space is aestheticized in very specific, if varied, ways. This aesthetic can be the globalized, homogeneous adherence to a certain set of trends—what the journalist Kyle Chayka (2016) calls 'AirSpace'—or the designated 'beauty' of noted landmarks such as churches, architecture or 'heritage', or the more colourful manifestation of diversity and proximity to the local, the authentic and the 'cultural'. Whatever the palette, however, within the discursive practice of cities the aesthetic is commodified and directed at a particular purpose. In city discourse, a city is a 'destination', somewhere to go, an aggregation of smaller destinations, of stadiums, concert halls, convention centres, museums, places to eat and drink and be seen, and multiple other 'attractions' which can be visited by the one who does the going. This sense of destination is captured in older ideas about seeking one's fortune amid the bright lights, opportunities and temptations of the city (Arden 1954), but it also has the more pointed connotation of a destination for particular things, primarily investment capital and tourists, and these situate the city according to the logic of competition and contestation. Each city is pitted against others fighting for the same attention and patronage and each city must therefore depict itself as the best and only possible destination for those things.

Global capitalism replicates itself through flagships, franchises and a proliferation of mobile yet carefully regulated brands (Klein 2001). In many cases, the consistency of the product regardless of the location is part of the brand's identity (the Big Mac, the IKEA bookshelf, the décor at Starbucks). But for competing cities, ubiquitous, homogenized aesthetics and experiences, while natural consequences of consumer capitalism allied to technological integration (see Chayka 2016), are problematic. To be a 'destination', a city must be inherently and indisputably unique—otherwise, why go *there*? The imperative to offer something different anchors the universal city to the specific and particular 'local' of its own geographical place. Thus the global city promotes itself as the entry point to local food and wine, culture, distinctive architecture, natural features, festivals and sporting events, things that cannot be replicated elsewhere. Such locality also manifests in claims to indispensability—the best, the only place to be for those wishing to undertake particular types of activities, such as financial trading, for example. This is a harder argument to make, because many such activities take place within a place-less electronic realm and are therefore not spatially fixed. So the attraction instead becomes the presence of like-minded others, and the agglomeration of interactions, innovations and talents that will result (e.g., Glaeser 2011).

The global cities of the world, even and especially the alpha ++ ones (Taylor et al. 2009), contain plenty of discount stores, factory outlets and franchisees, but it is not these more democratized and accessible brands that are most salient in the image projected outwards from London or New York. The imperatives of consumer capitalism also drive cities to embrace other qualities that play out in local spaces, qualities encapsulated by words like 'premium' or 'elite'. Pedestrian urban streetscapes are overwritten by outlets for high-end fashion, expensive restaurants, 'gourmet' grocers and other markers of gentrification which cater for the needs and demands of an increasingly wealthy minority of the population—the physical materialization of what Koh, Wissink and Forrest (2016, 30–33) have termed 'super-rich spatiality'. The spaces produced and practices enabled within them are exclusionary and unobtainable for the majority, but they function to push out the limits of individual aspiration (Hamilton and Denniss 2005; Kapferer and Bastien 2009). Ideas of 'the good life' are collapsed together with access to money, and through it, to consumer goods, comfort and leisure (Verdouw 2016).

The language of 'alpha' cities derives from research that has categorized world cities according to their size and influence. Those who have driven this research acknowledge that from such classifications, it is 'almost natural' to proceed to theories of competition and hierarchy, but they nonetheless reject these in favour of a cooperative, 'interlocking network' theory of city relationships which can be measured by examining the economic geography of transnational service firms (Taylor et al. 2009). In this network model, the classifications describe the level of relational integration between cities rather than implying some form of status. Of course, what is 'almost natural' is usually normative; it is not easy to displace ideas of intercity competition or the practices that feed them. However, the basis of this 'interlocking network' theory does point through to another characteristic of city discourse. This is the paradox that while cities are territorially situated (part of a nation-state), some are simultaneously transterritorial, nodes in a globalized economy in which advances in information and communication technology, mainstream access to travel and the commodification of leisure (Koh, Wissink and Forrest 2016) have made nationality and national allegiance less important.

That the transterritorial city is a space free from national parochialism and chauvinism becomes highly problematic as soon as the discussion turns to specific places and times (e.g., Malpas 2009). But the notion persists because of another set of ideas in which cities are inextricably associated with trade, and therefore with exchange, innovation and social progression. Such ideas are more compatible with—and therefore more 'true' according to— the discursive formation that produces 'the city' as a consumer object and a tradeable commodity. Trade, normatively declares the chief executive of the Business Council of Australia, leads to societies 'constantly learning and borrowing from other cultures, stimulating new advances in the sciences, philosophy, language and religion', while economic failure, due to lack of trade, produces 'failed states, and [. . .] conflict, with ordinary people suffering the most' (Westacott 2017). The convergence of financial exchange, innovation and progress in the discursive site of the city makes the city intrinsically directional and future-oriented. Cities progress, and progress is good; 'the country' is static, where nothing happens.

This series of ideas is activated in a series of practices that enable city identities to be leveraged into investment, wealth creation and status by organizing the components of the city according to certain 'grids of specification'. These include the 'organised networks of elements' (Foucault 2002, 47) that constitute technology, marketing and metrics. For example, as people upload their holiday snaps of city life to Facebook, Instagram and Tumblr, they are taking the individual elements of the city object and ordering them according to a particular mode of expressing experience—the curation of social media imagery is itself part of the performance and embodiment of the practice of being in the twenty-first-century city (as well as being a form of 'prosumption' [Ritzer and Jurgenson 2010]). Advertising, marketing and brand management techniques function similarly as a discursive surface upon which 'the city' can be arranged and specified, outwardly directed for the purposes of attracting tourism and inwardly, as part of the self-imaging, marketing and stakeholder management undertaken by city-level governments in order to present a city to itself. Both sets of practices curate reality, selecting, ordering and customizing the city for the consumption of a given public.

The most easily identified 'grids of specification', however, are the proliferating methods for ranking and comparing cities, such as *The Economist*'s

Liveability Index, under which Melbourne has been ranked the 'world's most liveable city' for seven consecutive years (*The Economist* 2017). There are others, of varying profiles and credibility—the 'world's most elegant city' (Paris), awarded by the 'Berlin-based online fashion merchandise store' Zalando (Trimble 2017); the 'world's most visited city' (Bangkok), identified by the Mastercard-sponsored Global Destinations Cities Index (Talty 2017); the 'world's least stressful city' (Stuttgart), awarded, following analysis of multiple 'sets of data', by the 'laundry services start-up' Zipjet (*The Local* 2017); and the 'world's most powerful city' (New York), determined by the Global City Economic Power Index of the Martin Prosperity Institute headed by 'creative city' guru Richard Florida (Florida 2012). The latter is itself a compilation of other indices—the Brookings Institution's Global Metro Monitor Map, the Global Financial Centres Index of Z/Yen (a 'think tank and consultancy'), *The Economist*'s Global City Competitiveness Index ('which includes 32 indicators of economic strength, physical capital, financial maturity, institutional character, human capital, global appeal, social and cultural character and environment and natural hazards'), the Global Cities Index produced by AT Kearney, a consulting firm, and the United Nations' City Prosperity Index which is formulated through consideration of 'five dimensions: productivity, infrastructure, quality of life, equity and social inclusion and environmental sustainability' (Florida 2015). Through layers of self-evidently 'objective' criteria, these metrics systematically define and interpret the city's 'success', while simultaneously producing versions of the city that can be reproduced in global sales pitches.

SUBJECTS OF THE CITY

Melbourne uses the 'most liveable' moniker in both internal and external place-marketing; the Victorian Government statement greeting Melbourne's most recent elevation to 'most liveable' status pointed to Melbourne's 'buzz', its attractiveness to 'the world's best' and the way it features '[t]he biggest exhibitions, the best events, world-renowned restaurants' (Andrews 2017). The government portal providing information for business, investors and skilled migrants uses the 'prestigious' ranking as evidence of 'Melbourne and Victoria's desirability as a migration destination for Significant Investors and other business and skilled migrants' (Live in Melbourne 2017). Invest Victoria (2018) contextualizes the *The Economist*'s ranking with information about where Victoria sits in relation to, among others, its popularity among expats (the *Expat Insider* 2014 Survey) and the Times Higher Education World University Rankings. But a different view was put by the head of the Victorian

Council of Social Service, Emma King, who told journalists that the title of 'most liveable' '[glossed] over the realities of life in Melbourne for many people': 'Did *The Economist* survey anybody who's living under a bridge or skipping meals to pay their power bill?' (in Chalkley-Rhoden 2017).

Yet while the heads of welfare agencies may be called upon, in the name of 'balance', to provide countercommentary in media coverage of the Global Liveability Index, their discursive authority and legitimacy is limited. That is, the subject-positions from which it is possible to subvert the successful, competitive, desirable city are subject-positions from which it is not possible to speak discursive 'truth'. That capacity is instead made available to other subjects. Political leaders, especially local representatives, can speak as promoters and defenders of their city—thus Melbourne's Lord Mayor speaks with discursive authority when he states that the 'most liveable' designation 'is an amazing feat' and 'an important selling point for Melbourne internationally: for businesses to invest or move here, for the best and brightest people to make Melbourne their home and for tourists to visit us' (in Chalkley-Rhoden 2017). Business 'leaders', entrepreneurs and investors, whose presence is used by indexes of achievement as a measure of a city's success, can speak, and have their speaking recognized as valid beyond their own self-interest. Thus property developers calling for changes to metropolitan policy and planning will be discursively situated as speaking for the city rather than for their own opportunity and profit (Jacobs and Flanagan 2018; cf. Clark and Moonen 2018; Bleby 2018; Condon 2018). Outside 'experts' are given status and authority precisely because they are externally situated. Their objective mastery of data and metrics, of indices and rankings, is not contaminated by the local and parochial. Their statements convey a 'widely accepted' 'accolade' while those of insiders and residents are the speech of 'naysayers and whingers' (Chalkley-Rhoden 2017).

Similarly, the unpalatable truths or unanticipated endorsements from other types of 'expert' are received as correct, credible and indisputable (e.g., as in Pryor 2018; Raabus 2010). Such 'expertise' may be deliberately introduced in order to generate connections and relationships between the city and its aspirations—the urban planning consultant or place management expert who will devise a new vision for a better (more walkable, more liveable, more vibrant, more cultural) mode of urban living (e.g., Raabus 2010). Though usually correlated with externality, such as through international university affiliations, this form of the 'expert' can include and overlap with the externally validated but internally situated entrepreneurial subject. The subjective functions taken up by (and assigned to) David Walsh, the owner of Hobart's Museum of Old and New Art, are a case in point (see, for example, Rentschler, Lehman and Fillis 2018).

The positions of 'expert', 'decision-maker' or 'investor' in relation to the discursive object of the city are relatively well-defined. But alongside these more established ways of relating to 'the city' there is a less formalized, less institutionalized category of speaking subject, one that has been established, promulgated and legitimized by the emergence of new ways in which to speak. Social media and the associated proliferation of 'likes', online reviews and user-generated content have enabled new forms of statement that were unimagined at the time Foucault developed his ideas on discourse. The subject that speaks through the Instagram dashboard, the Twitter hashtag and the Facebook page is one which I will somewhat clumsily label as 'authentic experiencer of the city'. It too is an expert subjectivity, but it is expertise derived not from external institutional authority or professional status, but from directly obtained experiences of occupying, embodying and performing city life.

Such democratization of the role of speaking subject is problematic in a discursive context, because discourse has power precisely because it is rare and scarce. The exclusivity of discourse is preserved by certain procedures that control and regulate access to it, enclosing and confining knowledge and its uses to particular statuses, functions and positions (Foucault 1981). It is one of these procedures that is called into play within the discourse of the city to manage the new, unruly proliferation of speaking subjects. Foucault (1981, 61–64) labelled it by reference to 'large social cleavages in what might be called the social appropriation of discourse'. He pointed out that although we supposedly have the 'right' to access any discourse via education, in reality, the distribution of education is 'marked out by social distance, oppositions and struggles. Any system of education is a political way of maintaining or modifying the appropriation of discourses, along with the knowledge and powers which they carry'. Use of Instagram or Facebook to post news and images about one's experiences of visiting or living in the city does not require entry to and negotiation of a system of education, but there are nonetheless forms of 'social distance, oppositions and struggles' in operation. Social media profiles are highly curated expressions of identity and allegiance, but their governing criteria are not necessarily user-defined. There is a small but growing body of research examining the complex dynamics of self-presentation and impression management in digital space (e.g., Hogan 2010; Zhao et al. 2013), including the 'visibility labour' of the Instagram 'influencer' (Abidin 2016), while in the popular media there is considerable scrutiny of the line between the depiction and the 'real' (e.g., Banks 2018; Bowen 2015). Such critique prompts questioning of the 'authenticity' of images which purport to show 'real' life but are in reality carefully refined, filtered and manipulated to show something else. But equally critical are the criteria by which the nature of that 'something else' is determined.

KNOWING THE CITY

Up to this point I have described the objects and subjects of city discourse. But the purpose of discourse analysis is not only to describe what is there but to identify how the relations that are established among subject(s) and object(s) enable certain ways of knowing and give certain things the status of 'truth'. So what is 'knowable' within the discourse of the city? In this section of the chapter, I identify three things about the city that are made knowable by the discursive formation within which it is situated and which are, in the discourse of the city, considered 'true'. Crucially, 'true' in this context does not mean 'right'. What is at stake here is not whether it is objectively correct to say a given thing about the city; rather, the emphasis is on how, within the discourse of the city, certain forms of knowledge are produced and validated, while other kinds are closed off and rendered less inaccessible. This is impor-tant because such a state of affairs produces consequences that are distributed among people and places in uneven ways.

Knowledge 1: The City Is Independent

When the Lord Mayor of Melbourne speaks of Melbourne's liveability, he speaks of Melbourne, not of the state of Victoria or the nation of Australia. It is not Victorians or Australians who 'should be extremely proud of today' but 'Melburnians'. This may be natural—the mayor is elected by Melburnians to govern the geographical location of Melbourne—but it is also inherently enabled by a discursive formation in which it is the city that is the source of authentic experience—not the nation, not the region, not, in most cases, the suburbs. It is the city within which experiences, events and spectacles are lo-cated, it is the city within which a particular lifestyle is available, it is the city to which investment, people and products are to be attracted. As cities aspire to—and attain—the status of being a 'global' or 'world' city, they aspire to exist beyond the national boundaries within which they are located and also to exist in spite of them.

Some writers, such as Catherine Fennell (2015), have linked this to the retreat of the welfare state, arguing that as both the ideal and operation of na-tionally funded, universally provided social security is eroded, the provision of social care is inevitably localized because the consequences—poverty, homelessness, crime—are most observable and felt at the local level. To create an environment within which such care can be extended, cities have to cultivate an identity that is municipal rather than regional or national. Of course, in many countries such a trend, if it exists, coexists with resurgent nationalist sentiments that explicitly reject claims to global connectivity, cosmopolitanism and diversity for their elitism, ethnic complexity and disconnection from the lives of 'real' people (see Malpas 2009). But this does not destabilize the discourse of the global city, because both city discourse and parochial nationalism affirm compatible identities for the city, albeit it for different reasons—whether the city is dissociated from the nation or transcends the nation, the city is different, separate and distinct.

Knowledge 2: The Outsider Is Better

The identity of a 'place', especially one with cultural, historical or aesthetic significance, is jointly constituted by the external gaze of the tourist and the place-attachment of the residents (Bernardo, Almeida and Martins 2017). But the discourse of the city does not situate both equally. Instead it privileges the regard of the tourist, the outsider-expert and the metric over the views of residents. In a globalized world, where there is 'tension within local places between searching out ever wider spheres of exchange and movement and simultaneously provoking an inward and deliberate search for authenticity, a conscious effort to evoke a sense of place and cultivate connections' (Williams 2002, 357), the discourse of the city which I am describing here takes sides.

Of course, the claims of locally situated subjects are not unproblematic— as Williams (2002, 352) notes in the context of the American West, 'who counts as a "local" and [. . .] what it means to be a local or an old-timer is problematic and often contested', given the history of itinerancy and mobility, the hierarchies set in place as a result of uneven access to wealth and property, and forced dispossession of the Indigenous people in that and other parts of the world (see also Rogers 2017). But within the discourse of the city that I am describing here, the subject-position of outsider-expert has greater authority than that of a 'resident' because of the different ways in which each is situated in relation to the object of the 'local'. For the latter, the 'local' is a contaminant—it makes them parochial and self-interested. For the former, 'local' is desirable: a conduit or entry point for outsiders looking to share what is 'local' as if they were locals themselves. This internationalizes the local, rather than protecting it, preserving it or keeping it secret. Local is valued only to the extent that it is globally accessible.

In practical terms, this means that local actors who, for example, oppose a new development on the grounds that it will change the existing character of the city will be cast into the subject-position of 'NIMBYs' or similar oppositional space. The 'NIMBY' (not in my backyard) is a caricature that has been extensively problematized (e.g., Wolsink 2006; Freudenburg and Pastor 1992; Wexler 1996), but it remains effective, partly because it is a moral label, applied to those who unreasonably object to socially necessary developments, such as safe storage of nuclear waste (Welsh 1993), affordable housing (Ruming 2013) or services for low-income households (Dear 1992; Gleeson and Memon 1994; Takahashi and Dear 1997), including mass transit (Weitz 2008). That is, the motivations of the NIMBY are easily attributed to the NIMBY's selfish and even ignorant regard for their own interests ahead of the collective needs of society (Lidskog and Elander 1992; Lake 1993) and at the expense of vulnerable groups (Gerrar 1994). The locally situated subject who seeks to resist local development becomes enmeshed in this charge of uncaring selfishness by association.

With regard to the discourse of the city, however, what becomes problematic is that NIMBYs are essentially arguing against change. Such arguments are inimical because the successful city is defined by its commitment to aspiration, progress and innovation; to the extent that they enable these things, tourist infrastructure, residential density and commercial redevelopment, however radically they rewrite the built and natural environments, become social necessities. This does not mean there is no space for resistance within the discourse, but those who wish to resist must appropriate elements of the city discourse to make their case in terms that are considered 'true'. For example, opposition can be successful if framed as a desire to ensure the city remains an attractive destination—that is, by remaining outwardly oriented—but it cannot be discursively legitimate if directed at decreasing the city's attractiveness to outsiders.

Knowledge 3: The City Must Compete

Academics may argue that competition is not the only way to read practices which classify and rank cities against each other (Taylor et al. 2009) but such calls carry little weight; competition is positioned as desirable and productive in many fields of human activity, and it is therefore entirely 'natural' in relation to the global city. But discursively, the configuration of object (the city) and subjectivities (the privileged expert, the political advocate, the entrepreneur) direct competitive expression in particular ways. Cities are places of excitement, innovation and activity, and thus cities compete to be exciting, innovative and active places. Cities are places where change is constant and valorized as a sign of open-mindedness, progress and technical prowess, and thus cities must embrace change to be successful competitors. Cities are destinations for the 'best' and therefore the experiences, goods and services on offer from competitive cities must be imbued with that quality, either due to rarity and exclusivity (to a place, to a certain kind of access), or value (cultural or economic), and preferably both. Cities are stages for a particular way of occupying urban space and thus successful cities must offer their residents and even more particularly their visitors a lifestyle that is compatible with city norms. Individual cities are the 'world's most' (insert: innovative, liveable, exciting, successful), and thus their activities are disciplined and directed by the configuration of variables in the various indexes, metrics and league tables which measure these qualities. To be such a city is a ubiquitous aspiration, but the point of aspiring to it is to be the only one.

CITY PRACTICE

Discourse, I argued above, is a set of 'rules' conditioning the production of truth. But truth on its own is not all there is to it. Discourse is articulated, expressed and put into effect through discursive practice, a form of 'thinking and doing' (Florence 1998, 463) which lies at the intersection between what is said (and known) and 'what is done' (Foucault 1991, 75). Drawing on Foucault, Reckwitz (2002, 250) defined 'practice' as 'a routinized way in which bodies are moved, objects are handled, subjects are treated, things are described and the world is understood [. . .] a "type" of behaving and understanding that appears at different locales and at different points of time and is carried out by different body/minds'.

In the discourse of the city, the primary way of thinking and doing, behaving and understanding is the urban 'lifestyle', a set of activities that are articulated and enabled through advertising, urban planning and popular culture, with disciplinary effects on discursive subjects. Lifestyle is performative and thus outwardly oriented, although at the level of the individual, practices may also be internalized and embodied. Importantly, 'lifestyle' is enabled by a certain kind of urban environment and inhibited by others. Lifestyle requires specific types of gathering places—cafés, bars, festivals—and these places are usually predicated on consumption of some kind. Lifestyle requires private space to be configured for public cultural display (the outfitting of rooms in the home for 'entertaining', the always-completed of landscaping rather than the work-in-progress of gardening). Lifestyle requires the provision of other facilities within which associated activities can take place—consumption of goods and services that are symbolically compatible with the city, which offer access to fashion, status and creativity. Thus 'lifestyle' and the discursive object and associated subjectivities of the city are interdependent; the former is the articulation and operationalization of the latter.

Lifestyle also excludes. The habitus of café culture acts to regulate and homogenize ways of being in public, both indirectly, through implicit social sanctioning of behaviour, dress or mannerisms that do not 'fit', and directly, through the efforts of proprietors to police the streetscape in order to protect their customers from unpleasant or uncomfortable sights that might detract from the quality of their experience. Thus gatherings of patients waiting for their daily pharmacotherapy treatment outside a local pharmacy become, in the view of traders overseeing pavement tables in the adjacent gentrified café strip, 'gang-like conversions' that are 'threatening' to patrons (see Duncan 2007).

Other, more technical modes of practice arise from the discourse of the city. 'City branding' is an assembly of professional expertise, knowledge production and governance techniques articulated on multiple platforms, including the promotional activities of the 'authentic experiencer', advertising, marketing campaigns, the replanning and rewriting of physical and cultural landscapes and the ritualized performances of exhibitions and promotional events. The 'fictive spectacle' (Boland 2013) thus crafted speaks to outsiders of a city's authenticity and identity but it simultaneously 'imposes' upon insiders a particular, 'frozen' version of the city that, while offering opportunities through which to display, preserve and express the value of local customs, culture and history, may simultaneously iron away fine local distinctions, historical tensions and socioeconomic grievance (see also Ooi 2011).

City branding responds to the 'true' fact of competition: cities are 'compelled' to 'establish a competitive, cosmopolitan identity in the contemporary world [. . .] to bring their "information flows" [. . .] in line with an urban population that is multicultural, mobile and frequently transient [. . .] [and] become part of those new linkages that bind them across national borders' (Paganoni 2012, 14). But if cities are competing against other cities, then both their engagement within the competition and their success or failure at it need to be demonstrable in some way. Thus the correlating practice of city branding is the practice of city ranking and indexing. Similarly complex, opaque and multiplatform, it simultaneously legitimizes the process of branding and regulates it.

The link that brings the urban lifestyle and the intercity competition into relation with each other is the practice of urban redevelopment. Spatial planning, argues Boland (2013, 269), has been co-opted as 'a significant accessory to the sophistry of city branding', and in allowing this to happen, spatial planners have become complicit in concealing, even ignoring, 'the acute social and economic malaise that scars large parts of our major cities'. This is a practice by which the built environment is rewritten to facilitate the city 'lifestyle'. Because this lifestyle is a highly urbanized one, because concentration and proximity of a diversity of experiences is central to it, this reconfiguring of the urban landscape involves the proliferation of hotels and apartment complexes, recreational opportunities and forms of retail and commercial space that enable and promote city-compatible forms of consumerism (Boland 2013). But the practice of urban redevelopment is directed at more than summoning outsiders. Branding may be 'principally about sexing up the city in the international beauty contest for investment, tourism, events, shoppers and new residents' (269), and it may colonize planning and development processes to achieve this, but it is also internally directed at targeting, classifying and reorganizing city residents.

That is, although in its effects the result of such redevelopment looks very like gentrification, alongside displacement that arises at a distance (because of 'the market' and its 'rising house prices' which 'price out' existing residents and consign them to other, less 'well-located' areas, to recite the usual explanation) come other strategies designed to more directly cleanse the city of that which is incompatible with it. Boland (2013) notes the emphasis on security and the social profiling activities which accompanied the regeneration and rebranding of Liverpool. In the same category are periodic 'crackdowns' on so-called 'rough sleepers' and the relocation of services that might attract unsightly clientele, like needle exchanges, pharmacotherapy services or homeless shelters, to less visible or populous areas. There are modifications to the built environment, such as so-called 'defensive' street furniture (also called 'hostile architecture')—seating purposefully designed to be incompatible with any use other than sitting, thereby preventing people using it to sleep on, or modifications to surfaces, such as edgings or spikes, to prevent people using them for skateboarding or for rest. Such changes represent 'the intentional "designing out" of certain identities, behaviours and categories of people from urban and public spaces' (Petty 2016, 68), and the crafting, instead, of 'an idealised and sanitised version of urban life' in which consumption is unimpeded, the unpredictable and unexpected have been 'disciplined', and architecture and urban design have been used to privatize the public sphere (Sandercock 1997, 30; also Coleman, Tombs and Whyte 2005).

However, the 'constructed aesthetic' (Petty 2016, 75) of the city depends for its legitimacy on more than just the facilitation of gentrification and the removal of rogue elements. Cities are also defined by their openness, their diversity and their cultural colour. These qualities are also appropriated into the practice of city 'planning' and rearticulated into certain genres of discursive knowledge, such as the glossy, high-concept community 'vision' that will convert an ordinary city into something significant (e.g., Gehl Architects 2010). They can also find their expression in a domestic form of city branding practice, through the commodification of cultural experiences—festivals, the use of street-art aesthetics, the 'pop-up'—which function as tangible demonstrations of the promise on offer within the city brand.

SILENCE IN THE CITY

Finally, in the city, as in many places, there are things that are not said. Such silences point to the possibilities and forms of knowledge that are not available within a given discursive formation, which are rendered as 'not true' by the rules of the discourse and which, if articulated and recognized, would make the formation unstable. There are two silences in the discourse of the city which I want to highlight here.

Silence 1: Exploitation

Contemporary urban life emerged from agrarian and feudal societies via a series of processes, collapsed under the term 'industrialization', which converted coal, gas and oil into energy and applied it to increasing the speed of communication and the mobility of people, products and information (Watson 1993, 3–4; Giddens 2009, 217–21). This much, of course, is not silent, although the normative interdependencies this narrative creates and maintains between 'the city', 'the modern' and Western history have been problematized, including for the ways in which they silence and limit theories and knowledge of the urban (Robinson 2013; Leontidou 1996) and the sociological (Connell 1997). We generally accept that the global city is possible only because people, things and knowledge can be extracted from different parts of the globe, assembled, disassembled, moved about and then reassembled at the site of their consumption, albeit in constantly shifting and irrepressibly mobile configurations. We see this as exciting and positive: it is to our benefit that there are now 'global supply chains in which Australian businesses— big and small—can find new customers and source productivity-boosting products from almost anywhere in the world, growing their companies and expanding the tax base that underpins the social safety net' (Westacott 2017).

But the chains of production and manufacture that underpin this mobility, and which produce the technical hardware, freight and migration that renders it all workable, are rooted in the Global South. Coffee, so central to so much city 'lifestyle', has a provenance that is inextricably entangled with the exploitation of and extraction from the Global South that began with colonization and continues today (Brockway 1983; Connell 2007; Rogers 2017). The link between rich and poor established by the chain of transactions leading from coffee plantations to café tables is itself evidence of the sustained and untenable global inequality generated and sustained by consumer capitalism. Further, many of the essential artefacts of modern life are constructed from resources that are limited and extracted in ways that cause unevenly distributed environmental and social harm (Klein 2001; 2014). The claim is that by bringing such conveniences to ever-widening audiences of consumers, capitalism is driving global improvements in living standards and quality of life and lifting people out of poverty. Yet if these are the ends, then the means are problematic, if for no other reason than universal attainment of the normative 'lifestyle' would bring discourse crashing into the limits of nondiscursive reality. (Bluntly put, there is simply not enough of anything—or if there is, the cost of extracting and exploiting it to full capacity would be unacceptably high—for the entire planetary population to live according to the ideal of the modern city.) This is the silence: the city, or at least, the city I am describing, is a product of consumer capitalism which rests upon a system of global relations that are exploitative, inequitable and unsustainable.

This is the case even within the city itself. The 'precariat' is a term used to refer to the growing segment of the working population structurally compelled to contingent, insecure and fragmented labour—people without access to the stable, regulated, adequately remunerated and fulfilling work which was the ideal of the social democratic, labour and trade union movements in the postwar period (Standing 2014). The visual image associated with the term is of a tenuous grip at the edge of a great height—of clinging, barely, to life. It is one of marginality and periphery. This visualization is a persistent one, despite the fact that the urban precariat exists in the very heart, physically, of the city. It is the precariat who clean the high-rise offices and drive their occupants to the airport. They are the childcare workers and disability support workers who tend to the bodies of the most vulnerable. They collect the sanitary bins from the women's toilet, sell petrol and chewing gum and wipe down the tables in the food court.

These two aspects of inequality intersect within the even greater silence on which contemporary processes of manufacture and production rest: colonialism, which made industrialization, and then postindustrialization, possible, but which is rarely acknowledged as a contemporary reality. It both enabled and depended upon the extraction and removal of mineral and agricultural wealth—and the labour with which to work it—from the colonies. The scientific disciplines which shaped modernity, such as cartography, biology, botany and astronomy among others, fed off raw material and data obtained without consent from the South (see Seth 2009; Connell 2007). The economies of colonial powers rested on multiple layers of violence: the violent invasion of occupied lands, slavery, penal transportation (Reynolds 2006; Hochschild 2005; Hughes 1996). All of this is known, and alleged to be in the past, but it isn't—it is unpalatable but accurate to say that the present distribution of wealth and status across the globe rests as much on these mechanisms of dispossession, land-claiming and violence as do injustices of the past (Rogers 2017).

The day-to-day social practices of everyday city life are rendered possible and pleasurable by these mechanisms but simultaneously depend on
them remaining invisible. Clearly 'invisible' is not meant literally. We know
about these things but not in ways that would make our current way of life
untenable. Our knowledge is instead made bearable because, discursively, it
is managed through the deployment of the anonymized subjectivity of a distant, unreachable 'them'. 'They' are victims of exploitative labour practices,
poverty and our own complicity in supporting the vast, unsustainable edifice
of cheap manufacturing, planned obsolescence and endless consumption.
'They' are helpless and valorized and cried over. But they are also denied individuality and agency—if they express resistance, it must be within confines
and expectations established by 'us', and if they express acquiescence, this
is simply an extended performance of their initial victimhood. And although
boycotts, fair trade campaigns and shareholder activism do try at various levels to draw back the veil of silence covering the global chains of manufacture
and production and the injustices that they create and perpetuate, the effect
is to further direct the gazes of those of us in the former colonies away from
ourselves and therefore away from the injustices created and perpetuated by
colonization. The idea that the lifestyle encapsulated in the act of drinking a
sustainably sourced, fairly traded latte in an inner-city hipster café in Sydney
or Melbourne (or Los Angeles or Miami, or Toronto or Christchurch or Rio
de Janeiro) is only possible because the land upon which the café stands was
violently wrested from its original, resisting occupants is unpalatable, even
preposterous. Why would one talk about land rights and suburbia in the same
sentence (unless doing so, as some Australian politicians did in the wake of
the Australian High Court's Mabo land decision, for the purposes of hyper-
bole and scare-mongering [in Fryer-Smith 2000, 35n5])?

The subjectivity of 'them' is increasingly enmeshed with the subjectivity
of the precariat. This is because 'they' are able to be mobile and therefore to
come to 'us' and be the taxi drivers, cleaners and security guards of the global
city (Sassen 1996, 2002; May et al. 2007). The precariat-subject brings together memories of the proletariat of Northern industry—the factory workers
who lived the squalor of industrial urbanization—and the modern exploitation of Southern sweatshops, piece work and pressure. The precariat identity
is, especially in large cities, very much a migrant one.[1] 'Their' presence in
'our' midst is made thinkable and doable because the migrant-precariat is a
moralized subjectivity—it takes on thankless jobs in the service economy
and exists on the fringes of the modern city, aspires to better, and makes
sacrifices in the hope of change. 'Aspiration' means, in dictionary terms, a
lofty or ambitious desire, but in discursive terms, it is a positive and desirable attribute held by docile subjects. Being 'aspirational' is to align with

governmental dictates that we regulate, improve and govern ourselves according to normative goals of home ownership, wealth, influence and social mobility. To desire something lofty and ambitious but not normative, such as knowledge disconnected from status or prestige or spiritual fulfilment, might be admirable, but it is not 'aspiration'.

Silence 2: The Periphery

As has been made clear, the city is marked by inequality, and frequently, this inequality is spatially distributed—in some parts of the city there is extreme wealth while in other parts there is dire poverty. But beyond this dichotomy, there are parts of a city that can be defined principally by their being 'not the city', at least, not the city of the city brand. These places are the suburban scars (Baum 2008) of deprivation, social exclusion and 'concentrated disadvantage'. They are, depending on one's political orientation, the collateral damage wreaked by economic restructuring, the victims of an eroding social safety net, or the product of indulgent overgovernment. If the city is an entity detached from its national and regional context, as argued above, then similarly, the city is rarely conceptualized as including those spaces in any city that are automatically, unattractively and tediously poor.

These places are broadly speaking an outcome of the postwar welfare state (although the precise sequence of causal factors varies according to the politics of the speaker). Many of them are the visible remnants of a postwar agenda in which the construction of housing for a social purpose was considered a core function of government. However, they are also fundamentally inconsequential in that the taken-for-granted history of the emergence of the city (industrialization, urbanization, suburbanization, re-urbanization, globalization) could have happened without them. Today, the projects, council estates and broadacres do not have a function in the aspirational, branded, destination city.

I will call these areas 'ghettos'. This is not because I think they are ghettos but because I need a term that encapsulates the way in which they are objectified—talked of—in this particular discourse. 'Ghetto', especially in contemporary usage, is a word that implies isolation, disadvantage and hopelessness in an urban context. The ghetto is a constellation of ideas: dependency (on welfare, the state, each other), the 'culture of poverty', immobility (in the sense both of individuals being 'trapped' in poverty and of a general lack of change and dynamism) and crime. It reclaims material out of the past, in this case, through the claim that these areas were once quite different—springboards for opportunity rather than traps of poverty and exclusion (Flanagan 2015a). That this 'springboard' was once conceptualized as centred upon the house itself—as opportunity within the dwelling—is overlooked; now, it is the need to remain in the dwelling, the immobility and inflexibility of the subsidy-tied-to-the-dwelling, which is the source of the dependency 'trap' (Flanagan 2015b).

The ghetto exists as an object within its own discursive formation—one which activates its own subjectivities and produces its own knowledge which is then enacted in its own discursive practices. It is not my intention to detail these here—rather, I want to emphasize one aspect of the ghetto which is significant to the discourse of the city. This is that, unlike the city, which is predicated on movement and change, the ghetto is static. This is partly because by its nature, aspiration and change are precluded. The ghetto is perpetual ('the poor are always with us'), excised (these are locations where outsiders do not go and are not brought to serendipitously—their existence rests on a lack of proximity) and hopeless ('a hopeless case'). Hope is about the future; the future does not exist for the ghetto, and therefore, by extension, it does not exist for its residents. The ghetto is immobile—it and its subjects are characterized by their incapacity to move due to the constrictions of poverty, the nature of the subsidies on offer to them, their own lack of ambition and the structural disadvantages that entrap them. It is also, simultaneously, in some ways infinitely mobile, at least within the confines of the city; the ghetto can move with its subjects because redevelopment can transform the ghetto but nothing can transform the people, so redevelopment produces displacement of the problem, further residualization of the other ghettos or, in a worst-case scenario, the contamination and decay of another, previously un-ghetto place.

In contrast, the precariat, like the city which it occupies and tends to, is oriented towards the future. Discursively speaking, it could be said that the precariat have children while the residents of the ghetto do not. More precisely, the children of the precariat embody potential (they are, at least according to the popular imagining of a migrant household, urged to succeed in school so as to have the opportunities their parents were denied and to contribute to society); the children of the ghetto are a scourge, associated with burnouts, graffiti and arson attacks. But despite their connection to aspiration and the future, the precariat remains spatially disengaged. The ghetto dweller, however unwanted, is fixed in space and circumstance, and indelibly linked to the materiality of vandalized playground equipment, overgrown gardens and rusting car bodies; the subjectivity of the precariat is the product of processes predicated on mobility, be it across the globe or within the labour market. Although they tend closely to the fabric of the built environment and the people who populate it, the materiality of this caring labour (see Fine 2007, 173–78) is not enough to anchor them to the place in which it is performed.

More specifically, the precariat are associated increasingly, in Australia and elsewhere, with migration, and migration of a particular kind—migration of 'them', of people of colour, people with different skins and religions and accents. This is not to argue that there are no nonmigrants in insecure or temporary work, or that all migrants come from the Global South, but to point to the importance of (specifically nonwhite) migration within the subjectivity of the precariat. This proximity to a migrant subjectivity is significant, because it associates the precariat subject with a kind of deliberate rootlessness—the migrant (versus the refugee) has voluntarily forsaken their own rightful place and this destabilizes their right to demand access to the regular income, stable housing and reliable social services that might serve as a pathway for them to leave the precariat and enter the city.

CONCLUSION

And yet—although the ghetto is excluded from the city by its lack of a future, and the precariat by its transience, the ghetto does undeniably have a presence, however curtained off, within the material of the city, and the precariat subjectivity is one which arises from movement and change and is directed at betterment and self-improvement, which is the goal of the city too. There is space, then, in the discourse of the city for the ghetto and the precariat to enter, and through this entry, to possibly transform its constituent rules in ways that cannot be foreseen but might enable more socially just ways of being.

In this extended exercise in describing 'the city' I have not included notions such as 'civic' or 'citizenship'; I have provided no sense of the city as a site for democratic exchange and contribution. The city I have conceptualized is a space of processes and practices that act upon subjects, making available subjectivities with respect to those practices that are predicated on the normalization of consumption, competition and a brand-able 'authenticity'—the norm of 'choice' creates the chooser, and similarly, the marginality of the unable-to-choose. Does this mean I think civic participation is undesirable and agency is impossible, or that I am rejecting the discourses of the 'right to the city' that other researchers have sought to use to counter the spatialized inequality of many modern cities (Harvey 2003)? I can see that my argument could be read that way, but I don't intend it to be.

I am not claiming my description is definitive. It is my focus on a particular form of the city that leads to these absences in my account. This form of the city is marketed partly through the implication that within a given city there is a vibrant local participatory culture that is inclusive of all ways of life, but although the city offers the freedoms of autonomy and choice, these are rarely conceptualized in terms of democratic choice or subsidiarity. There is a lot of value in conceptualizations of cities, such as that put forward by Catherine Fennell (2015), which examine how, as our world globalizes, local expressions of civic responsibility and civic care become more important. But examining how such expressions can be evoked is not what I am doing here. Because for those of us who live in cities, the discourse of the city is normalized, pervasive and overwhelming. If we also believe it to be inherently unjust, problematic or undesirable, we have to be able to see it for what it is before we can get rid of it and build a different kind of city in its place.

NOTE

1. Precarity is also, increasingly, becoming the dominant experience of young people (Sheen 2013).

Chapter 3

The City as Wild

Wendy Steele

We shape the city, and it shapes us.

—Vance, *The Continuing City* (1990, 4)

After all, cities would not exist without us.
The question of the moment is: could we exist without cities?

—Reader, *Cities* (2005, xiv)

What constitutes the 'wild city'? The uncivilized civilization? Natural un-settlements? Turbulent cohabitations? The very idea of 'wild cities' is trouble-some, highlighting at least in part the existential tensions around the human notion of progress and civilization: our aspirations; anxieties; passions and fetishes; our relationships with nature, the nonhuman, each other and other. How do we claim wildness as part of our innate selves, dismantling the notion of human exceptionalism, embracing our common role in our collective earth story? How do we free ourselves of what might be seen as the sanitized, moral-izing vision of humans as gods, the earthly middle-class elite—as prejudiced as it is delusional?

Cities have been described as 'the defining artefacts of civilization reflect-ing all the achievements and failings of humanity' (Norwich 2001, 1–2). The city emerges as a restless socio-ecological–politico system that defies conventional boundaries and borders. Perhaps the wild city with all its con-tradictions better represents this restless ambition than notions such as the 'good city' that long established pillar of urban planning normative visions. For what is the 'good city' representing? Good for whom? (The poor, the earth, nonhumans?) Good when? (Now? In the past? In the future? In our imagination?) Good by what standards? (The neoliberals? The technocrats?

The middle class?). The Wiki dictionary describes the word 'wild' as both an adjective and a noun. As an adjective 'wild' signifies the not tame, feral (as in animals), uninhabited, inhospitable, unmanaged, virgin (as in landscapes), stormy, turbulent, raging (as in the sea or wild weather), primitive, ignorant, uncivilized, uncultured (as in wild people), undisciplined, unrestrained, un-constrained, unbridled, unchecked (as in actions and deeds of wild capital-ism), violent and angry (as in emotions bound up in wild policies, politics). As a noun 'wild' is a descriptor for a natural state, uninhabited, unaltered, landscape absent of humans. At one level the wild city conjures up the fear of an inhospitable environment—menacing, sinister, uncivilized (riots). For some it represents the urban heart of darkness, a morally corrupt, unjust, un-kind, divided, prejudiced environment/settlement (terrorism, racism). More recently the wild city is considered to be increasingly uninhabitable through weather of mass destruction (instead of weapons of mass destruction) as part of the impacts of anthropogenic climate change.

How do we reframe what we mean by the wild city? Can we reclaim the wild without losing the good? This chapter offers three contrasting ap-proaches to the wild city (notions of wild and city separately and collectively) drawing on Manuel Castells's (1979) 'The Wild City', Hinchliffe et al.'s (2005) 'Urban Wild Things' and Susan Ruddick's (2015) 'Wild Worlding' in *Situating the Anthropocene: Planetary Urbanization and the Anthropo-logical Machine*. Collectively these three glimpses point to different orienta-tions and preoccupations with the nature of the wild city and our role within them. Beyond the oxymoronic, the wild city as an heuristic lens prods us to problematize cities—what and where the wild things are within the context of the Anthropocene. But first let us turn to the utopic notion and nature of the 'good city'.

THE GOOD CITY

Cities shape us and we shape them. A positive vision of the 'good city' as an achievable utopia has been a recurring idea of the ideal city and imaginaries of 'the good life' for human society. Models of the good city have certainly shifted—historical context, place and culture have generated different visions of what the good city looks/feels like over time. The politics of human proximity alongside the dynamics of spatial juxtaposition, flow and global connectivity have all served to reshape the urban ethic and good city imaginary. Key dimen-sions of the good city focus on the quality of the public sphere; good gover-nance; and deliberative, creative civic engagement. Common threads are a focus on urban civility, order, harmony and the enhancement of human experience.

More recently a range of good city values and principles have emerged from the urban literature in recognition as Amin (2006, x) notes 'that the concept of good does not track unmodified across space and time'. John Friedmann (2000), for example, argues that the good city requires intentional political practice (action/political praxis following Arendt) that is transformative. His focus is on human flourishing as a human right, which the good city must foster and enhance, the multipli/city as a goal that seeks an autonomous civic life free from surveillance and control, and good governance attentive to civic participation and the way decisions are made and carried out, by whom and for whom. For Friedmann the good city is an ongoing discourse intended to encourage progressive urban possibility and solidarity.

The good city as an ethic of care as articulated by Ash Amin (2006) involves the four Rs of repair, relatedness, rights and reenchantment and picks up this practical urban utopia agenda for defining human civility and prospect in cities. This 'pragmatism of the possible' is leveled at the fine grain of humans in cities—practice, place and circumstance—to enact transformative urban change. He invites us to rethink the idea of the good city as 'a challenge to forge a progressive politics of well-being and emancipation out of the urban experience', and asks 'how can care become the filter of urban experience'? To this end he argues that repair and maintenance of the urban infrastructure fabric are not an accidental agenda but at the core of wider transformative economic and social change. The good city has a duty of care to be inclusive and demand equity of rights for those most vulnerable and marginalized. This involves Lefebvre's idea of 'the right to the city' and the capacity to shape urban life and the benefits to be gained from city living. Finally through a process of reenchantment, the good city is one in which creative experiments around difference and multiplicity can be mobilized for the common good.

The city made us free and is our home, Brendan Gleeson (2010) reminds us in his book *Lifeboat Cities*. However, rather than hope, freedom and human flourishment in cities, he argues we have elevated hubris, exclusion, privatization and consumption to new heights, 'a crumbling over-extended empire' (183). For Gleeson the key watchwords of the good city are evolution and *resilience*, while the core values are threefold: justice (equity not law), modesty (restraint as the safeguard of civilization) and solidarity (the recognition and nurturing of human interdependence) (187). In good cities 'we will join non-human species and nature generally in a project of mutual evolution that sets its sights on peaceful co-existence as much as on the liberation of new human possibilities' (187). However, he cautions 'the good city will not be a society of saints' (192). It is with this in mind that we turn to the notion of the 'wild city' so often framed as the anarchic b-side to the ideal society, perhaps better understood now as part and parcel of our animal-human selves and city as human habitat. The 'nature' of the good city takes on new resonance and meaning when seen through the lens of the 'wild city'.

THE WILD CITY

Manuel Castells's (1979) essay on 'The Wild City: An Interpretative Summary of Research and Analyses on the US Urban Crisis' focuses on whether a new and more sinister city—the wild city—might be unearthed if civic and environmental resistance to market logic fails. In this article Castells seeks to move beyond what he describes as the myth of the urban crisis, which he sees as an ideological expression of the ruling class (political elite) to naturalize societal tensions and contradictions. For Castells cities are life and urban living is the condition across the globe.

There is a normative edge here that mirrors the good city discourses. The city should be a place of dignity, security and harmony where the greatest achievements of modern civilization should be available to all. His concern was that conventional urban problems (housing, transportation, pollution, urban renewal) had become subservient to notions of crime, violence, racial tension and public immorality. The roots of urban crisis, he argues, are produced by forms of spatial organization—a crisis of urban structure, capitalist accumulation, consumption and reproduction of social order and cannot be reduced to improper behavior in public places and the like.

At the heart of his concerns are capitalist accumulation and urban structure. The economic dualism and spatial segregation (capitalist concentration) of devastated regional areas; cities dominate over their hinterlands through structurally regressive mechanisms of redistribution. For example, local governments and provision of local community needs are separate and unequal, which prevents redistribution through public delivery and goods. Urban renewal is contested and should be seen not as a structural necessity but as a political struggle: a land claim. Urban renewal and social programs that are designed to improve the urban economic situation instead accelerate social conflicts and community mobilization against them.

Castells is particularly critical of the failure of urban policies to handle problems generated by uneven development and the breakdown of social order which leads to the development of community organizations and protest as the grassroots attempt to overcome elite models of collective consumption. The crisis, he argues, is in the system of production and distribution of critical infrastructure in key areas such as housing, transportation, health and education. Local governments generate a contradictory and uneven expansion of these critical services. Riots and breakdown of social order are what he envisages if this goes unchecked.

For Castells, the Establishment is violent in the development of repressive apparatus with a developing tendency towards urban policy that supports and promotes monopoly capital that requires grassroots challenges against such structural logic. In this 'top-bottom social order, urban movements repressed and discouraged and urban planners attending more international conferences in the outer, safer world. What could emerge of a failure of urban movements to undertake their present tasks is a new and sinister urban form: the Wild City' (68).

A quite different view of wild cities comes some thirty years later. In a paper titled 'Urban Wild Things: A Cosmopolitical Experiment', Steve Hinchliffe and colleagues draw on Bruno Latour's idea of 'wild things' to invoke assemblage theory which sees cities as made up of all manner of things and practices, many of which are unnoticed by urban politics, policy and planning. They make the case for a politics for urban wilds which sees urban living worlds as much more than simply human worlds, extending beyond the portal for human flourishment, enrichment and the pursuit of the good life. This is an urban politics 'without recourse to old binaries of nature and society' (Hinchliffe et al. 2005, 643) that have proven so inadequate within the context of climate change but instead made up of human and nonhuman ecologies. As Gleeson (2010, 182) warns, 'our towering Babels have become the monuments by which we have thumbed our noses at nature'. Drawing on Lovelock, he observes 'as human animals building and living in our city nests we are slowly severing contact with Gaia and ultimately in danger of becoming the real and predatory aliens on what has been the planet of our birth' (183). So what might a wild urban politics involve?

Are there spaces to be nonhuman in cities, and if so, what are the political consequences, are key questions posed by Hinchliffe et al. (2006). 'Nonhuman', they argue, is not the same as nature or wilderness, and we need to reach beyond 'crude maps and boundary markers' if we are to see progressive political struggle that fosters a wild urban politic and polity. They argue the term nonhuman is important and signals 'a worldliness of worlds, suggesting that culture and societies are shaped by more-than-human geographies [. . .] instead of human free choice versus the dead weight of matter we are interested instead in engaging with here things matter through the fraught processes of engaging with human and non-human worlds' (644).

Hinchliffe et al. focus our attention on interstitial urban space, former industrial land that has been left vacant (for human use) but is now earmarked for redevelopment in the form of a new privately financed 'super' hospital.

Over time the site has become the habitat for multiple forms of wildlife who make use of the patchwork corridors of abandoned urban land for habitats or passage. But the urban wilds in this context are largely disconnected from broader community dialogue around urban futures (Whatmore and Hinchliffe 2003). As Hinchliffe et al. observe, 'the economic rationality of hi-tech corridors seems more at home than talk of wildlife corridors and other forms of ecological space [. . .] not pure enough to be true and not human enough to be political, urban wilds have no constituency' (645).

In this sense the wild city seeks to politicize the nonhuman within the urban context. The emancipation of all—humans and nonhumans in the city—is the ideal here. This is not so much about politicizing the ecological, but rather as Latour suggests (1998, 235) a quest to ecologize the political. The aim, according to Latour (1999, 19), is not to extend the franchise to increasingly include nonhumans (a form of representation which leaves them looking like less-than humans), but rather 'to build one due process where the questions of what ties us all together things and people is explicitly tackled as politics'. This is a politics of entanglement, not representation, which insists that nonhumans and nonhuman spaces matter in cities.

Susan Ruddick takes this notion of human and nonhuman assemblages in wild cities one step further from the city to wild worlding within the context of the Anthropocene in her paper on 'Planetary Urbanization and the Anthropological Machine'. She argues that 'the anthropological machine is the discursive framework, the *dispositif* that grounds "Western man" in a sense of civility, secured through a violent division within and between the human and nonhuman: not the after-effect of the civilizing act but its very foundation' (2015, 1113). There is the question of how this exclusion is performed (e.g., through the benefits of law and of citizenship), but equally if not more importantly Ruddick suggests the question 'how does Western humanity imagine itself to be civilized, to be civil in light of these exclusions?' (1120).

Ruddick's interest is not just in the entrenched existence of the divide between human and nonhuman in urban spaces and places, but the work this divide does to create a particular kind of imaginary of what the urban is, or should be. For Ruddick, this approach renders the urban simultaneously 'placeless and pervasive' on a planetary scale, structured with a logic that asserts the urban is code for 'a way of life under capitalism' (2015, 1114). Urban galaxies and the perforation of traditional divides are now at a more than planetary scale as outlined by Brennan and Schmid (2014). The urban emerges as a chaotic construction, shape-shifting and unpredictable in form and content, everywhere and nowhere. Cities in this new imaginary are but one moment in the implosion/explosion process of planetary urbanization, a spatial landscape that includes, but is not limited to, cities. If the urban is both cause and cure for climate change, this logic will require rethinking and a new global urban politics to address the challenges of planetary-scale destruction.

Key to these shifts is the loss of a discernible boundary either in physical form, conceptual understanding or discursive community. The nexus of urban political economy and assemblage urbanism requires bridging the divide between the everyday lives of urban citizens (human and nonhuman), and critically addressing the role and nature of capitalist urbanization on spatial and temporal scales. This serves to legitimize/privilege particular understandings of the 'good life' based on largely capitalist notions of what constitutes human enrichment and flourishment.

A new conceptual frame or cognitive map for the urban is therefore required beyond the discursive framing of civilized life as a way of life under capitalism, ubiquitous now across the whole planet. For Ruddick (2015) this involves finding mondial ways to read/imagine the urban polity anew; 'the hauntology of the Anthropocene and the hauntology of the urban, [are] both implicated in a thinking of an ending: *the end of the wild, the end of a world*' (1118; emphasis added). To this end she invokes the words of Jean-Luc Nancy (2007, 35): 'we must ask anew what the world wants of us, and what we want of it, everywhere, in all senses, *urbi et orbi*, all over the world and for the whole world, without global capital but with the richness of the world'.

CONCLUSION:
The Binaries That Bind/Blind Us

Notions of the city and citizens are grounded in what it means to be human, with the ambition to be civilized as articulated by the 'good city' values and ideals. But if our concepts of civility are grounded in landscapes and discourses of exclusion, we need to ask the question, what has a focus on the good city obscured from our view and what new imaginary is now required within the context of a climate of change? How do we embrace the wild in cities rather than frame it as a state of fear from which we need to separate ourselves and defend? Beyond bifurcation what does the wild city mean?

The polarization of the 'good city' versus the 'wild city' must be rethought and rearticulated as part of an urban agenda that is the responsibility of and responsible for the world. Despite our attempts to break down and transcend the divide between the human and nonhuman, the urban wilds—when acknowledged—remain negatively, passively or weakly imagined in visions of possible urban civilization and futures. To make sense of our role, to reclaim and (re)make the wild city/earth story together will require a more nuanced,

Wendy Steele

inclusive approach to the binaries that blind/bind us. This will require a more thoroughly problematic glimpse of ourselves, our world, and our habits, and hubris—past, present and future—to politically rediscover and reengage with *the urban nature* of our wild cities and ourselves.

Chapter 4

Urban Time and the City as Event

Tony Fry

As is well recognized, the city, conceived as *polis*, is not just viewed as a situated material form, for it is equally understood as a collective animate body: the body politic. But more than this, the city is also a complex metabolic process: one of continuous and speeding creation and destruction. As such, the temporality of the city's relational ontological agents constitute it, as will be shown, as a designed and designing event.

To grasp the semblance of such a complexity is to acknowledge the error of an assumed commonality of meaning of 'city' as a conceptually unified, knowable and contained entity. My city lived and imagined is not your city. Situated experience certainly creates a difference of perception of place; individuated knowledge often takes and presents fragments as the whole, especially in those cities of an incomprehensible scale (like Tokyo with its population en route towards forty million); and then there are those cities of gross inequity, mostly of the Global South, wherein the division between the formal and informal is an absolute and spatially marked, thereby making the sociocultural divide clearly visible.[1] It follows that how the city is seen is always a matter of one's own sociohistorical placement.

The scale of the invisible dimensions, differences and intricacies of cities poses huge problems for phenomenological study, as does the notion of the city as a locus of social settlement (for in so many ways many are increasingly becoming viewable as epicentres of 'unsettlement' and places of passage). Thus clear distinctions between the visible and invisible, and settled and the nomad become indistinct and open to challenge.

In truth what a city actually is, especially viewed from the Global South, becomes increasingly unclear as rapid urbanization continues, and as megacities grow via disarticulated fragmentation, and with porous edges that exceed any defining spatial form, moment, formal acknowledgement or conceptual

51

construct (like the peri-urban). Substituting the designation 'the urban' for 'the city', and appealing to agglomeration, does not deliver coherence, unify fragments or resolve difference. Spatial ordering does not hold the city in place in a 'world' of urban (con)fusion and techno-panoptic immaterial social infrastructures. Everything 'bleeds'. The question 'what is a city' now cannot be met with a definitive answer. Maybe it never could; certainly when applied, the European model was a false norm. But notwithstanding, as the complexity and criticality of urban life and form continue to increase, in conditions of deepening global unsustainability, the imperative of questioning the place, nature and future of cities demands ever more attention.

The approach to responding to this imperative to be taken here centres on the city as a designing event—this from its very inception. This approach will lead to looking more closely at settlement, unsettlement and dislocation and how, against this backdrop, the idea 'event' is being understood.[2] Thinking event, design and the city will then be revisited. Finally the city will be considered as metabolic event.

FROM THE ORIGIN
TO THE DESTINY OF THE CITY

The European City is between two moments: its prefigured origin by the first cities of the ancient world, Eridu and Uruk (Samerian, 5400–5200 BCE) and Iken (Egyptian, 5000 BCE), as they commenced a developmental pathway to cities of the present; and the global displacement of the power and significance of these cities, this by emergent and coming megacities of megaregions and the defuturing fate that many cities now await.[3] Here then is a large framing of the city as object, gathering and fragmentation as it constitutes a designed and designing ontological event. One wherein there is an endless circling of people acting in ways that actively, or indirectly, design such cities. At the same time, the form, operational dynamic and life of cities design the disposition, ways of work, social relations and modes of life that in large part design people.

So seen the city is a worlding event (understood as the formation of a world-within-the-world) that acts to totalize 'the world' as 'standing reserve' endlessly and increasingly utilized by cities. The means sustained city life, and the 'appetites' of ever-larger urban populations heading towards ten billion, are metabolically unsustainable. This not least as depletion of resources ever outstrips their regeneration while at the same time causing potentially catastrophic damage to the biosphere.

This fundamental conflict between the 'worlds-within-the-world', epitomized by the city, and the biophysical world upon which all organic life depends is registered by deepening conditions of structural unsustainability that also enfolds threats of thermonuclear and technocognitive erasure.[4] The continuation of life so lived within a 'negative dialectic' cannot be viewed as anything other than a diminishment of our species finitude. Yet acknowledging this condition, one has to either abandon all hope of acquired agency, thereby fully embracing nihilism, or act on the basis that our existence is not completely fated and can be affected by affirmative action. Clearly finding transformative possibilities in 'dark times' poses a major question for the relation of philosophy to informed action (as praxis).[5] Whatever the form, the city is, unavoidably, central in meeting this challenge.

Within the long duration of our species (now being seen as two hundred thousand years plus) the existence of the city is but a fleeting moment. Against this backdrop, the realization that life now exists under conditions of erasure is being existentially deferred. Moreover, the actual possibility of life after the end of the city is a prospect not beyond imagination, as the world's displaced people evidence. Although urban populations of the Global North are yet to confront the reality, for many of them this is a future for their heirs already destined by the environmental dangers (including conflict)[6] of a changing climate.

One of the reasons why climate change gets disregarded is because it is believed to be a problem able to be solved by technology, if not immediately at least at some point in the future. Not only does such thinking not grasp the nature of climatic change in time (centuries), but it also fails to understand the problematic of problems. The assumption that every problem has a solution now, or at some moment in the future, is flawed. Notwithstanding the ability of new knowledge to change perceptions, and possible flaws in classificatory schema, there are three general orders of problems: those that can be solved (from the wicked to the evidently resolvable); those that may not be able to be solved but, by adaptation, can be lived with; and those that are impossible to solve and cannot be lived with no matter new knowledge and unconstrained imagination. In their difference cities occupy all three permutations. Some have problems that can be solved (which does not mean they will be), some have problems able to be dealt with by adaptation, but some are fated—like those that will not survive rising sea levels at the end of, and beyond, this century (at best they may be recreated but they will not be saved).

In recognition of the variable problems of cities, some with a dominantly defuturing propensity, how does one rise to challenge of thinking the city otherwise? This is a question obviously linked to the task of exploring what an 'urban' philosophy might be. From the perspective and concerns outlined, there are two directions able to be explored: first, going back to go forward to the origin of the city and the nexus between the polis and philosophy; and second, how thinking the city as 'event' changes what there is to think philosophically and so recasts what philosophy now needs to think.

PASTS, FICTIONS, FUTURES

To begin to think the city otherwise prompts revisiting that much earlier context and content of a similar project in the recognition that the Eurocentric 'fact' that philosophy began in Greece, thus the philosophy of city commenced in ancient Athens, stands on a fiction. One that rests with how the relation between Greece and Africa, especially Egypt, has been, and is now being, understood, be it not universally.

I want to view this fiction not just as a formative moment in how the city and humanity became viewed and thereafter represented, but as an example of the power of fiction embedded in history rather than as it is projected by utopias. To do this we will consider the relation between Solon, Plato and the *polis*.

Solon (c. 638–c. 558), from the fragments of his writings that survived, and what has been written about him, is mostly remembered as a statesman, lawmaker and poet.[7] Because of his ambitions and the configuration of his interests in Athens, law and politics, he became of considerable philosophical interest to Plato (c. 427–c. 347 BCE).[8] Solon, presented as a naïve visitor to Egypt in search of learning, has been linked to Plato's view of the importance of the wisdom of Egypt.[9] More specifically, his regard for Egypt's means of government and class structure has been shown to be a major influence upon his writing of *The Republic* (Stephens 2016). Likewise, his evocation in *The Republic* of the 'philosopher king' can be connected back to actual philosopher kings in Egypt.[10]

THE CITY AND/AS COMPLEXITY

Inchoate in *The Republic*, and its Egyptian traces, is the beginning of the city as an ontologically designing event via structuring of an ethos that realizes conditions of the common good (not to be confused with a design determinism). Cities come to be only by the design and construction of their material fabric, laws and codes of conduct, institutions and ways of life—historically such prefiguration was mostly via 'organic' development, with design prior to it becoming a division of labour. Latterly cities arrive by good or bad formal design practices formed by and for modernity.[11] Either way, an ontologically designing circle is established that fuses process with place.

Whatever is brought into being by design acts to incrementally design the *habitus* directive of the mental and physical practices of everyone that in part create, but are equally are created by, 'the everyday life of the city'. This schema of what is an unending process of design is obviously not based on understanding design as a professional practice. Rather, and more broadly, designing is understood as an intrinsic, if differential, ontological quality of our being: one that prefigures what is brought into being, and thereafter its ongoing designing agency.

Design, as ontologically intrinsic to our being grounded in the innate pre-figurative capability, goes ahead of our actions as a fore-having (*vorhabe*), a *something we have in advance* (Heidegger 1962, 190). As a 'something' lodged in our very becoming, that as designing technological being who created the world-within-the-world and within which the varied cultural modes of our being were formed and continue to be transformed. The scale and diversity of the forms of artifice of human creation, and volume and diversity of what has been produced, has created a relational complexity and unending process of ontological change that is literally beyond comprehension. As the familiar, but fundamentally unknowable and uncanny, the city is an object, gathering, layering the manifestation of this complexity. If we go back to the formative moment of our species becoming, we can gain a clearer view of this dynamic.

Our species came into a proto-world-within-the-world already in the making. From our progenitors we inherited stone tools and those of wood and bone that they made.[12] Consequently, not only was our technological being-in-the-world of making predestined but so also was a continual and unbroken circling of the ontological design of our becoming and being. Most immediately what this initially meant was that the use of tools advanced our tacit skills, modified our physiology (via muscular and tactile bodily changes), which thereafter resulted in increasing the conceptual complexity of to-be-made and making. We *Homo sapiens* were the recipients and contributors to the advancement of hominoid cognitive capabilities.[13] Besides the use of tools, what we made with them—hunting implements, cloths from cleaned and sewn animal hides, canoes, built shelters and so on—all contributed to the circling agency of ontological design. Thus our iterative development, and the development of the environments of our existence, were inextricably linked to each other.

Viewed from the present moment, the interactive, ontological designing of the material and immaterial world-within-the-world in which we come to be, and continually create, has become an immersive technospatial, artefactual, epistemic-communicative and symbolic environment of relational complexity beyond, as said, our comprehension. The scale, intricacies, rhizomic wanderings, interpenetration and continually changing, strange, but familiar, good and bad relational world cannot be arrested and observed.[14] Yet out of the necessity of 'being here', and partly as the continual makers of complexity, 'we' negotiate, experience and strive to meaningfully make sense of this our situated being-in-the-world.

For us complexity—city, technosphere, biosphere, semiosphere, the world-within-the-world—all fall in and out of focus according to our being in place, settled and functional and displaced, unsettled and dysfunctional. Not only does complexity beget greater complexity but it also constantly accelerates the speed of change: a condition indivisible from the un(der)-recognized complexity of unsustainability.

Placing the question 'What is a city?' in the frame of the complexity of complexity is a pragmatically appropriate question unable to be adequately answered that nonetheless continually begs a response. The challenge to urban philosophy so contextualized is to think how the beings that we are can live futurally negating the complexity of the unsustainable.

Not only are such 'hard times' unavoidable, but they have already arrived materially and emotionally for hundreds of millions of people. Like Lessing, one cannot feel at home in 'this world as it is' while, at the same time, ever remaining committed to it. What this means is finding the transformative potential of hard times and perhaps forging the realizable fiction of the polis remade. What now follows is to address how 'conditions of instability' are being understood, and how the indiscreetness of the city seen otherwise can be made present and engaged.

SETTLEMENT, UNSETTLEMENT AND DISLOCATION

The very notion of a confluence between the city, the urban and settlement is becoming undone. First in large part because of the conditions that *unsettle* any sense of certainty about a secure future, as with those conditions already posed.[15] Unsettlement in actuality is becoming a universally pervasive human psychology that simultaneously folds into a 'state of the world' and 'state of mind' producing a nihilistic way of life. This is an anomie mode of being wherein no matter what one does, nothing is seen to be able to counter the forces that are sealing one's fate.

Huge numbers of cities around the world have such unsettled populations occupying a 'city of panic'. Paul Virilio (2005) does not characterize such a city as one in which everyone is panicking: a city where people are running in the street screaming in fear, fighting to escape and looting supermarkets to stockpile food. Rather he defines it as a state of mind that knows that all that seems substantial, firm and certain is not. Panic is repressed not expressed, but felt as a condition of unsettlement and foreboding.

Second, it must be recognized that in the fastest-growing cities in the world most people live materially unsettled lives. These are the cities of rapid urbanization with vast and growing areas of informal 'settlements' in which there is no secure tenure nor adequate, or any, public utilities or services. In Asia and Latin America, 60 to 70 percent of cities can be informal. In Africa, with its even more rapid population growth, the impetus towards megacities is driven by informal construction on illegally occupied land. Of all houses built, 98 percent plus are now illegal (Fry 2017). These dwellings are built with a density and in conditions that create high fire and public health risks, and often on land subject to flooding or landslides (Fry 2017).

Unsettlement is a variable configuration of physical displacement, psychological insecurity and futural time. For instance, the inundation of the delta region of Egypt has begun; agricultural land is being lost, and people are being displaced. Not only is this having a psychological impact on these people but also it's making the entire agriculture community of Lower Egypt insecure. In turn, as the nation has a fast-growing population and now a diminishing agriculture sector, this situation will start to psychologically and economically affect the entire nation. As for time, here is a process that has started, the duration of which is totally unknown. Another of many and different examples is Miami. It is a fated city. It cannot escape the coming of the sea. The Everglades above it are already being salinated. Moreover, 'Miami stands to lose up to $3.5 trillion in assets by 2070 due to sea level rise, according to a new National Wildlife Federation report. . . . In Florida, $69 billion worth of property is at risk of flooding in less than 15 years, and beachfront property in Miami-Dade alone is valued at more than $14.7 billion' (Kallergis 2016).

While vast amounts of money will be expended to delay the inevitable loss of the city, the disaster will not wait for the arrival of seawater. Miami property values have already started to fall and at some point in the next few decades, or less, there will likely be a total collapse of values—a prospect that may well cause panic and a population flight. This will include tens of thousands of Cuban and Puerto Rican Americans creating a crisis by heading for New York and other major US cities with Latino communities. Another example of climate impacts with widespread consequences is the reduction in the volume of the rice produced in Southeast Asia and its nutritional value.[16]

Effectively all the problems that converge to constitute unsettlement elevate 'normal' human insecurities to produce what is likely to be a dramatically higher order of anxiety. Such a state of mind is just another, but mostly overlooked, expression of the unsustainable.[17] Obviously unsettlement will not be uniformly experienced: while existing everywhere, there will be a huge disparity between the inhabitants of wealthy techno-climate protection isolates, the 'concerned privileged' and the 'poor and desolate'.

Played out in and across cities is the conjuncture of unsettlement, the extent of coming enviro-climatic critical change, the increasing prospect of Orwellian panoptic societies existing in conditions of various levels of permanent war, the rise of megaregions and the decline of nations, the ongoing psychosocial impacts of hegemonic technology all converge to constitute that which is inadequately named as 'the unsustainable'. In asking, is there a way forward, one has to say yes, for the same reason that one has to embrace the world (within-the-world) as one recoils from its monstrosities.

Faced with this situation, philosophy per se remains held in check by extant divisions of knowledge. It is out of step with the scale and scope of the forces of the transformation of the human condition. Biocentric environmental philosophy, posthumanist philosophy, feminist philosophy, political philosophy et al. don't get it. Yet there are scatterings of minds trying to confront these unfolding 'hard times' recognizing a *negation* of *the negation* that they manifest has to be created, or discovered and exploited. In this context, is the city the place to be?

Three figures of thought that intersect with the urban and design have already been raised and now need to be reconfigured. These are fictions, complexity and event. Design commences with prefigurative fiction of the 'what might be' to be realized (or not); in this respect it has an understated political intent that mostly is modest and so goes unnoticed. But this is not always so: most grand design visions are equally political visions. A fiction arises out of the identification of the city as a designing event (its unstated ontological modality): it is of the city/*polis* designed as a designing event. The ancient view of the city as a place where events are created and happen and are public is one opening into the formation of an operable design fiction (in contrast to a utopia). Another is to make identifiable ontologically designing complexity present to assemble in new futuring combinations. Moving this thinking forward means saying more about the event and then the complexity of the city as a designing event.

HOW EVENT IS BEING UNDERSTOOD

How are we to understand precisely what an event is? Philosophically, one can start by recognizing:

- The specificity of our existence is 'the particularity of *the* event of our being in being' as it is constituted by, and punctuated within, our being-in-the-world.
- The temporality and causality of *an* 'event' is determined by the worlds of our existence. As such, ontologically events are both *cause* and *the caused*.

- The notion of 'event' is reflected in the very structures of language—they are named by nouns and constituted by the action named by verbs.

Yet such an introduction is insufficient, for there is no consensual philosophical understanding of exactly what (an) event actually is. As Alain Badiou (2007, 37) makes clear, the idea of event retains its 'original ambiguity'. Certainly as the discursive and epistemological contexts in which an event is brought to presence changes so does what it 'appears' to be. To acknowledge that thinking, the event began with the first question of philosophy: what is/ being and what is not/nonbeing? However, our concern here is not with how the event has been understood historically but with a contemporary understanding, and as such it has two moments, the first prefiguring the second. The first moment can be registered by what Alfred North Whitehead has to say in *Process and Reality* (1978): 'the actual world is built up of actual occasions', which he uses the term 'event' to name (37). A second registration of this moment emerges out of two linked works by Martin Heidegger: his *Beiträge zur Philosophie* (*Contributions to Philosophy [From Enowning]*), written between 1936 and 1938, and *Das Ereignis* (*The Event*), 1941–1942. Heidegger's concerns moved away from an 'organic philosophy of becoming' to thinking the 'event toward the beginning' via an 'appropriative event' (*Ereignis*).

Moment two situates the event in Continental philosophy and is perhaps best represented by a contested understanding of the event between Gilles Deleuze (1992), who draws a great deal from Whitehead when he sees event as that which comes to be in a 'chaotic multiplicity', and as such, is, as Badiou (2007, 38–39) describes that which is denoted by 'unlimited becoming'. In contrast, Badiou's own view (37) is that the event is created, as a composition, and, by implication, a making, which will take us towards a concern with remaking.

Clearly the issue of what (the/an) event is cannot be divided from the specific epistemology by which it is defined and then elaborated. None are exclusive, all are contingent. There are, though, two broad observations informed by Badiou (37) that are helpful to give the concept substance in relation to the city. The event is everything which is outside us (as subject), and the world outside us 'everything which happens'. These remarks converge with Heidegger's understanding of appropriation (*Ereignis*)[18] as an appropriative event, thus the appropriated and appropriation belongs to 'event'.[19]

The event can also be seen as political, but as Badiou (2005, 141) makes clear only 'if its material is collective', as qualified by his understanding that the collective is not as 'a numerical concept' but rather 'the vehicle for a virtual summoning of all' (141), which is to say socially 'a bringing together and a comprehending'. Events of course are not discrete; they exist in chains and flow into each other. Consequentially they are transitive, conjunctural and disjunctural.

While the city as a designing event requires theoretical framing, it equally needs to be grounded. Badiou as both a theorist of theatre and of 'the event' provides one way to do this. He views theatre as a form of action and 'the most political art form'; in so doing he understood theatre as the performative extending beyond the theatrical stage (2013, 2). Badiou makes the point clearly via Plato, who adopted an anti-theatre view of Aristotle's position on theatre while creating a theatrical mode of philosophy—as evident in his writing as based on scenes and dialogue.

The potential of an extended understanding of theatre for Badiou (2013) is as a situated extension of struggle wherein knowledge is created, encountered and contested as epistemology in action. What is at stake for him, as it was for Plato, is 'the transformation of the subject', and, following Socrates, 'a struggle over dominant opinion. To do this (echoing Sun Tzu and unrestrained warfare) one should 'adopt every possible means' (2). For Badiou, there is a direct link between his theory of event, as an exceptional occurrence, and theatre as 'an event' and a path to '*the* event' (the exceptional occurrence he privileges as revolution) (Puchner 2009, 261).

Object-things are events in so far as they act (Heidegger calls such action 'thinging'). Such action reveals the 'essence' of things as not lying within the object but phenomenologically through its performative attributes—the knife cuts, the mower mows, the aeroplane flies. So designed objects, as eventing events, go on designing, and as such this defines the nature of their ontological agency. This is the case irrespective of whether the object is material or immaterial (for instance, the essence of a message is its communicative/causal consequence).

From the perspective of the city as a designing event, it can be seen as a potential consciously assembled composition ontologically designing things that constitute 'the event of a drama of affirmative change' with redirective/remaking possibilities. The concept is one 'thing'; its realization is another!

Both Whitehead and Deleuze after him stated that the 'place on the creation of new events is both affirmative and productive' (Livesey 2010, 14). But events in themselves clearly do not have a reducible value. They can be good or bad, regressive or progressive, positive or negative, and, as argued elsewhere, designed as an ontologically designing event, can both future or defuture. This remark connects to a problem in the way 'becoming and creation' are presented by Whitehead and Deleuze (and others). That creation is dialectally indivisible from destruction is insufficiently recognized. Becoming is always an arising out of a displacement or negation, be it the destruction of idea, meaning, process or matter. The wooden chair arises out of destruction of the tree, the bird breaks out of the egg, the spherical planet displaces the notion that Earth was flat, the human via the overcoming of animality, the made world at the cost of the destruction of the natural and so on. Writ large, the failure to give sufficient attention to destruction, so characterized, is one of the main reasons why we anthropocentric beings are so unsustainable.

AGAIN THINKING
EVENT, DESIGN AND THE CITY

The city is caught up by speed as an event. Speed *drives* it as a change-event: one that is the locus of the becoming, arrival and departure of matter, commodities, meaning, information, capital, people as it functions with/as a synthetic metabolism.

Cities have always existed between what they were and what they are becoming. By degree this means they are situated in the betweenness of construction and destruction, care and neglect, preservation and transformation, futuring and defuturing. To realize this is, to repeat, to realize the multifarious forms of their ontological designing of being and beings that design. To understand cities so renders the division between their represented material substrate and economic, social, cultural and political superstructure in many ways as obsolete.

From the perspective of the city, it is important to remind ourselves that the object/event relation that ontological design exposes has always been present, and that the politics of the cities of 'democratic nations' is merely urban managerialism. Moreover, the essence of urban politics is not the plurality of opinion; rather 'it is the prescription of a possibility in rupture with what exists' (Badiou 2005, 24).

Every city is en route to its destiny. Every city, as event, has a birth, a life and a death—but their time is not as ours. A concern with architecture here confuses: there was the city before architecture (a category back-projection onto building; the city and architecture, and the city after architecture—in the face of complexity, the practice and its discursive practices will fail/is failing as they stand before extant and the coming forces of transformation). Posturbanism marks this drift in the Global North, and a coming hegemonic 'informalism' in the Global South.

Appropriately, as Emmanuel Levinas pointed out, 'The event of dwelling exceeds knowing' (1969, 153). Our being is not only often incommensurate with our knowledge, but the very thing that is most important of all to understand escapes us—'we' in our difference do not remember, or know, how to dwell (some cultures have forgotten, some never learnt and a few retain a trace). But what is now arriving is a displacement of the very sense, or possibility, of dwelling.

THINKING TOWARD A METABOLIC EVENT

The move from recognizing the city as a designing event with a defuturing propensity to remaking the city as a life-sustaining futuring event begins with considering the issue in general, but for thought to be turned to praxis a specific object of engagement has to arrive. The philosophical challenge hereafter becomes finding an appropriate starting point. Bending the urban metabolism towards a drama of affirmative change is put forward as one possibility to explore.

Understanding the metabolism of the city as an event within the event exposes the urban drama as another kind of circling wherein the familiar returns as the unfamiliar to be staged otherwise. Such an event requires thought, reflection, work and a refusal to reduce biological waste to a restricted instrumental problem.

Urban metabolism is not a new idea, but one whose explanatory value over time has been diminished. This is immediately evident if one, for instance, contrasts the importance given to the idea by Marx, who viewed metabolism as a way to comprehend and explore the relations between nature and society, labour and history, but with the views of Abel Wolman (1965), a key figure in establishing contemporary practice, the concept becomes shrunken and employed to make sense of problems of air and water quality in US cities. In a global review of this activity as a field, Kennedy, Pinceti and Bunje looked at around fifty articles (spanning 1965–2009) that focused on twenty comprehensive scientific studies. What this review exposed was just how limited the field of inquiry was. The social and cultural values that underscored the everyday life of urban population were totally overlooked.

There is nothing in the city to limit the growth of 'the organism'. Not only can waste not be eliminated or reintegrated but, in the current forms of the city, its rate of production or growth cannot be checked. The waste management industry is a marker of the failure of waste to be managed—a failure it has a vested interest in extending. All the thinking on waste, and restrictive metabolic processes, gets nowhere near the fundamental problems of the economy of desire that creates the dynamic of 'consumerism', this with the city as the prime and unconstrained site of its consummation.

Let's now go back to Marx. He used the concept of *stoffwechsel* (variously translated as 'material interchange', 'material reaction', 'exchange of matter' *and* 'metabolism' (the latter being used throughout the Penguin edition of *Capital* [1970]). Marx employs the term *stoffwechsel* in many of his publications, but most notably in his *Grundrisse* (1857–1858), *A Contribution to Political Economy* (1859) and in *Capital* (vol. 1; 1867) (see Hampton 2009). Common across all his comments was the recognition that what the concept allowed to be recognized was a relation between nature and society wherein human beings and nonhuman beings interact, with metabolism mediating this relation via human labour. Thus in Marx's theory of value, the use value of a material commodity always contains appropriated and expended natural elements. Marx held this to be independently true for every form of society (Hampton 2009). Marx's views were actually influenced by scientific developments of the day. In particular, the term *metabolism* appeared in a number of references he made to Justus von Liebig, who wrote on chemistry and modern agriculture, which Marx notes not only exploits the agricultural labourer but also robs the soil of nutrients (Marx 1957, 474–75). More than this, Marx placed this recognition of metabolic dysfunction in an urban context: 'Capitalist production collects populations together in great centres [. . .] on the one hand concentrates historical motive power of society; on the other it disturbs the circulation of matter between man and soil, i.e., prevents the return to the soil of its elements consumed by man in the form of food and clothing'. He then goes on to call for 'a restoration of a system' that allows for the 'circulation of matter' (474).

The observations made by Marx on these issues have provided material that has fuelled a vigorous debate on Marxism and ecology that, notwithstanding Marx's own concerns, were carried forward, not least by Friedrich Engels, William Morris and Rosa Luxemburg. Now the debate has been revived. Of particular importance in this has been the controversial writing of John Bellamy Foster (2013).

Without suggesting that Marx's views can simply be imported into a model for contemporary action, they do provide an opening into a broader vision that goes beyond the restrictive instrumental of the way the metabolic methods are currently being brought to the notion of sustainable cities (as it reduces the perspective to the waste stream management of material flows through the city). Not only is this perspective insufficient but it is also predicated upon a particular kind of city with a level of developed and functioning infrastructure, thereby excluding a vast number of cities on many continents. Obviously, there are huge sections of many cities with large informal settlements that are beyond the scope and reach of this type of management. In such contexts waste is both an urban problem and an economy of survival for 'wasted and abandoned' people.

In grasping the event of the urban metabolism, as but one event of the city as a designing event, a subterranean drama of appropriation, composition and decay starts to come into view that has the potential to animate the *polis* in ways that cut across spatial perceptions of the city, its political institutions and current objects of urban philosophical inquiry. The globalizing city laid bare exposes a nexus between an ancient (Egyptian) overwhelming fear of chaos and the imposition of a regulatory regime to check it (rule from the city of order); and the contemporary repressed fear of the unsustainable (a sanitized characterization of entropy/chaos) and illusions of control (urban design and tokenistically enforced environmental regulation).

NOTES

1. The exploitation of the informal economy by the formal does not disrupt the division. Not only is the evidence of the informal/formal relation enabling social mobility sparse, but the rate of influx in almost all such settlements exceeds departing numbers, as is acknowledged by even conservative studies. See, for example, Ivan Turok et al. (2017).

2. Comments here on the 'event' and 'the city as event' are especially drawn and developed from ideas initially outlined in Tony Fry (2017).

3. The view a decade ago was that megaregions, while accommodating 18 percent of the world's population, generate 66 percent of the world's wealth (Florida et al. 2008). Current economic trends would suggest a considerable increase in this figure. As such they and megacities become resource sinks that reconfigure the economic power of nations and diminish by degree urban economies. With reference to defuturing cities: large numbers of the major cities of the world were logistically sited in delta regions and are thus at risk already, and for many decades to come, from sea-level rises.

4. From the perspective of evolutionary biology, 'we' are not immune from an ecological correction, and are at the start of the sixth extinction event—see Elizabeth Kolbert (2014), a publication that triggered numerous other reports and serious media coverage.

5. A claimed relation between 'dark times and affirmed action' being an argument put forward by Hannah Arendt (1968) in her essay 'On Humanity in Dark Times'.

6. Gwynne Dyer outlined this possibility in his *Climate Wars* (2008). Subsequently strategic military planners have more seriously engaged the issue.

7. See 'Solon the Lawgiver' on the Athenian Agora Excavations website: http://www.agathe.gr/democracy/solon_the_lawgiver.html (accessed 18 January 2018).

8. Consequentially Solon figures frequently in Plato's dialogues in *Timaeus and Critias, The Laws* and *The Republic*—see Samuel Ortencio Flores (2013).

9. The relation between Greece and Egypt is said to have begun with Thales of Miletus (c. 624–c. 546 BCE), often claimed as the first Greek philosopher, this not so much because of what he thought but because of how he thought in order to in-

strumentally comprehend causal relations. Such thinking is regarded as marking the beginning of the end of the power of Greek mythology. Key to gaining this ability was that he studied at the Temple Waset in the City of Waset (was Thebes, now Luxor). Claims also exist suggesting the relation was established prior to the arrival of Thales.

10. The teachings of King Merykara (ca. 2150–2025 BCE), who authored a treatise on the conduct of kingship, being one example and *Akhenaten* (ca. 1352–1334 BCE), formally Amenhotep IV—a Pharaoh of the eighteenth Dynasty, who delivered a major critique of polytheism is another. See Obenga (2004) for a developed account of Pharaonic philosopher kings.

11. For example, the 1573 Laws of the Indies promulgated by Phillip III of Spain set out in fourteen ordinances an attempted structure of every aspect of the creation of a city for the administration of the indigenous populations of Spanish America, including its spatial and built form, laws, regulated everyday life, a form of labour.

12. The estimate is that by two hundred thousand years ago there were about seventy different stone tools in use, distributed in various numbers across many geographies (Fry 2012, 66–110).

13. From the first use of stone tools by earlier hominoid species over a period of at least six hundred thousand years prior to the arrival of *Homo sapiens*, brain size has been estimated to have increased by 30 percent. See Chris Stringer (2011).

14. Notwithstanding the insights of second-order cybernetics.

15. Added to which are changes in labour markets whereby AI systems and robotics are further reducing the use of the use of human beings. Job security is effectively a thing of the past.

16. Through heat stress, reduced rainfall and soil moisture, extreme weather events will significantly reduce food production and nutritional values globally, as the size of the global population continues to grow. This situation has been widely reported but largely ignored (see, for example, Thukral 2016).

17. Examples include a reduction in availability of planetary natural resources; geopolitical reconfiguration increasingly arriving, with some national borders being redrawn; and significant shifts in the power balance between nations. Some nations may even degenerate into dysfunction and break up.

18. In these two remarks Badiou's 'The Event in Deleuze' and Heidegger on *Ereignis* converge.

19. This understanding is central to the fundamental proposition underpinning Heidegger's *The Event.*

Chapter 5

The Immanent City

Simon Sadler

Two contrasting radical philosophies of the city sidewalk could be found in San Francisco in 2016. One called for renewal through 'tactical urbanism', the term lately adopted for creative, inexpensive and usually unauthorized approaches to urban improvement.[1] The other more starkly demanded the removal of the homeless from the city's streets. We could likely find any number of other variants, before or since, and from any number of other cities, of progressive and reactionary responses to the disorderly freedoms of the city. For the tactical urbanists, represented here by a San Francisco architectural practice called Rebar, the city offered 'good' disorder—in their best-known design, adopted by dozens of other cities, Rebar reclaimed car parking spaces as pop-up parks known as parklets.[2] Tactical urbanism was suggestive of governance-by-prototyping, or of anarchism or, in the words of a new sociological study of such practices, of 'DIY urbanism' (Douglas 2018). It implied that the city is a product of its own 'immanent' order that had no need for imposed order—this, at least, is the inquiry of this chapter. But in an open letter posted by a tech entrepreneur called Justin Keller (2016) and reported by outlets as far away at the *Washington Post* and the UK-based *Guardian*, the city was descending into a 'bad disorder' affecting the rights of urban consumers, impeding capital accumulation and degrading the public realm. In high-flown philosophical terms, he posted his grievances in an open letter to Mayor Lee:

> Democracy is not the last stop in politics. In fact, the order of progression according to Socrates via Plato in the *Republic* goes: timocracy, oligarchy, democracy, and finally tyranny. Socrates argues that a society will decay and pass through each government in succession, eventually becoming a tyranny. 'The greater my city, the greater the individual'.

This chapter very briefly accounts for the inversion of Keller's city of imposed order—the default of the Western urban ideal since Plato—into Rebar's 'immanent' order, a still-tentative default of the contemporary Western urban ideal identified in a 2016 lecture series on 'Immanent Urbanisms' by San Francisco's Red Victorian commune and hotel.[3] The Platonic ideal is the more easily visualized, theorized and historicized—for a half-century, Le Corbusier's 1925 Plan Voisin for Paris was the paragon of urban reform inspiring large-scale urban development like that of New York City master planner Robert Moses in the mid-twentieth century. It is sensed still in the high-tech eco-cities of Asia and the Middle East such as Masdar in the United Arab Emirates. The city of immanent, creative 'self-organization' is harder to depict, other than in vignettes such as parklets, the planting of urban communal gardens on vacant lots, the provision of street furniture by a sidewalk's users, or the claims made by some architects that their design is parametric. Immanent urbanism can be framed (as this chapter will attempt) by a theoretic and philosophical nexus that is as indeterminate as its subject. As nebulous a notion as it is, it is nonetheless conveyed by arguably the most important architectural polemicist since Le Corbusier, Rem Koolhaas, who in 2001 offered Lagos, Nigeria, as an exemplary urban 'mutation'. No more 'hand of god' gesturing over Paris (Le Corbusier's hand, gesturing in a well-known photograph at his Plan Voisin model)—no more plans, in fact: Lagos mutated through a million entrepreneurs, according to Rem Koolhaas.[4]

And yet the Plan Voisin could not be built, and Lagos is as much a catastrophic legacy of colonialism as it is a self-organized system. To see Lagos as Koolhaas sees it, for instance, requires a certain sort of apperception. What, this chapter tries to ask, constitutes an ontology of immanent urban order? It is to perceive the city as a self-organizing 'second nature' with a self-organizing populace—the city not just as the detritus of our own material culture, but as a medium with its own patterns and laws, by turns bucolic, garden-like and sublime; tended by communards, avant-gardists and entrepreneurs; its self-organizing capacities accelerating through technology and markets. In this ontology, the city shows Being *as* self-organization, a sensibility currently underwritten by the laissez-faire economics of neoliberalism, regarded as a quasi-natural force whose growth and natural wastage should not be controlled, but seeded. And while this sort of urban laissez-faire can be read as cruel neglect, or as class war, or as the sovereignty of capitalist development, it also has deep and utopian ancestry, since the spontaneist city also functions as a laboratory of reform. An ontology of urban immanence entails perceiving the city not as a space for the imposition of control *over* nature and anarchy, but *as* a natural anarchy, or as a self-organizing 'second nature' becoming a commons for a self-organizing citizenry.

Below I outline an ontology of urban immanence, before considering in conclusion whether the crisis of neoliberalism should prompt a reconsideration of governance, precisely to secure the conditions for immanence, top-down and bottom-up urbanism ever necessary to one another.

AN ONTOLOGY OF THE IMMANENT CITY

How and when was an ontology of urban immanence possible? It was, after all, anathema to the modern search for urban order. At the birth of the modern secular city, Lorenzetti's 1338–1339 frescoes *The Allegory of Good and Bad Government* in the Palazzo Pubblico of Siena measured the city's internal harmony against a nature unkempt and managed, walled off, so that public space could be foregrounded as a plateau of civilized collective life. (See figure 8.1 to view one of Lorenzetti's frescos [page 122].) In tandem with the centralization of political economy in the state, the reemergence of classically based urban planning allowed Renaissance, Baroque and Enlightenment architects to approach urban design as a coherent whole; by the eighteenth and nineteenth centuries, the city could be imagined as nothing less than a work of art, exemplified by Louis XIV's Paris. Art merged with function in the mid-nineteenth-century networked boulevard urbanism of Baron Georges Haussmann's Paris and Ildefons Cerdà's 1859 plan for Barcelona, so that the city could represent the distribution and growth of national prosperity through a coalition of capital, technique and government.

With that extension, the 'second nature' of urbanism replaced first nature. 'What are the dangers of the forest and the prairie compared with the daily shocks and conflicts of civilization?' asked Charles Baudelaire in 1867 (quoted in Benjamin 1973, 39). 'Men can see nothing around them that is not their own image; everything speaks to them of themselves. Their very landscape is alive'—so wrote situationist philosopher Guy Debord ([1958] 1981, 50–54, 51). He attributed the observation to Karl Marx, and although the quotation isn't found in Marx's authenticated writings, it helps periodize a moment, from the mid-nineteenth to the mid-twentieth centuries, when cities like London, Berlin and Los Angeles were without readily perceptible boundary, extending and densifying seemingly according to their own logics of development and communications, eroding much sense of an overall centered authority. It was as though the city was modernization's book of nature, and that it required new modes of apperception. In painting from the seventeenth century on, and later in photography, the motif of the city increasingly supplemented those of landscape, the nude, still life and portraiture to present viewers with sites of everyday beauty and moral turpitude.[5] Vermeer, for example, presented the delight of everyday life, actions, events and movements in the 'overlooked' places of the city; Canaletto found a means of registering, almost mechanically, the optical phenomena of the physical sites and visual sights of Venice and London. Impressionist painting gazed upon Haussmann's Paris with an almost Aristotelean disinterest, and the literary, cosmopolitan mid-nineteenth-century wandering of Baudelaire as *flâneur* would be described by Walter Benjamin (1973), a half-century later, as 'botanizing on the asphalt'. Benjamin was a fellow traveller with the surrealists, who in the 1920s were encountering Paris as a geological remnant of Haussmannization. After the Second World War, Paris was mapped by situationist successors to the sur-realists, the city conceived as the battleground between authentic life and the infrastructure of state and capital, the situationist as Rousseau-esque primitive, living wild in urban nature; much as the Romantics had sought to understand their emotional response to wild nature, surrealists and situationists wanted to understand their emotional response to second nature. In all, a mute *liking* for the inexplicability of the city's own logics, and a joyful surrender to them, becomes apparent in later twentieth-century culture—consider, for instance, the affectless unfolding of the photographic panorama *Every Building on the Sunset Strip* (1966), by Los Angeles artist Ed Ruscha. The city epitomized the impossibility of coherent cognitive mapping in a postmodern era, its subject lost perpetually in an assembly without beginning or end, centre or periphery, authenticity or inauthenticity (Jameson 1991).

That very loss was the *revelation* of a new whole: whatever order there was to the city was immanent to it, as in first nature, and was better cultivated than commanded. An aesthetics of cultivation assisted a shift in urban agency from the dead hand of dictatorial command to something thrillingly liberal and even-tually anarchic. Whereas Louis XIV could once command Paris and Versailles according to his will (as Le Corbusier somewhat wistfully showed his readers [1925, 285]), Marc-Antoine Laugier's keynote 1756 *Essay on Architecture* was already offering a city-making model of interacting entities, as in nature. 'We should look upon a city as a forest', Laugier (1756, 250) argued:

> That there may be order therein, and nevertheless a sort of confusion. That all be in a direction, but without monotony; and that from a multitude of regular parts, there results from it in the whole a certain idea of irregularity and a chaos, which suits so well to great cities. We should for this end possess in an eminent degree the art of combining, and have a soul full of fire and sensibility, which ceases lively the most just and the most happy.

Laugier's 'urban forest' thus combined governance with self-organization, aesthetically and, perhaps, politically. Joshua Reynolds (1907, 224), in his thirteenth *Discourse*, explained:

The forms and turning of the streets of London . . . are produced by accident . . . but they are not always the less pleasant to the walker or spectator, on that account. On the contrary, if the city had been built on the regular plan of Sir Christopher Wren, the effect might have been [. . .] rather unpleasing: the uniformity might have produced weariness, and a slight degree of disgust.

The pictorial break from grand, linear, classical tendencies emphasized instead growth and change, a visual analogy for political and economic freedom and satisfaction beyond utilitarian profit and loss, industrialization and statism. In England, indeed, the variegated, orderly disorder of the Picturesque aesthetic was transferred from landscape architecture to the city—Picturesque theorist Uvedale Price joined architect John Nash in the King's Office of Woods and Forests to style Regent Street in a sequence of asymmetrical 'natural incidents' as it wandered irregularly across London. Ebenezer Howard's late-nineteenth-century proposal for Garden Cities, notably, synthesized first and second nature using Picturesque visual vocabularies. Biologist and sociologist Patrick Geddes adapted the Garden City model to imagine the city as a holistic region holding its citizens, their freedoms, functions and networks in harmony with one another and with nature.

Geddes was interested in anarchism, which with its emphases on quality of life and association surely lurks in immanent urbanism's DNA. His espousal of architectural planning was in some sense an homage to a basic precept of anarchism—that we can live with ourselves, with one another, and with nature. Geddes's was a planned, immanent urbanism, if we can grasp that paradox, human history become natural history in his grand *Notation of Life* diagram, under development from 1904.[6] Especially after the Second World War, resource allocation in countless cities worldwide was handled through the growth of such giant planning apparatuses as Britain's Town and Country Planning Acts, but worries about authoritarianism, paternalism and the crushing of initiative were immanent even to the ascent of planning.[7] Nor need an anarchic interest in resource allocation be confined to the left, since repulsion at cultures of dependence, shared by the left and right, became more visible with the unpopularity in the 1960s and 1970s of the Welfare State and its architecture.[8] Ideally, the new commons of the city would provide a terrain in which our true nature could be discovered. How could resource distribution be managed in the absence of clear top-down authority? One way was to encourage an 'innate' proclivity for fairness, and rudimentary accounts of anarchism assumed a benign essentialism—that we are all by nature good, and that only something outside of us corrupts us. More precisely, and simply, anarchist Peter Kropotkin claimed we have benign human instincts and antisocial instincts, and that we should try to cultivate the good ones. Anarchism also suggested techniques for shaping the city without recourse to

Haussmann's wrecking ball or to top-down design and planning. Especially following its reinterpretation as a 'festival of the oppressed' by Henri Lefebvre and the situationists[9]—building in turn on the sympathetic accounts of anarchist geographer Élisée Reclus—the eruptive Paris Commune of 1871 has remained perhaps the single most beguiling instance of a city's immanent revolutionary power, an experiment in radical citizenry acting in solidarity with artists, poets and intellectuals, the city their new commons. The Commune remade the city in the now, and such 'prefiguration' (as anarchists would today put it) collapses the difference between means and ends by allowing citizens to live today as they might wish to live in the future.

The legacy for practitioners of a consciously immanent urbanism today (again, think of the maker of a parklet) is to insist on such exemplary citizenship, model behavior, participation, strategy, transgression and a festive, game-like quality to direct action, often with a concomitant aesthetics: if the aesthetic of control is the straight line and axis and hard, smooth surface, then the prevailing aesthetic of immanence is raggedly, fecund, in process. Anarchic creativity has enjoyed increasing cachet since the 1970s—urban sociologist Richard Sennett contemplated *The Uses of Disorder* in his 1970 apology for an anarchism of sorts, and anarchism's ecological inflection by Ivan Illich and Murray Bookchin gave it further reach. 'Social sculpture' was artist Joseph Beuys's term for artistic activity that strives to revolutionize society or the environment through language, thoughts, actions and objects. It fused Romantic belief in the innate creative capacities of humans with a program to initiate action, reform and even direct democracy, as where Beuys prompted the planting of trees at Documenta 7 in 1982, or organized a campaign for plebiscite. Anarchist assumptions allow that the Reclaim the Streets initiatives of the 1990s, or Critical Mass's demands for bike ways over roadways, or squatters' movements reclaiming and reusing houses, or unauthorized urban guerrilla gardening—the immanent urbanist practices of our own era—promulgate a common good rather than self-interest. All this implied an insight into the nature of order and the 'impossibility' of planning: in the early 1970s the possibilities of a rational, linear design process was dealt a blow by the discovery of the so-called wicked problem—that every imposition of order, it seems, engenders disorder (Rittel and Webber 1973). And, as Italian architectural historian Manfredo Tafuri claimed in the 1970s, 'architecture' per se provided a 'regressive utopia' of planned continuity at odds with the city's freedoms (1976). Immanent urbanism, on the other hand, contained a quixotic hope: that the city can be *changed* by small numbers of creative people, their work attaining some sort of 'butterfly effect', bottom-up and dispersed. An urban garden, say, makes gardeners who make more gardens.

Immanence implies a force that will carry us to an exhilarating condition because it is unplanned and ultimately unknowable: an exhilaration more of the *now*, of the lived moment, than of the future. Rooted in existentialism and anti-Hegelianism (recall Occupy, defying media pressure to state 'one demand'—for the Occupiers, the present was multiple in its grievances and possibilities), the disavowing of clear historical targets is nonetheless almost millenarian, a postmodern way of describing totality without resorting to grand narratives, plans or unitary aesthetics.[10] Whereas top-down agency was linear—Cartesian, abstract, the product of rational (and perhaps dictatorial) government—bottom-up agency would be webby, composed of interacting entities unburdened by the yoke of statecraft. But what should in theory be the increasing modesty of the ideology of urban reform became, through immanent urbanism, its *extension*, as an urbanist intelligentsia of activists, architects, critics, designers, boosters, sociologists, policy wonks, campaigners, academics, artists and so on, reimagined agency draining away from the state and corporations into a city operating according to some sort of quasi-natural law. Immanent urbanism therefore is urban design become exponential, seeing order in disorder, design in the undesigned. It accounts for complex relationships by living them and attempting to transform them. All this affirms that the city is as resilient as nature—a second nature of usable disorder that dispenses with any need for historical purpose (of the sort once described by Hegel), or for planning.

By the late twentieth century, the convergence of a poststructuralism (in part extrapolated from anarchism) with complexity science, networked information technology and, for some, free-market enterprise, promised an accelerated transition to self-organization. Rebar architects (2016, n.p.) explained that 'You normally have centralized, hierarchical, development-driven groups shaping cities, with the public bureaucracy trying to rein them in to generate public benefits. What if the whole financing mechanism for building cities is about peer network generated finance?' This 'hacking' of San Francisco approached space, infrastructure and capital as a ready-made waiting to be redirected. 'You can make an argument that the iPhone has had more of a radical effect on culture and society than any piece of architecture because it has enabled people to be networked and it has enabled all these other businesses', Rebar (n.p.) continued. This embraced the terrible logic of urbanism identified by Tafuri (1976, 120)—that modern urbanism, with its careful alignments and zonings, had hopelessly waged its plans against the chaos of capitalism and its technological innovations, and capitalism had won, because design and its plans could not change political economy—'The city of development does not accept "equilibriums" within it'.

Gilles Deleuze and Félix Guattari's philosophy was a gateway to this phase of immanence. Applied to the city, their image of the fluid materialist substratum of all existence, all ontology, as a 'Body Without Organs' negated any essential difference between nature and the city, or any other entities, since all was energetic matter, in becoming, with limitless potential for new conjunctions. And just as in the 'natural world', where seemingly stable entities like rocks and mountains are in reality very slow-moving flows with faster-moving biological material flowing around, then so too in cities buildings are in reality very slow-moving flows, and conduits for bodies and information. Picture an urban garden, or any 'bottom-up' urban practice, as Deleuze and Guattari advise on the good life in the Body Without Organs ([1987] 2004, 161):

> This is how it should be done. Lodge yourself on a stratum, experiment with the opportunities it offers, find an advantageous place on it, find potential movements of deterritorialization, possible lines of flight, experience them, produce flow conjunctions here and there, try out continua of intensities segment by segment, have a small plot of new land at all times. It is through a meticulous relation with the strata that one succeeds in freeing lines of flight, causing conjugated flows to pass and escape and bringing forth continuous intensities for a BwO.[11]

The search for new apperceptions of the city, from Vermeer and Canaletto to surrealism and situationism, might now be understood as the city's subjects gazing back upon the system from whence they hailed, and to which their lives were immanent, formed from it and its interactions with its entities and flows. Command of the system by one entity was unlikely, though a 'multiplier effect' of the few upon the whole was possible (in a further important extrapolation of this ontology, Michael Hardt and Antonio Negri explained the immanent political forces of the dispersed 'multitude'); the undifferentiated 'socius' of the city (or Earth) offered vast and unpredictable potential connections activated through conjunctions with other bodies, accelerated through the particles, connections and relations of networked computing. If the basic networks of Haussmannization had sped up Paris and hosted the unpredictable singularity of the Commune, what might San Francisco become, nearly a century-and-a-half later, with nudges from citizens proximate to the information revolution of Silicon Valley?

Indeed, the poststructural vision of self-organizing, indeterminate networks of forces, affects and becomings offered a philosophical accompaniment to the turn in the sciences to complexity. The city could be understood as a complex system like any other, as matter, energy and information coursed from node to node, the density of interconnections ensuring that pathways could not be determined in advance, but were capable of being adaptive or generative.[12] This was an alternative to design by planning, with its epistemology of predictability and transcendent teleological principles. In her pivotal study of the

The Death and Life of Great American Cities (1961), Jane Jacobs found in complexity science a bottom-up, self-organizing substitute to the total municipal planning of her nemesis Robert Moses. Unlike Moses's monofunctional and monocultural freeways and open spaces, the systemic density of Jacobs's idealized Greenwich Village could adapt (to waves of newcomers, say), and it could generate (new cultures, for example). In the early twentieth century, the Chicago School of urban sociology had described urban change in terms of the city's ecologies, but by the end of the century socio-spatial succession was generally assumed to be unending rather than headed for some climax state. What unimaginable effect could there be, then, from a pop-up parklet, as it extended a key social space of Jacobs's city, the sidewalk? A parklet city might self-organize into other new entities—more parklets, or festivals, or habitats.

Then again, it could lead to a catastrophic crash in order. Wouldn't that be a bad thing? Not necessarily, for the immanent urbanist, insofar as change is ever a cherished quality of modernity; from at least the mid-nineteenth century (think, again, of Baudelaire), the opportunities for transgression were central to a city's allure. In any case, contemporary urban immanence felt like a *bounded* risk—it was, frankly, difficult to imagine the transgression of the parklet triggering wholesale revolution, as the building of a barricade in Paris in 1871 or in 1968 would have signaled. When all entities are connected as in a lattice, why would just one or two social classes (workers, students, women, etc.) suddenly coalesce? 'A desire to transcend political contest altogether frames the vision of individual and collective life proffered by advocates of civic innovation', concludes geographer John W. Elrick (2017, 871) in a close study of San Francisco's governmental encouragement of technology. 'The demand that urban subjects see themselves not as political actors or members of social classes but as individual bits of human capital lies at the heart of campaigns to innovate the public realm in San Francisco'. The sort of Californian cyberculture from which Rebar drew, as they called for 'peer network generated finance', envisaged self-organization as postpolitical—'out of control', as the pun of cybertheorist and ecologist Kevin Kelly (1994) had it, in its organizational liquidity, beyond the reach of authority, a gloriously runaway technological aesthetic. The contemporary condition, as Kelly's fellow cybertheorist and ecologist Stewart Brand put it (quoted in Clark 2000, 29), was a 'carnival of constant innovation and surprise, with desired results and unexpected side effects colliding in all directions'. 'There are some traditional uses for public space—socializing, commerce, political activity—that are moving online', Rebar mused (2016, n.p.),

> So public space has been sort of 'freed up' from its traditional roles, and in this there's an opportunity. When painting was freed from its technological obligations with the invention of photography in the 1860s, it almost immediately

became nonrepresentational and then surreal and then everything else. So maybe the relationship between technology and public space is evolving in a similar process.

Kelly, Brand and Rebar looked to the operations of the neoliberal, networked free market, unhindered as far as possible by regulation, as the final element in 'natural' self-organization. Theories of architectural and urban self-organization had been propounded since the 1960s, notably by Christopher Alexander, who found innate patterns in environmental organization shaped by parameters (spacing, paths, orientation, custom and so on). A beginning of so-called 'parametric' design, this 'fitness' has been found, at one extreme, in informal settlements like the *barriadas* and, at another extreme—in the polemics of architect Patrik Schumacher, for instance—in the complex system parameters of economics. What to radicals is the urban site for the tacit or overt appropriation, seizure, occupation and unenclosure of property, for libertarians is a site of primitive accumulation. Troubling to progressives, for its advocates this unconstrained market is wholly ethical and necessary for human enterprise and sustainability, since the market, it is assumed, innovates and learns faster than government.

CONCLUSIONS: AN IMMANENT GOVERNANCE

On first reading, then, it was as though San Francisco c. 2016 was 1860s Paris redux—the emergent properties of the city as the basis for a social emergence enveloping all. But the new amenities of public space in San Francisco and elsewhere—bike lanes, urban gardens and the like—are not evenly distributed across social class (and correlated demographics like race). One problem is that dramatically increasing costs of living in a metropole like San Francisco make access to the new amenities inherently exclusive, and the amenities, in turn, increase the costs of living. This undermines the possibility of a universal immanence, then. Marx and Engels cautioned of the city's 'metabolic rift' with nature, and San Francisco can be compared to a body exchanging material and energy between nature and society, expelling its depleted materials, citizens and labor to the surrounding region.[13] Of particular consternation to Justin Keller, whose open letter to San Francisco's Mayor Lee began this chapter, was the continuing presence of waste life within his recently adopted city (2016):

> Every day, on my way to, and from work, I see people sprawled across the sidewalk, tent cities, human feces, and the faces of addiction. The city is becoming a shanty town [. . .] I know people are frustrated about gentrification happening in

the city, but the reality is, we live in a free market society. The wealthy working people have earned their right to live in the city. They went out, got an education, work hard, and earned it [. . .] I shouldn't have to see the pain, struggle, and despair of homeless people to and from my way to work every day.

Belief that a self-organizing city system is more and more inclusive (rather than more and more exclusive) is an ideological conceit; immanent urbanism is perhaps less an ontology revealing the truths of Being, and more a pleasing, privileged 'structure of feeling'. The Marxist cultural historian Raymond Williams claimed that before a community's worldview is formulated as ideology, it is sensed aesthetically, institutionally and experientially—as a structure of feeling. Williams focused his analysis on language and literature, but structure of feeling might run through material culture, too; the city, with its parklets, bike lanes and farmers' markets a 'relay machine' for taste formation and a contemporary bourgeois consciousness, encouraging social interactions with people of shared values and class background. This skewing of ontology into ideology can be illustrated when Koolhaas claimed to see in the Lagos crowd only pure morphogenetic becoming, freeing him of any transcendent judgements like hierarchy, right or wrong, Cartesian distinctions with their calculating ambitions, the better to meld aesthetic subjectivity and cognition as one. Koolhaas misread Lagos, geographer Matthew Gandy (2005) patiently explained: Lagos was not opportunity galore and self-organizing, but a tragic, historically explicable, postcolonial disorder. The capacity of something as artificial as capitalism to *look* natural was precisely something that Walter Benjamin tried to expose in his unfinished *Arcades* project. This naturalness romantically emphasizes the unpredictable afterlife, affordances and aesthetics of property, as if the instrumental role of material culture is the lesser part of its urban purpose. If the city seems quasi-natural, moreover, it can appear to be something untamable.

But there are potential pleasures in an ontology of moral judgement, restoring the Kantian distinction between the aesthetic and cognitive, in which an astonished perception of a second nature become wild makes us recoil to analysis. 'I am telling you', warned Keller (2016, n.p.), '*there is going to be a revolution*'[14]—Keller's reaction to the sight of homelessness and his apocalyptic sense of San Francisco inadvertently suggests that neoliberal second nature, with its pitiless extraction of surplus value to the exclusion of any social contract, is unsustainable. And that tactical urbanism might make the city greatly more convivial with no appreciable effect on escalating inequality—this, too, might make us recoil to redistributive economics and an economy decelerated to something progressive, ecological or socialist. Could Keller's angry petitioning of government make the case for a traditional social contract, and the social democracy that had once proceeded from it?

It's a less edgy urban ontology than that of a Dadaist tactical urbanism, of Koolhaas's gesturing at the Lagos crowd, or of Keller's righteous anger. From Dadaism on, argued Manfredo Tafuri in his milestone 1973 Marxist critique of urban design, the avant-garde became released from much sense of solidarity in favor of a more mystical spirit or *Geist* of a sort present in immanence. But since the Middle Ages, something like a social contract supported by a city's education, shelter, medicine, transportation and redistributive tax underwrote the *life* needed for immanence. At base the city is a system of clean water, from Roman aqueducts to John Snow's 1854 cholera map. While there is renewed appetite for governance through various strong mayors' initiatives in the United States and elsewhere, the enterprise of a properly immanent urbanism in the service of *people* needs a robust firewall against the enterprise of neoliberalism which approaches problems of the city only *economically*.[15] As sociologist Neil Brenner (2015) wonders, tactical urbanism might be ineffective against neoliberalism, and may even bolster it, proliferating to fill the gap created by the withdrawal of welfare programs, public services and environmental protection. The contaminated drinking water in Flint, Michigan, in 2014, and the deadly June 2017 blaze at Grenfell Tower, West London, both attributable to the fiscal restraint of small government, would be an appropriate point at which to categorically reject neoliberal urban reform.

More than the principally spatial disruptions illustrated by Rebar's work, then, a 'deep immanence' would require political, economic and infrastructural redress, accepting the curtailment of absolute personal freedom (of the sort demanded by Keller) in return for universal opportunity, fairness and inclusion. Rather than promulgate an ontology of the city as in a state of sublime emergence and becoming, governance can be another tactic of the immanent—this was, after all, something attempted by the Paris Commune—supplementing or foregoing vanguardism to foreground responsibility for big, long-term, collective and political decisions. (Lorenzetti's frescoes sandwiched the Sienese government between allegories from which to measure the intent or likely outcome of their decisions.) The city really is a philosophical problem, in which case: for its immanence to be harnessed, it might be necessary to rein in an ontology founded in anti-idealism.

NOTES

1. See for instance the Street Plans Collaborative (Mike Lydon et al. 2011).
2. The festive annual meter-feeding Parking Day, which creates 'parklet' public space from parking lanes and parking spaces, was popularized in San Francisco in 2005.

3. My thanks to Eric Rogers for inviting me to this conversation and for devising the term Immanent Urbanisms. This chapter draws on the talk I presented at Immanent Urbanisms, and on 'A Natural History of the City', presented at the Moderna Museet, Stockholm, Sweden, 2011.

4. See also the documentary film *Lagos/Koolhaas* (Van der Haak 2002).

5. The depiction of the city actually accompanies its entire history. Cities were widely depicted in the art of the ancient Near East, both in Egypt and Mesopotamia, especially Assyria. Hellenistic and Roman art established a tradition of the city view as a motif, where buildings were shown to provide a scenography for religious and mythical stories and for political and military propaganda.

6. The diagram was published in 1927 (Welter 2003).

7. The British planner Andrew Derbyshire (1996) recalled that his generation of planners in the 1950s had been extremely interested in anarchism.

8. An impressive intellectual skepticism spread across the political and philosophical spectrum encouraged a turn away from governance—from the classical liberalism of Friedrich von Hayek to the activism of Jane Jacobs and the design methods of Horst Rittel; from the neo-Marxism of Henri Lefebvre and Manfredo Tafuri to the poststructuralism of Michel Foucault, Gilles Deleuze and Félix Guattari; from the constructionism of Bruno Latour to the political and aesthetic philosophy of Jacques Rancière.

9. For a recent account, see for instance Gavin Grindon, 'Revolutionary Romanticism: Henri Lefebvre's (2013) Revolution-as-Festival', *Third Text* 27 (2): 208–20.

10. On this loss of near-future planning and a new millenarianism, see Guyer (2007).

11. Gilles Deleuze and Félix Guattari, *Mille Plateaux*, 1987, translated by Brian Massumi, *A Thousand Plateaus* (London and New York: Continuum, 2004), 161.

12. On self-organization see, for instance, Evelyn Fox Keller (2008; 2009) and Nigel Clark (2000).

13. On urban metabolism, see for instance Nik Heynen et al. (2006).

14. Keller was in part contending with the effects of the Lee administration's own policy of encouraging an innovation economy (for instance, by waiving payroll taxes for firms opening along the Market Street corridor), which helped drive income inequality in the city to the second highest in the nation. See Elrick (2017).

15. For further analysis of the fusion of nature, innovation, governance and neoliberalism in San Francisco, see Elrick (2017).

Part II

CITY LANDSCAPES

Experience, History, Identity

Chapter 6

Solar Le Corbusier

Allan Stoekl

I

In the crisis of the 1920s and 1930s, Europe faced not so much an awareness of the brute reality of insalubrious urban congestion and concentrated poverty (the awareness of that reality had been prevalent in cities for thousands of years) as the recognition of the need for a larger and coherent economic, social and urban transformation that would alleviate those conditions. But what type of transformation?

Of course, much of Paris had been razed and rebuilt in the mid-nineteenth century under Napoleon III, in the famous project supervised by Baron Haussmann (Pinkney 1958). But in those days the concern of urbanists was less with the crisis and transformation of the economic system than it was of the need to make the city accessible to the army (in cases of urban revolt) and to open it up to the rising middle class (what today we would call gentrification).

In Le Corbusier's day, seventy-five years after Baron Haussmann, urban transformation was to be accompanied by a greater awareness of economic and social crisis. Among many others, Friedrich Engels (1968) had certainly been aware of this crisis already in the nineteenth century, but for Le Corbusier and his contemporaries the central problem was not so much one of purely political and economic revolution implemented in the city, as it was a kind of spiritual urban transformation. Le Corbusier's urbanism, aware as it was of social ills (triggered and intensified by the global crisis of capitalism) and their spatial and 'hygienic' consequences, was in no way a model elaborated under the sign of egalitarian communalism. Rather, as I will point out in this chapter, Le Corbusier was driven by a desire to foster not just an intensely individual liberation, but one that was powered not so much by a desire for collectivist urban reform as it was by an all-powerful solar energy and all that it implied. Such reform, however, as we will see, was not without its problems.

For Le Corbusier, modernism is a *plan*. He was indeed connected with an avant-garde group in the 1920s, called 'Plans'.[1] '*Planisme*' was the doctrine of aesthetic, social, economic and political planning, the French corporatist equivalent of the Technocrats in the United States. All could be planned, had to be planned, to preserve the world from the chaos into which it was threatening to fall: economic disorder, urban decay and squalor, social unruliness.

Le Corbusier was of course a great architect, but the cities he designed—'radiant cities'—were never really built. Attempts by other architects after World War II, perhaps, but not by Le Corbusier himself. Of course there were a few buildings, or fragments—the *Unité d'habitation* of Marseille, some fragments of Chandigarh, in India—but his city truly came, and comes, to life only on the page. His cities are ultimately written, and drawn: they are narratives, sketches, plans.

Le Corbusier's artwork is total and totalizing: it is a total way of life, with every possible contingency foreseen and every unpleasantness deflected. His cities are written and drawn by the hand of the master. At every moment we sense his presence behind the word: he it is who tells us what is wrong with the current city—its congestion, its dirt, its inefficiency and squalor. And he too provides us with illustrations, drawn in his own hand. His drawings, his handwriting, which marvelously convey the plan of an old city center, a cathedral and its placement, the path of the sun across the sky, the structure of trees in relation to the architecture that he proposes. And the presence of giant housing blocks rising from the space of the transformed city.

As architect, as master, he is in touch with a deeper stratum—not just materials, but with a privileged way of accessing them. He sketches a nautilus shell, and its connection to a mathematical curve, and writes (1942):

> The law of numbers is inscribed in natural works (*oeuvres naturelles*).
> Man, a product of the universe, carries in himself the mark of numbers.
> He discovers them, he expresses them, he uses them to direct his enterprises.
> Laws are inscribed in mechanics and in the calculation of the resistance of materials.[2]

Laws, numbers: the master has privileged access to the unchanging basis of things, to the profound relations between matter and law. Hence architecture and cities too, via this access to the law of number, will excel as art: they will be in harmony with the ratios, the golden mean, the 'Modulor' that governs the harmony of the relations of all physical things. And the politics tied to this law of numbers will be equally precise, equally definitive. The inhabitants of the city will find their happiness in relation to this material and quantifiable law.

Le Corbusier's sketches, 'in his hand', are not impressionistic; they are quite precise, and his architectural drawings feature straight lines, perspectives stretching to infinity. This is the law of the city: to be seen. The planner separates, as he must, different urban spaces: delivery lanes below, walkways above. The delivery lanes make possible the quick arrival of people and provisions to their destinations: they assure that motorized transport never gets stuck in some urban irrationality, never leads to dirty and time-wasting congestion. Roads, multilane freeways, are always free, always open, always guarantee maximum urban efficiency. Above these, however, or beside them, connected to the green spaces opened up by the tower blocks that dominate Le Corbusier's urban space, there are walkways that give access to shopping areas, cafés, schools. One has the impression, looking at these drawings, that urban space is meant to be seen as a static and well-proportioned harmony. One does not drift like a Situationist, one is stationed, at a point, to witness the aesthetic effects the urban designer has provided. City space is not about facilitated movement and surprise: it is about movement to a precise point allowing the elaboration of a specific aesthetic effect. The urban dweller does not improvise, does not move to resist; on the contrary, the city is the law of material elaborated in such a way as to present the perfect view of material—constructed and natural, constructed as the perfect enhancement of the natural—from the perspective of the perfectly lived life in the perfectly ordered society. There is no 'psychogeography', no multitude of urban significations, because there is only *one* psyche and *one* geography.

Thus the swift and efficient movement of the car or truck is paradoxically inseparable from the stasis of the privileged observer. Both are creatures of the will, the law, of matter, of the architect. The motorized vehicle zooms through urban space, finds the right spot to take on or drop off cargo; then it disappears around the corner, or into an adjacent garage. The citizen of the city positions him or herself properly, among trees, on a playing field, in a café, to observe the city, in its relation to nature, in its elaboration in conjunction with the law of harmonized matter.

That is urban life for Le Corbusier: I do, I see, what has been prepared for me, what has been programmed. I exercise, I go to my job, I receive my friends, I go to the café, I play sports, I take my child to school, all in officially determined ways. There is nothing beyond or on the other side of this activity: there is no unconscious, no more radical communication, no death-drive or ecstasy: these only get in the way of a life that is self-evident, transparent. There is no alienation in the city because a properly planned city by definition does away with alienation. If this visual, walkable life is in harmony with the laws of numbers, of materials, then there is nothing else: the architect and urbanist is not just someone providing a neutral structure, something to be used and forgotten, or contested and ironized through inversion, but rather a philosopher who provides one's raison d'être, the very meaning of life. There can be no urban complexity of or in Le Corbusier's city: the planned city now saves us from complication, uncertainty, inefficiency, ambiguity of meaning, uncanniness, slowness, danger, exploitation, delirium, coincidence. It allows us to reside in our apartments, in peace, fulfilled aesthetically with a fine view of the sunny green areas around our building.

Thus the sketch 'A Contemporary City', in *Urbanisme* (Le Corbusier 1989, 246–47), translated as *The City of To-Morrow*. The caption tells us, among other things: 'We are in the center of the city, the point of greatest density of population and traffic; there is any amount of room for both'. In the distance, skyscraper housing blocks; on the right, below, a highway with cars; in the foreground, a café terrace, providing the perfect perspective to view the towers, the surrounding green area with trees; on a café table, a teapot and several cups; another table has a carafe and a water glass. In the sky, decoratively frozen, several biplanes, one seemingly headed, Icarus-like, down to earth. And yet we notice that this drawing does perfect justice to the scene, because it is the *only* perspective possible of this scene. It depicts the traffic and yet we see no movement, and we need to see no movement. There *can* be no movement; movement is transcended in a larger stasis. What's more, there are no people in the drawing. In fact there are practically never people in Le Corbusier drawings, except of course for the Gumby-like 'Modulor' figure of perfect human proportion who shows up in his own little proportion boxes (was there ever a Modulor woman?). Here the perfect proportion of the city replaces human spectators; the city observes itself, having programmed its own (self) observation. People are absent not because they are peripheral, or dispensable, but because they *are* the city, its permanent configuration. Cars and people are always the same, always in the same movement, and for this reason their movement does not need to be shown—it is unshowable, since what is different is always the same. Consciousness *is* the solidity of the city, capable of looking out but not in. The cars and planes are frozen, even in their descent, and the people are absent. The people are observers, and for that reason they see—from the proper perspective—rather than are seen. In the midst of the perfect architectural and urban harmony, there is a strict iconoclasm: the image of the person is always absent, invisible, for the same reason that the eye of the observing artist is absent from most paintings, or the camera lens of the photographing camera is absent from most photographs. The observer is on *this side* of the scene. The urban scene for this reason *is* the observing human, rather than humans observed; it therefore *is* the consciousness of observation, *is* the self-consciousness of the city dweller, which is the human *tout court*. The human is the autobiographical subject of the urban observer, the urban depictor: Le Corbusier himself, in the perfect stasis of contemplation of self through contemplation of city.

Le Corbusier's narratives of life in the radiant city also project this time-lessness, this absolute of perspective. Here the cessation of time touches its equivalent, the instantaneous. Nothing involves delay, any annoying separation of moments that could interrupt the perfect perspective, the perfect harmony of individuals perceiving perfect harmony, thanks of course to the urbanist. Just as Le Corbusier is as much a writer and polemicist as an architect, so too he is as much a narrative author as an expository one. The Radiant City is, first and foremost, a story: the story of how we move and live, and can finally rest, in the city. It takes very little to flesh the story out with people and social situations. It's a strange story, however, a paradoxical one, since Le Corbusier's narrative is one of absence of delay, in other words of the temporality necessary to all narrative.

Imagine, Le Corbusier suggests, life in one of the tower blocks he proposes, and in its surrounding green spaces. In *The City of To-Morrow*, Le Corbusier contrasts the city of today with what is to come. He writes of the angry and coercive concierge one has to deal with nowadays, the noise in the apartment, the impossibility of having parties for fear of bothering others, of trying to exercise in one's room because it's inconvenient to go to the health club. And it gets worse: 'As for food, your maid goes to the local store and wastes a lot of time, and everything is very expensive. As for your car, the garage is ten minutes away, and if it is raining you reach home soaked, in spite of having a car. And your children have to be taken to the Park to play: that is, if they have a nurse-maid or governess' (1989, 214). Le Corbusier goes on to ask: 'What if we could at one step wipe out all these difficulties?' and concludes: if only we could '*by order bring about freedom*' (214; emphasis in original).

What strikes one here, along with the obvious political implications of the *cri de cœur* of the bourgeois suffering from the tyranny of his servants, and the reactionary implications thereof (order brings about freedom), is the desire for a kind of domestic Taylorism, that would cut wasted time—not only that of the servants, but of oneself. All the domestic agony of current everyday bourgeois life comes down to waste: wasted effort, inconvenience, but above all wasted time. But unlike industrial Taylorism, whose purpose was to increase efficiency and thus profits by cutting wasted time on the part of workers, in this case the elimination of wasted time is a kind of narrative imperative applicable to all. 'Freedom' is the redefinition of one's life as a narrative in which, paradoxically, time does not pass. The leisure of the leisure class is inseparable from instantaneity. Delay as such, the gap between desire and its fulfillment, the gap between the consciousness and its wants, the free will and its exercise, is eliminated. Such a freedom would abolish narrative because it would exit from time and exist in a kind of glorious present. Or, conversely, a true not-narrative of freedom would somehow be elaborated in the *absence* of the passage of time between a want and its fulfillment. We see just this absence as Le Corbusier goes on to narrate life in the Radiant City.

We learn that 'grouping 660 flats' in a 'block of closed cell-like elements' will facilitate the organization of life: freedom through order. On the ground floor would be 'commissariat, the restaurant service, domestic service and laundering' (Le Corbusier 1989, 217). This pseudo-military organization, rather than breeding the boredom ('hurry up and wait') of the army, instead leads to the instantaneous satisfaction of needs:

> The kitchen would be capable of supplying meals of a simple or elaborate sort at all hours. If you desired to bring some friends back to supper round about midnight, say after the theatre, a mere telephone call is all that is needed for you to find the table laid and waiting for you—with a servant who is not sulking, as he happens to have just come on for the night shift. An experienced hotel manager, a specialist with a staff of specialists, would organize and see to the whole domestic economy of the block. (217, 220)

Upper-middle-class social life—that all-important dinner after the theatre—is now organized along factory lines, and the sulking servant has been replaced, through the miracle of correct architectural organization, by one who is happy at his job. That's Le Corbusier's story, but, like so many happy stories, it abolishes itself as a narrative: nothing happens, nothing can or ever will happen, as time is abolished in order's freedom. We have gone to a posthistorical realm, thanks to correct architecture, one where social tensions have been effectively done away with—the servants are now happy—and for this reason the possibility of revolution is banished (or, more precisely, made obsolete).[3]

At this point Le Corbusier's words and sketches join: the not-narrative is inseparable from the not-sketch, the sketch that represents the absence of any living (and moving) urban inhabitants. Time and autonomous individuals have been banished: the glorious perspectives and the perfect organization of commerce and entertainment have been shaped through the absence of the exercise of the human will (the absence of time) and the absence of the drift of nonauthorized perspective (the absence of people in space). All that is left is the figure of Le Corbusier himself, artist and technician, the last man hidden in the perfect plan, consciousness as the seen. Art as technics triumphs, on the other hand, because without will and drift, without humans to cause problems, total aesthetic organization—what Le Corbusier calls freedom—is for the first time possible. Total calculation is total freedom, minus the human. Or humans without the human, since Le Corbusier still needs at least the idea of functioning bodies in his cities, but humans stripped of their human-ness, of the delay represented by their unfulfilled desires and their irrational urges.

One should not judge Le Corbusier too harshly in this: after all, he has provided a valuable service by elaborating the most sophisticated version yet of a technically perfected esthetics (or vice versa), society, and even ecology (remember, his cities are 'green', bringing nature back to the city). If that perfection involves a certain subtraction, then so be it. I would go so far as to suggest that Le Corbusier's technocratic stance even serves as the unconscious of the Situationists—he is both what they hate and fear the most, and the bedrock of aesthetic and technical meaning they depend on if only to revolt against it. The spectacle at its highest point of development is after all the incessant consumption of images, divorced from historical time and assuring the perpetuation of social life in a bubble of alienation. Alienation, that is, from worthwhile human contact, communication, and productive, meaningful, historical labor. One could argue that Le Corbusier is the end-point of the completely alienated state of social being, of everyday life, that the Situationists love to hate. Nothing happens in his world, or everything happens immediately, without happening, without resonance: the world, that is, cities, are perfect spectacles without anyone there: imagine a Beckett play where there is no irony and everyone is happy. Le Corbusier's cities are perpetual motion machines in which there is no motion; when all motion is to be found in the technically perfected repetition of the same, motion itself is lost in synchronicity.

But what grounds the technical for Le Corbusier? In the seeming absence of so many institutions of civil society—Le Corbusier's cities seem to lack any third space: city halls, pool halls, fora, beer gardens, even cinemas—what motivates the Corbusian citizen besides wanting a quick meal? What is he or she supposed to do all the time? And what is the city as 'machine for living' supposed to do? Or is that the wrong question? If so, why?

II

In the early 1940s, under the occupation, Le Corbusier journeyed to the French fascist capital, Vichy, to try to convince the authorities—going all the way up to Marshall Pétain himself—of the values of his radical model of urban renewal. He was met, it seems, with utter indifference (Richards 2003, 54–65). Along the way, he wrote a book with a fellow French corporatist, François de Pierrefeu (1942), titled *La Maison des Hommes* [*House of Man*].[4] This is a fascinating book, not only for its political complexity but also for the questions it poses concerning authorship. If indeed we can take de Pierrefeu's argument as essentially representing Le Corbusier's—as Simon Richards (2003, 222), for example, does[5]—then we can follow the crucial step that Le Corbusier takes from a critique of contemporary life to the ultimate valorization of the sun. For, much like the American Technocrats of the same period,[6] Le Corbusier would ground his urban nonrevolution in a more efficient use of energy; his theory is, in effect, an energetics. This is of crucial importance because this gesture allows Le Corbusier to fuse technical solutions with what are essentially moral (and even spiritual) ones. And, as we'll see, this fusion will result in both the triumph of the technical and the elaboration of the most formidable challenge with which the technical can be confronted.

De Pierrefeu–Le Corbusier stresses that the current economic order is engaged in 'over-consumption'—that no respect is shown for the natural resources of the earth, and this leads to humans 'weighing down on the earth':

> Oil, coal, minerals flow from the flanks of the earth in streams that will never run out. All discretion has been abolished vis à vis mother nature; more than abolished, derided. [. . .] The dogma of the day is *the wastage of a cosmic reserve*, one irreplaceable and given one time only [. . .]. (1942, 31–32; emphasis in original)

So far we have a kind of proto–peak oil theory (shared, by the way, with the American Technocrats),[7] which is promptly tied to another kind of overconsumption—that of what nowadays we would call commodities, or rather commodity fetishes. De Pierrefeu: 'And let's note how false needs, artificially aroused, show a tendency to cause each other to multiply, which industry, operating in an additive manner, will only be able to satisfy in an ever more minimal way. From this, there will be disappointment, furor, and revolt. Until the nature of things, in the end, gets revenge, as it did in America in 1929' (1942, 34).

Where today is the 'spiritual house' in this world of 'imposed dreams'? Certainly not in the urban 'palace of mirages', which the author(s) associate with the current 'Modern city', since the latter, '[chasing] away the *sun*, also chased away the invisible radiance (*rayonnement*) of which it is the instrument and symbol, both of the morals of society and of the heart of the citizens' (De Pierrefeu and Le Corbusier 1942, 39–40; emphasis in original).

People might be the victims of the tendency to overconsume, to chase the mirage of the commodity fetish to the detriment of the city and society in general. This monstrous fetishization is given a double material basis: in energy, and in the city. De Pierrefeu and Le Corbusier would ground liberation from (bad) modernity in the revision of current modes of energy consumption and in the reconstruction of the city by the planner. For today's city, the bad, pre-Corbu city, is a mirage of false consumption, and it is *dark*; the essay suggests a reciprocal causative link between these two. The darkness of illusion is doubled by the darkness of the city, its congestion and blockage of sunlight. Since we are inattentive to things, since we waste them, since we misuse them by taking them to be the source of real happiness, we are inattentive to the origin of real health, and thus we live in, and maintain, bad cities. These in turn, through their gloominess and energy inefficiency, their fundamental wastefulness, only reinforce our delusions and immoral habits. We ourselves have created this blockage: if we are transformers of the sun, we alone, it would seem, of all animals are also the nontransformers of the sun, its blockers.

The sun is 'instrument and symbol', and for this reason the sun is both the origin and end of human, and of all life. Freeing ourselves from 'false dreams' means building the city and restoring its 'principal and key', which is the sun: 'the 24 hour cycle' and the 'radiation of the day' (De Pierrefeu and Le Corbusier 1942, 40). The radiant city is not just a metaphor: it is indeed radiant since the tower blocks designed by Le Corbusier are set at angles that allow for maximum sunlight. And, of course, they are set in parks, 'nature': there is an enormous amount of open land around the *unités d'habitation* which make access to the sun possible, as soon as one ventures out of the house (or rather apartment, 'cell'). Thus the sun is the central factor in what today we would call an ecologically oriented architecture: one attentive to 'natural' rhythms and natural energy sources. But the sun is more than this: it takes on a kind of existential originality, in that it serves not just a practical function in life in and outside of buildings—but it also defines man. De Pierrefeu and Le Corbusier write (1942, 44–46; emphasis in original):

> The reestablishment of fruitful labor, and a happier labor, imperatively demand the *radiance of the sun*. From the point of view of physics, the living being is nothing other than 'a transformer of solar energy', in the apt formula of Dr. Pierre Winter, and of all the many forms of this energy, it is light, from the infra-red to the ultra-violet, which constitutes its most indispensable nutrient. He absorbs it directly by the skin, through millions of papillae, tuned to the luminous vibrations like little precision tuners. He absorbs it directly through food—vegetables and meat—which are veritable 'stores' of light. Darkness, the sick light of cities, broken up by smoke and dust, are the very power of tuberculosis, rickets, and neurasthenia.

Dr. Pierre Winter is also quoted in *Destin de Paris*, where pretty much the same point is made, with the additional statement by Le Corbusier (1941, 15): 'The sun in every room, all year. Consequently, no windows facing north'.[8] There is one crucial difference between the two passages; in *Destin de Paris* Dr. Winter himself is directly quoted (15; emphasis in original): *'The human being* [l'être humain] *is only a tranformer of solar energy; life is only a circulation of this energy; light is one of our fundamental nutrients* [aliments].

(We absorb it through our skin, we tap into it every day in these 'reserves of light' constituted by the majority of vegetable and animal nutrients [Dr. Pierre Winter, fifth CIAM congress, Paris 1937])'.

De Pierrefeu and Le Corbusier in *La Maison des Hommes* write of the 'living being' as solar transformer; Dr. Winter writes of 'human beings' as doing the transforming. Certainly the paraphrase of Dr. Winter is appropriate, because humans are, after all, living beings; yet Dr. Winter's own stress on humans in *Destin de Paris* is decisive.[9] It establishes a contrast between, on the one hand, all natural systems, dependent as they are on sunlight, and human beings in particular: it stresses the link between the human as a natural system and the larger role of the sun. It puts the city, locus of the human, at the center of the relation between the sun and the ecology in which we thrive. The city of solar architecture is the differentiating space, the articulation point between simple nature and the human in all its complexity.

And yet there is something here that goes against the human, and this is what is brought out by the substitution by de Pierrefeu and Le Corbusier of 'the living being' for 'the human being'. The fact is that man is 'only' a 'transformer' of energy; the metaphor here is of a device, the transformer, that changes the wavelengths of electricity in order to get a job done. Here the transformer is the human, electricity is solar light, and the job done is survival. The word 'only' would seem to stress the fact that everything that all humans do—all their grandiose accomplishments—is reducible to a mere transformation of energy (a purely technical function, akin to the work of the transformer), and that, in the end, by tweaking the quote our authors suggest that this role of and for the human is itself not even human: after all, all living beings do it. They transform, they are transformers. And, presumably, they are transformed. And if humans block solar energy in their dark cities, they alone are the creatures who block their own nature as transformers. Hence their need for a conscious practice of architecture: that of Le Corbusier.

This is a revealing transformation: from human to all living beings. The transformation of solar energy cannot be seen as an anthropocentric gesture. In fact the ironic mode of Dr. Winter's original statement already stresses this kinship between humans and life in general, and the relative insignificance of the human: all we do is transform energy. But we alone as humans tend to block it. Hierarchies are reversed: man is not the author but a passive transformer, whether he knows it or not. Humans are at the service of energy, in fact that's what they do, or should do: serve it by transforming it. Dr. Winter's passage invites us to reverse the typical hierarchy: it is less a matter of humans using solar energy than it is of solar energy making use of humans. The human itself is de-anthropomorphized in this reversal: the human essence, if we can call it that, is not human at all (it is *only* solar energy), and the solar is fundamentally indifferent to the human. The solar expresses itself as solar in the human, by transforming itself, but does so in all other living beings as well. At best the human can be like all other creatures; at worst, it will try to block and deny solar energy. Thus de Pierrefeu and Le Corbusier's revision of the passage is 'spot-on'. It's just that the human is able to build . . . cities. Humans have to build cities in order to most effectively transform solar energy; they have to do consciously what all other creatures do unconsciously.

It's not, then, even a case of the solar becoming conscious of itself in the human. 'Man', the perfectly proportioned man of the Modulor, builds the world as nothing more than a solar transformer. Man is the conscious interruption in the solar that intensifies the solar, by placing it in a human narrative: the timeless narrative of the city. The city is the machine for living that makes possible the health of the human through the proper transmission of the solar; 'man' in turn builds the city to properly accumulate, transfer and transform the solar. The city is the transformer of the human transformer, from energy waster to energy transmitter. It seems that other 'living beings' can transform solar energy in the same way; bees or ants come to mind. Conversely, it would seem that the human is the only 'living thing' that can *not* transform energy: after all, humans are devoted to their bad cities, which ineffectively transmit solar energy, thus endangering human health, and presumably the health of other living beings as well. The book—Le Corbusier's book, his narrative—is thus necessary to transform the human into a proper transformer, by showing 'him' how to transform the city. It is the non-natural break in a circuit, which nevertheless aids in the functioning of a natural circuit (sun—city—human), since that circuit has been harmed, interrupted, by the bad human city. Where the human really distinguishes itself—is unique—is therefore not in the simple transformation of solar energy—the human shares that with all other living beings—but in the resistance to solar transformation, what we could call solar blockage, and to the eventual conscious undoing of this blockage through Le Corbusier. The human is limitation, not plenitude, the irrational production of scarcity and dirt, the production of narrative delay (the sulky servants, the wait for dinner after the theatre), but also and above all the overcoming of this limitation. The danger of the human lies in the diminution of solar energy, which can only be countered, in the human case, by the supreme conscious human creation: the architecture of the Radiant City. Sunlight for humans (unlike animals) is therefore a construct of consciousness—and ultimately of Le Corbusier's consciousness.

What is sunlight, exactly? Is Le Corbusier, channeling Dr. Winter, really even singing the praises of solar energy? Or is a humanized solar energy—presumably all we could know or experience—singing the praises of Le Corbusier (by consciously coming into itself, so to speak, through Le Corbusier, in the radiant city)? Is human consciousness, then, merely the vehicle by which intensified solar energy comes back to itself, after being interrupted by that same consciousness?

One notes a certain uncanny in this movement of solar energy. It is double, both more than human—encompassing the human and everything else—but strangely less than the human, too. It allows itself to be waylaid, interfered with, blocked. It risks finitude, limitation, being extinguished in darkness, dirt and disease. It allows itself to be tweaked, transformed, in a therapeutic way by Le Corbusier. It allows others, ignorant architects, non–Le Corbusiers, to transform its energy into bad architecture, self-defeating (and solar-defeating) cities. Uncanny solar energy talks through Dr. Winter and Le Corbusier (when he paraphrases Dr. Winter and is ventriloquized by de Pierrefeu); but it is not reducible to them. As such it can hardly be pinned down; it is in a constant state of appropriation, reappropriation, loss and rediscovery. And we could say it's not even a thing, but the very principle of the transformation of things, and thus their production, reproduction and recycling. It is what allows all the other things to grow, to be transformed, to be reconfigured. Solar energy is the 'origin', where everything comes from, what everything is transformed (back) into when it is eaten or lived in or built.[10] It is all the language necessary for these transformations through the human. It then must also be the negations carried out by language, the sign systems, the metaphors, that all refer back to the sun and represent it. It must be the human strategies, linguistic, narrative, architectural, necessary to rechannel the sun and defeat the bad architecture that would block it. But what then is the sun?

Primarily the sun would be not just the origin of life, what has to be transformed by life in order for life to exist, but the origin of all life, and all metaphor (the transformations of all things as carried out through the interventions of consciousness), since it makes possible, indeed mandates the human transformation of solar energy—under the aegis of Le Corbusier's architecture—which itself depends on language, signifying systems, complexes of metaphors.

Solar energy, then, doubles the human, talks, does things, transforms itself—it's the ultimate shape-shifter—but it is not human, not reducible to the human in any case, and even represents the demise of the human (or at least the finite, historical human) to the extent that the temporalized human is the prime author of the blockage rather than the transmission of energy. Or, conversely, the human is this blockage that always already, so to speak, invests the sun, in the movement that necessarily delays the sun, separates it from itself, in transmitting the sun in story and architectural plan—and which thereby, paradoxically, overcomes the blockage, and through the signifying practices of consciousness triumphs over it.

III

The sun, then, can be characterized as a master metaphor, the term which gives life, from which all meaning flows and to which all meaning returns. It is the emitter of the endlessly transformed energy that guarantees meaning and life. And yet while it generates human meaning—meaning is nothing more than the transmission and transformation of energy, both in life forms and in meanings—it itself resists reduction to meaning. It is not just human meaning; it is the generator of meaning, of 'existence' of all living beings. It is the blockage and unblocking of meaning. Solar energy can never be reduced to a single meaning, a single master metaphor, no matter how encompassing. As a source, *the* source, in order to be transmitted, elaborated, it has to differ within itself, open a gap, a space of not-meaning, out of which the differentiation of metaphor, the representation and constitution of the city, can take place. The sun itself is from the first a trope, since it stands for—by way of metonymy—its rays, which are themselves liable to endless substitution and transformation. In itself, so to speak, the sun opens the gap that constitutes all relations of signifier and signified: the gap of the not-being of the signified, its demise and/or proliferation, extinction and proliferation, and through that the unmooring of the signifier, its provisional status and endless duplication. Through that metaphorization the sun itself runs the risk of being just another metaphor, all the while playing the role of an element heterogeneous to the system, generating it, mastering it. At those moments when it falls, loses its privilege as primary and unitary source of all meaning, it becomes just another trope, just another term in the signifying chain of cities. At that moment the city darkens, grows dirty and corrupt; the sun is (temporarily, at least) just another object in the sky, just another signifier in the chain.[11]

Take, for example, the case of the automobile in Le Corbusier. The car is necessary to the radiant city; after all, what characterized the old city, epitomized by old Paris, the stinky and decayed first, second and third *arrondissements*, was the traffic tie-ups, the *maladies de circulation*. '*Circulation*' in French can, of course, mean both traffic and circulation (of the blood, for example), and condemning the fact that in large parts of modern cities traffic can't move is to diagnose the city as a body, with blockages of arteries and chronic inflammations. To open up the city, restore it to health, is to make efficient circulation possible, and this of course requires the car. After all, modern technology means speed, the speed of travel in the city, and it is a crime—literally, a crime against the sun—on the urbanist's part to resist it. All the dingy little streets do nothing more than impede the movement and necessity of the automobile, and deny its imperative, which, after all, must be the imperative of the sun: circulation, health, growth, life—the instantaneity of consciousness. Writing of the towers of his city, Le Corbusier waxes rhapsodic:

[Actually] these sky-scrapers [Le Corbusier's version, that is, as opposed to those of New York] will contain the city's brains, the brains of the whole nation. They stand for all the careful working-out and organization on which the general activity is based. Everything is concentrated in them: apparatus for abolishing time and space, telephones, cables and wireless; the banks, business affairs and the control of industry; finance, commerce, specialization. The station is in the midst of the sky-scrapers, the Tubes run below them and the tracks for fast traffic are at their base. There need be no limit to the number of motor vehicles, for immense covered parking areas linked up by subterranean passages would collect together the host on wheels which camps in the city each day and is the result of rapid *individual* transit. (1985, 186–88; emphasis in original)

No doubt one can criticize the bourgeois individualism on display here, the cult of the car linked, as in so much of today's American urban design, to the putative desires of the 'individual' consumer. But the cult of individualism obscures another, deeper question. If we return to our old friend the sun, we note the emphasis placed on the automobile here as solution to the city's antisolar bias is a paradoxical return to that which occludes the sun. The reason for this is fairly evident: if the city is the most efficient transformer, via the human (i.e., Le Corbusier himself) of the sun's rays, but the car is dependent on a fossil fuel, gasoline, which is nothing other than the capture, the hiding, so to speak, of solar energy. Solar energy in automobility is not just instantaneous, but it is elaborated in a temporality, stored; it leaves a trace or stratum that may or may not be deciphered and tapped. It may or may not be put to 'use', to 'work'. Fossil fuels, after all, are only ancient sunlight (Hartmann 2004), the manifestation of the simple fact that sunlight can be diverted, hidden, preserved, but also lost. Most ancient plants, after all, were not preserved; their carbon was fed back into the atmosphere. Only a small proportion were preserved, in bogs, then under great pressure, in such a way that their sunlight later could be 'liberated' in work (on the part of humans). This preservation/loss of sunlight has another feature: it is finite. There is only so much fossil fuel in the ground, and it is a precious resource, as de Pierrefeu and Le Corbusier have already reminded us. But its finitude is in direct contradiction to the infinity of solar energy, its endless stream that makes all life possible.

Fossil fuel, then, in a strange way is not solar energy but instead its doubling, its dead twin. Or its twin that, through its finitude, brings death with it: the eventual stagnation, the run-down of the old city when fuels become scarce and cars clog it. And not only cars do the clogging: the pollution produced from the burning of fuels clogs the lungs of the city's inhabitants. Fuel stands in for solar energy, represents it, but as a gap, a risk, a threat of scarcity, of extinction. Oil is a supplement to the sun, an added element that is apparently necessary to the city in its functioning, but which is outside the solar economy of plenitude and speed (if not instantaneity). Or, put another way, the sun evidently needs fossil fuel to complete the city—the solar machine man has created to transform the sun's rays into human life via petroleum— but that necessity introduces a gap, a moment of non-energy, non plenitude of meaning and life into the totality of the urban, and hence solar, energetic economy. This is the great un-thought of Le Corbusier's work, because it puts in question the totalizing potential of solar architecture itself. How can solar architecture be solar if the city in which it finds itself is driven by fossil fuels?

At the same time, this fossil-fuel finitude reintroduces the question of the metaphorics of the sun. Through its mortal double, oil, the sun reconnects to the necessity of its representation, its proliferation in metaphor. Oil is evidently necessary, since the privileged solar human, Le Corbusier himself, has incorporated it into the definitive city, given it a central role. But oil is not merely a stand-in, a substitute, for the real thing; *pace* Dr. Winter, the real thing in the new city, the sun, needs a substitute, it is not self-sufficient. It needs a representative, a double, oil. But that in turn means the sun is not just the author and guarantor of all things; it itself is just another source, just another disposition of energy, just another sense of what the city is and can be. Another, albeit privileged, symbol (of 'invisible radiance'). The closed economy of energy from the sun—always properly recycled by animals and sometimes by humans, always there when you need it, in infinite quantities— is conditioned by the very scarcity and loss that characterizes the old city, the human city as darkness and concealment. This loss serves as the signifying break, the gap in the circle of solar plenitude. The sun is a metaphor, then, that can only work in the best of circumstances, as all metaphors do, through loss and concealment, through what is not it. In this case, through oil.

The human is not just a signifier of the solar. The sun is a metaphor of the human, in all its ambiguity. The new human as transformer, but also the old human as loser, as principle of loss and obscurity. The sun runs the risk of doubling the death, the sheer bone-headed stupidity, that humanity represents and embodies. This explains, perhaps, the smiley face that Le Corbusier rather unconvincingly puts on the face of the sun, in at least one illustration (1941, 19). The sun is human, it smiles at us, but it's a human that is least human, most dead, most potentially absent, in its doubling of, in its representation of, the human. The inhuman sublime. The sun not a perfect origin of metaphor, but a prosopopeia, the dead subject speaking in a human voice, of the necessity of its own absence, its own death (De Man 1979). The infinite power, the sublimity, of the sun in this case is not its reassuring guarantee of the success of the city, of the Kant-fueled total mastery of human reason, but its uncanniness, the reminder that the solar is always doubled in itself (in its highest moment, the city) by fossil fuel, that the human as living conscious city is doubled by the profound absence of human comprehension: human mobility in pollution. The sun is the dead (represented) face speaking to itself as the death of the human, it's the image of the human in the absence of its volition, its loss of control of the city, and the city's future (its permanence). That loss of control, the return of the city to darkness, to energy waste, is ironically just another version of the human, the human as the finitude of fuel, as the 'use' of ancient, stored, traced, solar energy to the point of depletion. The happy face of the sun is a symbol of the human, the prosopopeia of the human reflecting upon itself, back to itself, as death, death speaking and shining, via the sun, in the sun.

The metaphorical nature of the sun is precisely what prevents it from being a benign natural force that generates and grounds meaning and guarantees humanity's centrality in the universe. This has profound ecological implications: rather than authorizing a harmonious eco-planet or eco-city in which all living beings have their place, validated by human management of sustainable systems, and ultimately grounded in solar energy, the sun is 'rotten' in Georges Bataille's (1985) sense. Or at least, as Bataille writes, it's double, one side friendly, the source of meaning, life, health, whatever, the other the point of oblivion, the blinding, pitiless disk into which the auto-mutilating madman stares. This second sun is not a happy smiling face/force through which we and 'nature' derive our full meaning together—but of course under our watchful and profitable management; instead the sun is profoundly indifferent, a metaphor incapable of arresting a labyrinthine movement in which tropes are constantly flipped, incapable of referring back to one stable meaning or sense at the top of the system. The indifference of metaphorical drift is a feature of a system characterized by the incongruous juxtaposition of a technically flawless system—Le Corbusier's city—and a profound and inhuman obliviousness marking the sliding of signifiers. The sun is a dead sun, its radiance the indifference of ruins, channeled through the endless proliferation of metaphors: the automobility of the sun.

Or perhaps we could say that technical perfection and metaphoric drift— what Jacques Derrida called 'dissemination' (1981)—are closely linked. And as Paul de Man pointed out, the movement of grammar—through which metaphors are coordinated in a syntagmatic linkage—is itself inhuman, a mechanism capable of running without human intervention.[12] This dream of the grammatical machine is also the dream of a perfect solar architecture: radiant cities could be put up, after all, following preestablished models (or computer programs) mechanically coordinating towers, the position of the sun on any given terrain, arterial highways, and so on. After Le Corbusier, you don't even need an architect; the appropriate software can do the job. Aesthetics, with the (Modulor) human at the top, the basis for the measurement of all things, is inseparable from the uncanny movement by which the sun's symbolic and moral radiance is doubled by the sun's knowledge of itself, and speech, as dead. The dead sun speaks—death. Aesthetics itself is now perfect, perfected and wholly irrelevant, since there is no place for a privileged humanity: the world can sustain itself perfectly well without human intervention, or with only the endless proliferation of metaphors whose author is dead and whose extension is infinite.[13] Humanity accomplishes itself in its subtraction. One thinks of Wall-E (2008), the little robot working on a depopulated planet, savoring the filmic fictions he finds on old cassette tapes, endlessly cleaning up crap whose meaning eludes him, crap whose forms saturate the world. His little corner of the world is perfectly ordered, a technically perfect dump: nothing ever happens there, and its irrelevance is sadly funny. The film of course has a happy ending, but one can just as easily imagine Wall-E's world ending with no change, and the utter indifference of the sun shining on whatever remains. History ends in the indifferent and atemporal repetitions of the machine, articulated through the movements of dead actors.

Just as the sun is double, Le Corbusier's city is double as well. On the one side, the city in the image of man, solar man, Modulor man, but a city devoted to this figure's comings and goings, whatever they might be, and for whatever (inscrutable) purpose. This most human of worlds is strangely dehumanized, it closes its circle of self-regard by embracing solitude and willed alienation. The model for this in Le Corbusier is, as Simon Richards (2003, 133–34) has pointed out, Blaise Pascal, the great seventeenth-century French mathematician and writer. It was Pascal who lamented all the world's 'diversions', the need for the distractions that keep us from going crazy. Pascal's solution is to argue the necessity of the rejection of all *divertissements* that block us from God. We must turn from the world, sit alone in our rooms. 'I have often said that the sole cause of man's unhappiness is that he does not know how to sit quietly in his room' (quoted in Richards 2003, 133).[14]

The problem with this, of course, is that focusing on oneself in one's room can itself become a diversion. What's needed, then, is the ability to isolate oneself, and then isolate oneself from oneself: thus Pascal (quoted in Richards 2003, 133) could write: 'we must love a being who is within us but is not our own self [. . .] and is both ourselves and not ourselves [. . .] True conversion consists of self-annihilation before the universal being'.

Richards stresses that Le Corbusier ultimately values in his city not the gregariousness of city life, the diversity and neighbourhood camaraderie championed by all the Jane Jacobses of the world, but instead its solitude. What can at first seem like an anti-urban critique of the city—in effect Le Corbusier redesigns the city in order to deurbanize it, because he profoundly distrusts city life in general (Richards 2007)—goes on to reveal itself instead as a method for deriving a kind of higher spirituality through a new kind of alienated city living. But it all depends on how one defines alienation. Many people are struck by the seeming sterility of Le Corbusier's notion of urban life; the Surrealists, Situationists, et al. would die of boredom in all that solar illumination. What do you *do* in a Radiant City?

For Le Corbusier, in effect, the point of the urban 'machine for living' is to make it possible to live a modern life, all the while withdrawing from the world and annihilating oneself. All the services that would be provided in the city, the ultimate conveniences of life in his city, have a larger purpose: they make Pascalian withdrawal from the world and human life itself possible. Hence Le Corbusier (1947, 18) could write: 'And since leisure will require a man to spend more time in his room (Pascal's *desideratum*), a new concept of home will arise; an extension of the idea of home to take in the sun, all space and nature's green'.

This is a brilliant passage, because it links Pascalian self-annihilation to the pleasure of sunning oneself in one's beautiful apartment. And once again the sun—never mentioned to my knowledge in a laudatory mode in Pascal—is at the heart of it. The ultimate gloom and doomster, Blaise himself, is transformed into a California hippie, basking in sun, space and green. That is what the city does: it turns the darkened, withdrawn Pascal into a solar transformer. Withdrawal itself is solarized.

A (non)society of Pascals living in *unités d'habitation* might sound a little strange, but perhaps the role of the sun will help us decipher passages like this. Since Le Corbusier does not write of God, we can assume that the mystical state of self-abstraction he is calling for is essentially godless, or, more accurately, that the place of God in Pascal is taken in Le Corbusier by sun, space and green. It is at this point that we start to see the logic of Le Corbusier's sun worship. The sun is less a plenitude than a movement of self-abstraction and self-abnegation. The ideal city dweller sits alone in the cell, the apartment in the *unité*. After working, whatever that means, he or she returns home and meditates, alone, in the sun. The technically superb appointments of the city and its dwellings make possible this meditation on, and before, the sun. The perfection of the city effaces itself, so to speak, before the 'self-annihilation' of the solar subject. This self-annihilation, as we've seen in the case of Le Corbusier's subjectivity, and in the case of his signifying machine, is of the instant, or of repetition within the instant; it's outside the temporal flow. In this atemporality, the city-subject melds with an uncanny sun, the sun as symbol of the inhuman, of that which affirms but defies the self-conception of the human as center of space and time.

The human is this darkness at the heart of solar signification, nevertheless at the heart of the signification (which dictates a gap), this not-knowing at the culmination of architectural-aesthetic reason. The ideal citizen of Le Corbusier sunbathes in this light of prosopopeia, the self-expression of the dead or 'rotten sun', fully darkened but made necessary—and hence contingent—by the diverting and antidiversionary human sign lolling beneath it. It is a social connection, an urban connection, that is at the same time a kind of mystical break and withdrawal to the point of human extinction. The machine for living is the privileged vehicle for this withdrawal. Bataille makes the connection between his decomposing sun and human sacrifice, and Le Corbusier's sun is not far behind: his sacrifice is less a bloody one than the simple extinction of the social subject at the moment of the most finely engineered urban sociability. The human erases itself in a being-toward-extinction, the repetitive effacement of the human in the spacing, the reconnection, of the sun. The most perfectly planned city, the most technologically developed and aesthetically urban space, stands naked and abandoned on the planet, under the rays of the mortal orb.

NOTES

1. On Le Corbusier's connection with the 1920s journal *Plans*, and his connections with Georges Bataille, see Allan Stoekl (1990).

2. All translations of this work are my own.

3. As in Alexandre Kojève's *Introduction à la lecture de Hegel* (1980), at the end of history nothing new can happen. Humanity dies, in effect, since it is defined by its historical project (human liberation), and that has been completed. Le Corbusier goes a bit further, implying that not only is historical transformation (i.e., revolution) at an end, but urban change is as well.

4. All translations of this work are my own.

5. De Pierrefeu, it seems, wrote the narrative text, Le Corbusier provided the sketches and commentary accompanying them. It seems that de Pierrefeu was serving mainly as Le Corbusier's mouthpiece: as Simon Richards puts it, 'even the most cursory reading reveals that [de Pierrefeu] has been deeply inculcated into the Corbusian creed [. . .] For this reason I will be treating de Pierrefeu's text as a reliable transcript of Le Corbusier's own ideals' (2003, 222). One should note, however, that de Pierrefeu emits a few openly fascistic and racist pronouncements along the way, which are not on display in Le Corbusier's other writings.

6. 'Technocracy Inc.' was a political movement (despite its name) in the United States in the early 1930s. It promoted a corporatist plan of government (run by experts, not politicians), and a revision of the monetary system that was to be based on energetic inputs rather than gold (Scott et al. 1933).

7. M. King Hubbert participated in the Technocracy movement of the 1930s. As a petroleum expert he plotted out a bell curve of natural resources, including petroleum, that any technocratic planning would have to take into account. His work became highly influential in the early 2000s (the 'peak oil' theory) since it promised to predict the imminent depletion of global oil reserves (1949, 103–9).

8. All translations of this work are my own.

9. As a contributor to planiste (corporatist, technocratic) journals such as *Plans* and *Préludes*, along with Le Corbusier, Dr. Winter was very much associated with the technocratic 'new right' tendencies that later attempted, without a lot of success, to gain traction at Vichy (see note 3, above). Dr. Winter's articles have as subjects topics such as the role of sports and labour, the psychological conditions of labour, the circulation of air (in homes), the importance of the peasantry, and the 'laws of nature' that determine planning (these works are cited on the final page of the 1941 edition of *Destin de Paris*). Dr. Winter's interest in solar energy was paralleled by other French thinkers of the period, such as Georges Ambrosino, a physicist who, like Le Corbusier, had connections with Georges Bataille.

10. Interestingly, Le Corbusier never writes about what today we would call a larger urban ecology, but only about the organisms—and primarily lawns, trees— which are expressly placed in the city (in parks surrounding the *unités d'habitation*) by humans, for the enjoyment of humans.

11. On the metaphoric of the sun, see Derrida (1974).

12. De Man (1979, 298) writes of the 'deconstruction of the figural dimension [. . .] as not unconscious but mechanical, systematic in its performance but arbitrary in its principle, like a grammar'.

13. This, of course, was a problem for Kojève (1947): the end of history also meant the death of man. His survival would be only as a kind of higher-level animal, engaged in purely empty and formal—if death-embracing—activities.

14. This passage starts the famous 'Divertissements' section in Pascal's Pensées (section 168 in the version edited by Philippe Sellier [Paris: Le Livre de Poche, 2000]). In French: '*J'ai dit souvent que tout le malheur des hommes vient d'une seule chose, qui est de ne savoir pas demeurer en repos dans une chambre*'.

Chapter 7

Escaping Mediocrity

Renaissance Florence and the Rejection of the City

Katie Campbell

In the jubilee year of 1300, the Florentine diplomat Giovanni Villani went on pilgrimage to Rome. Inspired by the city's great monuments and the famed deeds of its ancient citizens, Villani decided to write a history of his own hometown. In his *Nuova Cronica* or New Chronicle, he claimed: 'Florence, daughter and offspring of Rome, was mounting and pursuing great purposes while Rome was in its decline' (Levey 1996, 6).

With hindsight this pride might seem hubristic, as in 1333 Florence suffered catastrophic floods; in 1346 the crops failed, leading to famine and unrest; in 1347 the major banks went bust when the English King Edward III defaulted on his debts; and in 1348 the city was visited by a bubonic plague—known as the Black Death—which destroyed over half of the population. Three decades later, a strike by the wool workers in the summer of 1378—the Florentines generally revolted in summer—nearly sparked a revolution among the city's large population of disenfranchised, ghetto-dwelling labourers. Nonetheless, by the end of the century Florence had recovered its confidence and began to expand. In 1384 it conquered the neighbouring Arezzo; in 1390 it conquered the hill town of Montepulciano; in 1406 it conquered the port city of Pisa; and in 1421 it purchased Livorno, a small town on the coast, to supplement and protect the sea trade of the mercantile Pisa, whose port was beginning to silt up.

By the beginning of the fifteenth century civic pride was in full flow. In 1402 the city's chancellor, Leonardo Bruni, in his *Praise of the City of Florence*, compared his hometown, surrounded by its satellites, to the moon surrounded by stars. His successor, Coluccio Salutati, claimed that no city in all the world was 'as securely placed within its circle of walls, more proud in its palazzi, more bedecked with churches, more beautiful in its architecture, more imposing in its gates, happier in its wide streets, greater in its people, more glorious in its citizenry, more inexhaustible in wealth, more fertile in its fields' (Lewis 1996, 132). Twenty years later the scholar Goro Dati in his *History of Florence* praised the city in even more specific terms, detailing the layout, articulating the relationships between the spaces, and enumerating the features, which ensured beauty, wealth and security. Dati extols the city's wall with its strong towers and great gates; its wide straight streets; its four graceful stone bridges and its many mills 'which between them grind as much grain as the city needs' (Lewis 1996, 133). He also praised the city's conveniently placed market, its central square and the Signoria palace—the seat of the republican government, from which the city's elected rulers ruled. The city he proudly describes appears rationally designed for efficiency, comfort and delight.

Within a decade, however, the focus of civic pride would shift from the city to the surrounding countryside. By the mid-fifteenth century, Florence's intellectuals and scholars were turning their attention from urban to rural life, and specifically to rural villas.

The earliest Florentine villas were essentially fortified farms. Any urban dweller who could possibly afford to would acquire a small farm to supply wine and oil, fruit and vegetables, fish and meat, as well as culinary, medicinal and cosmetic herbs for his city dwelling. In those days of sudden drought, famine or crop failure, a small farm would provide the urban dweller with the security of a guaranteed food supply; this was especially important at a time when households were composed of extended family, guests, employees and servants or slaves, all of whom required feeding.

As it was understood in Classical times, however, the rural villa was much more than a mere farm. It was seen instead as a place of *otium*, or retreat, a place of leisure and scholarship, as opposed to the *negotium*, or business and busy-ness of the city. Thus the villa derived its meaning from the urban context; it was, in effect, an antithesis to city life. Over the course of the fourteenth and fifteenth centuries in early Renaissance Florence, the meaning of the rural villa gradually acquired these classical connotations. Rather than simply a farm to supply the urban dweller's need for food, the rural villa became imbued with virtue, it became the ideal as opposed to the real—urban—life.

This idea of the moral superiority of rural life had first been expressed by the ancient Greek philosophers and was taken up by the Romans of the Republican era (fifth–first centuries BCE). Cato the Elder (234 BCE–149 BCE) was one of its fiercest proponents; when not fighting for the Republic, this Roman senator and historian would retreat to his farm in the Sabine hills to work his land. In 160 BCE he compiled his thoughts on rural husbandry and villa life into an influential book, *De Agri Cultura*, which was to prove a great influence in the Renaissance fifteen hundred years later. Several generations later, Varro wrote his influential treatise, *Three Books on Agriculture*. By 29 BCE, when Virgil was writing his bucolic *Georgics*, rural life was already taking on an idyllic, almost elegiac, quality which was echoed in the *Odes* of his near contemporary Horace.

Ironically, the embracing of villa life and the pursuit of *otium* was most popular at the end of the Republican period. In 27 BCE, when Augustus over-threw the Republic and established himself as the first Roman emperor, the wealthy classes, which had formerly ruled, suddenly found themselves with little to do. Anxious not to challenge the authority of the emperor, they re-treated to their country villas and focused on architecture and horticulture, art, literature, poetry, scholarship and the other liberal arts which *otium* allowed. By the end of the first century CE, Pliny the Younger was admonishing his friends to quit the city and retire to the country to pursue 'a good life and a genuine one, a seclusion which is happy and honourable, more rewarding than any "business" can be . . . leave the din, the futile bustle and useless occupations of the city and devote yourself to literature or to leisure' (Acton 1973, 13).

A similar trajectory happened in Florence during the fifteenth century as the Medici autocracy gradually replaced the Republic. The twelfth and thirteenth centuries had been a time of great social change in Northern Italy. With the fall of the Roman Empire around the fifth century, the countryside had been taken over by feudal lords, who lived in fortified castles, served by serfs who exchanged their labour for the security provided by the master. When, in 1115, Florence declared itself a republic, the city became one of the major centres of Northern Italy. As the mercantile bourgeoisie began to gain wealth and power, the old, landed aristocracy became increasingly ir-relevant. Soon enterprising individuals, looking to expand beyond the city walls, began to purchase the neglected lands of the increasingly impoverished nobles. Investing in rural enterprises, they created brick works, potteries, fisheries, timber farms and stone quarries for the growing cities. But with an expanding population, food and wine became among the surest commodities to be exploited from the countryside. Productivity immediately improved when men began working their own land, either as modest farmers with their own small-scale farms or tenants to affluent landlords. Freed from medieval serfdom, many were taken on by large landowners on a share-cropping basis known as the *mezzadria*, or 'half-and-half' system, where all produce was shared between the landlord, who provided the capital, and the tenant, who provided the labour.

This shift in land ownership from the aristocracy to the bourgeoisie meant that rural land became primarily a source of income rather than an expres-sion of power and class. It also altered the appearance of the countryside as acres of wilderness and barren land were ordered into neat little farms. Over the fifteenth century these rural landscapes became a favourite subject of the early Tuscan painters who celebrated the newly tamed countryside in the backgrounds of their portraits and religious and historic works. From Paolo Uccello's 1435 *Battle of San Romano*, to Benozzo Gozzoli's 1459 *Adoration of the Magi*; from Francesco Botticini's 1475 *Assumption of the Virgin*, to Botticelli's 1475 *Portrait of a Man*, the Tuscan countryside features as a patchwork of woodlands, grazing lands, orchards, vineyards, cereal fields and vegetable plots, dotted with small farms, presided over by the occasional villa/castle and stitched together by a system of roads which imply the link to the urban centres.[1]

All economic advantages aside, the fifteenth-century celebration of rural life had a philosophical as well as a financial basis. It derived from the rediscovery of classical texts—the writings of Cato, Varro, Virgil and Horace, which had extolled rural life and deplored the compromise and corruption of the city. In the fourteenth century, Christianity, which had filled the power vacuum after the fall of the Roman Empire, began to lose its supremacy. After a thousand-year reign that came to be known as the Dark Ages, the Church was challenged by the rebirth—*re-naissance*—of classical culture. This arose partly from the archaeological excavations recently begun in Rome, which revealed the richness of the pre-Christian culture. It was also stimulated by the classical manuscripts being discovered in the neglected libraries of Northern Europe. It was further promoted by the classical philosophy, espoused by Greek and Arab philosophers, introduced to Europe by Crusaders returning from the Holy Lands.

Inspired by classical learning, Florentine scholars began to shift their focus from God to Man, from the spiritual to the secular, from faith to reason, and from superstition to science in a movement which became known as Humanism. It is unlikely that this shift would have occurred anywhere but Florence; brash, affluent and fiercely independent, the young Republic resisted the inhibiting orthodoxy of the papacy in Rome or the university in Padua. One of the key ideas to emerge from the rediscovery of the Classical world was a taste for rural life, a sense that the countryside was a place of spiritual renewal, not simply a site for agricultural exploitation. Three Florentine writers were particularly important in promoting this fashion. In 1302 the Florentine poet Dante Alighieri (1265–1321) was expelled from the city, having been caught up in the battles between the Guelphs—who supported the pope—and their rivals, the Ghibellines, who supported the emperor. From his banishment, Dante described nostalgically his lost homeland as 'the daughter and heir of Ancient Rome' (Sica 2007, 18), thus promoting the idea that Florence would recreate the glories of the classical world. Dante's famous *Divine*

Comedy, in which the author is led through Hell and Purgatory by the ancient philosopher Virgil, stimulated interest in classical literature while simultaneously celebrating the countryside around Florence.

In the next generation of Florentine intellectuals, the diplomat Francesco Petrarch (1304–1374) retired to the countryside near Avignon which was, at the time, the home of the pope. Here he built himself 'a small but pleasant house with olive groves and vineyards' (Sica 2007, 18). Inspired by classical celebrations of villa life, Petrarch wrote his influential *Vita Solitaria*, promoting the spiritual and physical benefits of rural living while pitting *otium* or rural contemplation against *negotium*—the corruptions of city life.

A third Florentine, Giovanni Boccaccio (1313–1375), promoted the sensual delights of rural life in his fiction. His 1343 *Fiammetta* denounces the city as 'full of pompous talk and cowardly deeds . . . teeming with greedy, proud and envious people and full of countless anxieties' (Boccaccio 1972, xxxix). His later work, the *Decameron*, pits the city as a place of death against the joy and vitality of country life. This extremely influential work describes the exploits of ten youths who flee Florence to avoid the devastating plague of 1348. Several miles into the countryside they find refuge in a hilltop villa where they cavort in a state of prelapsarian innocence, telling stories, gathering flowers, swimming naked, drinking wine and eating sweetmeats. Amid its endorsement of villa life, Boccaccio's novel also celebrates the liberal values of the budding humanist movement. While the humanist ethos promoted rural life, and the contemporary economic situation privileged rural investment, many historians also discern a political motivation behind the fashion for country living. They believe it was promoted by the brilliant banker Cosimo di Medici to shift the ruling classes from the city to their country estates so they wouldn't notice that he was gradually taking over the government, transforming the Republic into a Medici holding. As historian Harold Acton notes, 'Anti-Mediceans detect a serpentine cunning in Cosimo's cult for Platonism, as if he had a sinister intention to pervert the Tuscan character and distract it from political activity' (1973, 48). Acton's wry, almost sceptical tone might derive from the fact that he was a British aristocrat born into the privileged community of Anglo-Florentine expatriates, which rediscovered the Renaissance in the late-nineteenth century and celebrated the Medici—though admittedly more for their patronage of the arts than for their political machinations. The Italian historian Eugenio Garin is one of those who ascribes political motives to the Medici's promoting of classical philosophy. He claimed that, like Cosimo, his grandson, Lorenzo the Magnificent, promoted classical philosophy 'not only to add brilliance to his house, but also for insidious reasons of political propaganda' (Acton 1973, 48). Having been raised amid the horrors and humiliations of Italy's Fascist era, Garin looked back with pride to the civic virtues of the fifteenth-century Republic, before it was overthrown by the Medici autocracy.

Whatever one's feelings about the motives of the Medici, over the fifteenth century, as the Florentine Republic gradually ceded power to the Medici, the virtues of rural life were increasingly advanced by the city's leading philosophers, artists and poets, many of whom were supported by the ruling family.

Cosimo di Medici (1389–1464) was the first and the greatest of the Medici rulers. Through canny bookkeeping and brilliant diplomacy, he built up a fortune in banking and used it to finance his political career. A master of propaganda, Cosimo was careful to avoid provoking the envy of his fellow citizens. He upheld the rules of the Republic, but by carefully placing his friends, family, employees and debtors in positions of power, he ensured that the city was run in a way which suited his interests. Cosimo had been educated in the new Humanist ideas—and while his father, Giovanni di Bicci de Medici, bought up rural farmhouses, hunting lodges and lookout towers in the late fourteenth century as agricultural investments, it was Cosimo, in the fifteenth century, who transformed these into humanist villas. Like the classical philosophers, he promoted farming as a virtuous activity, especially when combined with scholarship and contemplation. Under his leadership, the rural villa became a place of noble pleasure, where the dignity of labour merged with the intellectual rigour of scholarship.

The earliest rural villas in the Medici portfolio were Cafaggiolo and Il Trebbio—neighbouring properties twenty kilometres north of the city in the Mugello—a fertile valley known for its rich harvests. Cosimo combined the two estates and transformed their dwellings into comfortable residences, filling in the moats, removing the drawbridges and piercing the towers with windows to frame views of the surrounding landscape. In both cases, however, he retained the high defensive walls and crowning battlements; coming from a virtually unknown family, he was keen to preserve the connotations of feudal wealth and power attached to such medieval features.

Despite his professed love of rural life, Cosimo's favourite villa was not these ancient and distant agricultural estates but the suburban villa of Careggi. In 1417 his father had purchased the property as part of his programme of rural expansion. Located just four kilometres northwest of Florence, it retained its rural character but was easily accessible. As at Il Trebbio and Cafaggiolo, Cosimo renovated the villa, removing the original watchtower but retaining the moat and drawbridge—a wise precaution at a villa so close to the city at a time when many resented the growing power of the Medici. He also extended the modest farmhouse to create a comfortable villa with two wings enclosing a central courtyard. Writing a century after its completion, the historian Georgio Vasari—ever keen to flatter his Medici patrons—describes the villa as 'very rich and magnificent' (Vasari 1987, 43); nonetheless, it was still essentially a working farm. Famously, Cosimo would rise early to plant his vines and prune his orchards before descending, by humble mule, to attend to affairs of state in the city below. His friend and biographer, Vespasiano da Bisticci, asserts: 'Of agriculture he had the most intimate knowledge, and he would discourse thereon as if he had never followed any other calling' (Hale 1977, 25).

In the peace and solitude of the villa, Cosimo lived simply, dressed modestly and dined austerely in the company of his friends. These philosophers, artists and intellectuals soon became known as the NeoPlatonic Academy because of their shared interest in the classical world. With the help of friends and foreign agents, Cosimo amassed a large collection of ancient texts which he kept at the villa, among which was a rare copy of Cicero's *Cato Maior de senectute* (Giannetto 2008, 35). In this discourse on aging, Cicero extols the beauty of a well-managed farm, claims the farmer's life is the happiest possible, and asserts that the pleasures of farming are particularly suited to the wise. Cicero also evokes Lucius Quinctius Cincinnatus who was ploughing his land when he was informed of his election as ruler of Rome—a story which provided a happy precedent for Cosimo himself. Indeed it is likely that Cosimo's conspicuous demonstration of his agricultural prowess was a deliberate attempt to associate himself with those ancient republicans, even as he was undermining the Florentine Republic.

Cosimo's devotion to villa life and classical philosophy is perhaps best illustrated in a letter he wrote to the philosopher Marsilio Ficino. In 1462, crippled with gout and troubled with intimations of mortality, he urges Ficino to visit: 'yesterday I came to the villa of Careggi not to cultivate my fields but my soul. Come to us Marsilio, as soon as possible, bringing with you our Plato's book, De Summo Bono. This I suppose you have already translated from the Greek into Latin as you promised. I desire nothing so much as to know the best road to happiness' (Ross 1910, 73). Two years later Cosimo died at the villa. It is said that Plato was being read to him in his final moments—though this too may be simply propaganda.

If Cosimo preferred Careggi to the earlier, more distant agricultural estates, in 1450 his son Giovanni commissioned another suburban dwelling: the Villa Medici, Fiesole. Located two miles north of the city, in the ancient Etruscan hilltop village of Fiesole, this was the first-ever purpose-built humanist villa; it wasn't adapted from an existing farm or fortress, it wasn't pretending to be an ancient feudal estate, and its purpose was pleasure rather than productivity.

Though Vasari later described it as 'an esteemed and magnificent palace' (1987, 43), the Villa Medici is, in fact, quite small and modest. Being a mere ninety-minute horse ride from the city, it didn't need to accommodate the large retinue of servants, family, friends and courtiers that a distant villa would have demanded. More of a gentleman's retreat than a rural estate, it reveals the shift from the communal, almost clan-like existence of the early Renaissance to the more private, individualistic lifestyle that evolved in the fifteenth century. It also marks the point when the villa shifted from being an essentially utilitarian space to being a place of leisure. Where classical writers had stressed the productive aspects of the villa, and the early humanists, like Cosimo, had used their villas for labour combined with scholarship, Giovanni's generation favoured friendship and pleasure over labour and utility. The Villa Medici was unashamedly a place of *otium*, removed from the commerce of the city, but also removed from the labour of the farm.

Perched on the edge of the steep hillside, the site had no agricultural potential and was chosen for its panoramic views alone. Unlike earlier villas with their sprawling additions and forbidding stone facades, it is a neat cube shape, covered with white plaster which emphasizes its dramatic simplicity. Dispensing with the traditional, inward-looking central courtyard, its rooms open out to the countryside, with large windows and loggias to draw the outdoors into the very fabric of the building.

Giovanni's humanist education gave him a love of the classics, and his villa contained his prized collections of antique medals and sculptures. He was also a connoisseur of music and art, and Vasari reports that among its handsome salons and commodious halls the villa had the novel feature of rooms devoted solely to music and to books. But Giovanni's overriding passions were women and food; unwilling to diet, he became dangerously obese and died of a heart attack only three years after the villa was completed. Nonetheless family and friends continued to use the villa as a convenient escape from the city, as indicated by a 1491 letter to Giovanni's nephew, Lorenzo, noting: 'I have followed your example and over the last forty days, almost as if I had fled the city, I have become an assiduous visitor of the Fiesole villa' (Mazzini 2004, 157).

The Villa Medici was extremely influential in shaping late-fifteenth-century tastes. Within a generation it had become a virtual emblem of Humanist affiliation and featured in many paintings of the time such as Biaggio's *Annunciation* (c. 1490) and Ghirlandaio's *Assumption of the Virgin* (c. 1486). In 1478, the poet Poliziano, who was tutoring Lorenzo's sons at the villa, wrote to the philosopher Ficino urging him to visit. After extolling the cool breezes, abundant shade and plentiful water he adds: 'The villa itself lies off the road, in a dense wood, but commands a view of the whole city, and although the district is thickly populated I enjoy that solitude dear to those who have fled from town' (Mazzini 2004, 157). When Giovanni first built on the steep hillside, few would have considered such an unpropitious site; Poliziano's letter, written twenty-five years later, indicates the presence of the Medici on the hillside had sparked a frenzy of villa building nearby.

In his fifteenth-century *Vite*, detailing the lives of his illustrious contemporaries, Cosimo's biographer Vespasiano reveals an almost fawning respect for villa dwellers. Writing of Agnolo Pandolfini, he notes: 'in the summertime he went to his well-ordered villa, a man in the fullness of his years . . . escaping the mediocrity that the townsman was obliged to support' (Sica 2007, 20).

While rural attractions might be obvious to a mature man 'in the fullness of his years', they also get an enthusiastic endorsement from the teenage poet Michele di Vieri (1469–1487). Before his death at the age of eighteen, from a blow to the groin sustained during a hammer-throwing game, Vieri described the joys of rural life in a letter to a friend. Echoing Pliny's first-century description of his villa life, also in a letter to a friend, Vieri recounts how he rises early to walk in the garden, then retires to his study to compose verse or read classical authors. After lunch he plays board games then reads in his vineyard, till the cool of the evening when he plays more games for exercise: 'This is how I spend the summer, while the spread of diseases in the city continues' (19). Vieri ends his letter in words which echo those of Cosimo a generation earlier, claiming 'I do not cultivate my fields but engage myself with letters', adding 'I do not have the library of the Sassetti or the Medici but I have a small shelf of the right books which are dearer to me than the richest possessions' (19).

Along with the poets and writers who sang the praises of rural life, one of its most persuasive promoters was the Humanist architect Giovanni Battista Alberti. His seminal *De re aedificatoria*, or *On Architecture* (written c. 1450, published 1485)—based largely on Vitruvius's first-century treatises—was the first text to interpret classical architecture for a modern audience. Although Alberti was not employed by the Medici, he would have been keen to remain in favour with the ruling family, and throughout the book Alberti endorses rural life, both implicitly and explicitly. After ranting against the restrictions of building in the city where one is constantly thwarted by 'party walls, dripping gutters, public ground and rights of way', he claims: 'in the countryside this does not happen, here everything is more open whereas the city is restrictive. Here all spaces are free, there they are occupied' (Sica 2007, 50).

Alberti suggests that the villa be sited close to the city so the patron can visit it effortlessly, 'on foot and with transport, both in winter and in summer' (50). This indicates that his market was urbanites—men who expected to flit from their city offices for a short rural respite before returning to the rigours of commerce. His treatise was aimed at members of the new bourgeoisie who would design their villas from scratch, rather than those of the landed aristocracy who had to fit their lifestyles into ancient feudal estates. Biasing comfort and convenience over commercial considerations, he recommends a site with good views and cool breezes rather than one whose main virtue is its fertility. Alberti's prescription for the villa layout reveals much about contemporary class and gender roles: he suggests that rooms should be used according to the season, with winter bedrooms facing the sunrise and summer bedrooms the midday sun, winter dining rooms facing the sunset and summer dining rooms overlooking greenery. Husband and wife should have separate bedrooms to allow both to sleep, but should have a common door. The wife should have an adjacent dressing room and the husband a library. The kitchen should be near enough the dining room that hot dishes don't cool in transit, but far enough to block out noise and smells, and domestic staff should be lodged in separate quarters, but near enough to hear their masters and to serve them quickly. Alberti also notes that the less prosperous should emulate their wealthier betters, adding that farmhouses 'should provide for the oxen and the sheep as much as for the wife . . .' (Sica 2007, 50).

Although Alberti's suburban villa was largely the preserve of the new, mercantile class, it was also a way for aristocrats—and those sons of merchants who had achieved enough wealth to retire—to distance themselves from the vulgarity of labour and commerce. Indeed much of the fifteenth-century discourse in favour of country life is presented as an antidote to the brashness and crudity of city commerce. In his *Libri della Famiglia*, Alberti describes villa life as 'a blessing' and 'an unheard of happiness', a source of health, profit, pleasure and honour, free from the trouble and anxiety of commerce:

> There is no need, as with other occupations, to fear deceit and fraud from debtors or suppliers. . . . You will not be cheated nor need to call upon notaries and witnesses, bring lawsuits or engage in other irritating and depressing matters. . . . You can live undisturbed by murmurs and tales and by the strife that breaks out periodically in the city. You can be free of the suspicions, fears, slanders, injuries, feuds and other miseries which are too ugly to mention. . . . The cultivation and management of fields does not give rise to envy, hate and malevolence . . . and what is more, while enjoying your estate you can escape the violence and unrest of the city . . . avoid seeing all the stealing and crime, and the great numbers of evil men who are always in sight in the city. (24)

This extraordinarily paean to rural life reflects the enduring tension between the need to make money and the longing to spend it in leisure and study far from the commercial centre. It is notable that those who sing the praises of rural life are almost always, like Alberti, urbanites for whom a visit to the country is a holiday, time out of their normal lives.[2]

By the late-fifteenth century, the appeal of rural life was reinforced once again, by financial considerations. The Ottoman Turks were interrupting Florence's trade with the Levant, and a series of wars between the various states of the Italian peninsula meant the city was repeatedly raising taxes to defend itself militarily. Though banking had been the mainstay of the Florentine economy for two hundred years, suddenly money was in short supply. At the end of the fourteenth century there had been seventy banks in Florence (Hale 1977, 12); by 1460 there were thirty-three; by the end of the century there were fewer than six (71). On Cosimo's death in 1464, the younger members of the family, having neither his diligence nor his cunning, began to diversify, shifting from banking and trade to exploit their rural properties. As the city's population grew, agriculture offered slower but surer returns than banking, manufacturing or trade. In the 1470s, Cosimo's grandson, Lorenzo, created a model farm at Poggio a Caiano, where he attempted such novel ventures as breeding Arab horses and raising exotic birds. Rather more successfully he imported Lombardy cattle and was soon supplying the city with nearly all her dairy needs, while at Cafaggiolo the family established a ceramics factory.

Towards the end of the fifteenth century, the banker Giovanni Rucellai advised his sons to get out of business, adding, 'I would not advise you to seek offices and political influence . . . there is nothing which I esteem less, nor which seems less honourable, than to be involved in public affairs' (Hale 1977, 57). A century earlier, public service had been seen as an obligation of wealth and power, as expressed in Paolo da Certaldo's pithy observation: 'a villa makes good animals and bad men' (Giannetto 2008, 32).

Whether this shift was driven by the Medici, it certainly served their purpose by moving the governing classes out of the city. While Cosimo operated discretely with the backing of the Republic, two generations later Lorenzo operated openly as the de-facto ruler of the city. Lorenzo's death in 1492, however, engendered a backlash against the family led by the fundamentalist Dominican priest Girolamo Savonarola. The Medici were exiled; the Republic was revived and political turmoil ensued until 1532 when Alessandro the Moor, reputedly the illegitimate son of the Medici pope Clement VII, was created hereditary Duke of Tuscany by Charles V, who virtually controlled the Italian peninsula.

The death of Lorenzo marked the end of Humanist era and its eulogies to rural life. Nonetheless the rural/urban divide continued to be explored by writers through the sixteenth century. In their treatises, however, rural life was seen primarily in commercial terms; the laudatory note of the fifteenth-century humanists was replaced with a more materialistic tone. And where the fifteenth-century humanists had wryly castigated the city as a place of casual cheating, in the sixteenth century it becomes a much more sinister place.

Where earlier writers tended to accuse urbanites of such foibles as ambition and slander, in his 1566 *Le dieci giornate della vera agricoltura e piaceri della villa* the Venetian agronomist Agostino Gallo provides a catalogue of veritable psychopaths. Claiming that country folk are free from ambition, pride, envy, vindictiveness, treachery and murderousness—and, rather perplexingly, that they are 'not cuckolded by their wives'—he goes on to describe city dwellers as bawling street sweepers, whores reeking of musk, sorcerers, cheats and cutpurses, bullying soldiers and swindling tricksters. Further, he claims that in the city one is subject to the sight of slanderers having their eyes put out, blasphemers having their tongues slit, malefactors being branded on the face, liars having their hands cut off, murderers being beheaded, thieves being hanged and traitors being quartered (Hale 1977, 129).

Gallo's treatise is presented in the form of a dialogue between two old men; buried deep in the conversation is the observation that two generations earlier the city had been a place of 'discipline', of 'peace, charity and faith'. One speaker asserts that many nobles had recently retreated to their villa to enjoy 'a sort of liberty' that they could not find in the city, and wishes that the elders of the past could return to punish those urbanites who make it impossible to live 'in peace and tranquillity' (130). As a Venetian, Gallo inhabited a Republic which was in decline and under threat, physically besieged by the Ottomans, commercially undermined by the shift in trade to the recently discovered Americas. His dystopian depiction of the city as a place in social meltdown might well be a coded reference to the contemporary political situation.

Gallo was not alone in his focus on liberty. In a letter, published in 1544, the Mantuan poet Alberto Lollio lists, among the consolations of rural life, the fact that at his villa he enjoys 'sweet liberty', living according to his own desires without fear of the 'ignoramuses' of the city (111).

Intellectuals in fifteenth-century Florence had embraced rural life as part of a rediscovery of nature through the new Humanist philosophy; their objections to the city were expressed largely in legal terms. Indeed Alberti's catalogue of debtors, notaries, lawsuits, slanderers and cheats could be a coded dislike of the new mercantile classes—epitomized by the Medici. The Medici, in turn, distanced themselves from their commercial activities with a conspicuous display of rural villa building and agricultural activity. By the sixteenth century the conversation had spread from Florence, and the countryside was depicted in more overtly political terms. It was seen as a place of liberty, in contrast to the city filled with traitors, murderers and gruesome tortures, which represented the tyranny that threatened the individual and the republic.

In practical terms, ever since Florence ushered in the Renaissance and with it modern capitalism, the city has been seen as the place where people make their money, while the country has been where they retreat to enjoy it. The city thus was seen to represent our venal selves, our guilt and fears, while the country represents our better—ideal—selves. The city is where tyrannies evolve while the country is where liberty thrives.

With its vigorous capitalism, global trade and cosmopolitan community, modern England has many parallels with Renaissance Florence. Like Italy's fifteenth-century Humanists, England's finest writers have promoted an idyllic image of country life: from Shakespeare's Forest of Arden—whose very title suggests Eden, where courtiers retreat from the evil of the urban court—to Milton's vision of Paradise which reads like a description of England's home counties. From Blake and Wordsworth to Thomas Hardy to E. M. Forster, rural life is presented as good and pure, while urban life represents temptation and corruption. In England today, nearly 85 percent of the population lives in an urban or suburban setting, yet the fascination with rural life endures. This is demonstrated daily in the BBC's iconic radio series *The Archers*—'an everyday story of country folk', the world's longest-running radio soap opera which has broadcast continuously since 1950.

As early as the sixth century BCE, in his fable of 'The Country and the City Mouse', the philosopher Aesop codified the idea of the country as a place of honesty, simplicity and safety, with the city representing riches, adventure and danger. This binary view fails to acknowledge that the countryside is largely shaped by urban concerns, its survival depends on urban markets and its depiction is largely dictated by urban intellectuals. Recently, *The Archers* has been rebranded as 'contemporary drama in a rural setting'; perhaps after five hundred years, the enduring fantasy of rural virtue as an antithesis to urban vice is beginning to be understood for what is: a fantasy.

NOTES

1. This celebration of rural life was not without its detractors. In the early fourteenth century, in his *Nuova Cronica*, Villani noted, disapprovingly, that many citizens, both grand and ordinary, were building large estates 'with an expensive layout and handsome buildings much better than in town', adding that because of the extraordinary costs involved, these misguided fools were thought to be 'mad' (Ackerman 1990, 64). Thirty years later, the Florentine merchant Paolo da Certaldo railed against the custom of spending time in the country. In his *Libro di buoni costumi*, or *Book of Good Manners*, he advises his fellow citizens to stay in the city and involve themselves in crafts or business, asserting 'a villa makes good animals and bad men' (Giannetto 2008, 32). These arguments were, in part, a continuation of the medieval

discussion about whether the active or the contemplative life was superior, but they also expressed the bias of the patrician, Republican class which favoured an active life of civic responsibility in which men lived in the city working for the common good.

2. The reality of villa life is often very different from the fantasy, as indicated in a letter of 18 December 1478, from the Humanist tutor Poliziano to his patron Lucrezia Medici. Stuck at Cafaggiolo with his restless charges and their dull, pious mother, he laments:

> [T]he rain is so heavy and so continuous that we cannot leave the house and have exchanged hunting for playing at ball so that the children should have exercise [. . .] I remain in the house by the fire in slipper and a greatcoat, were you to see me you would think I was melancholy personified [. . .] When at Florence we have some sort of satisfaction, if not else, that of seeing Lorenzo [. . .] Here we are in perpetual anxiety about everything [. . .] I am drowned in weary sloth, such is my solitude. (Ross 1910, 214)

Chapter 8

Justice as the Urban Everyday

Wendy Pullan

In the twenty-first century, justice and/or injustice has often been associated with the city. That this should be the case is not surprising: inequality of life and opportunity may be at its most acute in urban situations, and the demand for individual rights has become central to an understanding of identity. In parallel to this, the world's population is increasingly urban, reflected in the magnitude, sprawl and complexity of many contemporary cities. Nonetheless, the question of what, if anything, makes justice particularly urban is not fully understood. The focus is more commonly upon how systems of justice might respond to current problems that, almost by default, are found in cities. At the same time, judicial systems and the juridical tend to be associated with the powers of the modern state or regions, and since World War II, as a duty of international order. In comparison, the authority and meaning of justice in cities and the institutions of urban life may appear minimal, weak or nonexistent.

There is a paradox here. For most ordinary people, injustices are experienced in situations of everyday life, but if they are to be righted by legal systems this entails a far more abstract and remote process. We step away from the everyday in order to achieve justice, and typically, we go to court to do this. The disjuncture between the relatively tangible life of the city and the conceptual meanings of the justice system (Spaulding 2012) is demonstrated by the obscurity of the courthouse in the landscape of many contemporary cities; it is no longer the highly visible and recognized public building that played a key role in forming the civic centre as conceived in the nineteenth and early twentieth centuries. At the same time, the process inside the court has become rarefied and abstruse for laypeople (Spaulding 2012; Mulcahy 2007).

It is worthwhile to ask whether this apparent fissure between justice, in the ways that it is conceived and applied, and the myriad practices of everyday life, as they are found in cities, obstructs the role of justice as it pertains to particularly urban concerns, and if so, can it be overcome. This is an extensive and complex question, in some ways beyond the scope of this chapter. Most obviously, justice is primarily the concern of jurists and legal experts; but the matter of how justice is perceived and made real, ultimately the relationship between what is tangible and what is not, is clearly a philosophical problem. I would also suggest that there is an urban question here that has to do with the nature and capacity of the city as a tangible place that embodies more complex, abstract and ephemeral meanings.

In order to interrelate these various strands, the idea of *nomos* is helpful.[1] Legal theory and jurisprudence refer to nomos in its most basic sense translated as 'law', but in a secondary meaning as convention or customary practice. Legal scholar Robert Cover places legal systems within the context of the wider world in which they are generated and situated (Cover 1982). He refers to nomos as the 'normative world' and recognizes that 'in the normative world, law and narrative are inseparably related' (1982, 5). At its best, law and everyday life are intimately intertwined and law emerges from living values and practices rather than dictating them. Cover goes on to say that many aspects of a great legal tradition are constituted by a rich nomos, establishing 'paradigms for dedication, acquiescence, contradiction and resistance' (1982, 6). I would further the argument by saying that these paradigms exist not solely in the domain of legal jurisdictions but also figure in the practices found in cities and urban life. This begins to offer some basis for linking the life of cities with law where the understanding of nomos can be of help in trying to grasp how law in its broad normative sense can play a significant role in how and where we live our urban lives. Integral to this thinking, I suggest that many everyday practices have become so ingrained into regular urban procedures to form what could be regarded as a sort of customary law, understood as the intrinsic, accepted and expected conduct of a community, established over long usage, to be treated as expectation and protocol.[2] This chapter will consider how urban justice can be seen and understood on such a basis.

Scholarly investigations of justice that are particularly relevant to the emerging twenty-first century have been plentiful. John Rawls's (1999; 2001) idea of justice as fairness, as a way of addressing problems of distributive justice and inequality, has been exceedingly influential, and although sometimes criticized, it is reflected in many of the discussions of social justice today. Much of the concern for justice in cities has been regarded in terms of social justice, often following Marxist interpretations, especially Henri Lefebvre's plea on behalf of all citizens for the reconstitution of cities in order to establish the right to urban life and David Harvey's (1973) vision of the overturn of urban capital and production as the central requirement for political justice. Much of this thinking has been based upon the relationship between individual rights and the collective, or the interface between individuals, their differences and their distinct rights, with the focus on social justice within cities following important research by Mitchell (2014), Fainstein (2011), Soja (2010), Marcuse (2009) and others. Themes have centred on the problems of neoliberalism that have been highlighted by Marxist critique or activism, emerging from unreasonable authoritarian control and lack of democratic accountability. The role of individual and group identity as something to be asserted and protected to become a key feature of a just society is a recurring and significant feature of modern societies all over the world.

As intense and pervasive as this thinking has become, there are identifiable gaps with respect to the place of justice in cities. First of all, it is not clear how we can describe justice as particularly urban, opposed to what is oriented to other collective bodies, for example, the state, the tribe, the community or a particular ethnic or religious group. Justice is regularly regarded as a function of nations or states, or even internationally, but the idea of the city as a just body in modern times remains elusive. If we are to encounter cities as specifically just or unjust places it is useful to consider whether we can also speak of particular urban places in these terms. Harvey (2012, xii) has stressed the importance of locating urban social movements in the streets,[3] but he sees this as social and political interactions with little regard for how these particular urban spaces may help to embody justice and its activities. The abstract nature of justice does not translate well into concrete city spaces, and we have a poor sense of where to look for justice inside cities. Likewise, the representation of justice and injustice in ways that are visible to citizens in modern settings is not obvious. Certain processes of justice may be at work but are often not recognizable to most people. Finally, to what extent are these questions and problems to do with historical changes in cities? Are there points in urban history that particularly reveal how justice plays a role? These are large and complicated questions, and I can only begin to introduce them in this chapter. However, it is my contention that one way of approaching these issues together is in the relationship between justice and urban praxis or everyday urban life, the latter being characterized by tangible practices that are rooted in particular urban conditions and places, habitual although subject to change over time and recognizable in some way to most inhabitants.

The discussion here is rooted in the collective notion of civic life rather than individual rights. Shifting the key relationships to the city as an entity, where certain events and relationships are possible, is an approach taken by

Paul Ricoeur in his consideration of *The Just* (2000). Describing justice as 'an integral part of the wish to live well' (xv) he reminds us that Aristotle saw justice in the context of the city. He goes on to interpret Arendt where 'it is as citizens that we become human. The wish to live within just institutions signifies nothing else' (xvi). This is a broad reading of justice, but there is no question that public life and institutions are key to its meaning. Such a reading of justice does not focus on individual rights or individuals within a collective but, rather, key relationships within the corporate body that interacts in varied and complex ways. The pursuit of 'living well' may be experienced and evaluated by individuals but the prime locus for it is a collective one that today is commonly embodied in the public life of the city.

REPRESENTING JUSTICE IN THE CITY

If we are to investigate the relationship between justice and cities in concrete places, it is worthwhile to first of all consider where justice can be seen to take place and the efforts made to represent it. One of the most visible attempts to physically embody and represent the practice of justice in the city is in The Hague, which has been dedicated explicitly to the processes and manifestation of international justice. As such, efforts have been made to render justice taking place to all peoples regardless of who they are and where they come from. The irony here is that such an all-encompassing international justice system has been riddled with tensions between the international and the domestic (Dickinson 2003, 296), making it one illustration of the distance between the specificity of situated urban life and the more abstract juridical concepts. Nonetheless, we also find the specific adoption of a city as a destination for justice: the international court system is often referred to as simply 'The Hague', and the city itself is seen as an arbiter for the whole world.

As the principal judicial organ of the United Nations, where rulings are made for both individuals and states, the primary institution is the International Court of Justice, located in the 1913 Peace Palace. Although this institution is most well known, there are a number of other courts and tribunals located throughout The Hague, established as needed, mostly due to wars or ethno-national conflicts; together they form an urban topography of institutions dedicated to international justice.[4] More informally, the official courts and tribunal systems have spawned a proliferation of unofficial groups and NGOs for justice and democracy, contributing further to the urban topography of legal and quasi-legal institutions and encouraging lay participation and wider understanding by the public.[5]

As such, The Hague is one of the most concrete attempts to pursue and represent justice in the city. However, the drawbacks are fairly obvious: as the global international court it is unique with no reason to replicate it in other cities. As much as the elaborate system of courts and unofficial centres have become representative of the city, there is also a sense that they are an essentially artificial and mannered addition to the city; justice is laid down as a weighty layer over and on top of the city rather than emanating from particular concerns within it. The Hague's nature as an international court removes it geographically and culturally from the disputes, crimes and atrocities on which it focuses (Dickinson 2003, 302–3), and although some of these are urban, many are not. To some extent the urban topography of The Hague has become contrived in order to support its judicial institutions, and the constant focus upon the ethical expectations associated with these activities places an extraordinary burden on the more quotidian functions of the city. While these problems do not necessarily detract from the fascination and value of The Hague as the international court, they do not bring us much closer to understanding everyday justice in pursuit of a just city.[6]

Rather than establishing a centre for justice, I would instead like to turn to an example that is intentionally rooted in local customs and situations; this is Siena in the Middle Ages. Located in the Campo, Siena's enormous shell-shaped central piazza, the council chamber of the city's Palazzo Pubblico, accommodated a rotating body of the Nine Governors and Defenders of the Commune and People of Siena, known simply as the Nine, or *Nove* (in power 1287–1355). Referred to by Bowsky (1962, 369) as an 'urban oligarchy', the governing body was drawn from groups of merchants and bankers, lesser nobles and scholars, elected for terms of only two months in what he described as coming 'close to the ideal of a balanced communal government, keeping in mind that we are not referring to a twentieth century democratic ideal' (Bowsky 1981, 313).[7] In Siena the Aristotelian idea of the 'common good' was adopted to also mean the 'good city', and the two meanings may have been used interchangeably in some circumstances.[8] Via Thomist thought and contemporary usage of jurisprudence, much of this thinking was interpreted through the theme of justice, both as a means and an end in the city (Rubinstein 1958; Frugoni 1991, ch. 6).

Perhaps better known than the Nove is a cycle of frescoes by Ambrosio Lorenzetti that describe urban government and life in Siena in the fourteenth century. In their council chamber, or Sala dei Nove, the Nine deliberated the city under the shadow of these images.[9] On the two long walls of the room, two cities face each other, together intended to inform and inspire enlightened governance in Siena. The images show two versions of the walled city of Siena and its *contade*, or dependent countryside: on the room's eastern wall, the Allegory of Good Government or Justice shows a city that is secure and

Figure 8.1. Ambrosio Lorenzetti, *The Allegory of Good Government*, Sala dei Nove, Palazzo Pubblico, Siena; detail showing the good or just city.
Source: Wikicommon.

prosperous with impressive buildings, flourishing agriculture and participative citizens; on the western wall, the Allegory of Bad Government or Tyranny portrays a derelict city where buildings crumble, soldiers fight on the streets and agricultural fields fall into neglect.

The detailed frescoes depict two visions of urban praxis, stemming from the direct effects of government and the people, either good or bad. At the same time, the frescoes also function as moral tales illuminated by allegorical personifications of tyranny and justice, virtues and vices. While it would be unreasonable not to see some evidence of propaganda on behalf of the rule of the Nove (Skinner 1999; Frugoni 1991, 161ff.), it is also one of the most detailed and didactic representations of the period to show aspirations for a city where 'the aim was a form of obligation in communal service directly encouraged by the frescoes' (Bowsky 1981, 309).

Depicted on the north wall and enthroned as emperor/magistrate/Christ figure, an enormous man is flanked by the virtues, human figures about half his size. He presides over the room, both above twenty-four Sienese citizens represented below him in the fresco, as well as over the human beings—the actual citizens of Siena—who would have occupied the floor of the Sala dei Nove in front of him. Lest there be any doubt about what makes a good city, Justice sits, a slightly smaller female figure but also enthroned to balance the Common Good/Good City from other side of the fresco. In fact, Justice sits apart where she alone is understood to descend directly from God's intervention (Polzer 2002, 89); in such a setting, she trumps Peace, who reclines as only one of the virtues. In medieval Siena, justice was possible but peace remained elusive, hence the need for the agonic space offered in the Sala dei Nove itself, just in front of the fresco.

The Sala dei Nove is embedded in the Palazzo Pubblico to act like a pivot point of political responsibility at the centre of Siena. On one side is the Campo, where all of the city's *contrade*, or neighbourhoods, came together in ritual and informally. Towards the southern end of the frescoes, each of the two urban depictions transitions into painted countryside beyond their city walls. This corresponds to the actual *contade* topography of Siena, still seen directly through the window at the end of the room. The sense of the paintings merging with the geography is particularly potent at this point—from working city we move to working countryside; governance and justice sits in the key location of the Sala dei Nove in between. Concurrently, this important relationship is rooted in deeper associations: from the city, with its history and conflicts, debates and laws, the topography extends outward into nature, where human time and culture becomes displaced by a more fundamental timelessness. *Nomos*, which dominates the room, is oriented in a primary ontology by *physis* beyond it.

With the city to the north and the countryside to the south, the actual topography was directly represented in the two images of the city on either wall. The dialectical possibilities for what a city can be, so clearly illustrated in the frescoes, are heightened by the direct relationship between the representational mode and city; this was centred upon the Nine, as the governing force in Siena. The question of a just city, seen in Siena to be equated with a good city, came down to one room oriented to all the primary aspects of the urban conditions. For every Sienese the city's place and significance would have been made visible and recognizable through painted representations of everyday life and morality.

CITIES AS LEGAL BODIES

The representations and the practices of Siena were typical of the medieval European city-state in the late Middle Ages and Renaissance. They emerged from a long tradition rooted in the Aristotelian understanding that regarded cities as fundamental for politically engaging activity that aspired, ultimately, to a higher ethical good. Such cities were formed in what Engin Isin (2002) refers to as corporations enjoying independent political and legal status with reference to the citizens themselves. People inhabited cities where their primary affiliations as citizens were often derived from the ways they made their living; in other words, legal identity was incumbent upon what people did in their lives as urban citizens. Put simply, the status of a city depended on its citizenship and citizenship depended on what people did. Isin (2002, 124) points out that the emphasis upon occupation and activity endowed some level of visibility and inclusivity upon marginalized groups such as Jews and Muslims, peasants and the poor, resulting in multiple and overlapping power structures and jurisdictions, even though cities also remained fragmented and hierarchical in many areas. Nonetheless, we cannot underestimate the importance of concrete and visible activity that was seen to foster prosperity and well-being. Direct representation of the city in terms of its praxis through architecture, art, religious ritual, processions, festivals and other events, commerce, fellowship and various institutions was a regular way of demonstrating the identity of different urban organizations, such as guilds, trusts, brotherhoods or neighbourhoods, as well as the city as a whole. The physical nature of such representation was identified with the political being of the city (Trexler 1991, 213) and projected the virtues of citizenship (Isin 2002, 137). Urban praxis—simply and usefully understood as 'what people do' (Carl 2000, 328)—was central to the defining of cities; as we have seen in Siena, everyday life in all of its diversity was the primary way of embodying and representing the city.

As modernity crept in, cities and the perception of them changed in two interrelated ways that are significant for this discussion: firstly, cities became generated as corporations by the state, removing political and juridical power from the citizens and the locale of the city; and secondly, the urban entity as a state-created corporation became regarded in abstract legal terms rather than by everyday praxis through the various roles of the inhabitants (Isin 2002, 168ff; Isin 1992, ch. 2). The changes were initially represented ceremonially in the person of the ruler in order to take possession of and assume authority over the city where such acts as 'presenting the keys to the city gates by the mayor was one of the external signs expressing the transfer of power' (Chroscicki 1998, 207). Eventually the legal basis of the city became rooted in the nation-state. In so doing the distance between ruler/state and citizens was substantial and intentional, and key features of the city instead of being ensconced in everyday praxis became routed through legal doctrine. Treatises and charters were the primary references. Otto Giercke (quoted in Isin 1992, 24) explains the transformation by distinguishing between de facto corporations where the 'actual members came together to achieve an end determined by themselves' and de jure corporations where association was imposed 'from outside and above'. Isin refers to the 'de jure corporation' as a legal invention that was 'an abstract and subordinate body politic' (2002, 168). With the advent of the nation-state the de jure corporation became the blueprint for early modern cities and is still the basis for the formation and governance of cities today, even with the ramifications of increased globalization. The changes were stark, as Isin (2002, 168) states: 'any group of people who might gather and define themselves as a corporation, exercising powers that were not prescribed by law, was declared illegal, and in time, became unthinkable'.

The replacement of de facto corporations rooted in praxis by the de jure corporation rooted in codes of law led to a greater universalization of urban practices and justice. It also meant that everyday life slowly became less respected and less viable as an arbiter for urban justice. This was manifested in fundamental changes in spatial thinking that not only affected cities but were conducive to the primary characteristics of the modern nation-state. John Locke defined political power as the 'right of making laws . . . for the regulating and preserving of property [. . .] all this only for the public good',[10] where fenced or bounded territory is understood to constitute the primary socio-spatial order.[11] This is typified by the early modern preoccupation with demarcating and mapping political boundaries of the new nation-states. Borders and boundaries become seen as what is just, good, legal and ordered. In the transition to a more abstract legal system oriented by the state, it is possible to recognize James C. Scott's (1998) notion of new state controls that removed much of everyday human experience to that of instrumental state procedures. Scott regards these changes as part of developing modernity in a process of limitation and abstraction that we find in the modern corporation of cities; he states: 'these state simplifications . . . did not successfully represent the actual activity of the society they depicted, nor were they intended to; they represented only the slice of it that interested the official observer' (1998, 3). He demonstrates that such a transformation was underpinned by various modern systems such as mapping, urban planning, slum clearance, systems of measurement and standardized technology, all of which became central to modernizing cities. These systems afford a shorthand description of cities that becomes a way of observing and understanding them, where urban order 'easily legible from the outside [. . .] has no necessary relationship to the order of life as it is experienced by its residents' (Scott 1998, 58). It is therefore not surprising to remember that the period of early modernity heralded the fascination with ideal cities, these summarized simply by geometric shapes as circles or stars, stripped down to a utopian form and devoid of any hint of the richness and complexity of urban everyday life.

This brief account has focused on European and Western cities, but it is worth noting that through the imposition of the nation-state and globalization cities across the world are generally conceived in the same legal fashion. Scott shows that the phenomena related to 'seeing like a state' are relevant to a variety of examples all over the world. Today, the antipathy between city and state is pronounced. In what has been referred to as the 'unmaking of the post-colonial city', the polarization of city and state has become particularly pronounced in which 'urban spaces provide the location where past struggles and present ones become entangled in mobilization against the state and global institutions of capital and their governance projects' (Agathangelou 2018, 350). We have become accustomed to cities where the everyday life of citizens and common urban practices are no longer regarded as defining characteristics. Such practices have not, on the whole, disappeared, but they are submerged in bureaucratic systems and undervalued in comparison with more regulated, distant and abstract systems of justice. Yet in terms of human activity and urban life, cities tend to be understood through their centres and meeting places, connecting paths of movement that underlie urban narratives. At the risk of overgeneralizing, it is possible to say that states may be described by their boundaries, but cities are revealed by their centres, where people work, live, shop, meet, etc. Applying abstract state standards to urban spaces is problematic and there remains the need for representing urban spaces through recognizable urban narratives based upon everyday life.

NOMOS AND URBAN SPACE

There are affinities between the two different legal structures for cities—de jure and de facto—and the two meanings of *nomos*—law and custom. As a modern term, nomos has had a varied and somewhat strained history. There is reasonable agreement that it refers to law and order derived from legal and/or cultural structures, but beyond that it is controversial.[12] My own employment of nomos stems from three possibilities the term offers: (1) a dialectical relationship within its two meanings rooted in the statutes of law and in customary practices or culture; (2) the reciprocity of present and past found in the aspects of custom in the second meaning of nomos; (3) nomos as a normative world in which to illustrate complex difference and diversity. Robert Cover's (1982) work is instructive. Although he approaches nomos from the law and is not particularly interested in cities he also points out the significance of the wider culture in its dialectical capacity when he states: 'No set of legal institutions or prescriptions exists apart from the narratives that locate it and give it meaning. For every constitution there is an epic, for each decalogue a scripture. Once understood in the context of the narratives that give it meaning, law becomes not merely a system of rules to be observed, but a world in which we live' (1982, 4–5).

I have already suggested that narratives exist in the everyday activities found in urban spaces and I place a primary significance on the physicality of those spaces. But like Cover, I would also suggest it is the dialectic between everyday urban practices in their physical contexts and the laws and formal systems of justice embedded within the corresponding society that are necessary for our ability to live in an effective way. When the dialectic collapses so does a full urban life.

Cover values narratives or mythos as establishing 'paradigms of behavior [. . .] between the constraints of reality and the demands of an ethic [. . .] that may be combined into meaningful patterns culled from the meaningful patterns of the past' (1982, 9). I would argue that the enduring and concrete aspects of cities renders them one of the main vehicles for this to happen. The ability of architecture and the urban fabric to absorb and manifest the many possibilities between reality and imagination derives from a productive spectrum of precedent and potential to be taken into account in any compilation of urban justice.

Too often the reciprocities break down and the inherently universalizing aspect of formal legal systems becomes detached from human conditions. One common result is that which is considered just for one individual or group is regarded as unjust by others (Cover 1982, 7). We see this regularly in cities, as is demonstrated in the many works on urban social justice and inequality. The gaps in reactions to justice by groups with conflicting interests is more often revealed in wider life experience or the 'normative world' than in the law itself; in other words, we tend to observe and understand major differences and conflicting interests in the context of everyday life and not in prescribed laws. In fact, prescribed laws in their universalizing aspect can sometimes obscure key discrepancies. As well, conflicting interests are often complex and nuanced and it is only through wider cultural experience that they can be understood fully.

We have seen that much of urban praxis has been submerged or degraded to become the prerogative of states when the legal status of cities changed in the Renaissance; concurrently, the dialectic between nomos as law and as custom has also become obscured. Nonetheless, the spectrum between the two does remain available in potentially infinite examples of everyday life in cities, where behaviour, rooted in concrete places and specific activities, develops its own expectations and meanings that underlie what can be described as protocols of everyday justice. Take for example a vignette in the Palestinian market in Jerusalem's Old City showing one village woman selling herbs to a townswoman on the street in the Muslim Quarter.[13] Their respective homes and social classes are evident not just through their stance in the street as vendor and shopper but also from their clothing, one wearing the embroidered garment of her village and the other in more somber urban clothing. In this simple transaction, the protocols of the market—the variety and quality of the herbs, the customary bargaining and whether the price is

Figure 8.2. Transaction in the market of the Muslim Quarter in Old City, Jerusalem.
Photo by Wendy Pullan.

fair, the relationship between the women, long term or not, etc.—pertain to their long-established understandings and expectations as well as wider ethical positions. The vendor sits in an opportune place in the street; it is a Friday after Muslim prayers, and she is likely to find a number of customers at that time. She has found a location where there is a slight indentation of the building line that affords her a sense of prominence, presence and protection in the street; but she is carefully located not to cross the line in the stone paving behind her lest she invade private property. I could describe the scene in more detail; however, it is probably enough to say that this scene is typical of long-established everyday market dealings which, through their habituality and repetition, contain a level of fair negotiation that is well established, expected and understood as 'meaningful patterns culled from the meaningful patterns of the past'.

What is not evident in the photo and can only be surmised through other forms of experience based upon inside knowledge or research is that the seller is illegal, in Israeli terms, and prohibited from entering Jerusalem from the West Bank by a law that is detached from the human conditions relevant to the Palestinians and their normative world. She does so by relying upon an elaborate series of transactions that involve assistance from a number of other people, various means of transport, negotiations established and officials turning a blind eye to allow her and her goods to come to the city so she can make a living.[14] These transactions represent a different form of justice, here withheld by the state and then circumvented through inventive means. In recent times such a process has become part of the praxis of the city, responding to new conditions.

This example can be interpreted in different ways depending upon one's experience, knowledge and opinion of the situation. Palestinians and Israelis may have opposing views of the situation. Through the example we can discern various aspects of urban justice embedded in and revealed by the local culture and supplemented by our more universal experience of markets. Much of this justice is rooted in long-term precedents, but some of it has been recently established, jolted into a more difficult and contested present. Because of Jerusalem's current geopolitical situation, the small situation I describe here is an example of far larger problems and potential ramifications. We see the second understanding of nomos at work as an expression of the conventions of cultures, in this case, clashing ones; with deeper knowledge we can also see the first and primary understanding of nomos as law, determined by the state, which here is contested and in certain ways inadequate. However, the dominant aspect of nomos could be referred to as customary rather than juridical and without it (the customary) the first aspect of nomos (the juridical) lacks critical aspects of reality. Scott (1998, 7) explains such a situation very simply when he points out that 'formal schemes of order are untenable without some elements of the practical knowledge that they tend to dismiss'. Most significantly for this discussion, we see how everyday acts in the city spaces represent elements of justice, both granted and withdrawn. Although far less inclusive and grand than the Siena frescoes, these acts, like the frescoes, illustrate an agonic quality situated within Jerusalem's urban structures and meanings. The city is the critical locus for this to happen.

CONCLUSION

What I describe here is not a system for justice or absolute equality. Rather it articulates the significance of urban praxis as a living repository for practices that interact and adjust over time in order to ensure a context for difference and diversity. In many ways the argument comes down to incompatibilities between equality as (ideally) aspired to in the law and diversity as embedded in culture and custom. Paul Ricoeur (2000, 78) follows Aristotle's under-standing and points out that absolute or 'simple equality'—arithmetically the same share to everyone—is a hallmark of a repressive society and to everyone's detriment. Rather, he suggests 'complex equality' as a corrective and in doing so refers to Michael Walzer's (1983, ch. 1) argument that for equality to be complex it must depend upon differentiated social goods where no one interest dominates the whole. Ricoeur (2000, 78) points to complex equality in 'the intersection between the project of combating domination and the program of differentiating spheres of justice [. . .] [where] the concern for differentiation will win out over that of integration'. This intersection can be fruitfully located in the city and everyday life. In the potentially infinite scope of urban praxis, with its complexity and variety but also its precedents and order, difference is most immediate and, arguably, most compelling. It would then be fair to say that for a just city the most relevant significance of the urban everyday is in its capacity for structured differentiation.

NOTES

1. *Nomos* (νόμος) is an ancient Greek term where it was often seen as one of the two world forces and conditions: *nomos* (law, order, custom) and *physis* (nature). In modern times it is used in law, philosophy, religion, sociology, but it is rarely found as part of urban studies or urbanism.

2. Customary law is usually regarded as traditions based in indigenous groups and first nations; however it can also refer to quotidianal practices, especially to do with local communities (see WIPO 2013).

3. Harvey sees this in terms of gaining state rights for cities, by means such as urban participation in allocating municipal budgets. This is, of course, important, but it does not address the physical embodiment of cities.

4. At present these include the International Court of Justice, the International Criminal Court, International Criminal Tribunal for the former Yugoslavia, Iran-United States Claims Tribunal, Permanent Court of Arbitration, Special Court for Sierra Leone, Special Tribunal for Lebanon (near The Hague) (see Hague Justice Portal n.d.).

5. https://www.peaceportal.org/web/exploring-peace-and-justice-in-the-hague.

6. There is a branch of international law based upon customary justice but like other aspects of The Hague, it is removed from local conditions.

7. For two months, members of the Nine lived in the Palazzo so as not to be exposed to corrupting influence from outside the city.

8. Aristotle, *Nichomachean Ethics,* 1094a29–1094b12. See also Gadamer (1986). The ambiguity of the terms is more obvious in medieval Latin where *bonum commune* could mean either common good or good commune (city). See Rubinstein (1958, 185).

9. On the Internet there are many photos of the Lorenzetti frescoes in the Sala dei Nove. A good selection, including views of the room, can be found at Khan Academy, 'Ambrogio Lorenzetti, Palazzo Pubblico frescos: Allegory and effect of good and bad government', 14.1.13.

10. John Locke, *Second Treatise on Government*, para. 3.

11. Ibid., para. 22.

12. A detailed discussion of the modern understanding of nomos is beyond the scope of this chapter. Its interpretation by Carl Schmitt, associated with German National Socialism, has tainted its meaning, although more recently Schmitt's ideas have been seen more positively by some. Nonetheless, his work remains disputed. For an interesting recent article that summarizes commentary on Schmitt's idea of nomos as well as Hannah Arendt's criticism of it, see Jurkevics (2017).

13. Photographed in 2009; the conditions and transactions refer to 2007–2009 when the research was carried out.

14. Since 2005 Israeli closure laws have forbidden most Palestinians living in the West Bank from entering Jerusalem without a special permit.

Chapter 9

Gardens, Cities and Timescapes in South Asia[1]

Smriti Srinivas

A curious excavator of traditions stumbles over something protruding above the surfaces of the commonplaces of contemporary life. He scratches away, discovering bits and pieces of cultural design that seem to elude coherent reconstitution but which leads him deeper into the past.

—Schama, *Landscape and Memory* (1996, 16)

At the capital [. . .] I had a dream: It seemed to me as if three silver trays of fresh dates known as *ratb* were brought and placed before me. The dates were each of the size of a span. They were fresh and full of juice. It was reported to me that they had been reared in the garden. At that moment I awoke and found it was morning. This servant of God interpreted the dream as follows: That by the grace of merciful God the dominions and homes of all the three *Kafirs* shall fall into his hands. On the third of the month mentioned above news arrived that Nizam Ali was dead.

—Husain, *The Dreams of Tipu Sultan* (1900, 87)

Like Simon Schama's excavator in *Landscape and Memory*, through the soil of the commonplace—the spaces of gardens and parks in South Asia—I try to unearth designs of thought, practice and culture constituting and framing the relationship of gardens to cities. I look for ways to bring into view what may have disappeared, what lies within ritual practices, renatured landscapes or old texts, for other avenues for creating relationalities, and the modes through which gardens become repositories for the senses, experiences, imaginations and concepts. As the vivid dream of garden-grown dates of Tipu Sultan (1750–1799) encapsulates, our ideas of allies, enemies, empire or divine grace nest within certain landscapes and their fruits.

133

Before revisiting the cities and gardens that Tipu Sultan traversed, I turn to some literary and historical evidence of gardens in South Asia that may serve as signposts in these explorations. Gardens—and by extension, trees and plants—seem to play an important role in Buddhist traditions. Apart from the several gardens and parks that signal key events in the Buddha's life—Lumbini or Sarnath, for example—the Buddha appears against the identifiable backdrop of several named groves, discussing religious topics. These groves are urban retreats for the peripatetic Buddha. In the *Mahaparinibbana Sutta*, for example, the Blessed One stays in the Pavarika mango grove in Nalanda; in Vaisali, at the courtesan Ambapali's grove; at the mango grove of a smith in Pava; and at the Sala grove of the Mallas near the Hiranyavati River (Rhys Davids 2000, 14, 28, 70, 85). These Buddhist scriptures preserved in Pali seem to describe a society in north India between 500 and 400 BCE. Five cities are of significance for 'Buddha's ministry': Sarnath, a suburb west of early Varanasi, or Banaras, where the Buddha gave his first sermon; Kausambi; Sravasti; Vaisali; and Rajagriha, capital of early Magadha and close to the sylvan location at Gaya where he achieved enlightenment (Heitzman 2008, 15). These five cities—which appear numerous times in the early texts—occur within a hierarchy of other settlements, reminding us that these groves and greens appear amid an urbanizing world. The gardens and groves, like Buddhist monasteries, were separate but proximate to urban and courtly space and, thus, emphasized the Buddha's miraculous life, separating it from secular lords; plant and flower motifs were perhaps also symbolic of a new social order (Shimada 2012; Hawkes and Shimada 2009).

Among more contemporary gardens, Mughal gardens have received a great amount of attention. Under Mughal rule, gardens found a place within the vast corpus of buildings and urban sites, which include residences, palaces, forts, mosques and funerary structures constructed from the early sixteenth century until the middle of the nineteenth century (see Koch 1991; Westcoat and Wolschke-Bulmahn 1996). Babur (who ruled from 1526 to 1530 in India) is associated with gardens such as the Char Bagh (Four-Fold Garden) and Bagh-i-Hasht Bihist (Garden of Eight Paradises) at Agra, introducing the scheme of a subdivided walled-in garden with walkways and canals. The tomb of Humayun, built by his son Akbar (r. 1556–1605), and Akbar's tomb, built by his son Jahangir (r. 1605–1627) in Sikandra near Agra, has a similar fourfold pattern. Other elaborate garden schemes emerged under Shah Jahan's rule (1628–1658), such as the Taj Mahal funerary structure at Agra or the famous Shalimar gardens in Lahore. While Mughal gardens have been most discussed, peninsular India or the Deccan region also contains many kinds of landscape practices within the built environment as well as in literary, poetic and visual contexts; these include pre- and non-Mughal gardens as well as traditions that were outside, or on the periphery of, Mughal rule. Gardens appear to be key institutions of rulership and elite practice but there are references to charitable gardens that were open for public enjoyment, for food, and medical uses (Ali and Flatt 2012).

As these literary and historical examples show, gardens spatially materialize the labor of both state and non-state, elite and non-elite actors in South Asia. In this chapter, I approach gardens and cities to ask, do gardens also materialize timescapes in the city? By 'timescape', I mean the experience of other or multiple times in the present by where and how we are positioned in or move through the city; the ways in which 'landscape is the work of the mind' before 'it can ever be a repose for the senses' (Schama 1996, 6–7); but also the moment of 'recognition' when 'a place suddenly exposes its connection' (Schama 1996, 16) to other places and times through dreams, rituals, growing practices, walks or trails of memory. Taking cases from two south Indian cities—Bangalore and Madras or Chennai—I will suggest that at least three timescapes—mnemonic, spiritualist and cohabitational—emerge from distinct pathways. These pathways include the ritual life of an old community of urban gardeners, the life and writings of a Ceylonese Theosophist for whom the Buddhist *sangha* included a 'brotherhood of venerable trees' (No Author 1975, 148), and the practice of walking in the city. These timescapes facilitate the experience of nonlinear time in the city or the multiple temporalities copresent with city life.

Bangalore, in Karnataka state, has long been associated with horticultural gardens tended by Tamil-speaking migrants who identify themselves as 'Vahnikula Kshatriyas' or those who belong to the lineage of fire. In fact, I have suggested that four elements were central to the spatial order of Bangalore from the middle of the sixteenth century until about 1800: a complex of a fort (*kote*); a settlement market (*pete*); a reservoir, lake or tank (*kere*); and the horticultural garden (*tota*) provided its design (Srinivas 2001). The horticultural gardens, in which grew a variety of fruits, vegetables or flowers, were interspersed with the city's terrain and organically linked to water-harvesting regimes such as tanks or ponds and feeder canals that carried water or organic waste from the city. Remnants of these gardens appear today as nurseries and small gardens in the city that supply citizens with seasonal produce—winter fruits such as oranges or vegetables such as gourds—or in larger tracts in the metropolitan region given to the cultivation of grapes, betel nut, pomelo or other plantings. The significance of gardens and horticulture in this region should not be underestimated: Karnataka, for example, accounts for almost 75 percent of the floriculture industry in the country, and Vahnikula Kshatriyas are specifically renowned for their expertise in growing flowers.

Legally regarded as a Backward Class numbering about 250,000 in Bangalore and surrounding areas, Vahnikula Kshatriyas are commonly called 'Tigalas', a local term used to refer to Tamil speakers who migrated into Bangalore. The first wave of migration may have occurred in the period after the tenth century when the Bangalore region became a frontier zone for Telugu, Tamil and Kannada-speaking groups. Another wave of migration appears to have occurred during the late fourteenth and early fifteenth centuries when groups such as the Pallis, Padaiyichis and Vanniyar were inducted into the armies of the Vijayanagar Empire and those of local chieftains. The third wave of migration is associated with the continued importance of recruitment of these groups in the eighteenth century as the needs of militia and trade revenues increased in significance for three powers—the rulers of Mysore, the Nawab of Arcot, and the British East India Company. In the armies of Haidar Ali and Tipu Sultan, these groups of the Pallis, Padaiyichis or Vanniyar (regarded as Vahnikula Kshatriyas today) found their way into Bangalore district from settlements in North Arcot, Salem and Coimbatore. A popular narrative about their origin runs as follows:

> When Haidar Ali was warring with the Nawab of Arcot, he camped in some fields near the site of the battle. By day, only some gardeners were working there and Haidar Ali imagined that his camp was secure. But by the next morning, he found his camp ransacked. This happened three nights in a row. Finally, he kept watch one night and found that the lowly gardeners working innocuously on the fields by day carried torches of fire, 'ti', by night showing them in their dual incarnations of gardeners and soldiers. He realized the value of these men, carriers of fire ('Ti-galas'), and invited them to settle in his dominions. (Interview with a Vahnikula Kshatriya male, 3 March 1996)

Apart from gardening, the corporate identity of the Tigalas/Vahnikula Kshatriyas is associated with the Karaga performance, Bangalore's central civic ritual occurring for nine days in March or April every year in the calendar month of *Chaitra*. The key moment within the performance is the incarnation of Draupadi, the polyandrous wife of the Pandava brothers in the Sanskrit *Mahabharata*, as a goddess. She manifests herself first in the form of a sacred icon, and second within the body of a male priest from the Tigala/Vahnikula Kshatriya community, who, by carrying this object, becomes conjoint with her. The word 'Karaga', therefore, has three levels of meaning in the Kannada language. First, it refers to the nine days of festivities in the city—a genre called *jatre*. Second, the word 'Karaga' indicates the sacred icon—an earthen pot—that embodies the power (*shakti*) of the goddess. Third, it refers to the male priest when he carries the icon on his head on the final day of the festival under a floral headdress made of jasmine.

The Karaga festivities tie closely with Bangalore's historic tank culture. For instance, the annual 'birth' of the sacred pot occurs every year on the seventh night of the Karaga performance at the Upnirinakunte (a saltwater pond) in Cubbon Park bordering the Kanteerava Stadium. It is brought to a pillared hall in Sampangi tank and revealed to hundreds of excited devotees. Upnirinakunte today is a small, covered well unknown to passers-by, and there are few signs to remember that the site of the Karaga's unveiling was an extensive tank. Early in the twentieth century, the tank had partly gone dry; authorities drained it to create the monumental Kanteerava Stadium for the Indian Olympics in 1946. Despite this, the Vahnikula Kshatriyas who undertake to host the Karaga return every year to the locations of key water bodies in Bangalore to perform rituals over nine days of the festival. In addition to the fate of the Sampangi tank, the Dharmambudi tank is now the central bus station of the city and the Kempambudi is partially choked by sewage and urban construction.

The dramatic transformations of the city in the last hundred years help contextualize the performance's role. In 1901, the population of the metropolitan area (including the area of the old city and British military cantonment) stood at 228,000 persons; today it is about 10 million. Perhaps one of the greatest impacts of population growth, public and private sector investment, state policies and urban development has been the steady decline of Bangalore's ecological base in the twentieth century: B. N. Sundara Rao reports that in 1830 the Mysore region as a whole had 19,800 tanks, many of them built in pre-British times (1985, 326). The British continued to build tanks in the Bangalore region, constructing the Miller and Sankey tanks, for instance. In 1987, the Lakshman Rau Committee reported that of the 390 tanks within the jurisdiction of the Bangalore Development Authority, 127 tanks lay within the conurbation limits; of these only eighty-one tanks were 'live', the others having been breached after independence due to public housing, home construction and urban infrastructure projects.

Within this terrain, the Karaga performance produces a timescape we may describe as an urban mnemonic. In contrast to dominant visions that represent Bangalore as a 'garden city', or the 'Silicon Valley' of India, the Karaga performance produces and celebrates the 'gardeners' city' or the 'city of the children of fire'. The performance recovers architectural fragments, spatially peripheral tracts and older axes of the city from a zone of urban amnesia linking these to contemporaneous axes and institutional sites in other patterns of meaning. The protocol of memory activated in the Karaga performance, unlike the archives of a museum, is a protocol of enactment and embodiment occurring through two devices.

The first device is kinetic and includes movements in time and space in the city through ritual events and the routes taken by the Karaga priest, his

retinue and citizens. In addition to the rituals performed over nine days at
the site of several water bodies and temples, after the Karaga icon's birth,
'Virakumaras', sword-bearing men of the Vahnikula Kshatriya community
who act as protectors of the Karaga priest, bring the Karaga icon to the pillared hall near the Kanteerava stadium. Two days later, the procession of the
priest with the Karaga on his head leaves the Dharmaraja temple, the central
site of the Karaga performance, for a tour of the old city. Apart from visits to
various temples, the procession also visits the tomb of the Sufi saint, Hazrat
Tawakkul Mastan. The ritual players have to move through 'actual' space,
through certain streets, across parks, through milling crowds, between buildings. Within these spatial and temporal constraints, there are also 'virtual'
spaces and times activated by the procession and the places where rituals
occur, charging some sites—temples, water bodies, the Sufi shrine and others—with greater significance than others.

The second device is the recitation of an epic, the *Karaga Purana*. This
is the source of a unique *Mahabharata* story describing the origin of the
Vahnikula Kshatriyas from Draupadi, a fierce goddess in the forest, during her battle against a demon. Although some of the characters present in
the *Karaga Purana* are common to the Sanskrit *Mahabharata* attributed to
Vyasa, many themes found in it are independent of the classical epic, such
as the formation of an alliance between the Pandavas with a local ruler of a
city-fortress, Potha Raja. A mixture of songs and prose, the two languages
of the *Karaga Purana* are Tamil (for the songs) and Telugu (for the prose).
The epic is an origin story for the community but also depicts the city and the
forest as part of the same landscape of memory.

The Karaga performance relies on the image of the wild goddess surrounded by a group of male protectors/offspring, who together roam a region
between the forest/exile and the city/battlefield. In spite of these martial
representations, the ritual players and Vahnikula Kshatriya community associated with the performance face fierce struggles over the city's production base. In the last several decades, they have been trying to consolidate
themselves through a wider political alliance between different groups in the
city—castes who also regard themselves as belonging to fire lineages or who
have fiery ancestors—who constitute part of the urban informal economy
or the lower end of the formal sector. This alliance, which draws from the
performative terrain, has a complex relationship to the cultural and economic
policies of the state, other elites and power brokers.

If horticultural gardens, gardeners and their practices point us to a mnemonic timescape, my second timescape—a spiritualist one—emerges from
a Buddhist past, in networks of religious transculturalism that bridged South
Asia, Europe and North America, and in the life and writings of C. Jinara-

jadasa (1875–1953). This timescape has linkages to cognate terms and global histories of 'spirits', 'spiritualism' and 'spirituality' (van der Veer 2001, 2009), other teachers such as Sri Aurobindo and the Mother in Auroville, as well as New Age ideas in contemporary South Asia. As I have discussed in detail elsewhere (Srinivas 2015), Jinarajadasa, more than anyone else in the Theosophical Society, made a refuge for the ecological and utopian potential of Theosophy in soil, trees, gardens and locality. The Theosophical Society continues to bear a material and vital imprint in Madras/Chennai because of the existence of its gardens that probably comprise the second largest green space in the city after Guindy National Park. Shortly after arriving in India in 1879, the founders of the Theosophical Society—Madame Blavatsky and Colonel Olcott—purchased a small estate of twenty-seven acres called Huddleston Gardens south of the Adyar River for the Society's international headquarters in 1882. By 1925, the estate had grown to 262 acres, and it is about the same area today.

The estate contains a number of separate areas such as Blavatsky Gardens (after Madame Blavatsky) and Besant Grove (named for Annie Besant) and many landmarks. It is home to the famous banyan tree under which the philosopher and teacher J. Krishnamurti gave several inspired talks and where he opened services at the shrine called the Bharata Samaja in 1925. In the same year, C. Jinarajadasa began construction of a Buddhist shrine near the Olcott Memorial in a beautiful palm grove. In 1950, a Bodhi sapling that came from the original in Bodh Gaya was planted. Other planned shrines included a Masonic temple, a Zoroastrian temple, a Christian church, a Jewish synagogue and a Muslim mosque. After the estate expanded, a library, a publishing house, Society headquarters, and other buildings appeared on the grounds but abundant space existed for trees, plants and flowers. If you walk through the Adyar gardens today enclosed on one side by a wall and bounded on another by the river, you encounter a landscape where brush jungle prevails. Local species, rocks and roots back exotic species to make the landscape look like 'original' forest. There are also plants and trees arranged in formal and informal beds, a walled lotus pond and other watery arenas, separate sections for cultivating different trees such as coconuts, and, of course, the various shrines.

Much of the renaturing of the Theosophical Society/Adyar gardens was the project of Jinarajadasa. A modest being, his uniqueness is generally occluded in normal histories about the Theosophical Society that are focused on high-profile figures such as Annie Besant or J. Krishnamurti. He usually receives mention for the fact that in the Silver Jubilee year of the Theosophical Society, he planted mahogany seedlings to form an avenue running through the estate. Soil from various countries was put into pits prepared for the seedlings in 1925 so that today, if you walk down 'Founders Avenue', you can still read the names on the plaques—Brazil, Puerto Rico, Ukraine and so on. While these trees did not survive, his efforts were part of more extensive labors. In a reversal of colonial journeying to the tropics and the South for the collection of flora and fauna but in concert with the expansion of a global network of botanical gardens in the colonies, Jinarajadasa brought to Adyar about 300 species of seeds and plants from various countries. He writes, for instance, that in his Latin American tours of 1928, 1934 and 1938 alone, he collected 229 varieties. Some were planted in Adyar and some distributed to other gardens: for example, the Victoria Regina lily that he brought from a visit to the Amazon was gifted to the Victoria gardens in Bombay. Of the many plants, he delighted in two varieties of bougainvillea, one a brilliant crimson brought from Australia and another a rose variety from Panama (No Author 1975, 151).

Long before he became president in 1945, Jinarajadasa supervised the vast acreage of the Adyar gardens. Although there were some trees that were grown for fuel, most were allowed to grow to their fullness without much tending and flowers were not plucked indiscriminately; Jinarajadasa himself would not accept garlands. While the official policy against tree cutting could perhaps be traced to a letter that C. W. Leadbeater wrote in 1909 to Annie Besant, Jinarajadasa long before that certainly believed that trees and plants had souls, were home to nature spirits and communed with them. In an article about two banyan trees in *The Theosophist*, he describes how he could see that the tree spirit of an eighty-year-old banyan tree that had to be removed in the estate was alarmed. When Jinarajadasa came near it, the tree sensed that he was a benefactor and displayed a rosy aura; he persuaded the tree spirit to move out of the tree onto two branches before it was felled. Replanted, the branches coalesced and grew into 'a beautiful banyan tree in which the Tree Spirit is indeed happy in his more youthful form' (No Author 1975, 149). Gardens and landscapes for him were 'windows through which he looked out of this sensuous world of ours into a supersensous world, which to him was the real world and his real home' (No Author 1975, 151).

I argue that the Theosophical Society gardens were the outcome of the refashioning of at least three norms (Srinivas 2015): First, there is what I call the 'South Indian Victorian', which drew on European nineteenth-century wild and pastoral visions of arcadia, along with South Indian designs for horticultural gardens, and the scrub jungle typical of the area. Second, there is a 'greening of the idea of comparative religions', their study and their practice, with religious shrines from several world traditions set amidst nature. Third, this garden is rooted in the idea of a Buddhist fellowship of all living organisms including trees or plants that are evolving into sentient beings.

While we can explore any of these in detail, of the last we can see multiple expressions in Jinarajadasa's writings. He writes, 'God's plan is evolution' (2007, 18). By this, he means that life is everywhere, there is 'no dead substance' (18), and that the life of the plant, animal or man is not different from the stone. Corollaries to this are that Life never dies, death is only a change of form and that Life evolves. Nature thus involves the flow of Life through its various forms: 'Reincarnation is a fact in Nature' (Jinarajadasa 2008, 3). Nature, thus imagined, is not mechanical but 'ethical' (Jinarajadasa 2005, 29), and we can approach and sense the 'rhythm in life' (41) through worship of nature, its study, the love of nature or by refashioning it, for instance, through art or a garden.

In *Flowers and Gardens*, Jinarajadasa writes of the religion of a dream community: 'They think of each individual as having a flower within him which is slowly opening' (2006, 8). They speak of the flower in man, of man dying and meeting his flower, and the Flower of Flowers. People surround themselves with flowers and in the garden children are the gardeners. This vision of the utopian community as garden parallels the association of childhood with flowers. A cognate of Jinarajadasa's vision is the imagination of Maria Montessori, who spent several years during World War II as a guest of Theosophical Society in Adyar, of the nurture needed during childhood so that the soul of the child can flower. Another direct cognate is the educational philosophy of the philosopher J. Krishnamurti (whom Jinarajadasa had mentored for some years while Krishnamurti was still associated with the Theosophical Society) for whom the landscape situating his schools—whether in Ojai Valley in California or Rishi Valley in India—have a pedagogic value. They offer a utopian place of contrast to a degenerating world where questions of knowledge and freedom can be explored in relationship to the environment, seasons, open air, trees and other beings.

Finally, the Buddha occupied a central position in Jinarajadasa's world of spiritualist fellowship. Some of this was biographical: Jinarajadasa was born in 1875 in Ceylon of Sinhalese Buddhist parents. The turning point in his life came at age thirteen when he met C. W. Leadbeater, who was in Ceylon assisting the Buddhist educational movement. In 1889, he accompanied Leadbeater to England and became a member of the Theosophical Society in 1893; however, the Buddha continues to appear in his thought and writings. The interpretation of the Buddha and the Buddhist *sangha* in his work should also be located in the institutional links of Theosophy with Buddhism. Both Theosophical founders had converted to Buddhism, but through Colonel Olcott's central efforts for the revival of Buddhism in Ceylon from the 1880s onward—which included founding schools (in one of which Jinarajadasa studied, becoming its vice principal in 1900)—the tracks between Theosophy and Buddhism crisscrossed in several personal and institutional histories. The founder of the Maha Bodhi Society, Anagarika Dharmapala, for instance, was inspired by Olcott and Blavatsky and maintained close relations with the Theosophical Society for many years. Jinarajadasa's interpretation of the Buddha, however, was a counterpoint to Dharmapala's more nationalist Buddhist project.

This brings me to the last timescape—one of cohabitational or coeval time—through our experience of trees and gardens. In some ways, the iconic form of this is the Bodhi tree under which the Buddha sat about 2,500 years ago; a sapling from that tree was brought to the Theosophical Society garden from Bodh Gaya. Offshoots of the Bodhi tree grow in many locations globally from Anuradhapura in Sri Lanka to the Foster Botanical Garden in Honolulu (a gift from Anagarika Dharmapala, it is said, to Mary Foster in 1913), bridging the time from the Buddha to ours through many shoots and roots.

However, a more mundane tree triggers my final reflections on timescapes and emerges from my knowledge and analyses of the South Asian city accrued through walking. I have walked regularly in many cities including Bangalore, Chennai and Delhi. Walking through and traversing the city in order to carry out activities becomes a methodological tool to observe regularities on one's path as well as unexpected events, movements, sights and emerging structures. Getting to the market, taking a bus part of the way and then walking the rest to one's destination, walking because there is no way in which one can take an auto-rickshaw on a particular stretch, picking a trail amidst exposed pipes and cables on a partly dug-up road; I have argued that pedestrian-quotidian living is a method of inquiry into the urban (Srinivas 2015). The pedestrian is an urban actor rather than a flaneur or a tourist and in many urban areas across the world, this kind of practice allies one with the large numbers of non-elite actors who use streets, parks and other public spaces to pursue daily activities. Pedestrian-quotidian movements in streets, parks, residential communities, crossroads or markets—captured in their ritual, associational or everyday aspects—allows us to register place histories, shifting maps, encroachments, contingencies, flows of public and domestic activities or urban subcultures.

Some of my girlhood walks in Bangalore—with my grandfather and his mixed-breed dog, for example—included long peregrinations from his home in Shantinagar, up the tree-lined Double Road, past a still existing cemetery to Lal Bagh, presently a 240-acre botanical garden in the center of the city. Built on Tigala/Vahnikula Kshatriya gardens that sold to private developers in the early 1950s—about the same time that the nearby Sampani Tank was drained and converted into a stadium—my grandfather's neighbourhood was part of the spatial and demographic transformations of the postcolonial Indian city, which would only accelerate in the next few decades. Lal Bagh in the mid-1970s was already the site for annual flower shows, a destination for ardent walkers, for tamed bears and their retainers performing tricks for children (this occupation has now disappeared from the urban landscape), for eating at a restaurant famous for its Art Deco-like design and tasty *dosas* (this was later torn down).

On a recent walk four decades later in Lal Bagh, a small mango from a native tree (*Magnifera indica*) fell on my head as I passed under it. As I held the fruit, an encounter seemingly demanded by the tree, I noticed for the first time that the path I was walking on accommodated the tree's trunk, which jutted into the path unlike the other trees and plants in the garden. The tree obviously predated the path and a notice next to it stated that the tree belonged to Tipu Sultan's time. Had the notice always been there, or did the Director-ate of Horticulture insert it more recently given that the garden had become a huge tourist attraction for national and international visitors in recent years and the location for 'green heritage walks'?

Tipu Sultan, whose record of dreams with which we began, perhaps set down to record his dreams in the mid-1790s; feeling increasingly isolated in his efforts against the British, he could have been searching for meanings in, and guidance through, his dreams (Brittlebank 2011). The account of his dream of fresh dates ends with news of the death of the Nizam, another regional ruler, whom he counts among the unbelievers and probably dates to 1797. In 1796, Tipu records an earlier dream of riding on an elephant in a mango grove. While his military exploits, the nature of his relationship to Islam or his position as an early modernizer have dominated scholarship, there is more to Tipu Sultan's role than meets the eye within the evolving landscape of Lal Bagh.

My inquiries reveal that the area we know as Lal Bagh today originally contained mango orchards. Haidar Ali established a garden there in 1760 inspired perhaps by his visit to the French colony of Pondicherry or more directly by the gardens in Sira that may have been influenced by Mughal pro-totypes or other Deccani landscapes. A cypress and rose garden overlaid the mango orchards and Haidar Ali's son, Tipu Sultan, supplemented it with plots and plants from the Indian Ocean world and beyond. For instance, he issued instructions to two embassies sent to Turkey and France in the 1780s: these briefs reflect his interests in enlisting diplomatic-military assistance against the British, but also in overseas trade, ports, artisans, fruits and trees. From Jedda and Musqat, Tipu Sultan also sought seeds and saplings of almonds, pistachios, walnut, pear, dates and yam, along with silkworms and gardeners.

Tipu Sultan's gardens in Bangalore and Srirangapatna 'were the nurseries in which seeds and saplings from various countries around the world were obtained and planted' including pine and oak from the Cape of Good Hope (Hasan 1971, 340).

After the last Anglo-Mysore war and the death of Tipu Sultan in 1799, the British consolidated several plots including Lal Bagh into the Government Botanical Gardens in 1856. Hugh Cleghorn, Conservator of Forests, Madras Presidency, wrote: 'The object in view is not merely to improve the culture of indigenous plants, but at the same time to naturalize exotics, and prepare both for introduction in the plains' (1865, 331). One might explore whether this horticultural norm differed from the Sultan's and the circulation of ideas and practices between Victorian England and the colonies. It appears from my initial research that what was equally, if not even more significant, was the movement of plants, personnel, technologies and techniques in the Indian Ocean world that also penetrated the Royal Kew and other British gardens. By the end of the nineteenth century, the newly constructed 'Glass House', a modern engineering feat of cast iron and sheet glass, became a major focus of Lal Bagh. While this structure—later the site of numerous flower shows and exhibitions—could be directly connected to its more famous Victorian counterpart, the Crystal Palace in Sydenham, the reality was that glasshouses and conservatories by then had become very popular in England and elsewhere because of new technologies and cheaper materials. While in Tipu Sultan's time, Lal Bagh may have covered an area of about 40 acress, by the time of Cleghorn's report, it had expanded to 99 acres, and at the end of the twentieth century stood at about 240 acres.

Much can be said about the temporal transformations of Lal Bagh in post-colonial India: its role as Bangalore's premier public garden and the singular place it occupies in India's science city as a showcase for visiting dignitaries, floriculture or horticultural production. Numerous publics use Lal Bagh daily—joggers, lovers, children, tourists, green heritage walkers, botanists and others. In the context of this chapter, my mango tree encounter suggests that walking in the South Asian city allows us to note a large range of extant and extinct garden designs that have been altered in complex ways over time and which have shifting relationships to urban space. Even within Lal Bagh, boundaries of paths have changed, structures have been covered by moss, buildings have been removed, trees have fallen and many non-native ones have been planted. Walking, then, provides us with experiences of topologically layered time in the city through gardens and the time of real trees. With some of these trees, we cohabit other times in the present but gardens are also cohabitational timescapes opening out to other gardens and garden designs within and beyond South Asia.

NOTE

1. This chapter was first conceived as a presentation for a pre–conference session on 'Time and the South Asian City' at the Annual South Asia Conference in Madison, Wisconsin, 26 October 2017. My thanks to the preconference session organizers, especially Sneha Krishnan, for the invitation, and the other participants for a lively discussion. The chapter draws from research done for two of my previous books (2001; 2015).

Chapter 10

A Vertical Melbourne

Megan Nethercote

High-rise towers congest the skies of cities around the globe. As new towers have proliferated at record rates, scaling ever-higher heights, the urban morphology of many previously low-rise cities, such as Melbourne, has radically and abruptly transformed. High-rise towers and vertical living are themselves far from new, but they are now, along with the stacked societies they create, a ubiquitous and almost exclusively urban phenomenon. Since the orchestrated demise of mass vertical social housing, with its attempts to democratize vertical living across many Western cities, property developers have furnished the seemingly insatiable private market appetite with an array of apartments ranging from prosaic, 'investor-grade' stock, through to ultra-exclusive vertical enclaves for uber-wealthy elites.

Surprisingly, given this epic vertical expansion of cities, perspectives on human societies in leading academic debates about cities and urban life have remained resolutely 'flat' (Graham 2016, 1). Geography and urban studies research explores the structuring of 'horizontal aspects of cities stretched across the earth's surface', yet when it comes to the third dimension—to the vertical axis—exploration of the structures of cities and urban life is 'patchy and limited', especially in Anglophone debates (7). This 'horizontalism' is perhaps especially persistent in understandings of urban inequality, which is 'almost always imagined to be constituted horizontally rather than vertically' (12). Again, geography and urban studies, which have much to say about urban inequality, are testament to a steadfast reliance on traditional top-down cartography and horizontal geographic frames of reference (Graham and Hewitt 2012; McNeill 2005). It is not that the third dimension has been altogether ignored: architecture, archaeology, climatology, geology and philosophy, for example, all embrace more fully three-dimensional perspectives (Graham 2016, 3). From studies of modernist mass social housing to

147

contemporary 'super-talls', urban and architectural historians continue to contribute hugely to exploring the vertical dimensions of urban life through the changing designs and symbolisms of stacked housing. Yet these are typically less attentive to the 'broader geographies, sociologies, and politics of verticalizing cities' (Graham 2016, 8–9).

In trying to understand contemporary cities as they rise ever-upwards, the persistent 'flat' perspective or 'horizontalism' is deemed inadequate and flawed (Graham 2016; Harris 2015; McNeill 2005). Part of the urgency for a more fully volumetric perspective arises from the contradictions of contemporary capitalism that manifests, for instance, in the elite ascent and secession into vertical enclaves of the super-rich, while residents struggling to remain housed are pushed towards the urban fringe, with all the disadvantages this entails. Pervasive vertical metaphors for social hierarchy and difference— 'upper class', 'high flier', 'ivory tower' and so on—which themselves are so deeply entrenched, naturalized and taken-for-granted in our everyday language, allude to the connection between vertical structures, vertical ascent, and social stratification, wealth, elitism and power (Haacke 2011). The starting point for this chapter then is the view that as cities expand vertically at greater intensities reaching ever-higher heights, more than ever there is a need to grasp our cities more volumetrically (e.g., McNeill 2005; Graham and Hewitt 2012).

This chapter explores why this vertical dimension of cities is now so vital. Focusing on Melbourne, this exploration weaves through Melbourne's high-rise housing history and its culmination in an unprecedented proliferation of towers, especially in the wake of the financial crisis. Indeed this is a city well suited to this task: an 'inner urban "gold rush" of high rise development' (Buxton et al. 2016, 153) has seen, since the turn of the century, a remarkable reversal of its long-dominant penchant for suburban development. Moreover, this high-rise development has occurred at such intensity as to position Melbourne as a global front-runner in vertical expansion (outside of China) (71).

I begin by focusing on questions of 'how': outlining two parallel high-rise narratives that took shape around the 1970s, whereby high-rise social housing was pathologized, while private high-rise was progressively lauded by an urban consolidation planning consensus. In the second part, I turn to consider *why* high-rise development is so ubiquitous today. Here I depart from the emergent critique of high-rise Melbourne as a frenzy of 'neoliberal' market-led development, introducing Marxian perspectives to begin to position high-rise housing within financialized capitalism. This perspective has the potential to sharpen our understanding about why this vertical expansion continues apace despite questioned social and urban benefits. However, this chapter is necessarily but a first tentative step towards this task, and is subsequently more explorative than comprehensive in this regard (see later refinements in Nethercote 2018), tracing conceptually and through secondary data on Melbourne, some of the non-shelter functions played by high-rise housing. The conclusion echoes important calls from verticality scholars across the social sciences by pointing towards a more volumetric reading of the socially regressive outcomes produced by this political economy of apartment development, including new verticalized stratification. Paying attention to the vertical in this way offers to augment the critical, yet essentially horizontal schema, of socio-spatial polarization produced by high-rise development located only in high-amenity, job-rich inner-city areas where land prices dictate it remains prohibitive but to investors and wealthy homeowners.

PATHOLOGIES OF HIGH-RISE PUBLIC HOUSING

Melbourne's first public housing high-rise towers were built under inner-city slum reclamation programs that targeted dire housing conditions, and the social deficiencies believed to fester within these (Tibbits 1988; Hayward 1996). The scale of vertical development was extensive: the Housing Commission of Victoria's (HCV) high-rise program delivered forty-five high-rise towers across twenty sites in fourteen suburbs in inner Melbourne. Between 1962 and 1974, 7,834 new apartments housed roughly 14,000 public housing tenants. Most towers ranged between twenty and thirty storeys; in the biggest estates four buildings were clustered together, such as Elizabeth St, Richmond; Atherton Gardens, Fitzroy; and Racecourse Rd, Flemington. The seventeen-storey Emerald Hill Estate was completed in 1960 in South Melbourne, followed by a proposal for the thirty-storey award-winning Park Towers, which was completed in 1969, and the highest of the towers erected by the HCV.

The rise of mass social housing in Melbourne is often explained, not unlike in other Western cities between 1930 and the 1970s, as the product of the advent of industrialized prefabrication, lift technologies and steel-frame engineering, and its collision with the sway of modernist ideas. New vertical landscapes were proclaimed as a salve for industrial poverty, urbanization and the ravages of war, including a huge housing backlog.

Modernism touted vertical living as revolutionary: the means to engineer a new socially progressive society through elevated high-rise living. The modernist imperative—to 'erase the traces' (tabula rasa)—urged the construction of a new world on the ruins of the old (Hatherley 2009, 3). New vertical technologies, such as lifts and reinforced concrete, would 'lift' people into light and air, removing them from ground-level afflictions of pollution, disease, industrial poverty and social disorder. More than simply shelter, the high-rise was to offer a 'kind of membrane between humanity and nature', through which 'planning and design [provided] a way to bring the two into balance and order after decades of disordered urban development' (Zipp 2012, 367–68). The 1944 report of the Commonwealth Housing Commission, which was established to investigate housing problems, reveals the grip of such ideas. It was 'suffused with a modernist confidence in the rational efficacy of planning and engineering to overcome a myriad of social and environmental problems' (cited in Hanna 1991, 87). Indeed the commission was perceived to be so enchanted by these modernist ideals, that its officials on their European tour are said to have glossed over Britain's struggles with mass high-rise housing (Dalton 1988; Tibbits 1988). For the HCV, convinced as they were that 'bad houses made bad people' (cited in Costello 2005, 72), new mass high-rise housing would address its 'implicit objective' to 'improve the moral fiber and health of tenants' (Hayward 1996, 13).

These modernist ideas are argued to have coincided with local postwar advocacy for the modernization of the building industry in order to remedy the seventy-thousand-dwelling backlog in Victoria (O'Hanlon 1998). This was to be achieved through industrialization, prefabrication and new architectural forms. Local 'six-pack' low-rise flats were deemed uneconomic and inadequate to deliver the dwellings required. High-rise by contrast not only embodied the new spirit of rational, 'scientific' mass production of the industrial era, but it necessitated new mass-produced materials such as steel and reinforced concrete. In Victoria in 1946, Canadian Stanley Lang, as director of the State Material Procurement Directorate, and charged with approving construction materials, urged Premier Cain Senior, based on his experience in North America, to urgently commit to a program of mass production of housing for the mid to lower end of the housing market, expecting production of 37,500 homes annually (O'Hanlon 1998). High-rise public housing was thus as much a part of HCV's 'commitment to concrete housing' (1998, 111), with a local factory in Homesglen revitalized by increased demands, including for the twenty-two-storey Atherton Estate in Fitzroy and the thirty-storey Park Towers in South Melbourne.

The legitimacy and funding of high-rise public housing was ultimately short-lived in Melbourne. It was, as proved to be the case further afield, no more than an '"interregnum" of socialism or social democracy' (Hatherley 2009, 9) and, by May 1971, the Victorian government announced the end of high-rise public housing development (Hayward 1996). In the orchestrated local demise of high-rise social housing, its successes and its failings were subsumed into an enduring mythology in which its architectural form—and its verticality specifically—was the prime root of its failure. Jones's (1972) study of Australian poverty reinforced government and social reformers' determinist arguments about buildings as a cause of social problems, and the economics of high-rise. Jones (216) emphasized the social 'costs of an ideology' as high-rise failed to provide adequate flexibility, privacy and homes for families:

> Coupled with the cost disadvantages of high-density living are the social effects: the loss of privacy; the inflexibility of the dwelling unit to changes in the life cycle; the difficulty of controlling children where there is no secure open space; and the many other features of high-density accommodation that make it unsuitable for families with young children [. . .] It is ironic that for all the professional talk about high-density accommodation, very few private flats or home units are used by families with young children. It is most unjust that poor families with children should be forced to bear the costs of an ideology which is not only false but is not followed by other sections of the community. The Commission can do it only because they are dealing with people in desperate situations.

By the end of the 1970s, bureaucrats and politicians were described as similarly convinced that high-rise housing was high-cost and socially problematic. Meanwhile, the stigma perceived and experienced by residents grew. Melbourne's pathologies of high-rise public housing, as in the United States and United Kingdom, have been 'one of the crucial manufactured realities' to elicit the systematic dismantling of public housing provision (Graham 2016, 184).

Nonetheless, suburbanization also provides an important backdrop to the demise of high-rise social housing. The postwar population explosion had coincided with prolific 'motorized suburbanization' (Dodson 2016). This suburbanization was encouraged by new housing estates planned and built by state agencies. In Melbourne, a US Fordist spatial ordering was evident: manufacturing employment was located on generous greenfield locations and supported by macro policy providing higher-wage jobs aimed at stimulating consumer spending (Dodson 2016; Spiller 2013). Expansive suburbanization ensued, and homeownership rates soared from 52 percent postwar (1947) to 70 percent by 1971 (Badcock 2000). This was the long boom: unemployment was low, wages were high, financing was readily available and the construction sector responsive throughout the 1950s and 1960s (Dodson 2016). And overall, this urban form, with the dispersal of jobs, made for a fairly inclusive city with relatively equitable access to jobs, services and amenities (Spiller 2013).

Some local accounts of public housing make clear the conflicted position of the state between administering a viable public housing system and promoting homeownership. These were resolved to some degree by the signing of the second CSHA agreement, which ironed out tensions between public housing support and the government drive for homeownership by facilitating the sale of public housing assets and so providing another avenue to homeownership. High-rise housing was problematic, since this strategy favored the 'best' properties and those in the most desirable locations, often leaving high-rise housing stock in the hands of the HCV. Meanwhile, suburbanization prompted the exodus of many working-class and migrant households from the inner city and raised alarms that Melbourne might soon transform into a US-style 'donut' city with only the most marginalized and vulnerable residents remaining in its core (Spiller 2013).

However, by the 1980s, the postwar suburbanization model was under strain: poor state coordination and financing had crippled the timely delivery of suburban infrastructure and servicing, and the first wave of deindustrialization from the 1970s meant householders were increasingly troubled by a mismatch between their employment and housing locations (Dodson 2016). This raised concerns about 'locational disadvantage' throughout the 1980s and 1990s, especially in the context of rising unemployment, as those less well off were increasingly confined to the outer suburbs (Badcock 1994). As we shall see, an initial policy consideration of urban form and urban densities emerged that saw metropolitan planners attempt to consolidate urban footprints, although suburban development remained singularly dominant until the turn of the century (Buxton and Tieman 2005).

CONSOLIDATION CONSENSUS

The rise of private apartment developments in Melbourne since the postwar period has coincided with the widespread and wholesale subscription to urban consolidation ideas (analogous with 'smart growth' or 'compact city' models), including among policy elites. This persistent policy consensus broadly considers that housing and urban planning problems faced by contemporary cities, including unprecedented population growth, issues of housing access and affordability and suburban sprawl, could be remedied through higher intensities of land use, and especially higher residential densities in inner-city areas. In Melbourne, this policy paradigm emerged in the late 1960s in response to an emergent suburban critique. Deregulatory measures, such as provisions for subdivisions, were subsequently introduced to promote intensity of land use at the plot scale. By the turn of the century, the relative disregard for organizing where this 'consolidation' was occurring prompted increased strategic oversight to target intensification around 'activity centres' (Dodson 2012, 25).

High-rise housing in particular has successively replaced medium-density as the typology of choice under this consolidation paradigm, especially in the inner city from the 1990s. While residential high-rise was relatively rare even in 2002, today the once unthinkable is now the status quo. The 1990s saw the redevelopment of Melbourne's core, spurred initially by the 1991 recession which led to high vacancy rates in commercial city tenancies. The municipality's Postcode 3000 program incentivized developers to undertake significant conversion of high-rise commercial properties in the CBD, as well as 'new build' construction projects. From the mid-1990s a new wave of high-rise apartment construction was under way. Since the financial crisis, this apartment stock represents an ever-larger share of the housing yield, especially in the inner city. This urban development subsequently prompted steep local population growth; during the last decade of the century, a fifth of the metropolitan population growth occurred in the inner city, amounting to an increase of seventy-five thousand residents, and today the City of Melbourne is among the fastest-growing municipalities nationally. In and around the CBD, the designation of the 'highly permissive' Capital City Zone planning positions development approval under the sole jurisdiction of the State Planning Minister who has approved, often at breakneck speeds, numerous skyscraper developments, irreversibly transforming the core's urban structure through vertical expansion (e.g., Buxton et al. 2016, 141–42; also Nethercote, forthcoming).

The value and efficacy of Melbourne's own 'containment, consolidation and centres' planning consensus (Forster 2006, 179) has been widely challenged, especially within planning (e.g., Gleeson 2012, 121), including authoritative critiques of its proclaimed environmental benefits (Gleeson 2012), and the lack of mechanisms for its implementation. The strongest criticisms challenge its faulty premise, arguing that increasing urban density through high-rise development overlooks the complex social and political forces that shape how urban housing is produced and consumed. Providing high-rise housing only in inner-city areas with great amenity and job access means density will be 'effectively "wasted"' (Dodson 2012, 29), since high land prices translate to relatively high-cost apartments that cater only to the housing and investment needs of relatively better-off households. In the absence of adequate mandates for affordable or public housing, this high-rise housing then only exacerbates the growing inequalities between those wealthy enough to make profits (and live in) in these apartments, and lower-income households who are 'stuck' in job-poor (outer) suburbs, where lagging public transport infrastructure ensures car dependency and limited access to jobs and opportunity (Dodson 2012, 29).

The planning orthodoxy of higher-density development has nonetheless maintained traction. It remains the well-rehearsed policy response to a growing population, to demographic trends, to smaller household size (and subsequent assumptions about housing demand) and to concerns about the outcomes and costs of suburban sprawl, including infrastructure provision costs and socio-spatial disadvantage and exclusion. Melbourne is far from alone in the uptake of these ideas, instead pursuing its variant of a globally influential manifesto of densification through vertical urban extension, with its well-worn claims to economies of scale and proximity.

The unwieldy proliferation of high-rises has meanwhile been blamed on state subscription to 'neoliberal' logics that ascribe planning regulation as inimical to much-needed vertical growth (Buxton et al. 2016). The prevailing critique of vertical Melbourne indeed emphasizes the diminished control of a state government who has ceded control to the market: the enduring image is of Melbourne under a 'facilitative planning system' (71) left to the whims of profit-driven developers who have run amok, building taller towers to fill their pockets, dramatically transforming Melbourne despite questionable urban and social outcomes. Buxton and colleagues, for instance, stress how government has 'opted for a market-led approach, which has diminished the legitimacy and efficacy of state-led planning for a sustainable future' (153).

> The high-rise model is promoted by a powerful network of high-rise and big-city advocates. New towers are a symbol of urban corporate domination, fuelling serious land speculation and reducing housing affordability. Financial and property interests, the construction industry and high rates of foreign investment are, in effect, deciding the urban form of large areas of Melbourne. A lack of regulation provides an artificial stimulus to destroy the city's existing urban fabric. (82)

The question, given the contested rationales and outcomes of Melbourne's high-rise expansion is, as local planning academic Buxton (2016, n.p.) queries: 'Why would any government collude in such destruction, contrary to the public interest, when other housing alternatives are widely available?' Some accounts have pointed to the changing lifestyle choices of 'new urban dwellers' or emphasized repeated planning policy 'failures' that have produced today's high-rise Melbourne. There have also been important technological advances in construction and building, particularly elevator design, and legal provisions (e.g., strata title regulation) that explain the 'nuts and bolts' of *how* residential towers have been able to rise ever upwards. A Marxist perspective by contrast emphasizes the structural drivers of urbanization, and thus helps place (high-rise) housing within the current political economy. It is engaged here to begin to sharpen our understanding of why government appears so 'permissive' of this vertical expansion, even when its housing and urban benefits for city residents may be questionable.

HIGH-RISE HOUSING UNDER FINANCIALIZED CAPITALISM

High-rise housing has sometimes been crudely reduced either to an 'Orwellian' demonization and pathologization (typically of high-rise mass social housing as outlined above), or an 'Olympian' glorification, that 'celebrates them as totems of financial vibrancy' (McNeill 2005, 52). The political economy of high-rise production and consumption can complement existing scholarship and understandings of Melbourne's rising skyline by paying more attention to the significance of vertical expansion under capitalist political economy.

Housing's enduring function under capitalism has been to provide shelter that allows for social reproduction. In this way, housing has always been essential to protecting and reproducing capitalist systems of production. But since the 1980s/1990s there has been an historic shift in the underlying structural process of capital accumulation itself, as the influence of financial capital has grown, relative to production (Lapavitsas 2013). Capitalism has become financialized as 'non-financial companies increasingly make profits by speculating in capital markets; banks in turn have transformed acting largely as agents converting assets into loanable funds for producers and consumers; and workers have sought assets and credit to finance consumption as wages have stagnated' (Moreno 2014, 247; Lapavitsas 2013). Residential real estate provides a vital 'spatial apparatus' for this financial accumulation, through which capitalists transform the city into real estate controlled and managed within financial networks (Moreno 2014). The term 'asset price urbanism' (Byrne 2016) invokes the contemporary feature of this mode of accumulation whereby urban space and its relationship to finance is managed to optimize the relationship between credit and real estate. Three additional functions of high-rise housing emerge from this interdependency between financialization and urbanization under financialized capitalism (Moreno 2014). I will describe these in turn. These do not indicate a 'one-size-fits-all process' of (high-rise) urban development since this is necessarily fragmented, path-dependent and variegated on the ground. Accordingly, these are discussed within a rough conceptual schema but illustrated via Melbourne's distinct vertical expansion.

PRODUCTIVE ECONOMY

Beyond providing shelter, perhaps the most tangible economic function of housing is as a productive economy. Large high-rise construction projects are hugely labour intensive and thus support a thriving construction sector as a major local employer. High-rise development also requires a raft of other secondary services, thus securing employment for architects, project managers and quantity surveyors, estate agents and solicitors for property transactions, and so forth. Outside the sphere of production, high-rise development is also hugely capital intensive: it requires project financing from financial institutions, and other finance and intermediaries to support its consumption, including mortgage brokers and lenders.

At the macro economic level, Australian cities have routinely been a central platform for national economic growth; however, their role in facilitating economic growth has intensified since the GFC, the contraction of the resource boom, and with falling commodity prices. Cities, and specifically city building, now represent significant policy levers for federal government and for state governments as they seek economic expansion (Ruming and Goodman 2016). High-rise residential projects are an important part of this; a city skyline littered with cranes has come to signal a thriving economy. Nationally, the number of apartments built each year has tripled since 2009, and in 2016 apartments constituted roughly a third of all residential building approvals, though they still represent less than 10 percent of the dwelling stock (RBA 2017, 1). In Melbourne, apartments now constitute the main form of new housing construction, surpassing previously singularly dominant suburban growth, with over twenty thousand apartments under construction in inner Melbourne, almost all initiated by private developers.

At the state level in Victoria, the 'permissiveness' of the planning system toward high-rise has thus been linked to the state government's 'addiction' to land-related tax revenue (valued at approximately $7.6 billion p/a), and its 'desperation' to maintain the construction industry share of 7 percent of state production (Buxton 2016). State Premier Daniel Andrews conceded as much when recently endorsing Melbourne's latest 'tallest' tower as part of Crown Casinos complex (ABC 2017): 'What we're really approving is 4,000 jobs . . . for construction workers and for those in the hospitality sector, in the construction phase and for the future'.

The ability to bring capital 'in' to cities through high-rise projects requires local knowledge, but the production of high-rise housing especially during real estate bubbles is detached both from *local* housing need—often neither directly prompted by it, nor a salve for it. Planning policy in turn does not restrain this developer activity; planning controls fail to impose height restrictions, and a 'bonus' scheme permits ever-taller towers in exchange for questionable public benefits. Hardly surprising then, Melbourne's high-rise development is producing some of highest site densities in the world (e.g., plot ratios of 18:1), and subpar housing and urban outcomes. Overall, these conditions recall neoliberal urbanization as characterized by the late Neil Smith (2002, 443) who remarked: 'real-estate development becomes a centerpiece of the city's productive economy, an end in itself, justified by appeals to jobs, taxes, and tourism [. . .] become an increasingly unassailable capital accumulation strategy for competing urban economies'.

Foreign investment has been crucial to Melbourne's vertical expansion. The state has long facilitated individual foreign investment in Australian real estate, and this continues on the basis that direct investments from overseas into local real estate, and new construction projects in particular, benefit the construction sector through increased employment and (questionable) boosts to local housing supply. Since the GFC, the share of Asian (Chinese) investors has grown, replacing other investors who pulled out following the downturn. Foreign/global investors in Australian real estate range from the middle classes to the super rich, all jointly motivated by investment, but also by migration and child education prospects, albeit the opportunities for these respective investors differ. For example, visa and immigration privileges are handed out to investors of over $5 million through the Significant Investment Visa (SIV) program. Rogers and colleagues (2015) identify a continuing upward trend in overall individual foreign investment, and in Chinese investment, with conservative estimates of a 400 percent increase between 2006 and 2014. Positioned within treasury, the Foreign Investment Review Board shows that approved foreign investment in Australian real estate by Chinese investors has indeed grown exponentially since the GFC, from A$712 million in 2006/7 to $4.2 billion in 2011/2012 (Rogers et al. 2015).

The presence of foreign capital in Australian real estate is significant not only because it contributes to the financing of high-rise projects, but it may shape the appearance of Melbourne's skyline. Fincher and Costello (2005) suggest apartment production in Melbourne is shaped by narratives circulating about the 'dwellers' ethnicities', including those of immigrant 'outsiders'. Roger and colleagues (2015, 16) meanwhile urge further consideration of how foreign investment might be shaping our cities, since we know little about how 'the cultural profiling of foreign investors by real estate, immigration, financial and developer interests' is 'undertaken or used to inform the building practices of developers, the financial products of investment professionals, or the sales strategies of real estate agents'.

HIGH-RISE ASSETS

Second we have witnessed the intensifying and global commodification of real estate (Marcuse and Madden 2016). High-rise has been a key part of this, as Graham (2016, 177) describes:

> The urban growth skyward often thus becomes merely a process of the marketization of land and real estate organized more for the 'housing' of elite capital than for a city's people (let alone a city's poorer population). New condominiums for elites in cities like London, Vancouver, Toronto, San Francisco, Miami, Melbourne, Sydney, and New York thus needs to be understood primarily as what Paul Goldberger in *Vanity Fair* has called 'tradable commodities, perfect for the speculatively inclined'.

Melbourne's vertical ascent has been phenomenal and intense, most occurring in the past fifteen years and intensifying since 2009. The new vertical housing stock is far from uniform: prohibitively priced, luxury high-rise residences stacked in ever-taller towers, themselves seeking questionable accolades and prestige, jostle alongside small, poorly designed and built, 'investor-orientated' apartments in more prosaic tower forms. The latter have been described as 'built to the lowest standards on every criteria, which few people will want to live in or own' (Buxton et al. 2012, 153). These towers cluster together across inner-city precincts, such as Docklands, and are blamed for creating windy, soulless and sometimes desolate urban realms.

These apartments are generally cheaper than other forms of neighbouring housing, since they use land more intensively. Yet with a median price of half a million Australian dollars, they are rarely 'affordable', especially given their desirable locations (RBA 2017). Melbourne's new high-rise stock is brimming with small, one and two-bedroom apartments, priced for and lapped up by an investor market, that rents to a largely transient demographic of international students and professionals.

Local investor activity is part of Australia's longer history of 'petty' ('mum and dad') landlordism, under a taxation regime that continues to incentivize such consumption. Offshore buyers, who are restricted to purchasing new dwellings under current regulations, are attracted to this new stock in central urban locations. Low interest rates have only sweetened the appeal of these housing investments for purchasers and developers alike. Under these conditions, housing market inflation has become untethered from the local wage economy, while city residents are increasingly pushed out of the inner city, homeownership or both. This commodification is inherently problematic since it stems from the favoring returns on capital rather than the housing needs of a city's residents. As Buxton recently decried, 'it does little for Melbourne's real housing needs and is likely to become unlivable and be demolished within a generation, a shocking legacy to shortsightedness' (2016).

In Melbourne, ineffective and permissive planning controls for height, design quality and building performance are blamed for further fuelling this inner-city speculation frenzy (Buxton et al. 2012). State government response to these perceived 'natural "growing pains"' of intensive urban development resulted in new apartment design guidelines (DELWP 2015, 5). If these provide any reprieve it will be largely cosmetic, detached as they are from the more substantive issues of housing distribution and commodification that are shaping who consumes these high-rise assets.

SITES OF HYPERCONSUMPTION

High-rise housing also serves a symbolic function. Moreno (2014, 248) has argued that under financialized capitalism, architecture (along with art and culture) has been mobilized in complex ways to embody 'the cultural logic of [capital] accumulation'. This represents a shift, whereby architecture emerges today as 'operative rather than a merely ornamental feature of financial capital' (263). And indeed this is part of what makes the present commodification of urban property more than simply a revival or intensification of the land plundering of nineteenth-century London and Paris; for ever-taller towers are more than simply an extension and intensification of a longer history of capitalization of urban land. Moreno elaborates that it is 'no accident' that the radical shift towards financialization coincided, for instance, with a 'surge in theoretical interest in exploiting the microeconomic qualities of urban places—location, proximity, clustering—as a kind of technological instrument of competitive advantage', or that the urban regeneration paradigm emerged asserting that economic growth could be produced by attracting and relocating 'creative' professionals in ex-industrial locations. In these ways, 'Urban space now provides [. . .] a complex apparatus through which the interlocking forms of landed, financial and technological capital construct a new kind of "spatial-cognitive fix'" (Moreno 2014, 264).

In this context, high-rise housing towers, as part of contemporary architecture and urban culture, thus become 'a kind of "pattern language," a new urbanism funded by the circulation of financial claims on the future but articulating the ebb and flow of contemporary consumer needs and desires; whose mix of weak and strong signals are constantly "swept" to identify sources of business advantage' (264).

Residential high-rise appears to work in at least two ways in this regard. The first is apparent in the inane, and sometimes dangerous, pursuit of ever-greater heights. Extreme towers such as the Burj Khalifa and the proposed Freedom Tower in Saudi Arabia, which will surpass one kilometre in height, are not designed and developed to reap immediate returns on investment. Instead these aim to 'lubricate the worlds of tourism and hyper-consumption', acting as 'catalysts designed to add value to vast malls and [other neighboring] real estate projects'; these are deliberate ventures to capitalize on the prestige accorded by their record-breaking heights (Graham 2016, ix). Melbourne too has been drawn by similarly mindless development logics. Australia 108 will be Melbourne's tallest tower upon completion, shamelessly marketed as the 'highest residences in the Southern hemisphere'. Rising to 319 metres, the 1,105-apartment tower was designed by local 'starchitect' Fender Katsilidis with a development consortium, and then sold on to a Singaporean developer for $42.3 million. Katsilidis champions the tower's multi-million-dollar apartments as 'an opportunity to buy into history and own a trophy sky home', with its penthouse selling for AUD25 million (Royall 2017). Far from remedying urban housing pressures, towers like these create luxury vertical enclaves. For Graham (2016, 197; also Atkinson 2017), these towers provide the means for an 'elite takeover of the urban skies [. . .] eyrie-like refuges for the world's super rich'. That some of these elite residences will be used only sporadically reinforces a current development trajectory far removed from planning rhetoric of densities, efficiencies and accessibility invoked within consolidation debates.

More prosaic apartment towers serve a related function. This is most unmistakable (and most considered) in the case of Vancouver, where the apartment boom reflects the real-estate complex—one altogether out of kilter with the city's economy and labor market. High-rise is central to Vancouverism's 'global-city discourse-complex for its winning combination of density, livability and sustainability—all rendered seductively real in the forest of glass-walled condominium towers that has colonized the downtown core since the late 1980s', and the 'value of which is largely registered in the symbolic realm of "cognitive-cultural" capitalism' (Peck et al. 2014). As Peck and colleagues (Peck et al. 2014, 388) have argued: 'City boosterism is nothing new, but green-tinged and market-friendly readings of Vancouverism have begun to coalesce into a pernicious urban paradigm'. Vancouverism makes clear an operative role for an altogether more mundane and formulaic form of high-rise development, beyond the super-tall, super-exclusive futuristic Shards, and Burj Khalifas of the world. These skyscrapers are far more pedestrian in form, not so dissimilar from their modernist and much pathologized forebears (Graham 2016, 201), though still far from 'affordable'. Peck and colleagues deride the staid 'tower-and-podium format that has been pushed to the point of parody', arguing that it is producing in Vancouver a 'suburban involution' whereby inner-city towers embody the 'multi-dimensional (re)production of suburban spaces':

> If the condos of Vancouverism were once seen as edgy and innovative, by virtue of their challenge to North America's picket-fence hegemony, their subsequent commodification, materially and culturally, is reducing them to vehicles for capital gains accumulation and marketing clichés. Reassuringly standardized— right down to the granite countertops, top-of-the-range stainless-steel appliances and hardwood floors—Vancouver condos have become highly fungible and slickly marketed investment commodities. (404)

For although high-rise development has circulated globally as an apparently 'winning formula' for city development, as Peck and colleagues (2014, 402–3) have argued, 'rather less is said about the fortuitous and inherently non-replicable location of Vancouver at the confluence of accelerating flows of wealthy migrants and speculative capital', which ultimately provided the means to 'regenerate' the urban core in this way. Melbourne's high-rise is by no means a Vancouver replica, but it may fast become vulnerable to some of the same criticisms. Much like Vancouver, Melbourne now faces concerns about 'ghost' apartments left uninhabited. Property vacancies rates rose by 19 percent in the past five years, with the state government recently legislating an 'empty homes' tax that follows similar approaches as Paris and Vancouver, despite its questioned effectiveness (Pawson 2017).

Overall, while financialized capitalism actively stimulates high-rise development, this spatial 'fix' is always only a temporary salve to capitalism's crisis-prone tendencies. Mounting competition over profits within the built environment encourages increasingly speculative behaviours that edge the housing market towards crisis point. These crisis moments do not signal some inevitable and total collapse; their form is rather more multifaceted and varied, providing opportunities for different responses. But they do clearly expose the inherent discordance between the welfare needs (including housing as home) and the needs of finance capital, the necessity for state intervention to mediate these, and their embeddedness within urban space.

CONCLUSION

The marketing of apartments in Australia 108 relies unapologetically on claims to exclusivity achieved through vertical ascent. Their allure, according to their local 'starchitect' designer, is the chance to 'be part of a world that few others can imagine'; Katsilidis (2017) elaborates:

> We are all born with the ability to soar, but only the brave trust their wings. Australia's tallest tower will go where no development has gone before, offering a cloud-breaking lifestyle 319 metres above the glittering Melbourne streetscape. [. . .] As Melbourne's highest tower, Australia 108 will form a bridge between earth and sky. When low cloud rolls in from the ocean, *you will enter what seems another realm*. A sky that appears grey at street level will reveal itself as a misty dreamland, a breath-taking spectacle unimaginable to those on the ground. Australia 108 presents the Sky Rise Residences. These exclusive apartments are found *above* Melbourne and offer a luxury lifestyle never experienced before.

Intriguingly, this unashamed attempt at vertical urban segregation from a fear-inducing terrestrial city is marketed in combination with an appeal to amenity and centrality within that very same city. The appeal of being cocooned luxuriously high above is perpetuated alongside, somewhat ironically, by promises of the conveniences of the city's amenities 'within easy reach below'. Indeed Australia 108 is marketed through the shameless marshalling of a hyperbolized image of Melbourne's urban status—'home to the most fortunate people in the world [. . .] holds the crown as the most livable, lovable city on the planet' (Katsilidis 2017).

The crowding of towers across city skylines signals an important politics of verticality. This chapter aimed to look beyond the prevailing high-rise narratives outlined in its first half, to explore some of Melbourne's skyscrapers' multiple non-shelter functions. These functions have, for the most part, been largely disguised by sustained appeals to urban density and associated consolidation rhetoric on the grounds of demographic change, worsening inequality and ecological sustainability.

Whether exceptional and iconic or mundane and midrise towers, Melbourne's vertical sprawl risks producing socially regressive outcomes. Indeed the nascent critique of high-rise Melbourne has at times already been damning. Most tangibly, 'developer-friendly', 'permissive' planning controls that once permitted the Docklands waterfront redevelopment—and which are now cementing a contentious high-rise future for the vast Fishermans Bend redevelopment—are criticized for producing substandard housing in apartment towers that cluster in windy and sometimes soulless urban precincts.

In addition to these undesirable, if localized outcomes, there is a broader, citywide fallout from this vertical expansion. This vertical urbanization risks reinforcing through Melbourne's urban morphology stark socio-spatial inequalities between low-income households 'stuck' within job-poor outer suburbs, and those who can afford this new centrally located housing (Dodson 2012; Buxton et al. 2012, 109–11; Spiller 2013). For the concentration of high-rise development in high-amenity, job-rich inner-city locations (and to a lesser degree in established middle-ring suburbs) necessarily caters only to relatively wealthy households since high land prices dictate higher housing costs, and provisions for affordable or social housing are lacking. While accepting that high-rises are contributing to Melbourne's housing stock, the spatial distribution of this development currently reinforces a less-than-inclusive monocentric urban morphology. Demographically, the 'revitalized' inner city and the middle ring more broadly, have become home to higher levels of higher-income, highly educated professionals, alongside more transient renters. The outer suburbs meanwhile typically house those on relatively lower incomes, with relatively lower levels of tertiary education. This urban demography is not new per se—a spatial divide was embedded through deindustrialization and the subsequent regeneration of the inner city from the 1980s—but it risks being cemented further by the current high-rise trajectory. This is especially so since suburban fringe residents today have 'relatively fewer choices' than early generations, who once experienced relatively greater parity in access, with relatively less sprawl, less congestion and decentralized employment opportunities (Spiller 2013).

The vertical character of Melbourne's expansion, however, also insists that to this still largely horizontal conception of urban socio-spatial inequality, we pay more attention to how and, more significantly, why the vertical axis has been co-opted, and how it is creating, embedding and exacerbating new urban divisions (Graham 2016; Graham and Hewitt 2012). This initial consideration of the economic functions of high-rise housing under financialized capitalism points towards potentially compelling incentives for vertical expansion that have little to do with producing housing for the city's residents. It appears that within these and other non-shelter functions, we may find better clues to understanding why this proliferation of towers continues apace despite its questionable housing and urban benefits (for further discussion, see Nethercote 2018; forthcoming).

If high-rise towers create exclusive communities just as powerfully as exurban gated communities, then it is worth thinking more about the distinct *vertical* manner in which this is achieved, including how the vertical ascent into secessionary vertical landscapes stratifies the city from ground-plane lobbies to sky-high penthouses (Graham and Hewitt 2012; Graham 2016). It also calls on us to evolve our largely horizontal conception of urban socio-spatial inequalities, to account for these vertical stratifications. Only then can we grasp the fully three-dimensional ways in which urban inequalities are now written into and experienced across the verticalizing city.

Chapter 11

The City's Other Face

Modern Ruins and Urban Endings

Emma Fraser

In the imaginary of the city, there are certain recurring images and common urban characters. The thronging American metropolis, New York, Chicago; the modern industrial city, the 'Cottonopolis' of Manchester, the 'steel' cities of Pittsburgh, Sheffield (UK), and Newcastle (Australia). The old European city, with winding cobbled streets and historic architecture—Amsterdam's canals and art galleries; London's boroughs, bridges and high streets. The high-rise urbanism of Hong Kong and Dubai. Increasingly, these imaginaries are also hypertechnological—a 'cybernetic urbanism' (Krivý 2018) of global smart cities founded on algorithms and populated with automated machines (Foth, Mitchell and Estrada-Grajales 2018); digitally securitized city centres designed for control and surveillance (Krivý 2018) transformed by mega-projects visioned through digital and 3D renderings of future development (Melhuish, Degen and Rose 2014).

In reality, many cities are hybrids, new and old together—gridded streets forced onto the landscape to reorder the vernacular, like Haussmann's new Paris, built on the ruins of the 1871 Commune and erasing many ancient parts of the city; or Robert Moses's Cross-Bronx expressway, blamed by Marshall Berman for leaving the South Bronx as a 'modern ruin' in the 1950s and beyond (Berman 1982). So often, we call on a conception of the ideal city—clean, safe, new—as if this conception *is* the city, but it is also a place of endings and chaos and disorder; a place where things are torn apart and scattered, and forgotten and left behind because of relentless forces that push (things and people) ever onward. Many cities have experienced mass decay, the destruction of war and population decline leading to abject ruin—and destructive renewal. In the same year as the Paris Commune, the Great Chicago Fire razed a third of the city, and a hundred years later inner-city neighbourhoods were overwhelmed with abandoned buildings as populations shrank and urban blight set in; Manchester's industrial growth gave way to postwar ruin and later postindustrial decay; Melbourne's now revamped docklands were derelict for decades. Many cities—like Detroit, Pittsburgh or Leipzig—have yet to fully recover from a long period of decline characterized by the decay and ruin of vast industrial complexes. This chapter considers these kinds of modern ruins—ruined architecture, derelict wastelands and mass destruction—as an unavoidable part of urban life, arguing that the city is a place of ruins as much as a place of advancement and development.

The persistence of sites of modern ruin is at odds with how we see the city and ourselves. Urban ruins in particular are so often perceived to be within, but not of, the city, aberrations that don't belong there—the furnishing of gothic underworlds, or markers of deprivation and failure, rather than an inherent character of the city. Modern ruins are sites that mark out truncated futures—blunt urban endings figured in broken windows and rubble, which at their most extreme present a counter to mantras of perpetual growth and seamless order. The ordered city is the aim of urban planners, city councils and governments, but also the dream of those who wish to address the traditionally negative impact of rapid urbanism. Historically, the 'new' city is forged on the unfortunate ruin of the old; for Le Corbusier, the old city was Paris, with its medieval backstreets (Kasinitz 1995, 101). For Jane Jacobs, it was the more organic form of the city prior to active planning (1972, 50). Jacobs identified urban policy in American cities as the source of cycles of 'slumming and unslumming' (284), generating decay and destructive redevelopment, the life and death of urban neighbourhoods. According to Robert Fishman, Frank Lloyd Wright foresaw the 'death' of the modern city in urban sprawl, making what was a new city to those like Le Corbusier a rapidly declining 'old' city, 'the centralised industrial metropolis' (Fishman in Kasinitz 1995, 395), which fell to ruin as populations moved out to commutable suburbs, and heavy industry declined—the (Western) industrial city has become old, even endangered (407).

Often-romantic visions of the modern city as a planned behemoth of efficiency and order frequently obscure a countervision, a contrasting imaginary, whether gothic, noir, steampunk or dystopian—the materiality of urban decay and destruction, and the fictions of imagined apocalyptic ruin. A counter-city that is run-down, dusty and forgotten, disordered, eerie and strange, and which reveals a vision of the modern city that is ruinous and crumbling, a place of endings and disintegration. This fragmented and ruined concept city corresponds to the shattering experience of modern life as one of wreckage and dislocation, and stretches from the slums and boulevards of early modernity (Benjamin 1983; 1999a), to the liquid and quartz forms of late modernity

(Bauman 2000; Davis 1990), and Berman's reworking of Marx's expression of modern transience, 'all that is solid melts into air' (Berman 1982), or Schumpeter's 'creative destruction' (Hetherington and Cronin 2008). The modern imaginary of ruins derives from colonial and imperial ruin gazing (Hell 2008; Stoler 2013), and the eighteenth-century obsession with the fall of civilization, 'this earlier imaginary of ruins haunts our discourse about the ruins of modernity [and yet] the twentieth century has produced a very different imaginary of ruins', one which moves away from the return to nature of the romantic sublime, and dwells on the inherently destructive nature of progress, working at a frenzied speed to unravel and reconstruct in perpetuity (Huyssen 2008, 18).

Marshall Berman used the term 'modern ruin' to describe both the urban decay of the Bronx and the underbelly of urban modernity as a churning destructive force, exemplified in urban decay:

> Among the many images and symbols that New York has contributed to modern culture, one of the most striking in recent years has been an image of modern ruin and devastation. The Bronx, where I grew up, has even become an international code word for our epoch's accumulated urban nightmares: drugs, gangs, arson, murder, terror, thousands of buildings abandoned, neighborhoods transformed into garbage and brick-strewn wilderness. (1982, 290)

Berman's vision of the Bronx as a modern ruin shows the 'other face' of the modern city that is the central concern of this chapter. The emergence of urban modernity—and the concept of the modern city—is associated with ruins; that is, with material, metaphorical or allegorical ruination. The interpenetration of ruins, the city and modernity is established across multiple registers of fragmentation and decay. Theories of the urban have been intertwined with such visions of ruin (symbolic and actual) by a number of writers including urban sociologists like Georg Simmel, who wrote *The Ruin* in 1911; and by Jane Jacobs, who focused on urban blight and regeneration in *The Death and Life of Great American Cities*. In Berman's work, the end of the city is an inevitable and haunting possibility of modernity, even in the present; made visible through modern ruination, urban decay and destruction.

Perhaps the most detailed philosophy of modern ruins is put forward by Frankfurt School theorist Walter Benjamin, described by Andreas Schönle as a 'founding father of ruinology' (2006, 651). Benjamin famously critiqued the construct of linear historical time with references to Paul Klee's painting *Angelus Novus*, in which Benjamin perceived that Angel of History held aloft, looking upon the wreckage of the past, unable to make it whole, as the winds of progress blew the Angel towards an unknown—but implicitly

destructive—future time (Benjamin 2003, 392). But Benjamin also repeatedly cited the Janus face of capitalism as a contrast between progress looking
forward and ruin strewn behind—the latter is the 'other face' of perpetual
progress that the Angel can only look upon in frozen horror—and this other
face persisted, for Benjamin, in outdated fashions, relics that seemed out of
time, the outmoded and forgotten remnants of an era—most notably, the then-
decaying Paris shopping arcades.

Despite the unfinished nature of the voluminous and fragmented *Arcades
Project* (Benjamin 1999a)—and, indeed, Benjamin's collected writings
generally—Benjamin's writing consistently and movingly evokes a kind of
shadow world of urban life, haunted by the advent of modernity, but also by
its own present and future ruin. As Susan Buck-Morss states in *The Dialectics of Seeing, The Arcades Project* 'broke radically with the philosophical
canon by searching for truth in the "garbage heap" of modern history, the
"rags, the trash", the ruins of commodity production that were thoroughly
tainted with the philosophically debased qualities of empirical specificity,
shifting meanings, and above all, transiency' (1989, 218). To understand
the city—and by association, past and future historical constellations, as
well as material encounters and the visual regimes of modernity—Benjamin
had to tear the city apart, to see the city not as a composite whole but as a
profoundly fragmented place. In doing so, Benjamin produced a vision of
modern ruin: what Max Pensky calls a 'disruptive-constructive strategy'
(2001, 154), that is allegorical 'insofar as it consists of the wilful wresting
of fragmentary images and textual elements from their place in the history
of literary reception and the construction of montages or constellations from
these fragments, montages that are intended to illuminate the object truth of
contemporary social reality' (154–55).

The strategy was not restricted to works of art, texts or media, however.
Benjamin also sought this illumination of reality in real material decay, in
the modern urban ruins of his era. In *Ruin and Rubble in the Arcades* Tyrus
Miller suggests that destruction and progress go hand in hand, observing
that Benjamin's method stemmed from the contemporary historical tendency towards obsolescence and swift decline, a method focused on 'the
ruined hopes of the past' in the arcades; those 'things, impulses, objects
and matter' in a state of decay and fragmentation (Miller in Hanssen 2006,
93). As Miller states, 'Benjamin follows the surrealist procedure to the letter, montaging a pile-up of disparate industrially produced fragments' using
'the same uncanny jumble of outmodedness that attracted the surrealists'
(Ibid.), and which is also found in urban ruins and relics—the other face of
the modern city.

A (SHORT) HISTORY OF
MODERN URBAN RUINS

If we date the phenomena of urban ruination from the advent of modernity, up to the present day, urban endings in cities take many forms beyond postindustrial decay. These include slum clearance and revitalization, disappearing entire communities and ways of life under the rubble of demolition; or the devastating aerial bombardment and firestorms of modern warfare in Dresden during World War II, or in Aleppo since 2013; or even further back to the ruins of the American Civil War, or the War of 1812, in which American government buildings were reduced to smouldering wrecks. Modern ruins include the wreckage of depopulated disaster zones like Pripyat, near Chernobyl, or New Orleans following Hurricane Katrina. Even small transitions—a few derelict shops or a burnt-out building—can be understood to be ruinous in nature, not aberrations in the fabric of the modern city, but constituent parts of urban life.

Ruins are a fundamental aspect of the city, as it is lived, as it is dreamed—abandonment, dereliction, devastation and demolition characterize different phases in a city's development. This vision is nothing new—it's as old as cities themselves (Woodward 2002). The ruin imaginary—though possessing a particular contemporary form—reaches back to antiquity, to the fall of Rome, and Carthage, and forward to the speculative ruination of contemporary cities. Ruin gazing also produces a certain kind of imperial imaginary, from Shelley to Speer, that sees ruins as part of the rise and fall narrative of the West, in which history ends in the destruction or disintegration of great monuments (Hell and Schönle 2008, 2)—this is one key way in which the city is imagined, through urban endings in ruins. At the same time, although the imaginary has a long historical trajectory whose clichéd forms can be traced to a distant past, it is also something embedded in postwar modernism, in the form of speculative realism, science fiction and apocalyptic urbanisms (Vidler 2010). Simultaneously, the modern urban ruin is embedded in what Sharon Zukin would call a postindustrial, post-Fordist, even postmodern imaginary of place as a fragmented pastiche of disintegrating forms (1991).

In the case of London, the ruinous alter ego appears, for example, in Gustav Dorés's 1872 etching of Macaulay's *New Zealander* gazing out at the future ruins of St Paul's, or Joseph Gandy's *A Bird's-Eye View of the Bank of England* in ruins from 1830—but also in the postwar ruins and bomb sites of Rose Macaulay's *The World, My Wilderness* (1950), with former landmarks transformed into rubble-strewn wastes. Paris's ruins also haunt the city through the surrealist and situationist preoccupation with the torn-up cobbles of revolution and forgotten and neglected passages and side streets—one of the key influences of *The Arcades Project* was Louis Aragon's account of the *Passage de l'Opéra* on the verge of demolition (Aragon 1994, 14). Paris's counter-city also features in Hubert Robert's reimagining of Parisian monuments as ruins of antiquity—but also in photographs and artworks displaying the destruction of the city following the Franco-Prussian war and uprising of the Paris Commune—including the Tuileries Palace, which stood as a ruin for more than a decade. For contemporary city governments, underlying planning and branding are fears about the 'haunting spectres of crime, corruption, and decay' (Huyssen 2008, 5) that are associated with urban ruination and decline.

A ruinous, alternative image of the city thus goes far beyond the imagination—the reality of the down-and-out city in ruins was lived contemporarily in Benjamin's times, and in many ways his vision was driven by his own despair over the destruction of Berlin, his home city much diminished following the economic crises of the 1930s, threatened by war, and to which he was unable to return from his exile in Paris. Benjamin's perception of the modern as inextricably linked to destructive change in experience culminated for him in the destructive energies of the First World War, revealing a profoundly altered world over a short period:

> A generation that had gone to school in horse-drawn streetcars now stood in the open air, amid a landscape in which nothing was the same except the clouds and, at its center, in a force field of destructive torrents and explosions, the tiny, fragile human body. (Benjamin 1999b, 732)

These destructive elements encompass both the literally destructive forces of modern warfare, but also the nature of change, accelerated in Benjamin's lifetime by progress and development, in such a way that experiences of a recent past appeared impossibly dislocated from the present. But even immediately prior to this destructive period of history, central Paris—where Benjamin lived at the end of his life, and where he tried desperately to complete *The Arcades Project*—had been in a state of ruin for much of the 1920s, caught up in cycles of decay and reconstruction as the economy fluctuated, and the last of Haussmann's plans came to fruition. Paris was one of the first cities in which mass urban ruin was photographically documented, with postcards of the burnt-out Hôtel de Ville and other ruined Paris landmarks widely distributed in the years following the uprising in 1871 (Luxenburg 1998; Przyblyski 1995). Similarly, the American Civil War and Crimean War generated what Susan Sontag considered some of the earliest ruin photography, 'anonymous' and 'epic [. . .] depictions of an aftermath' (Sontag 2002, 86), showing landmark buildings of Atlanta and Charleston reduced to rubble, or the streets of Sebastopol hemmed in by ruins (see also Ginsberg 2004, 488).

In this context, modern, urban ruins are those architectural structures that persist in every city—no matter how well developed or densely populated—which are visibly affected by material decline and neglect, or destruction. Not ancient ruins, but those of a recent and recognizable past—those of living memory—as well as the imagined ruination of the contemporary moment, envisaged through decay and a return to nature. Materially, such a ruin may be rotting away and empty, wide open for anyone to wander into (like the arcades of Benjamin's time). A modern ruin may be in a secured area, off-limits to the general population—like the vast field of ruins that sat between East and West Berlin for decades. It is important to note (as Benjamin did in relation to the arcades as obsolete ruins that revealed the forgotten parts of the city) that such urban endings present vital sites of contrast to the vision of the city as new, planned, and seamless—and increasingly, as technological, shining and smart.

THE POLITICS OF MODERN URBAN RUINS

Walter Benjamin was drawn to the Parisian arcades as they fell out of fashion, were neglected and became ruinous havens for forgotten and outmoded fashions and objects. These arcades were, for Benjamin, conceptually attached to the vagaries of commodity fetishism, but also the very nature of modernity, and the modern city. For Benjamin, abjection and abandonment went hand in hand with the churning production of 'up to date' objects and styles—clothing and consumer goods, but also interiors, architectural forms and technology. The gaslight that illuminated the earliest arcades in their heyday became models for a kind of critical illumination of history itself, and their afterlife, lingering uselessly on the interior walls of barely trafficked passages. The arcades at the end point of their popularity also exemplified the increasing destructiveness of progress-driven history, pointing to a politics of (particularly urban) ruins. The arcades, in this sense, were quintessentially modern ruins in the making—covered passages intended for an emerging class of consumers; swiftly outmoded by the energies that produced them, abandoned by the crowds and left to fall to pieces by the ever-churning drive towards newness—a drive that continues to characterize (and ruin) modern cities.

Louis Aragon, in his surrealist semifictional work *Paris Peasant*, suggests that such ruinous sites, the unusual, 'the unthought of' (1994, 11) parts of the city, can be mediations on the mythologies of an era. Aragon gives credence to the personal experience of spaces of decline as destinations that reveal something about the present—in his case Paris of the 1920s—but also something about the past, and something about the city itself. Benjamin was drawn to Aragon because of his aptitude for imbuing various spaces of Paris with an otherworldly sense of being stranded between life and death:

> Although the life that originally quickened them has drained away, they deserve, nevertheless, to be regarded as the secret repositories of several modern myths: it is only today, when the pickaxe menaces them, that they have at last become the true sanctuaries of a cult of the ephemeral, the ghostly landscape of damnable pleasures and professions. Places that were incomprehensible yesterday, and that tomorrow will never know. (Aragon 1994: 14, also quoted in the *Arcades Project* [Benjamin 1999a, 87])

In transience, the myth of the modern is revealed—the city is not whole and shining, it is fundamentally ruinous, constantly out of fashion and routinely torn apart. For Benjamin, the idea of being outmoded or old-fashioned is exemplified in the arcades' life and death. As Benjamin states in *The Arcades Project*: 'Not long ago, a piece of old Paris disappeared—the *Passage de l'Opéra*, which once led from the boulevards to the old opera theatre. Construction of the Boulevard Haussmann swallowed it up. And so we turn our attention to the [. . .] often empty and dust-covered arcades of more obscure neighbourhoods' (Benjamin 1999a, 923). Not only do the arcades physically manifest the past in the present, they also contain a configuration of past-present relations. They hold outmoded objects and dreams from a recent past, appearing 'old-fashioned in comparison to the new' (2014). Furthermore, the architecture of the arcade itself, as a construction in iron and glass, evidenced a sense of the archaic or obsolete.

A similar analysis of modern urban ruins might now include other popular spaces of consumption: strip malls or suburban shopping complexes that are swiftly going out of fashion as online shopping expands; the useless machinery of twentieth-century manufacturing, stranded in inner-city brownfields; the foreclosed homes of the subprime mortgage crisis, boarded up and left to rot; smashed-up shopfronts that once displayed videos, and later, DVDs and games, for hire. To use Benjamin's critical formulations: the process of decay and obsolescence embodied in rejected objects and places stands for the more abstract ruin of the collective past, driven by a destructive present and future. Modern ruins bring into being a revolutionary mode of comprehending the space of the modern city, through things and places that are in the process of 'being no more' (833), politicized by the material transience that comes to bear in abandoned, disused, derelict and obsolete urban spaces that are left to their inevitable ruinous end.

In *The Ruin*, written in 1911 (notably, before World War I), Georg Simmel makes a particular point of referring to 'urban ruins' left alone by people to fall apart, as a 'more meaningful, more significant' phenomenon than the ruins of antiquity, or even war (Simmel 1959, 261). For Simmel '[t]he inhabited ruin loses for us that sensuous-suprasensuous balance of the conflicting tendencies of existence which we see in the abandoned one. This balance, indeed, gives it its problematical, unsettling, often unbearable character. Such places, sinking from life, still strike us as settings for life' (261). As in Benjamin's arcades, Simmel suggested that urban ruins have a particular capacity to unsettle us, to generate contemplation of modern life through abandoned architectures. At the same time, however, Simmel warns of the nostalgia of ruins, and particularly abandoned architectures, in which the contrast between human ingenuity and the persistence of nature appears as 'a cosmic tragedy which [. . .] makes every ruin an object infused with our nostalgia; for now the decay appears as nature's revenge . . .' (259).

Nostalgia brought on by modern urban ruins isn't necessarily a problem, however. As Dianne Chisolm suggests in relation to Benjamin's constellating method and allegorical destruction, nostalgia can be a way of imagining, through the assemblage of historically loaded fragments, alternative histories and futures (2001). As an example, Svetlana Boym's retrospective nostalgia is directly linked to the political capacity of 'ruinophilia' (2017, 43), which, rather than presenting catastrophe and ruination as inevitable violence, instead links ruin (including the end of the city) to freedom and possibility. 'A tour of ruins leads you into a labyrinth of ambivalent temporal[ities. . .] that play tricks with causality. Ruins make us think of the past that could have been and the future that never took place [. . .]' (43). Rather than a return to nature, or an imperial or colonial nostalgia, a *critical* nostalgia through ruins 'condenses alternative senses of history. Ruination is a corrosive process that weighs on the future and shapes the present' (Stoler 2008, 194); it understands modern ruins to be political.

This need not be a hopeless vision of pending catastrophe (the sort of 'postmodern' apocalypticism that Henri Lefebvre and others have rejected [see for example Lefebvre's 1996, 31]). Instead, it is more like what Svetlana Boym terms the off-modern, in which 'the ruins of twentieth-century modernity [. . .] undercut and stimulate the utopian imagination, constantly shifting and deterritorializing our dreamscape' (2017, 44). The nostalgic vision triggered by a conceptualization of the city-as-ruin is more of a 'prospective vision' that is 'connected with an orientation towards the future' (Boym 2017, 39), than a hopeless and clichéd nostalgia for the past. The city-as-ruin links across 'sites of different modernities—industrial, post-industrial, digital, post-digital' (40), through multiple citations of fragmentation and destruction, the mutuality of modernity and ruin, and the imagination of something beyond the present moment. Moreover, '[r]eal ruins of different kinds function as screens on which modernity projects its asynchronous temporalities and its fear of and obsession with the passing of time. Benjamin says that allegories are, in the realm of thought, what ruins are in the realm of things' (Huyssen 2008, 19). This reference to allegories and ruins is often, in Benjamin's work, directly related to a representation of a lived history and language from his *Trauerspiel* study (Benjamin 1998), but—as in the example of the arcades and Aragon's work, above—there is always a significant blurring between what Benjamin saw and experienced and how he conceptually imagined the world through fragmentation and ruin.

Tara Forrest uses Benjamin's work to describe the capacity of the imagination to open up a faculty or perception within cognition, a politics of possibility that generates understanding beyond the literal representation of what is seen (2007). For example, Benjamin's ruin and rubble can be situated in symbolic and speculative registers, as well as in the material, through film's capacity to explode our perceptions of urban life, revealing the world as a rubble field (74). Not only is the figuring of the city as a ruin capable of counterproducing possibilities for the world at large, but an imagination of rubble and fragments derives from a tendency to reconstruct and oppose aesthetic regimes through the fantastical (Jameson 2005). As Joseph Tanke asserts, the notion of the imagination 'breaks the habitual sensory frameworks that prevent the full flourishing of human capacities, ushering them into new space-time configurations' (Tanke 2011, 157). The power of such imagination to impact the everyday experience of the viewer—by distancing, transfiguring—may also be transferred to material encounters and experiences in the city, but especially in modern ruins.

Benjamin's ruinous method is a reworking of the imagination of the cities of modernity; of the life of the commodity; and of the future of the present as a counterfactual history, where the city is imagined more in the form of the trash heap of history (Pensky 2001, 211) than as a beacon of unproblematic future progress. Here, lived encounter and the moment of reading flash up together with a multitemporal recognition of the present moment through the ruinous allegorical mode. This is the true essence of experience, for Benjamin. 'Modernity's constant assertion of the ever-new cannot prevent its collapse into the ever-same. It too will decay, its monuments will fall into ruin, even when the monuments of modernity least expect it' (Frisby 1985, 235).

The cyclical loss embedded in the modern must be opposed by redemption, and the fragmented allegorical mode is potentially redemptive, even in ruin, as Graeme Gilloch suggests:

> The allegorical gaze, like the magical gaze of the child-as-collector, is the salvation of the thing. Ruination and redemption—these are the Janus-faces of allegory. The allegorical vision as the overcoming of myth and the moment of

historical redemption contains within it the qualities of the dialectical image, and hence becomes the fundamental basis of Benjamin's critical historiography. (Gilloch 1996, 138)

While Benjamin resisted the baroque conceptualization of melancholy and eternal transience uncovered in his study of German tragic drama (Benjamin), and considered the destructive aspect of modernity in terms of catastrophe, he did not necessarily frame decay and decline as solely negative: the ruination caused by the push for progress and desire for increasingly fetishized commodities could, in fact, be opposed in ruin. That is, the myth, the illusion constructed by the increasingly detached material products of an era, can, in their decay, reveal the dreams of the era as just that—improperly invested imaginings. It was ultimately Benjamin's reimagining of the concept of the city, through modern urban ruins and urban endings, that generated his critical and philosophical politics of history and progress—a profound understanding of the cities of modernity as cities of ruin.

CONCLUSION

In 'Convolute N' of *The Arcades Project*, Benjamin describes 'The pathos of this work: there are no periods of decline. Attempt to see the nineteenth century just as positively as I tried to see the seventeenth, in the work on *Trauerspiel*. No belief in periods of decline' (1999a, 458). Later, Benjamin writes that '[o]vercoming the concept of "progress", and overcoming the concept of "period of decline" are two sides of one and the same thing' (460). As Susan Buck-Morss clearly articulates, Benjamin argued that no city, no moment, is more important or significant than the last—he was concerned with overcoming progress and its polarity, decline; and they are related tasks, for:

> The debris of industrial culture teaches us not the necessity of submitting to historical catastrophe, but the fragility of the social order that tells us this catastrophe is necessary. The crumbling of the monuments that were built to signify the immortality of civilization becomes proof, rather, of its transiency. And the fleetingness of temporal power does not cause sadness; it informs political practice. (1989, 170)

To value modern, urban ruins as political objects is not to invest in nostalgia, but to unlock an imagination that resists the supremacy of perpetual growth—the project that Benjamin was working on for most of the last decade of his life. Not just resisting the corrosive power of eternal novelty, but, through urban endings, in ruins, understanding the fundamentally illusory nature of the modern city as a site of reification and commodification. The link between ruins and the myth of progress is particularly evident in the creative destruction of urban regeneration: 'As a classic example of reification, urban "renewal" projects attempted to create social utopia by changing the arrangement of buildings and streets—objects in space—while leaving the social relationships intact' (Buck-Morss 1989, 89). What Benjamin sought was not the 'illusion of social equality' that such aesthetic and spatial renovation provides (89), but rather the alternative vision of modernity as one of decline and ruin.

This vision is evident in the emphasis that Benjamin placed on a fragmented and figurative perception of modernity as both a process of ruination and disintegration of experience, which seeks to redeem the past via a reevaluation of the ways in which we recall, preserve and inhabit a space of 'what has been', particularly through urban encounters with the traces of the recent past (Benjamin 2003, 183–84). Seeking these traces in actual ruins may seem to be an excessively literal, even blunt reading of Benjamin's work; however, Benjamin certainly centred his investigations in the material remains of the nineteenth century that persisted in Paris's decaying passages, where he encountered forgotten and neglected objects that he saw as the refuse of a churning, destructive modernity. Modern urban ruins are such rejected, ephemeral refuse, less a reflection of Benjamin's repetition of the ruin motif than a reference to the relationship between ruins and a culture of consumption or history-as-progress—whether cities ruined by war and revolution or the abandoned remnants of obsolete industries or outdated fads. As Benjamin's eclectic collections in *The Arcades Project* demonstrate, almost any category of remnant—books or toys, secondhand clothing, aging technology—might have similarly political import. However, by emphasizing ruined architecture, the other face of the increasingly seamless city emerges in ever-present urban endings that can be directly related to everyday life in the city, and, moreover, to the conceptualization of the city itself as a place of modern ruin.

Part III

CITY FUTURES

Power, Risk, Value

Chapter 12

Beyond Differences of Race, Religion, Class

Making Urban Subjects[1]

Saskia Sassen

Cities have distinctive capacities to transform conflict into the civic. In contrast, national governments tend to militarize conflict. This does not mean that cities are peaceful spaces. On the contrary, cities have long been sites for conflicts, from war to racisms and religious hatreds. Yet militarizing conflict is not a particularly urban option: cities have tended to triage conflict through commerce and civic activity. Even more important, the overcoming of urban conflicts has often been the source for an expanded civic sense. And more generally, the daily dynamics and interdependences of life in the city contribute to the making of an urban subject, as distinct from an ethnic, religious or racialized subject. I think of the possibility of an urban subject not as one that erases these powerful markers, but repositions them. This repositioning is likely to take on many diverse forms and involve diverse spaces, depending on a city's trajectory. Notwithstanding this variability, we can conceive of the urban subject as one who can experience the urban context as such, as urban. It signals that urban space is an actor in these dynamics, a thesis I explore in 'Does the City Have Speech?' (2013).

Today cities are at risk of losing this capacity and becoming sites for a range of new types of conflicts, such as asymmetric war, ethnic and social 'cleansing' and class wars. Dense urbane spaces can easily become conflictive spaces in cities overwhelmed by inequality and injustice. The major environmental disasters looming in our immediate futures could lead cities to become the sites for a variety of secondary, more anomic conflicts, such as drug wars and other nonurban conflicts that merely use the city as a deployment space. All of these challenge the traditional commercial and civic capacity that has given cities tools to avoid falling into armed conflict, and to incorporate diversities of class, culture, religion, ethnicity.

179

The question I examine here is whether this emergent urban future of expanding conflicts and racisms contains within it those conditions and urban
capabilities that have historically allowed cities to transform conflict. In the
past, urban capabilities and urban subjects were often crafted through the
struggle to address challenges larger than our differences, our hatreds, our
intolerances, our racisms. Out of this dialectic came the open urbanity that
made many cities historically spaces for the making of the civic and commerce, from historic Jerusalem, Baghdad and Istanbul, to modern Chicago
and New York. One factor feeding these positives was that cities became
strategic spaces also for the powerful and their needs for self-representation
and projection onto a larger stage. Both the modest social classes and the
powerful found in the city a space for their diverse 'life projects'. None of
these cities and projects was perfect. Each saw hatreds and injustices. But the
complex interdependence of daily life in cities was the algorithm that made
them thrive.

I will argue that today's unsettling of older urban orders is part of a larger
disassembling of existing organizational logics and hence unlikely to produce
urbanities that resemble the shapes of our recent past. This disassembling is
also unsettling the logic that assembled territory, authority and rights into the
dominant organizational format of our times—the modern nation-state.[2] All
of this is happening even as both cities and national states continue to be major building blocks of the familiar geopolitical landscape and the material organization of territory. In this sense, the urban order that gave us, for instance,
the open city in Europe is still there, but increasingly as mere visual order and
less so as social order, an order that can enable the making of urban subjects.

In what follows I first elaborate on dynamics that are altering the familiar
urban order and then argue that this is also a moment of challenges larger than
our differences. Confronting these challenges will require that we transcend
those differences. Therein lies a potential for reinventing that capacity of cities to transform conflict into openness rather than war. But it is not necessarily going to be the familiar order of the open city and of the civic as we have
come to represent it, especially in the West.

WHERE POWERLESSNESS BECOMES COMPLEX

Cities are one of the key sites where new norms and new identities are made.[3]
They have been such sites at various times and places, and under diverse
conditions. This role can become strategic in particular times and places, as is
the case today in global cities. Current conditions in these cities are creating
not only new structures of power but also operational and rhetorical open-

ings for new political actors who may long have been invisible or without voice. A key element of the argument here is that the localization of strategic components of globalization in these cities means that the disadvantaged can engender new forms of contesting globalized corporate power, including right there in their neighbourhoods.

Critical in this process is the capability of urban space to produce a difference: that being powerless does not necessarily mean being invisible or impotent. The disadvantaged, especially in global cities, can gain 'presence' in their engagement with power but also vis-à-vis each other. This differs from the 1950s to the 1970s period in the United States, for instance, when white flight and the significant departure of major corporate headquarters left cities hollowed out and the disadvantaged in a condition of abandonment. Today, the localization of the most powerful global actors in these cities creates a set of objective conditions for engagement. Examples here are the struggles against gentrification—an encroachment into minority and modest neighbourhoods that led to growing numbers of homeless people beginning in the 1980s—the struggles for the rights of the homeless, or demonstrations against police brutality against minorities.

Elsewhere I have developed the case that while these struggles are highly localized, they actually represent a form of global engagement; their globality takes the form of a horizontal, multisited recurrence of similar struggles in hundreds of cities worldwide. These struggles are different from the ghetto uprisings of the 1960s, which were short, intense eruptions confined to the ghettos and causing most of the damage in the neighbourhoods of the disadvantaged themselves. In these ghetto uprisings there was no direct engagement with power on its terrain. In contrast, current conditions in major, especially global, cities are creating spatial openings for new political actors, including the disadvantaged and those who were once invisible or without voice.

The conditions that today make some cities strategic sites are basically two, and both capture major transformations that are destabilizing older systems organizing territory and politics. One of these is the rescaling of strategic territories that articulate the new politico-economic system and thereby at least some features of power. The other is the partial unbundling or at least weakening of the national as container of social process due to the variety of dynamics encompassed by globalization and digitization. The consequences for cities of these two conditions are many: what matters here is that cities emerge as strategic sites for major economic processes and for new political actors.[4]

Against the background of a partial disassembling of empires and nation-states, the city becomes a strategic site for making elements of new, perhaps less partial orders. In this larger disassembling new sociopolitical orderings can coexist with older orderings such as the nation-state, the interstate system and the older urban order of a hierarchy dominated by the national state. Among the new orderings are global cities: these have partly exited that national, state-dominated hierarchy and become part of multiscalar, regional and global networks. The last two decades have seen an increasingly urban articulation of global logics and struggles, and an escalating use of urban space to make political claims not only by the citizens of a city's country but also by foreign firms and the global rich.

What is being engendered today in terms of political practices in the global city is quite different from what it might have been in the medieval city of Weber. The medieval city was a space that enabled the burghers to set up systems for owning and protecting property against more powerful actors, such as the king and the church, and to implement various defences against despots of all sorts. Today's political practices, I would argue, have to do with the production of 'presence' by those without power and with a politics that claims rights to the city rather than protection of property. What the two situations share is the notion that urban space enables also the weaker actor and that through urban practices new forms of political subjectivity (i.e., citizenship) are being constituted. Both the medieval and today's city are leading sites for this type of political work. The city is, in turn, partly constituted through these dynamics. Far more so than a peaceful and harmonious suburb, it is the contested city where the civic is getting built. After the long historical phase that saw the ascendance of the national state and the scaling of key economic dynamics at the national level, the city is once again a scale for strategic economic and political dynamics.

Two rescalings have repositioned cities. On the one hand, several strategic components of economic globalization and digitization concentrate in global cities and dislocate and destabilize existing institutional orders that go well beyond cities.[5] On the other hand, some of the major legal, regulatory and normative frames for handling urban conditions are now part of national framings—much of what is called urban development policy is national economic policy. The concentration of such global and national dynamics in these cities forces the need to craft new types of responses and innovations on the part of both the most powerful and the most disadvantaged, albeit for very different types of survival.

But what happens to these urban capabilities when war goes asymmetric and when racisms grow in cities where increasing numbers become poor and have to struggle for survival? Here follows a brief discussion of two cases that illustrate how cities can enable powerlessness to become complex. In this complexity lies the possibility of making the political, making history.

URBANIZING WAR:
Making Visible the Limits of Military Power

The pursuit of national security has become a source for urban insecurity.[6] In earlier wars, large armies needed large open fields or oceans to meet and fight. But nowadays, when conventional armies go to war their enemy is likely to consist of irregular combatants, and major cities are likely to become frontline space. This turns the traditional security paradigm based on national state security on its head. What may be good to protect the national state apparatus may come at a high price to major cities since that is where most asymmetric war is enacted. One component of asymmetric war is terrorism. Since 1998 most terrorist attacks have been in cities. This produces a disturbing map. Access to urban targets is far easier than access to planes for hijacking or to military installations. The US Department of State Annual Report on Global Terrorism allows us to establish that today cities are the key targets for terrorist attacks, a trend that began before the September 2001 attacks on New York. From 1993 to 2000, cities accounted for 94 percent of the injuries resulting from all 'terrorist attacks', according this report, and for 61 percent of the deaths. Second, in this period the number of incidents doubled, rising especially sharply after 1998. In contrast, in the 1980s hijacked airplanes accounted for a larger share of terrorist deaths and destruction than they did in the 1990s.[7]

We can see this urbanizing of war in the invasion of Iraq, which became largely an urban war theatre. But we also see the negative impacts of this war on cities that are not even part of the immediate war theatre—the bombings in Madrid, London, Casablanca, Bali, Mumbai, Lahore and so many others. The new urban map of war is expansive: it goes far beyond the actual nation-states involved. The bombings in each of these cities have their own specifics and can be explained in terms of particular grievances and instruments. These are localized actions by local armed groups, acting independently. Yet they are also clearly part of a new kind of multisited war—a distributed and variable set of actions that gain larger meaning from a particular conflict with global projection, the so-called War on Terror, beginning most visibly with the invasion of Afghanistan and Iraq.

A defining feature of asymmetric wars is that they are partial, intermittent and lack clear endings. There is no armistice to mark their end. They are one indication of how the centre no longer holds—whether the centre is the imperial power of a period or the national states of our modernity. We can see all these features in the US war on Iraq. It took the US conventional military aerial bombing only six weeks to destroy the Iraqi army and enter the country. But then asymmetric war set in, with Baghdad, Mosul, Basra and other Iraqi cities the sites of conflict. A second feature of contemporary wars, especially evident in the less-developed areas, is that they often involve forced urbanization. Contemporary conflicts produce significant population displacement into cities; however, when the armed conflict takes over the whole city (e.g., Mogadishu in the 2000s), we also see flight out of cities. Also common today is for the warring bodies to avoid battle or direct military confrontation, as Mary Kaldor (2006) has described in her work on the new wars. Their main strategy is to control territory by expelling people of a different identity (ethnicity, religion, politics). The main tactic is terror—conspicuous massacres and atrocities, pushing people to flee.

These types of displacement—with ethnic/religious 'cleansing' the most virulent form—have a profound impact on the cosmopolitan character of cities. Cities have long had the capacity to bring together people of different classes, ethnicities and religions through commerce, politics and civic practices. Contemporary conflicts unsettle and weaken this cultural diversity of cities when they lead to forced urbanization or internal displacement. Belfast, Baghdad or Mostar each is at risk of becoming a series of urban ghettos, with huge implications for infrastructure, the local economy and the civic. Baghdad has undergone a deep process of such 'cleansing', a critical component of the (relative) 'peace' the US government claimed it had secured in the mid-2000s.

The systemic equivalent of these types of 'cleansing' in the case of very large cities may well be the growing ghettoization of the poor and the rich—albeit in very different types of ghettos. It leaves to the middle classes the task of bringing urbanity to these cities. The risk is that they will supplant traditional urban cosmopolitanisms with narrow defensive attitudes in a world of growing economic insecurity and political powerlessness. Under these conditions also, displacement from countryside to town or within cities becomes a source of insecurity rather than of rich diversity.

Today's urbanizing of war differs from histories of cities and war in modern times. In the two so-called world wars, large armies needed large open fields or oceans to meet and fight and to carry out invasions. These were the frontline spaces of war. In World War II, the city entered the war theatre not as a site for war making but as a technology for instilling fear: the full destruction of cities as a way of terrorizing a whole nation, with Hiroshima and Dresden the iconic cases.

This comparison of conventional and asymmetric war brings up a critical dimension: under certain conditions, such as asymmetric war, cities can function as a type of weak regime. The countries with the most powerful conventional armies today could flatten a city whether Baghdad, Gaza, the Swat valley or so many other urban conflict zones.[8] Yet in many ways they cannot. They can engage in all kinds of activities, including violations of

the law: rendition, torture, assassinations of leaders they don't like, bombing of civilian areas and so on, in a history of brutality that can no longer
be hidden and seems to have escalated the violence against civilian populations. But superior military powers stop short of pulverizing a city, even
when they have the weapons to do so. The United States could have pulverized Baghdad, and Israel could have pulverized Gaza. But they didn't. It
seems to me that the reason was not respect for life or the fact that killing
unarmed civilians is illegal according to international law—they do this all
the time. It has more to do with a vague constraint that remains unstated: the
notion that the mass killing of people in a city is a different type of horror
from allowing the deaths of massive numbers of people year after year in
jungles and villages due to, for instance, a curable disease such as malaria.
I would posit that pulverizing a city is a specific type of crime, one that
elicits a horror that people dying from malaria does not. The mix of people
and buildings—in a way, the civic—has the capacity to temper destruction,
if not to stop it. History repeatedly shows us the limits of superior power.[9]
In an increasingly interdependent world, the most powerful countries find
themselves restrained through multiple interdependencies. To this I add the
city as a weak regime that can obstruct and temper the destructive capacity
of a superior military power. It is one more capable for systemic survival
in a world where several countries have the capacity to destroy the planet
(Sassen 2008, 378–96).[10] Under these conditions the city becomes both a
technology for containing conventional military powers and a technology of
resistance for armed insurgencies. The physical and human features of the
city are an obstacle for conventional armies—an obstacle wired into urban
space itself.[11]

CITIES AS FRONTIER SPACES:
The Hard Work of Keeping Them Open

Historically, cities have evinced capacities to go beyond conflicts—conflicts
that result from racisms, governmental wars on terror and more. This implies
the possibility of making new subjectivities and identities. For instance, often
it is the urbanity of the subject and the setting that mark a city, rather than ethnicity, religion or phenotype. But that marking urbanity of subject and setting
does not simply fall from the sky. It is made, through hard work and painful
trajectories. One question is whether it can also come out of the need for new
solidarities in cities that confront major challenges, such as violent racisms or
environmental crises. Their acuteness and overwhelming character can serve
to create conditions where those challenges are bigger and more threatening

than a city's internal conflicts and hatreds. This might force us into joint responses and from there to emphasizing an urban rather than individual or group subject and identity (such as an ethnic or religious subject and identity).

Immigration gives us a window into these types of possibilities. It helps make visible the work of making norms, of making open cities, and of repositioning both the immigrant and the citizen as urban subjects. In becoming urban subjects they can transcend this differentiation of immigrant versus citizen in spaces where it does not help or is not necessary. In the daily routines of a city the factors that rule are work, family, school, public transport and so on, and this holds for both immigrants and citizens. Perhaps the sharpest marking difference in a city is between the rich and the poor, and each of these classes includes both immigrants and citizens. It is when the law and the police enter the picture that the differences of immigrant status versus citizen status become the determining factor, but most of daily life in the city is not ruled by this differentiation.

Here I address this issue from the perspective of the capacity of urban space to generate norms and subjects that can escape the constraints of dominant power systems—such as the nation-state, the War on Terror, the growing weight of racism in a national political culture. The particular case of immigrant integration in Europe over the centuries is one window into this complex and historically variable process, with diverse outcomes.

In my reading, both European and Western hemisphere history shows that the challenges of incorporating the 'outsider' often became instruments for developing the civic and, at times, for expanding the rights of the already included (Sassen 1999). Responding to claims made by the excluded has often had the effect of expanding the rights of citizenship. And restricting the rights of immigrants has been part of a loss of rights by citizens. This was clearly the case with the immigration reform act passed by the Clinton administration in the United States, which shows that a Democratic Party legislative victory for an 'immigration law' had the effect of taking away rights from immigrants and citizens.[12]

Anti-immigrant sentiment has long been a critical dynamic in Europe's history, one mostly overlooked in standard European historiographies until the 1960s.[13] Anti-immigrant sentiment and attacks occurred in each of the major immigration phases of the last two hundred years across Europe. No labour-receiving country has a clean record—not Switzerland, with its long admirable history of international neutrality, and not even France, the most open to immigration, refugees and exiles. Critical is the fact that there have always been individuals, groups, organizations, and politicians who believe in making our societies more inclusive of immigrants. History suggests that those fighting for incorporation have succeeded in the long run, even if only partially. Just to focus on the recent past, one-quarter of the French have a foreign-born ancestor three generations removed, and 34 percent of Viennese are either born abroad or have foreign parents. It took active making to transform the hatreds towards foreigners into the urban civic. But it is also the result of constraints in a large city; for instance, to have a reasonably fast public transport system means that it is not feasible to check on the status of all users. A basic and thin rule needs to be met: pay your ticket and you are on. That is the making of the civic as a material condition: all those who meet the thin rule—pay the ticket—can use the public bus or train, regardless of whether they are citizens or tourists, good people or not-so-good people, local residents or visitors from another city.

'European history' is dominated by the image of Europe as a continent of emigration, never of immigration. Yet in the 1700s, when Amsterdam built its polders and cleared its bogs, it brought in workers from northern Germany; when the French developed their vineyards, they brought in Spaniards; workers from the Alps were brought in to help develop Milan and Turin; as were the Irish when London needed help building water and sewage infrastructure. In the 1800s, when Haussmann rebuilt Paris, he brought in Germans and Belgians; when Sweden decided to become a monarchy and needed some good-looking palaces, they brought in Italian stoneworkers; when Switzerland built the Gotthard Tunnel, it brought in Italians; and when Germany built its railroads and steel mills, it brought in Italians and Poles.

At any given time there were multiple significant flows of intra-European migration. All of the workers involved were seen as outsiders, as undesirables, as threats to the community, as people that could never belong. The immigrants were mostly from the same broad cultural group, religious group and phenotype. Yet they were seen as impossible to assimilate. The French hated the Belgian immigrant workers, saying they were the wrong type of Catholics, and the Dutch saw the German immigrant workers as the wrong type of Protestants. This is a telling fact. It suggests that it is incorrect to argue, as is so often done, that today it is more difficult to integrate immigrants because of their different religion, culture and phenotype. When all of these factors were similar, anti-immigrant sentiment was as strong as today, and it often led to physical attacks on immigrants.

Yet all along, significant numbers of immigrants did become part of the community, even if it took two or three generations. They often maintained their distinctiveness, yet were still members of the community—part of the complex, highly heterogeneous social order of any developed city.

Today the argument against immigration may be focused on questions of race, religion and culture, and might seem rational—that cultural and religious distance is the reason for the difficulty of incorporation. But in sifting through the historical and current evidence, we find only new variations on an old passion: the racializing of the outsider as Other. Today the Other is stereotyped by differences of race, religion and culture. These are equivalent arguments to those made in the past when migrants were broadly of the same religious, racial and cultural group. Migration hinges on a move between two worlds, even if within a single region or country—such as East Germans moving to West Germany after 1989, where they were often viewed as a different ethnic group with undesirable traits. What is today's equivalent challenge, one that can force us to go beyond our differences and transform ourselves into urban subjects?

CONCLUSION

The particularity of today's emergent urban landscape is profoundly different from the old European tradition. This is so even though Europe's worldwide imperial projects remixed European traditions with urban cultures that belonged to other histories and geographies. Yet it shares with that older time the fact of challenges larger than our differences. Therein lies a potential for reinventing that capacity of cities to transform conflict and difference into at least relative openness rather than war and intolerance. But it is not going to be the familiar order of the open city and of the civic as we have come to represent it, especially in the European tradition.

My sense is rather that the major challenges that confront cities (and society generally) have increasingly strong feedback loops that in fact contribute to the disassembling of the old civic urban order. Asymmetric war, as discussed earlier, is perhaps one of the most acute versions of this dynamic in cities that are part of the active theatre of war. And the 'War on Terror' at home extends the distortions of war deep inside the United States and Europe.

Yet this mix of conditions can generate ironic turns of events. These challenges affect both rich and poor, immigrants and citizens, women and men, and thereby contain their own specific potential for making novel platforms for urban action. Addressing them will demand that everybody joins the effort. Further, while sharp economic inequalities, racisms and religious intolerance have long existed, they are also local mobilizers for civic participation in a context where the centre—whether the imperial centre, the national state or the city's rich and powerful—no longer holds in the old ways. Similarly, the abuses of power by the state on its own people in the name of fighting terrorism can create coalitions, bringing together residents who may have thought they could never collaborate.

These negative conditions can forge a process that can transcend class, race and religion in particular settings and dynamics. But it cannot easily do this in a large California corporate farm or a suburb. It is a process that needs the city, and there it can make subjects that are above all urban subjects.

NOTES

1. This text is based on two publications in which the reader can find extensive bibliographic and empirical materials: Sassen (2008, 277–398; 2010).

2. The emergent landscape I am describing promotes a multiplication of diverse spatio-temporal framings and diverse normative (mini) orders where once the dominant logic was oriented towards producing (grand) unitary national spatial, temporal and normative framings (Sassen 2008, 378–419). This proliferation of specialized orders extends even inside the state apparatus. I argue that we can no longer speak of 'the' state, and hence of 'the' national state versus 'the' global order. There is a novel type of segmentation inside the state apparatus, with a growing and increasingly privatized executive branch of government aligned with specific global actors, notwithstanding nationalist speeches, and a hollowing out of the legislature whose effectiveness is at risk of becoming confined to fewer and more domestic matters (148–203).

3. With globalization and digitization—and all the specific elements they entail—global cities do emerge as such strategic sites for making norms and identities. Some reflect extreme power, such as the global managerial elites, and others reflect innovation under extreme duress, notably much of what happens in immigrant neighbourhoods. While the strategic transformations are sharply concentrated in global cities, many are also engendered (besides being diffused) in cities at lower orders of national urban hierarchies.

4. In contrast, in the 1930s until the 1970s, when mass manufacturing dominates, cities had lost strategic functions and were not the site for creative institutional innovations. The strategic sites were the large factory at the heart of the larger process of mass manufacturing and mass consumption. The factory and the government were the strategic sites where the crucial dynamics producing the major institutional innovations of the epoch were located. The large Fordist factory and the mines emerge as key sites for the making of a modern working class and a syndicalist project; it is not always the city that is the site for making norms and identities.

5. Emphasizing this multiplication of partial assemblages contrasts with much of the globalization literature that has tended to assume the binary of the global versus the national. In this literature the national is understood as a unit. I emphasize that the global can also be constituted inside the national—that is, the global city. Further, the focus in the globalization literature tends to be on the powerful global institutions that have played a critical role in implementing the global corporate economy and have reduced the power of 'the' state. In contrast, I also emphasize that particular components of the state have actually gained power because they have to do the work

of implementing policies necessary for a global corporate economy. This is another reason for valuing the more encompassing normative order that a city can (though does not necessarily) generate.

6. For a fuller development of this subject, see Sassen (2010).

7. I derived these numbers from the annual country reports. US Department of State, Annual Report on Global Terrorism (Washington, DC: Bureau of Public Affairs, Office of Strategic Communications).

8. Even if the nuclear threat to cities has remained hypothetical since 1945, cities remain highly vulnerable to two kinds of very distinct threats. The first one is the specialized aerial attack of new computer-targeted weaponry, which has been employed 'selectively' in places like Baghdad or Belgrade. The second is terrorist attacks.

9. A separate source for unilateral restraint is tactical. Thus theorists of war posit that the superior military force should, for tactical reasons, signal to its enemy that it has not used its full power.

10. And, from a larger angle than the one that concerns me here, when great powers fail in this self-restraint, we have what John Mearsheimer has called the tragedy of great powers (2001).

11. This dual process of urbanization of war and militarization of urban life unsettles the meaning of the urban. Peter Marcuse (2002) writes that 'the War on terrorism is leading to a continued downgrading of the quality of life in US cities, visible changes in urban form, the loss of public use of public space, restriction on free movement within and to cities, particularly for members of darker skinned groups, and the decline of open popular participation in the governmental planning and decision-making process'. Second, it questions the role of cities as welfare providers. The imperative of security means a shift in political priorities. It implies a cut or a relative decrease in budgets dedicated to social welfare, education, health, infrastructure development, economic regulation and planning. These two trends, in turn, challenge the very concept of citizenship (Sassen 2008, 277–327).

12. For a diversity of other domains, besides immigration, where this holds, see Sassen (2008, 148–276).

13. This section is based on Sassen (1999).

Chapter 13

Cities Remade

On Deciding the Fate of Building in the City

Janet Donohoe

The last few decades have seen a revival of American city centres. Many cities struggle with a scarcity of space and attempt to be ever more dense in efforts to reduce sprawl, to preserve nearby wilderness and to promote community. While these are perhaps laudable goals, they frequently lead to conflict between those who promote tearing down neighbourhoods for the sake of high-density housing and those who call for historic preservation. This chapter provides a phenomenological look at this tension and provides an analysis of possible responses through Edmund Husserl's work on historical sedimentation and Paul Ricoeur's work on narrative identity. I argue that the roles of testimony and collective memory as supported by a shared world yield a framework whereby the tension between replacing or preserving can be mediated. Drawing upon examples from my home city of Atlanta, Georgia, in the United States, we can explore the efficacy of this framework to real situations.

One might wonder why we would be so interested in whether neighbourhoods in cities are bulldozed or not. Cities, after all, are constantly changing entities that grow and change of their own accord. Whether they do so with the use of a bulldozer is hardly a philosophical project. Such a laissez-faire attitude about city neighbourhoods and philosophy fails to grasp the importance of place to philosophical thinking. For Husserl, the importance of place comes down to a question of layers of sedimentation that provide a frequently unacknowledged foundation for experience. For Ricoeur, the importance of place contributes to the work of testimony. These are the issues we will be exploring here. And as the world's population becomes increasingly urban, it is important to explore the role of cities in both the testimony of who we are and the experiences we have of the world. The question of whether to encourage or discourage the rebuilding of city neighbourhoods is not simply a question of social justice, or even aesthetics, but is a question of communal identity and experience.

As Robert Mugerauer would have it, we can think of the city as parallel to the stages of development of a human being. The city needs to accommodate both the stasis and quiet of rest, but also the delight and challenge of newness where 'one could experience the new, unsettling, and strange without its destroying the self with chaos or inassimilable shock' (Mugerauer 1994, 163). Moreover, this development of the self is not something that happens in isolation, it is always a communal, connected self. For Mugerauer, this leads to the question of how we would 'nurture both concretely enriching differences and also a generally intelligible social identity? This is the issue of the truly particular and the still shared, an issue of many distinctive places which yet make one place' (163).

This tension between the heterogeneity and the homogeneity of a city manifests itself in the tension between the desire to tear down and the desire to preserve parts of cities. It is at the same time a tension between a constant drive for 'progress' towards the future and nostalgia for the past. What I am arguing here is that phenomenology and hermeneutics are helpful in understanding and mediating these two desires. In planning, we do not want to be so focused on preservation that our neighbourhoods become stultified, nor do we wish to be so prone towards the new that we destroy any connection with the past at all. What we must come to realize is the dynamic nature of cities that can be thought in terms of a kind of narrative identity as provided for through the works of Paul Ricoeur. To think such allows us to maintain a living city that supports our sense of ourselves while incorporating a multiplicity of perspectives and allowing for the renewal and critique of each new generation.

While at one extreme we have processes of gentrification that are completely disrespectful of the history and culture of neighbourhoods, at the other extreme we have processes of preservation that are meant to secure neighbourhoods against change of any kind, but which frequently are a manner of excluding certain populations by restricting construction of equal access housing, or keeping property values in a neighbourhood elevated. Both processes frequently have classist and racist underpinnings. What should we do in the face of such injustice in urban housing and development? Should we allow any and all development without restriction, or are there good reasons for certain restrictions upon development? If change is a natural part of any city and neighbourhoods ebb and flow in popularity and capital investment, how do we determine policy that regulates whether and what kind of development should be allowed in a city? Two concepts in particular are helpful from Ricoeur. One is the idea of narrative identity. The other is the idea of concordant discordance. I would like to explore the use of these two concepts in helping to navigate the middle path between the preservation of city neighbourhoods and their demolition. We will begin with an overview of the role of place in communal identity and the sedimentation of history and tradition. Then we will examine the two extremes of gentrification and preservation in order to finally carve out an understanding of a middle path that can be described through Ricoeur's notions of narrative identity and concordant discordance.

PLACES AND COMMUNAL IDENTITY

Paul Ricoeur presents narrative as a means of providing unity for a fractured temporality. Ricoeur less frequently acknowledges the role that narrative plays in organizing our spatial experiences. This failure can be rectified by paying attention to the fundamental importance of place to narrative. As we know, plot requires setting. The setting for our lives is not inconsequential. It often goes unnoticed, but the setting for our lives is itself a dynamic and integral part of each experience. Where we are frames how we experience and frequently what we experience. Our embodied style of being in the world is structured in part by places that we inhabit. We focus on things that are important in our world without even realizing that in the simple constitution of the world around us we are enacting a system of valuation that means we see some things and not others. Much of what we see is based upon what has been passed along to us from prior generations through the world in which we find ourselves. The stories that we tell reflect the valuation and those communal habits that have been passed along because of and through places. We frequently know where important things happened and the fact that we know *where* is a hallmark of the event's importance. The event is associated with the place, the place is associated with the event and we easily come to understand that the event is important. Likewise, those events that are unimportant do not have a place that gets passed along from generation to generation.

The passing along of places of import does not happen without change of place, however. In other words, places do not remain static. Just as narratives of the past change, so do the places of those narratives. The Ford Theater where Abraham Lincoln was shot is certainly not the same place that it was on the evening in question even in spite of efforts to preserve it for history's sake. It is not hard to imagine, then, that places that do not undergo such deliberate preservation are equally not the same places that they used to be. Consider the grassy knoll of Dealey Plaza in Dallas, Texas, where John F. Kennedy was assassinated. It immediately fell into disrepair following the assassination as a city that was shocked and shamed by what had happened there turned away from the tragic place. Only in most recent years has Dealey Plaza begun a return to its prominence in the city. The narrative it supports now is quite different, however, than the one it supported prior to the assassination.

Traditions have been written onto the landscape itself in layer upon layer of history. The history becomes sedimented in a place allowing the past of the place to be narrated in its buildings, streets, parks and back alleys. The city becomes a palimpsest with some aspects being covered over while others are brought to the fore until a shift causes other areas to become prominent.[1] These shifts that we frequently see in city neighbourhoods where some places become trendy while other places grow stale may seem cyclical as populations move and demographics change. These are obvious ways in which the neighbourhoods are subject to change. If place supports the narrative, then changes to place involve changes to the narrative and vice versa. The neighbourhoods themselves reflect these changes in physical manifestations, the material reality of the place, in the communal narrative of the place, which reflects the community. The social traditions and manners of understanding become sedimented in the place.

Consider the layout and placement of roads and commercial districts of our cities. Roads are a simple way to recognize the layering of culture upon the earth. I have described elsewhere how in many cities, newer roads are built on top of older roads which were built to improve the lot of locals taking goods or livestock to the village for commerce.[2] This obvious layering and keeping with tradition also expresses the values of generations of people who take up prior traditions without real cognizance. Of course there will be and should be roads, we can imagine someone saying. People must be able to get to the city to sell their goods. Roads are conceived as there for the promotion and ease of commerce, not for artistic expression or experience of nature. Roads may have begun as cow paths that were later paved to make automobile traffic easier, thereby cementing the importance of these traversals and writing the history on the place. It is hard to imagine doing without roads, and even if we imagine a world of flying cars where we might be able to tear up all the roads, the paths of air travel might also follow the same kinds of arterial systems as roads, transferring that tradition to a yet future generation.

According to Lewis Mumford, one of the most important roles of the city is the transference across generations of a complex culture. As he writes (1989, 30), 'By means of its storage facilities (buildings, vaults, archives, monuments, tablets, books), the city became capable of transmitting a complex culture from generation to generation, for it marshalled together not only the physical means but the human agents needed to pass on and enlarge this heritage. That remains the greatest of the city's gifts'. Mumford is stressing here the importance not just of the physicality of the city, but the human narrative and human readers of the city as well. Furthermore, he underscores the importance of the city in the preservation of culture, suggesting that 'The invention of such forms as the written record, the library, the archive, the school, and the university is one of the earliest and most characteristic achievements of the city' (30–31). James Conlon (1999, 45) further argues that 'the city does not merely collect a culture's achievements; it also teaches them, passes them on to successive generations. Through its art and architecture, a city infuses the complexity of culture into the very bones of those who daily walk its streets. Living literally in the shadow of the Parthenon, the Athenian learns the complex meaning of Athena in a way inaccessible to the village peasant'.

What we see here is that place, given its importance to tradition, is more than merely the material plot of land. Place transpires between those who experience it and its materiality. What is remarkable about cities that were heavily bombed in World War II is not simply the devastating loss of life, but the loss of culture that is represented by the architectural gap in the city's narrative. To stroll the streets of Berlin or Cologne, Germany, is to be confronted with postwar construction. While we may disagree about the aesthetics of this architecture, what is apparent is that the reconstruction of these cities has meant the loss of periods of narrative history. The city itself suffers due to that loss. Parts of its own story have been irrevocably altered in the extreme alteration of its architecture and structure. Reconstruction has replaced the thickness of a narrative with a much simpler and less complex one—that of destruction by blanket bombing in World War II.

In war this kind of destruction of material culture is often used as a tactic to demoralize a population, but it also functions more radically than that to effect genocide. There are a plethora of contemporary and historical examples of the attempt to destroy a population through the destruction of its cultural artifacts and thereby a destruction of it memories, traditions and means of transference of the same. ISIS has done their utmost to destroy world heritage sites in Syria and Iraq, including the ancient city of Palmyra. The Taliban blew up Bamiyan Buddhist statues in Afghanistan.[3] Hitler's Krystallnacht aimed its destruction at Jewish synagogues. Sherman's total war approach to bringing the South to its knees during the American Civil War was focused on destroying southern culture by destroying its hallmark plantation homes. The aim of these types of actions is not so much for military advantage as for the erasure of a culture from the land.[4] Implicit in such tactics is the recognition of the importance of place to the identity and culture of a people. To destroy the place is to go a long way towards destroying the people. While city planners are not bent upon genocide, there can be similar effects through what I have called 'collateral' erasure of communities.[5] The construction of an interstate highway through a neighbourhood does not directly aim at the destruction of a community, but it is deemed acceptable collateral damage by those who are usually not members of the affected community and who, by being willing to accept it as collateral damage, clearly do not care enough for the community being destroyed. Wholesale destruction of a neighbourhood, whether as a deliberate act or uncaring 'collateral', is tantamount to genocide.

Even partial destruction of neighbourhoods is suspect. And yet, if the places of cities are so important for cultural transmission and reflect traditions and values to such a degree, then it might seem obvious that we should be doing everything in our power to preserve those places. We should hold firm against the changes of style and to reclaim areas that have begun to forfeit to the natural erosion of time. Our very culture seems to be at stake. Yet what we will see in the following is that rather than retrench we must recognize the importance of concordance of discord for maintaining a character that accommodates change.

A complicating element is the heterogeneity or diversity of a city. Cities are by definition diverse. This is both the richness and complexity of the city. We might be inclined to think that a narrative requires a certain homogeneity. We must all have the same story to tell, and that story provides us with a kind of identity that is singular. But I would argue that the singularity of the narrative is shot through with heterogeneity in that the story to be told is broad enough to encompass a multiplicity of perspectives. Place is not static. In its dynamism, it unfolds as any character in a narrative does. There are inconsistencies and changes that are fundamental to it, but that do not so radically alter its character as to make it unrecognizable.

REVITALIZATION, GENTRIFICATION AND NARRATIVE

Redevelopment of cities includes both the residential rehabilitation of neighbourhoods that were run down, preserving and revitalizing the old buildings but has also included the wholesale destruction of areas to make way for completely new construction. The argument is frequently made that in the interests of gentrification we need to demolish the old houses to make room for the newer construction that will satisfy the desires of the 'urban pioneers'. But gentrification then takes on an element of 'taming'. Frontier language is used that implies the conquering of savages. As Neil Smith suggests in *The New Urban Frontier* (1996, 117), 'The frontier imagery is neither merely decorative nor innocent [. . .] but carries considerable ideological weight. Insofar as gentrification infects working-class communities, displaces poor households, and converts whole neighbourhoods into bourgeois enclaves, the frontier ideology rationalizes social differentiation and exclusion as natural, inevitable'.

In a city such as Atlanta, Georgia, the increase in urban pioneers since the mid-1990s has entailed a complete overhaul of inner-city neighbourhoods primarily by upper-middle-class whites who in many cases rip down forty- to fifty-year-old modest homes to put up much larger contemporary houses. Neighbourhoods that for the past fifty years have been primarily working-class African American neighbourhoods are no longer that.

Smith describes this kind of activity, which is by no means unique to Atlanta, as the production of the revanchist city. This he describes as a kind of second-wave gentrification that transpires in response to former calls for more equitable housing practices that drove conservative whites to the suburbs. It is where 're-venge against minorities, the working class, women, environmental legislation, gays and lesbians, immigrants became the increasingly common denominator of public discourse' (1996, 44). Moreover, it is a hallmark of 'the rise of white supremacist militias, the vicious anti-corporatist right-wing populism of Patrick Buchanan, the intense emotion around anti-immigrant campaigns and the call for revenge against beneficiaries of affirmative action' (Smith 1996, 45).

The narrative, the ways in which we speak about the redevelopment of such downtown neighbourhoods, is revealing. We use the language of fron-tier and of pioneers. We speak of those who are willing to brave the frontier against the inner-city savages in order to bring order to the chaos, to conquer the wilderness and make it a safe home. Such language contributes to an at-tempt to eliminate aspects of the city's narrative, to cover over the sedimenta-tion of history that contributes to a city's identity. Instead, as Smith reminds us, 'the myth of the frontier is an invention that rationalizes the violence of gentrification and displacement, the everyday frontier on which the myth is hung is the stark product of entrepreneurial exploitation' (25).

Furthermore, Smith (26–27) argues: 'The new urban pioneers seek to scrub the city clean of its working-class geography and history. By remaking the geography of the city they simultaneously rewrite its social history as a pre-emptive justification for a new urban future. Slum tenements become historic brownstones, and exterior façades are sandblasted to reveal a future past'. This is a process of attempting to rewrite the past by remaking the place. In an effort to make the past more to our liking, we attempt to make the place more like us, more like our places, thereby suppressing certain social histories for the sake of others.

If, as we described above, places upon this earth secure the stories that we tell about who we are, then each time we bulldoze a building or a neigh-bourhood, we destroy a part of the story of ourselves. When we choose to bulldoze certain neighbourhoods and not others, then we are making choices about what will be remembered of who we are. This is frequently done with complete disregard for the history of racial minorities or the poor in favor of wealthy whites.

Atlanta's Summerhill district serves as a telling example. The local story is that this neighbourhood of Jewish immigrants and freed slaves arose in the period following the Civil War. It was one of the oldest black neighbourhoods that arose precisely because freed slaves were allowed to live there. It was a diverse and flourishing community of professionals and their families with Jewish synagogues alongside black churches. The neighbourhood had been neglected since the 1920s, however, and attracted the attention of those who wanted to improve Atlanta in the 1960s. At that time, roughly 65,000 primarily black residents were removed and their homes bulldozed to make room for a highway, a major-league baseball stadium and whites-only apartments. While the stadium served as home to the Atlanta Braves professional baseball team, the area surrounding the stadium never quite recovered, and the community that once flourished was scattered and destroyed. By the 1990s only about 3,500 residents remained in the neighbourhood, which became ridden with crime and poverty. While the Summerhill neighbourhood has been on the rise since the early 2000s, it has not yet fully recovered, and, of course, its character has changed significantly. With the removal of the Atlanta Braves baseball team to a northern suburb of Atlanta, the neighbourhood is the focus of much real estate speculation. One can only wonder at this point what will become of its narrative. What is certain is that it will never be what it was. The character of the neighbourhood was deliberately erased in order to replace it with a white narrative that ultimately never prospered. Instead, the neighbourhood now struggles to rebuild and rewrite without full benefit of the narrative history that would have been written upon the landscape had it not been deemed more worthwhile as an interstate.

We might decide given this discussion that the gentrification of neighbourhoods ought to be halted. It leads, after all, to all sorts of social injustice economically and politically. The elements that do not get so much attention are the ways in which this complete overhaul of city spaces leads to a loss of identity for many communities. The affront to communities is twofold. It is not simply a matter of being pushed into the farther reaches of the city that are food deserts, where public transportation is frequently more difficult and green spaces are lacking. It is a problem of loss of communal identity. Without places to support them, the narratives of communities are lost. If we understand the relationship between identity and place to be as strong as I have asserted here, then a forcible move from one area of the city to another can have resounding impact upon a community's conception of itself and the conception of that community throughout the city. The narrative is disrupted to such a degree that character cannot be maintained, the concordance is shattered.

In response, we might be inclined to allow the pendulum to swing to the opposite extreme which is to restrict changes that can be made to neighbourhoods. We shall see that this extreme has its own social justice and identity difficulties.

HISTORIC PRESERVATION
OR SOCIAL STULTIFICATION?

Historic preservation districts became useful tools for maintaining the integrity of neighbourhoods in the 1960s. The Druid Hills neighbourhood in Atlanta, Georgia, is one such historically designated area added to the National Register of Historic Places in 1975. The neighbourhood was designed by Frederick Law Olmsted in 1893 as Atlanta's second suburb. It comprises a number of mansions that were built in 1905 for prominent Atlanta families. In 1979 the historic area was expanded to a total of 1,300 acres, which now includes modest midcentury ranch homes in addition to the many turn-of-the-twentieth-century mansions.

The regulations governing changes that any homeowner can make to the exterior appearance of a home are extensive. Any property owner wishing to make changes must appeal to the Historic Preservation Commission—a group of seven volunteers who determine whether the proposed change is in keeping with the regulations. This group of people is imbued with a great deal of power and represent a limited demographic. While many of the guidelines are sound, their enforcement is frequently whimsical and the level of detail in many cases is extreme. What we see in the Druid Hills Historic District is one extreme of the preservationist attitude that is an attempt to sustain a singular narrative that appeals to a wealthy, white upper class. It reflects a misunderstanding of the narrative of the city, I would argue, in that it focuses almost entirely on consistency and coherence without any appreciation for the necessity of difference or change within a community. The absurdity of preserving a half-moon window in a front door with exactly four panes of glass must be counterbalanced by a willingness to allow for some change of style that comes with time, but also allows for change of population.

The Druid Hills example is not unique. There are many such neighbourhoods across the United States and not surprisingly, those neighbourhoods are characterized for the most part by their affluence. Rarely do we see fit to preserve the immigrant neighbourhoods or the working-class neighbourhoods.[6] Instead, we uphold the property that supports a narrative of prosperity and wealth rather than a narrative of struggle in spite of the fact that some of the strongest communities are actually those where struggle is the common mode. While historic districts were originally conceived as a response to the perceived 'rootlessness' of American city dwellers, we can query whether they offer any kind of amelioration of that rootlessness and for whom.

It is no accident that in looking at these two neighbourhoods, Druid Hills and Summerhill, one remains and is a source of pride for the city of Atlanta while the other is nearly unknown to most Atlanta residents. The destruction of the Summerhill neighbourhood is the destruction of a part of the narrative of Atlanta that is not seen to deserve protection and preservation. In Summerhill entire blocks were torn down in order to make way for an interstate, while in Druid Hills one cannot get a new front door without a multipage application and a public hearing. It is not coincidental that the Summerhill neighbourhood of homes that was torn down belonged to some of Atlanta's poor and black citizens while the Druid Hills neighbourhood was home to Atlanta's wealthiest families. Repeatedly in America we present poverty as shameful and blackness as something to hide while we valorize whiteness and wealth even if that wealth was acquired on the backs of poor blacks. The ways in which we structure our cities are all too often an attempt to erase the history and culture of the nonwhite, and the nonmoneyed. Instead, we should understand our cities and create policies in our cities that celebrate the complexity and richness of the wide variety of stories that can be and should be told. In the following section we will explore what constitutes the narrative of the city and how to use that narrative to adjudicate the tension between historic preservation and gentrification.

Robert Mugerauer (1994, 164) has suggested that 'While we want to design for coherence and stability rather than chaos, we also need openness and variety so as not to become fossilized and sterile, as happens when cultures and "places" become too closed in on themselves, too homogeneous or absolute, rejecting anyone new as an "outsider"'. For Mugerauer, as well as for others, historic preservation is not meant to tell a singular story. It is meant to allow all inhabitants of a city to take pride in the city. To recognize that the inheritance of what is passed along through place does not commit us to repetition, but allows for the transformation to reflect the changes of our cities means that we need a way to discuss the narrative identity that does not hold too strictly to the identity. This is where Ricoeur's notion of concordant discordance is helpful.

NARRATIVE AND COMMUNAL IDENTITY

Ricoeur argues in his essay 'Narrative Identity' that the role of a narrative identity is the creation and preservation of a character. Character, however, is not something that is to be judged by strict constancy or coherence. Rather, it is to be judged according to what Ricoeur calls the concordant discordance. The story can be critiqued or embraced from a whole host of different perspectives thereby undermining any kind of dominating hegemonic story. Ricoeur (1991, 80) suggests that 'the self does not know itself immediately, but only indirectly, through the detour of cultural signs of all sorts, which articulate the self in symbolic mediations that already articulate action, among them the narratives of daily life'. While Ricoeur ties this to plot, suggesting that it is in the plot that we identify the mediation between permanence and change, I would insist that in being tied to plot, it is also tied to setting. For Ricoeur (77–78), 'the advantage of this detour through the plot is that it furnishes the model of discordant concordance upon which it is possible to construct the narrative identity of a character. The narrative identity of this character will only be known correlative to the discordant concordance of the story itself'. Ricoeur explains that if a character takes an extreme action that we would deem to be completely out of character, the plot of the narrative breaks down. At the same time, if the plot loses its thread, the character becomes unbelievable. If we weave place into this understanding of narrative, then we begin to understand the necessity of providing a continuity of place for the narrative to make sense and a continuity of narrative for the place to be a place. This is not strict constancy or even identity. It is character.

This notion is not unlike what William Gavin (2008) has described as the aesthetic category of 'harmony'. For Gavin harmony includes 'the greatest amount of diversity with the fewest assumptions for unity; . . . maximum feasible participation; . . . [and] a creative tension of opposites'. Like Ricoeur, Gavin recognizes that this must be a dynamic notion that can accommodate change without giving up its unity. He explains that 'The city in this sense would not be a group of buildings, but a continuously changing pattern, a cultural matrix in and through which many undergo the process of self-realization' (141). Gavin perhaps stresses the unity more than we would like here, but the sentiment helps to understand why Ricoeur's conception of concordant discordance is so apt. It allows communities to tell the story of their connection to the neighbourhood or the land in such a way that it justifies some level of preservation without limiting the growth and change of that plot. There needs to be some kind of strain by which the narrative can be held together, but it needn't be unchanging nor does it need to lead to constant renewal of limited traditions, but allows for critique and newness within a continuous narrative.

This understanding of narrative creates the ability to cope with the dissolution of a center, and the disbursement of power spread out across a multiplicity of ways of living. To recognize that the city is characterized by such a multiplicity is to shake the foundations of any kind of singular narrative about the city and its people. This allows for an altogether different approach to planning that paves the way for nuance and the concordance of discordance. There is not unity, no totality, but there is still a story to be told that creates a rich understanding of neighbourhoods in change.

There isn't anything particularly new in thinking of the city in terms of a complex narrative of possibly conflicting discourses. What is new here is the focus on the idea of the concordant discordance as a way to navigate the tension between those who view the city as a singular narrative seeking to erase any elements that do not fit that narrative as opposed to those who view it as lacking any coherence at all. By focusing on the concordant discordance, we have the ability to allow for a variety of narratives without sacrificing the character of the city. We can acknowledge the contributions of many different neighbourhoods and areas of the city that contribute to an overall narrative by recognizing the importance of places of all kinds. We can open the restrictive preservation areas to elements of change without destroying their character while at the same time being more sensitive to the need to preserve elements of the lesser-valued, lesser-moneyed neighbourhoods that contribute to the historical sedimentation of communities.

Moreover, when we speak of the hermeneutics of the city, we mean not only the interpretation of the city itself, but also the interpretations of ourselves through the city. As we tell the stories of ourselves as city dwellers, we necessarily engage in a hermeneutic process that entails both testimony and archive as it is discovered and written upon the landscape of the city. That story is told through the buildings and parks, the streets and highways, the suburbs and exurbs, the waterfronts and bridges. The story tells us of ourselves, our values, our conflicts, but it does not always tell us those things transparently. The history of city and neighbourhoods is frequently not on the surface. It requires a hermeneutic engagement, a reading and rereading of the palimpsest that is the city. And so often, we can and do get it wrong. We fail to recognize our own biases in telling the story of the city. We misrepresent the characters. The city becomes merely the place of the storytellers, those with means and education. But the city itself does not fail in this way unless we deliberately allow it to fail by covering over the places of despair, demolishing the neighbourhoods of our shame and replacing them with the gloss and gleam of our false prosperity.

Just as with any tradition, our engagement with it requires that we take on a phenomenological position of renewal and critique, so it goes with the city. In addressing whether to preserve or make room for something new, we are called to query whether the place encourages our dwelling and whether the traditions that it supports are those we as a people choose to renew. If we take such an approach then I would wager that neighbourhoods such as Druid Hills would be less inclined to so strictly regulate what can be done to the historic houses in the neighbourhood. While the maids' walks may seem quaint, they hearken back to an era of racism and even slavery that is embedded in the landscape simply by the preservation of the name 'maids' walks' and the paths themselves. Maids' walks, then, if they are to be preserved at all, should be preserved only with an eye to transformation, acknowledgement, and reflection of a rejection of racism, rejection of extremes of an economically divided city. At the same time, as we consider the gentrification brought about by 'brave' urban pioneers, or the 'progress' brought about by the construction of an interstate, we can put in place additional policies that would reflect the need for preservation of places that support the narratives of nonwhite communities, that celebrate the once-vibrant inner-city neighbourhoods such as Summerhill, and that acknowledge the cities' poorer communities. The concord of Druid Hills's narrative should accommodate the discord of other styles and populations while the discord of shattered neighbourhoods like Summerhill can acquire more concord through more reluctance to erase their history from the landscape.

Places of the city serve as both testimony and archive. They are archival in that they preserve, often in some kind of physical form, the story of an event. They are testimonial in that they speak silently of that event without being asked. As Ricoeur (2004, 151) suggests, 'Each new building is inscribed in urban space like a narrative within a setting of intertextuality. And narrativity impregnates the architectural act even more directly insofar as it is determined by a relationship to an established tradition wherein it takes the risk of alternating innovation and repetition'. The palimpsest of the city allows for the coexistence of different ages, different histories and different communities. It can be, if we let it, a rich source of complexity for how we understand our communal selves, offering a possibility for the concord of discordance through the narrative it reveals.

If we can instead understand our cities through the language of hermeneutic narrative, we should have a method by which we can make decisions about whether and how to allow rebuilding of neighbourhoods and buildings. By stressing the embeddedness of narrative in places, but also recognizing that narrative character as one of concordant discord, we can give voice and place to a much richer and more complex conception of who we are and what we value.

NOTES

1. For more on the palimpsest of place, see Donohoe (2014).
2. See Donohoe (2017).

3. For more on these first two examples see Donohoe (2017).

4. For more on the genocidal impact of destruction of material culture, see Bevan (2006) and Turku (2017).

5. For a more complete explanation of the categorizing of types of destruction, see Donohoe (2017).

6. It is true that we have seen some change in this impetus in recent decades. Consider the New York Tenement neighbourhood or Detroit's Greektown neighbourhood.

Chapter 14

The City as a Construct of Risk and Security

Yosef Jabareen and Efrat Eizenberg

Contemporary cities appear as highly demanding entities. They are constantly thought of and reshaped by abundant and diverse social, urban, physical, economic and environmental plans and programs. What accounts for this endless production mode? What makes the contemporary city a restless and never-ending project?

To address these questions, we build on Lacan and Lacanian scholars, mainly Stavrakakis (1999; 2007), in terms of the development of the concepts of lack, desire and fantasy, and on Laclau and Mouffe's (1985) discursive social reality approach. Based on these scaffoldings, we propose a new conceptualization of the city: *the incomplete city*. We suggest that the city is a discursive social reality and that its constitutive ontology is lack.

Laclau and Mouffe (1985, 107) envisage social reality in terms of discourses, where 'every object is constituted as an object of discourse'. A discourse is the structured totality resulting from *articulating* both linguistic and nonlinguistic elements and 'is the primary terrain of the constitution of objectivity as such' (Laclau 2005, 68). Laclau and Mouffe (1985) suggest that all social subjects are the result of political and discursive processes. This does not mean 'that external reality has no independent existence' (Laclau and Mouffe 1985). However, people's perception of reality and the character of real objects is mediated entirely by discourse. Laclau (1990, 217–18) suggests that subjects are discursive, historic, open systems and cannot be viewed in 'essentialist' terms or as a 'totality'. Thus, Laclau and Mouffe's (1985) theory is suitable for understanding the struggle for social power and the struggle over meanings in general (Carpentier and Spinoy 2008) and for conceptualizing contemporary cities, in particular.

Accordingly, we assume that the city is a discursive social entity. Following Glynos and Howarth (2007), we contend that any legitimate approach
to conceptualizing the city requires at least some ontological assumptions.
Ontology proposes what types of things exist and how they exist. This perspective enables us to articulate the 'incomplete city' while remaining faithful to our ontological commitments. Our ontological framework provides
the conditions for developing an alternative approach to city theorization.
Furthermore, we identify two main logics: the logic of risk and the logic of
ontological security, which together articulate the discursive identity of the
incomplete city.

Thus, this chapter presents the concept of lack as our ontological framework and the two fundamental logics with which we articulate the incomplete
city. It begins by outlining the theory of 'lack' and applies it to the city. It
then presents the two logics and elaborates on the practices that reflect and
are attached to these logics. The final section of this chapter discusses the new
framework of the incomplete city and draws some theoretical conclusions.

THE CONSTITUTIVE LACK
OF THE INCOMPLETE CITY

Following Lacan, at the heart of our conceptualization stands the constitutive
lack, which is the ontological foundation of the incomplete city. Lacanian
theory is decidedly relevant for our social, political and spatial analysis of
contemporary cities because it offers a 'sociopolitical' conception of subjectivity, where the 'subject is equivalent to the lack which stands at the root of
the human condition' (Stavrakakis 1999, 38). Thus, we suggest that the city
is a 'lacking subject' with deep sociopolitical and spatial implications for the
way the city operates and the way we perceive it.

Lacan suggests that at the 'mirror stage', a child in its early months 'pri-
mordially identifies with the visual gestalt of his own body. In comparison
with the still very profound lack of coordination in his own motor functioning, that gestalt is an ideal unity, a salutary imago' (Lacan 2006, 113). In this
way, 'the infant acquires its first sense of unity and identity, a spatial imaginary identity' (Stavrakakis 1999, 17). It appears that from the very beginning,
we are able to conceive of our 'own failure' as an 'irreducible gap'.

The difference between the whole, total and ideal image and the fragmented
experience of the infant constitutes *lack* (Lacan 2006, 186), which must be
understood not as 'lack of this or that' but as 'the lack of being, properly
speaking' (Lacan 1988, 223). Furthermore, 'lack' is always related to desire,
and it is a lack that causes desire to arise (Lacan 1988). Thus, desire is related

to the existence of lack (Lacan 1988), a metonymy for the '*lack of being*'. The desire of being is to 'fill' the 'lack' and become 'whole' and 'complete'. Therefore, 'desire is the metonymy of the want to be' (Lacan 2006, 623).

In its fundamental use, fantasy, another central concept to Lacan, 'is the means by which the subject maintains himself at the level of his vanishing desire, vanishing inasmuch as the very satisfaction of demand deprives him of his object' (637). Thus, fantasy is what sustains the subject as desiring and is related to ontological lack. Its aim is not to ratify the fulfillment of desire but to sustain the subject's desire by telling it *how* to desire (Glynos 2001). According to Žižek, 'desire is not something given in advance, but something that has to be constructed' and articulated through fantasy (1991, 6).

In our conceptualization, we propose to understand the city as an ontologically lacking social reality. Its failures are constantly surfacing, and its 'harmony' is disrupted by various risks. Its goals always fall short from achieving. Thus, the city is in a constant state of desire for harmony and completeness. However, since the desire is never fulfilled, actions are taken regularly in the hope to fulfill it.

Desire and reality are intimately connected, and the nature of their link can only be revealed in fantasy (Stavrakakis 1999). Thus, 'when harmony is not present it has to be somehow introduced in order for our reality to be coherent', and 'it has to be introduced through a fantasmatic social construction' (62–63). The two logics that we will describe have crucial roles in generating the needed fantasmatic social constructions for introducing harmony.

Furthermore, the city as an ontologically lacking social reality is based on the Lacanian perception of 'the disruptive presence of "the real" in any symbolic order, that is, a presence that marks the impossibility of any putative fullness of being, whether at the level of structures, subjects or discourses' (Glynos and Howarth 2007, 11). The fantasy or the fantasmatic mode responds to the 'ontological lack' and its desire to become 'full' and 'complete'. Glynos and Howarth (130) suggest that fantasy, as a narrative, 'covers-over or conceals the subject's lack by providing an image of fullness, wholeness, or harmony on the one hand, while conjuring up threats and obstacles to its realization on the other'. Thus, the fantasmatic mode would 'consist of those discursive forms through which a society tries to institute itself as such on the basis of closure, of the fixation of meaning, of the non-recognition of the infinite play of differences' (Laclau 1990, 92).

Therefore, the city as a social reality is constructed around fantasies about achieving a sense of completeness, harmony or wholeness (see Gunder 2003). Thus, formally planned social and spatial programs contribute to the sense of filling the perceived voids in the city. Desires are repeatedly articulated as visions, goals and objectives aiming consciously and unconsciously to overcome its lack. However, completeness can never be achieved, as voids, gaps and disharmony are inherent to this entity. The city is like the Lacanian 'subject'; an entity that 'does not only invoke lack but also all our attempts to eliminate this lack which, however, does not stop re-emerging' (Stavrakakis 1999, 35). Stavrakakis suggests that lack continuously reemerges in the effort to consolidate the identity (35). However, all attempts to bridge the lack through identifications and to achieve a complete identity are doomed to fail. This failure repeatedly reinstates the irreducible character of the lack, which in turn reinforces attempts to address it. All efforts to fill the voids are in fact a 'circular play between lack and identification which is marking the human condition; a play that makes possible the emergence of a whole politics of the subject' (35). Similarly, we argue, this circular dynamic makes possible the emergence of the dominant logics that constitute the discursive arena of the city.

THE *JOUISSANCE*
OF THE INCOMPLETE CITY

In his *The Lacanian Left: Essays on Psychoanalysis and Politics*, Stavrakakis (2007, 182) suggests that 'the conflict between knowledge, reason, rational will, on the one hand, and irrational passions, pleasures and appetites, on the other, constitutes a central theme throughout Western theological, philosophical and political reflection'. As Žižek succinctly notes, 'today's politics is more and more about the politics of *jouissance*, concerned with the ways of soliciting or controlling and regulating *jouissance*' (quoted in Stavrakakis 2007, 181).

The city is a discursive construct with 'particular historical and *semiotic* conditions of possibility' (see Stavrakakis 2007, 193). Like nations, cities are presented as 'ours', 'our city', where a specific uniqueness characterizes our way of life. In some aspects, our enjoyment is organized around 'our city', 'the unique thing that we enjoy, that others do not have' (Žižek 1993, 201). Žižek applies the idea of enjoyment to the nation. Using the same analogy to the city, we suggest that the city 'exists only insofar as its specific enjoyment continues to be materialized in a set of social [and spatial] practices' that are continuously transmitted through urban 'myths that structure these practices' (202). Stavrakakis and Chrysoloras (2006, 157) suggest that 'what gives consistency to the discursive construction of the nation is a fantasy promising our encounter with the fullness of enjoyment located at the roots of national history'. Such enjoyment is obtained from certain practices and reproduced through our everyday life and other social and spatial practices.

Moreover, the fantasmatic mode is related to the existing mode of enjoyment and has the power to illuminate the way we perceive 'our city', ourselves, and the 'others'. The enjoyment of the residents of the city and its decision makers constructs the fantasmatic mode. There is a loyalty to an imagined city, a city of enjoyment. The lack, according to Lacan, is first of all a lack of *jouissance*, and the fantasy is the promise to overcome the lack and regain *jouissance* (Stavrakakis 1999). The lack of real enjoyment is always posited as something lost—the lost harmony and fullness. Within this mode, the need to protect our city from the 'others', for example, the immigrants, minorities or different people that are perceived as threatening the enjoyment of the city, is activated. As Žižek explains, ethnic tensions are always about 'the other' who 'wants to steal our enjoyment (by ruining our way of life)' (1993, 203).

THE LOGICS OF THE INCOMPLETE CITY

The city as a discursive social reality, we claim, is most strongly articulated through two logics: the logic of risk and the logic of ontological security. The Lacanian lack is constitutive to these two logics, thus making the city always incomplete.

The Logic of Risk

Risk is a constitutive concept of the incomplete city, since the perception of risk, or people's perceptions of risk, reproduces a persistent sense of lack by constantly impeding the *jouissance*. The discourse of social, environmental, economic and spatial risks is phenomenally broad, making the logic of risk a dominant logic of thinking and practice in today's cities. This logic captures the perception, manipulation and management of conflict over the meanings and interpretations of diverse social, environmental and security risks that every city faces. It is about uncertainty, and as such, the incomplete city always operates under uncertainty conditions.

It is true that to a certain extent, cities have always been about coping with risk, as expressed in the following words penned by Aristotle more than two millennia ago: 'Men come together in cities for security; they stay together for good life' (Blumenfeld 1969, 139). Indeed, cities have been facing environmental, health, social and security threats for centuries and have always strived to reduce risks by means of various spatial, physical, social and environmental measures (Jabareen 2015). However, with the rapid development of technology and modernity, this aspect of cities has intensified greatly, as reflected in their increasing occupation with interrogating, estimating, preventing, managing, accepting, denying and seeking to manipulate and cope with risks.

Giddens (1999) and Beck (1992) conceptualize modernity and modern societies in terms of risk. Giddens (1999) views risk as inseparable from modernity and as the mobilizing dynamic of societies that are bent on change and determined to control their own destiny rather than leaving it to religion, tradition or the whims of nature. Prior to the modern era, cultures possessed no concept of risk and 'lived primarily in the past', invoking 'ideas of fate, luck or the "will of the gods" where we now tend to substitute risk. Giddens argues that risk has replaced this kind of notion in modern, future-oriented societies interested in change. Beck (1992) defines the *risk society* in terms of risks that emerged beginning in the 1960s. Modern society, he maintains, 'has become a risk society in the sense that it is increasingly occupied with debating, preventing and managing risks that it itself has produced' (Beck 2005, 332). From his perspective, this was 'an inescapable structural condition of advanced industrialization'. For Beck, the concept of 'risk' replaces the concept of 'class' as 'the principal inequality of modern society, because of how risk is reflexively defined by actors'. The theory of the world risk society, however, maintains that modern societies are shaped by new types of risks and that their foundations are shaken by the worldwide anticipation of global catastrophes.

The logic of risk captures the conflict over the meanings and interpretations of the risk that a city may face. Each city has its own conceptions of risk based on its own understanding and interpretation of uncertainties, knowledge, political organization and values, political and market powers and resources. Risk means different things to different people depending on their social, economic and political capacities, and their political allegiances and social conditions. Risk is interpreted differently and manipulated by different people with different interests and different backgrounds. For the most part, knowledge regarding risk is questioned and challenged not only by the public but also by the experts themselves, dooming the city to operate in a shadow of unstable, challenged and incomplete knowledge. Risk is 'a virtual threat'; it is 'not an objective condition, but a social construction of reality, which starts with the question of how people explain misfortune' (Hoogenboom and Ossewaarde 2005, 606). Members of the same societal group are likely to adopt certain values and reject others, and this process of adoption and rejection is understood as determining the perceived acceptability of a risk (Snary 2004).

Therefore, social scientists have argued that risk perceptions can neither be understood nor analysed outside the social and cultural contexts in which they evolve (Douglas and Wildavsky 1982; Sommerfield et al. 2002). In this way, risk perception varies according to historical traditions and cultural beliefs, as well as political and administrative structures (Healy 2004; Jasanoff 1986; 1999; Rohrmann 2006).

From the perspective of risk, some risks may be conveniently ignored while other risks are emphasized. In this way, risk is about social power and resource allocation in our cities. In *The Risk City* (2015), Jabareen suggests that politicians typically confiscate the right to re frame risk because risk reduction and treatment entails resource allocation and consumption. Experts and scientists usually reframe risk settings as a science and powerful stakeholders typically hijack the right to reframe the acceptable level of risk. Thus, decision makers and politicians prioritize risk based on political, economic and social considerations. It would be naïve to suggest that politicians and decision makers consider scientific facts alone in their dealings with risk and the risk city. According to Beck (2006, 333), 'even the most restrained and moderate objectivist account of risk implications involves a hidden politics, ethics and morality'.

For several decades, contemporary cities have taken the lead in dealing with various risks at the local and at extra-local levels. Neither the state nor the society in general (as Beck puts it) have the capacity, organization, and urging drive (what we understand as an inherent need and desire) to put the different risks at highest priority. People are aware of global risks and sometimes even intervene and make risk mitigation their personal cause. However, people are most concerned with local risks, the risks that directly influence their life and enjoyment, the quality of the air that they breathe and the level of violence around them. Since the discourse of risk is so prevalent, life in the city is entangled with a strong sense of risk, with a perception of an imminent threat. Efforts to confront risks, which will never succeed in fully eradicating the risks, in themselves contribute to a greater awareness and preoccupation with risk.

The Logic of Ontological Security

The logic of urban ontological security captures the relatively new but existential drive of the city for inner consistency, for creating and maintaining itself a whole, as having a real substance, as offering a certain genuineness. In our elaboration of this logic, we build on R. D. Laing (1969; 1973) and Antony Giddens's (1991; 1996) concepts of ontological security. They conceive ontological security as a psychological superstructure that sustains our very basic sense of our being as real, as alive and whole, as continuous in time, as having an inner consistency, substantiality, genuineness and worth. This structure protects us from ontological insecurity, which is the disintegration of the self and which can actually be understood as schizophrenia—a state of constant but infertile battle to produce a sense of being. Laing (1969, 41) argues that the individual with a secure core is one who:

> experiences his [or her] own being as real, alive, whole; as differentiated from the rest of the world in ordinary circumstances so clearly that his identity and autonomy are never in question; as a continuum in time; as having an inner consistency, substantiality, genuineness, and worth; as spatially coextensive with the body; and, usually, as having begun in or around birth and liable to extinction with death. He [or she] thus has a firm core of ontological security.

Laing and Giddens understand ontological security as a psychological need of the everyday life, the need to experience 'being-in-the-world'. Ontological security is, then, based on the belief that a person maintains in the stability and consistency of his or her action in the world. In the extreme cases of ontologically insecure individuals, there is a lack of a consistent sense of biographical continuity and a failure to achieve an enduring conception of aliveness. In such cases, there is an obsessive preoccupation in apprehending possible risks to their existence. Giddens describes this state as 'inner deadness'.

Most people function somewhere between the firm core of ontological security and 'inner deadness'. These two poles are considered abnormalities. Thus, as Stavrakakis (1999, 29) argues, for the majority of people, the pursuit of 'the fullness of identity [. . .] introduces lack and makes identity ultimately impossible. For even the idea of identity to become possible its ultimate impossibility has to be instituted. Identity is possible only as a failed identity; it remains desirable exactly because it is essentially impossible'.

In the same way that Giddens (1996) expanded Laing's concept from an inner structure to one that is produced predominantly in relation to the outside world, we further extend it to explain the logic of contemporary urban social reality. Contemporary cities are preoccupied with having an internal identity that is whole, consistent and anchored in its historical biography. They desire to have their own substantial character that is genuine, unique and differentiated from other cities. This desire exists at the level of planners and policymakers, restlessly working to imagine this fullness of identity and take the needed measure to stand up for it. However, it is also the desire of the people to have a good match between their everyday life reality and a certain image of the place they live in. A constitutive lack, then, is at the core of ontological security, manifested by the ongoing effort to bring the different parts together into the same meaningful whole, which is the city. The 'story' of the city, its identity project, is never completed but always reinvented and reimagined; at the same time, it is always at work by adjusting unfitted pieces to the whole.

The ontological need of security is articulated in many ways. It might be mostly evident in the vision documents for the city and its branding as a certain type of city. These means are in themselves constantly updated to fit the changing reality and to stand up to other cities in the competition over uniqueness and wholeness. However, the constant maintenance of a stable and consistent whole is a vigilant task of planning and policy drafting at different scales of everyday practices. These various acts, whether yielding the intended results or not, are in themselves a firewall against an anxiety stemming from salient raptures of the wholeness, of an ongoing, well-functioning city. However, they are in fact a fixed mode of being and doing, as the task of achieving fullness and harmony never ends—hence the incomplete city.

Elsewhere we have discussed the importance of trust in urban ontological security (Jabareen et al. 2017). Trust, according to Jabareen and Carmon (2010), is based, among other things, on shared spaces with shared everyday practices, shared basic beliefs and a shared perception of the interests of the community as well as the risks and threats it faces. Residents of the city, diverse as they may be, are identified by their shared place identity—as being part of the same locale. Trust is also maintained in the city's operational and its planning apparatuses; these have an important role in keeping the city going, whole and harmonious.

For Giddens, one of the driving powers of ontological security is trust. First, a trust in others, starting from our caregivers, our parents; this is a trust that they will nurture and love us, and with the passing of years, it becomes a trust in wider social circles. Second, there is a trust in abstract systems and contemporary technologies. He writes about 'confidence in the reliability of a person or system, regarding a given set of outcomes or events, where that confidence expresses a faith in the probity or love of another, or in the correctness of abstract principles' (1991, 30).

These apparatuses and systems always lack the capacity to bring together all the different parts of the city as fitting into a consistent whole, but they are nevertheless trusted and at work. The physical environment of the city, its fabric, which is comprised of land use, building types and their organization, streets and driveways, and their hierarchy and meeting points, comprises the basic ingredients of the identity of the city, its uniqueness. Altogether, they structure the setting of everyday life of the city and determine in many different ways the habits, activities and experience of people in the city. As such, the script of the city, its 'identity', begins with these building blocks, and actions that change, improve and adjust these building blocks are constantly applied.

Urban ontological security assumes that 'identity necessitates security' and that threats to identity at the urban levels can come from various sources. These sources can be military, or environmental threats, or can also be constant threats, such as violence, crime and disinvestment as exemplifications of the logic of risk. However, the logic of urban ontological security is about maintaining a coherency of the place and its vision, making sure the achievement of a certain positive image will not be damaged, that the story will survive until there is a need to replace it with a better, stronger image. When the physical and social environment of the city are efficient in supporting the story and the experience and opportunities it unfolds, this is a state of natural attitude that dispels away all doubts and anxieties. Unfortunately, this 'equilibrium' state is a momentary disrupter in an ongoing state of disequilibrium and disruptions. There is always a better, more competitive and fitting script and more actions that are needed in order to fulfill it.

CONCLUSION

We conceptualize contemporary cities as incomplete cities—a discursive social reality that is always lacking. The incomplete city exists as a constitutive lack. As a discursive social reality, it is articulated through two main logics, that of risk and that of ontological security. These logics articulate multiple discourses around the incomplete city, among them, a dominant hegemonic discourse and various countering hegemonic discourses.

The logics of risk and of ontological security operate within 'a system of meaning' saturated with politics, situated on a ground of ongoing 'war of positions' among different peoples, groups, scientists and practitioners regarding its current conditions and future scenarios. As such, this city appears to be historical and not fixed in terms of time; it is evolutionary, instable and lacks any 'sutured totality' or 'full identity'. Thus, it is constituted as an arena of political contest and struggles between social, political and professional groups regarding the articulation of the nature of the city.

As permanently lacking, the incomplete city seeks to overcome its social, economic and environmental risks and to maintain its secure core through various social and spatial programs and practices. However, it will never achieve its desired completed identity. Indeed, it will 'continue to plan for certainty, even if we know—in our heart—that it is merely illusion and rationalization' (Gunder and Hillier 2009, 29). The search for completeness is a permanent and endless action that generates in itself new voids and complexities. In this way, the city is incomplete, as it is in a constant drive towards something, a need or a desire. These actions are in themselves a tool to overcome risk, disharmony and incompleteness—they are conceived as freedom, granted by the mere capacity to begin a new action (Arendt 1967).

Fantasy also plays a powerful role in the incomplete city. The fantasmatic mode is there to draw a trajectory for the future of the city, for possibilities of overcoming risks and achieving wholeness. Under this mode it is possible to find far-reaching fantasies, such as the 'zero-emission city' or 'cities without violence' or more modest ones, such as 'the green city'. These fantasmatic scenarios not only aim to propose overcoming the different lacks of the city but also direct the desire and teach the people how to desire and what to desire. In Lacanian terms, these fantasmatic scenarios define what the desired jouissance is and suggest the way to get there. The fantasy is related to 'harmony' and 'wholeness', which are always desired and unachievable targets. Thus, the incomplete city is about unfulfilled fantasies and desiring. However, fantasy as such helps transcend the lacking, unfitted and sometimes dire social or physical conditions of the city.

The incomplete city is always attempting to overcome its lacks through social and political practices, through representations and discourse, and through maintaining a certain fantasy. However, the continuous failure to fill the voids and bridge the gaps fuels the desire to continue and thrive for completeness. Within this cycle of failure and re-desire the city is always incomplete.

Chapter 15

Philosophies of Commensuration, Value and Worth in the Future City

Rethinking the Interdisciplinary

Michael Keith

THE ARCHITECT AND THE ECONOMIST[1]

How do we think about the future city in a fashion that owes more to academic scholarship than journalistic speculation? What are the claims made on behalf of the science of cities? The ability to gather large amounts of data, to measure behavioural patterns through indirect forms of monitoring and the technologies of the Internet of things have propelled many claims in the name of the 'smart' city. But historians of science and anthropologists of technology might warn us against the resurrection of the city as an object so easily known. They caution us against a sense of the future that is based principally on extrapolation from trends measured, however sophisticated the mechanisms of measurement or the algorithms of prediction (Urry et al. 2014).

Consequently, scholarship of the future city depends on combining different traditions and approaches of humanities, natural sciences and social science scholarship: the propensity of certain modes of commensuration between philosophies of knowledge production but also an understanding of the coexistence of different regimes of value and worth in the measure of city life. Scholarship needs to make visible the forms of irreconcilable and at times incommensurable combinations of nature and culture, competing domains of urban 'expertise', material and immaterial forms and the ethical dilemmas and choices they present to the deliberative metropolis.

Two unconnected events in the autumn of 2013 punctuated curiously some of these core questions about how cities might shape themselves in the twenty-first century in the decade that followed the global financial crisis of 2008. They exemplified a generational moment in city talk and also challenged an international audience to consider how philosophies of the emergent city make sense of the history as well as the future of the globe's metropolitan present.

The first was an exhibition in the Royal Academy of a retrospective of the work of architect and public intellectual Richard Rogers, celebrating his eightieth birthday. Rogers has been responsible for numerous signature urban interventions that range from the Pompidou Centre in Paris to the Lloyds insurance building in the City of London, the master plan of Shanghai's Pudong District and a massive new terminal at Beijing airport. He has built beautiful buildings and even more beautiful models of buildings that have never been built. He has dedicated a great deal of his time to making us think about the city as a public good; a built form and a way of life, an ethical project as much as an environmental construction. At the back of the Royal Academy, room after room was filled with diagrams, images and models but also with invocations, manifestos and calls to understand the city as a form of commons, a liberal space mapped by private property rights but also working in the name of a collective public good. The exhibition claimed that London could readily accommodate two million more people within its boundaries and ecological footprint. In the front courtyard Rogers curated an uncanny 'ready made' dwelling, appealing for creative, innovative ways to generate the two hundred thousand new homes that the United Kingdom needs to be built each year to address the current housing shortage that has since 2013 risen even higher on the national political agenda. A few years after the Royal Academy retrospective Rogers published a cross between a manifesto and an autobiography that built on the exhibition (Rogers and Brown 2017) to argue that cities should be 'places for all people', the common destiny of the globe.

When the city is seen *in toto* in this way, viewed in its entirety as some vaguely assembled form of commons, its successes and failures lie in the facility to balance public and private interests, maximize the positive externalities of the economies of scale, scope and skill that come from the creativity of the metropolis and minimize the negative externalities of pollution, rent seeking and excessive regulation. But this generic optimism is nuanced by the manifest inequalities that are fashioned in and shaped by the dynamics of urban transformation. 'In whose image the future city is to be made' is a question that takes us from Aristotle's Athens to David Harvey's landmark volume of Marxian theorizing in the 1970s (Keith 2014). The emergent city prompts us to understand the metropolis as flux, an extension of time as much as a distribution of space. So, for example, the arrival of new people in the city—international migrants in twenty-first-century London as much as rural migrants in the 'arrival cities' of the Global South—highlights the difficulties of getting this balance right. At which points do the freedoms of individual actions—cultural shapers and market makers alike—foreclose the options to rethink, repurpose or retrofit the future city, remake it as fit for another age? And how do we measure the values through which such a balancing act might be achieved, identify synergies, trade-offs and contradictions between economic prosperity, social justice, ecological sustainability and alternative narratives of the good life?

In this sort of discussion the unintended consequences of particular interventions in the externalities debate tends to be confined to occasionally esoteric corners of economic thinking, policy framing and planning practice. But in the welter of literature that asserts, invokes, supposes or far too often crassly universalizes and reifies the existence of a putatively neoliberal age, one intellectual trace influentially shaped global thinking about the logic of externalities. This was identified with the life's work of Ronald Coase, another British intellectual figure with a contrasting biography to Rogers. On 2 September 2013, this Willesden-born Nobel-Prize-winning economist, slightly older than Rogers but also a major twentieth-century figure, died at the age of 102 after coauthoring his last book *How China Became Capitalist* at the impressive age of 101. The child of public sector workers in the British postal service, life took him from a London grammar school to a prestigious chair in the Chicago School of economics. In contrast to Rogers, Coase was skeptical about the regulation of some public goods and services. After studying the role of public utilities, he published his landmark paper 'The Problem of Social Cost' in 1960, questioning the effectiveness of government intervention in the public realm, leading to his assertion that it should be possible to price externalities. In the 1991 Swedish Academy of Sciences citation for his Nobel, Coase was said to have discovered a 'new set of elementary particles in the economic system' through naming the concept of transaction costs in his 1937 paper 'The Nature of the Firm'. This insight informed the 1960 paper and led him later to suggest that minimizing transaction costs and maximizing the clarity of property rights provided an alternative frame to incentivize the use of market mechanisms to mediate the costs of the unintended consequences of utility optimizing economic behaviours. His influence is commonly credited with the growth of the law and economics movement that informs some of the key concepts and received wisdoms of economic governance today and in particular the claims that pricing signals might be more effective than state intervention in the regulation of the commons, what some economists in the twenty-first century choose at times to characterize as 'natural capital' when seeking a calculus for the value of nature. In reality, Coase himself was said to question the value of the Coase theorem; the interpretation of his own work by a subsequent generation of economists who cited his 1960 paper as evidence against state measurement and valuation of externality costs (Cassidy 2013). But he was certainly openly interested in how the logical register of economics could at times trump the arguments of legal statute and normative jurisprudential debate and—possibly apocryphally—he was at one point alleged to walk up to the nearby department of law in the University of Chicago to tell colleagues their time had come.

THE CITY OF EXPERTS

There is a self-evident sense that when an architect and economist talk of the city they might be reflecting on a shared subject made visible through very different lenses. The object made visible may be the same but the lens creates a very different figure, a figure made knowable through structures of knowledge informed by very different philosophical foundations and with very different disciplinary roots appealing to and sustaining very different forms of professional expertise. Where the values of Coasian economics were very much tied to the logic of utility maximization, the values of Richard Rogers's city links to a normative register with a very different philosophical genealogy. But what is 'value' in this contrast? And how does the act of valuation impact on the juxtaposition of values; the worth we attribute to different city futures?

One way of thinking about this might be through an understanding of how knowledge not only makes claims about the world but also performs as different kinds of *expertise*. A second way might be to think slightly more carefully about the philosophical basis through which we measure *value* in different intellectual traditions, how regimes of value and worth and the very process of valuation itself might have consequences that are powerful economically and significant ethically. In both cases we need to think about how knowledges translate between domains, how they are made commensurable between themselves or resist the process of commensuration.

We know that ways of framing the city depend on many different kinds of plausibility. Academic credentials may lend sheen in some quarters but are never sufficient. We also know that what qualifies as the sort of evidence that would falsify the claims about the future city of either Richard Rogers or Ronald Coase might look very different for each of them. How we recognize *evidence* in the disciplines of economics and architecture might map discrete intellectual cartographies. In the first part of the rest of this chapter I examine the manner in which the social construction of academic expertise on the city is germane. In the second I address how this in turn might lead us to a consideration of how we define *value* in measuring such evidence and why the notion of *commensuration* becomes central to an understanding of an emergent interdisciplinary study of city life.

PRECRISIS PERFORMANCE
AND HER MAJESTY'S TREASURY

During the Blair/Brown years of the Labour Party in government from 1997 to 2010 in the United Kingdom, the ascendance of certain forms of economic governance made themselves visible in curious ways that reflected both political power and the status attributed to different traditions of knowledge production over time. Partly in recognition of the internal politics of the government, subsequently described in detail by the two principal protagonists (Blair 2010; Brown 2017), major strands of domestic policy in domains far beyond the merely financial were dictated by the Treasury, where Brown became the longest continuously serving Chancellor of the Exchequer for two centuries. Brown's claim that Blair had willingly ceded to him the principal elements of economic and social policy was restated in his memoirs of 2017. The Treasury, invariably a powerful controller of purse strings, found enhanced legitimate reason to colonize large swathes of government.

Much of this is normally narrated through the frivolous frame of personal political rivalry. But the political land grab was also justified in terms that reflected less the history of personalities than a broader global trend in the performance of economic expertise. Tellingly, the manner in which Treasury policed its new domain was significant. Numerous reviews were commissioned on matters deemed of significance to the national interest. Notwithstanding the importance of judicial inquiries into Bloody Sunday, the death of a government scientist implicated in the search for weapons of mass destruction in Iraq and the multiple murders of a mistrusted GP, the judge-led public inquiry became much less significant in the period from 1997 to 2010. Whereas in the postwar years' 'law', when the judge-led public inquiry and a legal *modus operandi* was privileged in structuring the public interest and government policy, it became increasingly common to turn to senior neoclassical economists to examine the evidence and generate certain kinds of knowledge and policy options in shaping government interventions. Numerous reviews were commissioned by Brown's Treasury, most often headed up by an economist and commonly making visible future logics through an economist's calculus. Reviews on subjects as diverse as science research funding, low-carbon cars, mortgage debt, climate change, planning and land use, housing supply, stem cell innovation and public health research cast a wide Treasury net (H.M. Treasury 2007). In this sense economics territorialized a certain function of expertise within the mandate of the liberal state.

But more straightforwardly the generation of objective knowledge about a discrete array of social problems was funneled through the disciplinary framing of neoclassical economics and its accompanying epistemics and preceding philosophical roots. As well as allowing economics to perform in public through shaping policy, the role of Her Majesty's Treasury depoliticized *evidence*, displacing the disputatious forensic arena of the judicial inquiry, erasing the normatively problematic with the clinical reason of the dismal science.

At stake here are two connected but slightly different processes. First, the performative power of economics as a discipline may render as purely technocratic processes or phenomena that are simultaneously both analytical and normative. This is part of a global trend to use market logics to identify preferred outcomes. Economics needs consequently to be understood both in terms of the social and political context in which its credentials are established and also the consequences this has for shaping public policy. Secondly, there is a more deeply rooted historical challenge that focuses on how we come to *value* different things, objects and measurements in providing evidence through which private deliberations and public outcomes are justified. Economics itself rests fundamentally on the powerful notion of utility, a commensuration itself of accumulated indicators of usefulness whose evidential value is measured by the surrogate of behaviour. Both of these processes demand a combination of historical sensibility and philosophical reason in making sense of the shaping of the contemporary city. The first process demands an understanding of the generation of urban expertise, the second an understanding of the measurement of city values.

PROCESS 1:
Market Logics and the Generation of Expertise

Market logics and the associated pricing mechanisms can crowd out nonmarket values. As Michael Sandel has argued in numerous interventions over recent years, there are many situations when is it not appropriate to use price mechanisms to incentivize and govern behaviours. Price mechanisms make certain behaviours open to purchase by those that can afford them, ranging from tax evasion and corporate misbehaviour through to fining mechanisms used to 'nudge' parents picking up their children late from school (Sandel 2013). The former might more appropriately attract prison sentences rather than cash fines, the latter may accidentally normalize paying for proxy childcare for late school pickups.

In part this raises the core distinction between the Adam Smith of his earlier work on *Moral Sentiments* and his later work on the *Wealth of Nations*. The former was more concerned with the most logical and fair way of aggregating individual preferences and allocating values in a fashion that was fundamentally ethical. The latter was associated more directly with the role of governments, the value of competition and the imperative to privilege consumers over producers through undermining forms of political capture (Rothschild 2002). Smith saw the two works as continuous with one another. What they shared was a sense of valuing outcomes through the loosely defined philosophical notion of utility, a sense that we might measure outcomes through aggregated behaviours that served as a reliable measure of rational preferences.

Expertise thus creates its own objects through the lens of its disciplinary subject. Places and spaces are made knowable through a sense of disciplinary performativity. Famously, this is examined historically in the techno politics of development in Egypt in the landmark work of Timothy Mitchell's (2002) 'Rule of Experts'. For Mitchell, development economics was used to create its own space and logic of government intervention and state fabrication of markets where 'in each case the place and the claims of expertise are constituted in the separation that seems to open up, opposing nature to technology, reality to its representation, objects to their value, and the economy to the science of economics' (15). Modes of economic reason for 1980s Egypt became a programme of social reconstruction, liberal governmentality and international alignment as much as matters of scientific hypothesis testing.

And so the performative power of the discipline of economics rests not only on the claims to predictable truth implicit in the subject's epistemology but also on a combination of the interests that privilege its particular (utility maximizing) cognitive logic of behaviour, the institutional basis through which such expertise is articulated, and the modes of communication through which wisdoms become received.

In this context it is possible to map the structure of urban studies expertise through two slightly different lenses. The first of these is closely identified with structures of scholarly learning and privileges a conventional academic division of labour. Economists must compete with engineering, sociology, history or ecology in narrating the urban and generating social theory of the city. Economics may trump law at times, as Coase imagined, but occasionally the hubris of architects or the crisis of everyday mobility may privilege alternative ways of knowing the city and discrete urban disciplines.

The second lens foregrounds the array of more ostensibly technocratic challenges. The city needs to be governed, secured, mapped and made healthy. It is possible to draw the boundaries of urban studies slightly differently to include forms of expertise that have frequently been 'professionalized' over time and are represented by professional associations and credentializing bodies. In this sense we might speak of the 'urban professions'. They vary in status, reward, history and roots in the academy. But they share a practical and utilitarian function in academic training, as well as becoming sites for particular forms of research expertise. They would include professionals and training bodies in the fields of—*inter alia* but not exclusively—the study of housing, town planning and development control, architecture, chartered surveying, civil engineering, policing, transport planning, health planning and local government. In the British tradition such institutions are frequently institutionalized by their roots in the industrial city and the sovereign's seal of approval as with the Royal Institute of British Architects (founded in 1834, Royal Charter in 1837), the Royal Institute of Chartered Surveyors (founded in 1868, Royal Charter in 1881) and even the Royal Town Planning Institute (founded in 1914, Royal Charter in 1959).

These institutions create their own regimes of measuring value and worth. And, as Espeland and Stevens note (1999), struggles are often found at the borderlands of institutional influence over how commensurable these regimes might be. Struggles over commensuration—how we measure the city—may be surrogates for this struggle, reflecting and resisting forms of institutional power. Commensuration in this sense reflects and resists forms of institutional power. Claims about the incommensurable are often to be found at the borderlands of institutional spheres; commensuration 'transforms qualities into quantities, difference into magnitude' (332 and 316).

So in terms of a philosophy of the city it is possible to understand the urban as a subject that is made knowable differently by a range of these forms of scholarship both disciplinary and technocratic. For example, Ebenezer Howard and the optimists of the land use planning decades of the early twentieth century might have made claims for the strengths of their own ways of thinking about city futures, but their claims on the imaginations of politicians and publics alike were generally diminished by the rising skepticism around the well-ordered city. The city of planners may have reached its peak in the postwar years of the mid-twentieth century, a time in both its socialist and European liberal formations when planners more often trumped economists. The tide of disciplinary futures may both ebb and flood.

PROCESS 2:
On the Measurement of City Values

The links between the origins of social scientific reason and agglomerations of large numbers of people in the industrial metropolis have long been noted by historians of ideas. The city was in part where *the social* was explored, invented and subjected to various forms of governmental intervention (Rose and Osborne 1999). But the city was also the site where the phenomena that would be measured by social science were to be counted and numbered. For feminist historian Mary Poovey, the first industrial cities were where the 'modern fact' was discovered and defined in terms of how 'knowledge was understood so that it seemed to consist of both apparently non-interpretative (numerical) descriptions of particulars and systemic claims that were somehow derived from those particularized descriptions' (1998, xii). In part this reveals that numbers are never preinterpretative or noninterpretative. What should be counted and how we count are clearly constitutive to the foundations of knowledge making. But equally how we attribute numbers to values and values to numbers is always worthy of examination in and of itself in its specific historical and geographical context.

The historical procedures of double-entry bookkeeping, land ownership and political economy all involve regimes of numbers that on close inspection demand that we rethink the nature of *evidence*. Historical roots for Poovey are uncovered by an understanding of the foundations of merchant trading practice and situated reason that were later realized at the heart of the enlightenment project and the fountainhead of the British empiricist tradition. In the writing of scholars such as Francis Bacon (and also Robert Boyle and Thomas Hobbes), writing in the shadow of the seventeenth-century English civil war (and regicide) and the foundation and their engagement in the Royal Society (founded in 1663), a notion emerges that one should try to gather data free of theory but that 'all knowledge should be formulated in such a way as to serve the state which, in a period in which both religious and epistemological heterodoxies proliferated, meant supporting the monarch's ability to adjudicate and judge what counted as truth'. This doubled sense of simultaneous plurality of theoretical reason and an attempt to free data of theory is the heart of what Poovey describes as the paradoxical character of the modern fact (95 and 97–98).

In a similar register to Poovey, Desorisières has argued that the history of statistical reasoning invariably implicates relations between science and the state. More powerfully, he suggests that this creates 'a political space (that) involves and makes possible the creation of a space of common measurement, within which things may be compared, because the categories and encoding procedures are identical' (9, and quoted in Adkins and Lury 2012). Desorisières's space of comparison has informed a lively trend within the new economic sociology of the last decade (Callon and Muniesa 2005; MacKenzie et al. 2007; Muniesa 2012; 2017; Stark 2011b) that has considered how in the modern world there is a proliferation of information, data, calculative and other research instruments, measurements and valuations that may become recursive in their actions and consequences, something of profound importance in making sense of the 2008 global financial crisis (Adkins and Lury 2012). Drawing on a Callonian sense of the economy as produced, performed and curated, Muniesa suggests that in the world of financial services financial valuation was neither objective nor subjective but a practical activity, and moreover an activity that was openly performative in character (2012). He characterizes the work of ratings and analysis agencies such as Fitch, Moody's and Standard & Poor's when valuing anything from corporate entities to national economies authoring financial valuations involving practical processes that recursively generate value. These processes 'think of value as an activity rather than a thing, but also shows how this activity is itself a source of (economic) value' (Adkins and Lury 2012, 8).

In the last two decades a wider genre of social inquiry has developed a new consideration of categories value and worth that in part returns to measures of value in some of the founding texts of social inquiry such as Marx, Durkheim and Weber but also translate the registers of value into this new economic sociology (Beckert and Aspers 2011; Espeland and Stevens 1999; Çalışkan and Callon 2009; Lamont 2012; Stark 2011a). In their interest in regimes of value and worth, economic sociologists such as Lury, MacKenzie and Stark make the point that the topological interdependencies of social and economic worlds are intimately connected to the formation, legitimation and efficacy of institutions of calculability (Lury et al. 2012). These regimes of value and worth might lead us back towards the grounds of Desorisières's space of comparison. When trying to make sense of city futures there is an inevitable urge to make commensurable different regimes of value in the act of combination; combining both the different sources of expertise (historically contingent as they may be) alongside the available modes of scientific knowledge. So from the smallest unit to the grand plan, attempts to *design* the city necessarily invoke many different skills and many different values. For example, drawing liberally on the social theory of Peter Sloterdijk, Bruno Latour (2008) has asserted that we need to understand five principles of such design that combine humility, attentiveness to detail, a recognition that the tabula rasa is a fiction in any urban context, and understanding that design always invokes symbolic meanings, and an ethical as well as a functional question. Latour and Sloterdijk echo the two-thousand-year-old principles of the Roman architect Vitruvius who suggested that every building can be assessed by three different measures of 'value': durability, utility and beauty. We may measure a building by its capacity to last (*firmitas*), a measure of whether it is functionally fit for purpose (*utilitas*), or how beautiful it is (*venustas*). But these are very different measures. They are not always commensurable one with another; we may privilege one over the other two depending on our choice, and the basis for the evaluation may change over time as public preferences shift, catalysing demands for adjustment in the urban system.

Of great significance for the new urban sciences, this dilemma of commensuration is central to a scholarship of future cities; how they are planned, how they shape themselves autonomously and how they might be shaped by others, deliberately or accidentally. In the city, autonomous mutation, strategic and tactical interventions and disruptive technologies all share a propensity to generate emergent urbanisms and set up puzzles of metropolitan commensuration that are simultaneously analytical, instrumental and ethical. They demand an understanding both of how technology disrupts the logics of city form and urban life, and how we make visible and try to make commensurable the DNA of such logics in urban transformations that are always simultaneously economic, social and cultural.

For some, commensuration should be central to the academic labour that makes such combinations functionally possible and instrumentally optimal. The economist Amartya Sen is perhaps most famous for his attempt to recognize the radical incompatibility of certain measures of the good life and his analytical structure of a regime of *capabilities* that brings together different measures of the moral significance of individuals' capability of achieving the kind of lives they have reason to value, an approach that has become central to development studies scholarship and practice. Sen's approach has attempted to bridge philosophical foundations and economic reason and has found social theoretical echoes in the philosophy of Martha Nussbaum, her attempt to catalogue the unequal freedoms of women within a developmental context and the imperative to synthesize different measures and values of the good life (Sen 1979; 1999; 2009; Nussbaum 2000; 2004; 2006).

Philosophically, capabilities debates in the 2000s moved significantly from roots in Sen's attempts to synthesize different measures of the good life in pursuing 'development' to major philosophical literatures on the relative ordering of different capabilities and the variously intuitionist, procedural, Aristotelian and communitarian strategies through which such valorizations might be generated. There is no argument here about the importance or validity of such discussion. In a sense, it is a form of writing back the economic reasoning of Sen, almost *post hoc*, into the philosophical traditions that preceded it. Reading the literatures of the early 2000s a decade later, it has the appearance of a genealogy after the fact.

But it is instead the intention to suggest that alongside attempts to make different regimes of evidence commensurable we can also trace what is epistemologically incommensurable. It might be helpful in distinguishing the alternative genealogies of justifications, a consideration of how knowledges *perform* as well as they *predict* and *analyse* (Boltanski and Thevenot 2006). Callonian new economic sociology has highlighted the performativities of economic reason, how in some senses economists 'make markets' (MacKenzie and Muniesa 2007), the economy becomes a discursive object through which actions, practices and institutions might be justified. This powerful strand of social science literature does not always recognize that the same epistemological choreography can work for other measures of value and worth. We need to consider how regimes of value and worth are tied to histories and sociologies of justification that look backwards to the city that has arrived as well as to scientific models that attempt to predict the city that is yet to come. Looking both ways demands an analysis of the sorts of evidence that counts in academic analysis.

To recognize the performative dimensions of knowledge production is to say nothing—either positively or negatively—about dilemmas, configurations and shibboleths of cultural or epistemic relativism. It is instead to suggest a methodological exercise to analyse the performative power of particular statements that are made and knowledge claims advanced in the idiom of specific urban disciplines, akin to the *performative* rather than the *constative* elements of Austinian speech acts. Whether the chartered surveyor is right or the risk analyst measured probabilities accurately or mistakenly are different kinds of questions than those forms of study that consider whether chartered surveyors or risk analysts are listened to more carefully in deliberative arenas that shape tomorrow's cities. How we test our hypotheses about whether chartered surveyors or risk analysts are more powerful in the corridors of city power says nothing either way about whether chartered surveyors' or risk analysts' ways of representing, knowing, measuring and counting the world are more accurate. It speaks instead to the powers of different kinds of expertise.

In this sense we may need to be both imaginatively creative—in the spirit of Sen and others—in making different knowledge forms commensurable. At the same time we may demand a Kantian skepticism about the moments at which such commensurability is counterproductive. Is it truly valuable to consider the city commons—so valorized by Richard Rogers, so analytically dissected by Ronald Coase—as 'natural capital', measured, valued and priced in instruments that reconcile some innately contradictory forms of calculability? In each case we need to ask what constitutes evidence, not just whether economics trumps law, engineering trumps climate science or architecture trumps planning; let alone how we generate systems that synthesize each pair or all six measures of value simultaneously in the complex systems of systems that constitute the socio-technical metropolis of the twenty-first century.

RETHINKING THE INTERDISCIPLINARY:
On Returning to the Exchange between
the Economist and the Architect

When scholarly disciplines sit in an uneasy relationship with one another through alternative definitions of value, then how do they compete in a defence of disciplinary truth? If economics can use cognitive behaviourism and measures of utility to trump the moral order of legal reasoning, then how might alternative truths constitute themselves and be considered legally viable? And when epistemological diversity is the source of radically different measurements of 'value' and 'worth' how are the numbers, information and results of different traditions of scholarly inquiry rendered equivalent, comparable, measurable and tradable? Commensuration is the process through which different forms of information are transformed into comparable measurement or data. But how does a new urban science think seriously about the procedures through which the multiple forms of data are rendered comprehensible as *evidence* without succumbing to the disciplinary sovereignty of any particular regime of valuation?

In an engaged practice that describes itself as 'Forensic Architecture', a group of contemporary research architects proffers one answer to this question. They consider how new forms of data (big and small), information, imagery, testimony and digitized matter constitute themselves through the built environment in an argument about the nature of *forensis*; the practice through which evidence is shaped and the arenas in which such evidence is contested. The initiative, led by Eyal Weizman, uses architectural tools and techniques to reconstruct contested events and consider how novel forms of information can be generated and structured in a fashion that might enter legal contest.

In an exhibition at the ICA in the spring of 2018 in London, the Forensic Architecture team curated a consideration of the 'the modes and means by which incidents are sensed and evidence is presented'. In this setting, 'aesthetic considerations traverse all dimensions of forensic operation'; the philosophical foundations of law are shaped by narrative forces that transcend the merely epistemological.

In a series of stunning interventions the forensic architecture programme used the medium of architectural practice to consider arenas in which hard truths are remembered, recorded and reconstructed in an array of contexts damaged by massive injustice and abuses of human rights. From a racist murder in Kassel in Germany, through systemic state erasure of Palestinian land rights and illegal shelling in Gaza, through the testimony fashioned reconstruction of a Syrian torture cell, to the meticulous fabrication of the city landscape from which forty-three Mexican students were extracted and disappeared in Ayotzinapa, the team uses data mining, images scraped from the Internet, testimonies of victims, the lies of state actors and the truths spoken by objects to create a forum through which the past can be understood; events can speak through data.

The cultures which make visual data, reconstruct and make visible computer-aided design models, simulations, and real-time reconstructions of time and place generate a set of fields and forums through which we can reimagine how past matter speaks back to the present day. Fields and forums, fields the sites of investigation, forums the places where the results of investigation are presented and contested. The field is a dynamic and elastic space, the forum a composite apparatus that is constituted as a shifting triangulation between a contested object or site, 'an interpreter tasked with translating the language of things, and the assembly of a public gathering'. For Weizman '*forensis* thus establishes a relation between the animation of material objects and the gatherings of political collectives' (2014, 9). Digital recording equipment, satellite imaging, platforms for data sharing, open-sourced material and state recording of phone logs, witness statements, and signaling and communication networks, commonly accompanied by geospatial data with time signatures, all generate diverse categories of information that can (at times contentiously) be assembled as evidence.

As argued in this chapter, philosophically the city is a socio-technical system that is made visible as an object of knowledge that is in turn the function of disciplinary lenses that measure *value* differently. Ronald Coase and Richard Rogers both found fame, but their generation of influence peaked at a moment where economics more often than not trumped law. Coase's foundation of the law and economics and movement, its eponymous journal and his role in the Mont Pelerin Society privileged economic reasoning on the public stage and played a pivotal role in postwar twentieth-century public life (Davies 2014; Gane 2014; Mirowski 2014; Steadman-Jones 2012), translating the ordoliberalism of the victims of Hitler and Stalin into the received public policy nostrums of Reagan and Thatcher. Their practices of valuation, spawned in the mid-twentieth century, privileged the logic of utility optimizing, the philosophy of cognitive rationalism and behaviourist empiricism as a primary source of *evidence*.

And so the notion of commensuration is historically important because of how it served this territorialization of expertise. It is philosophically important because it frames the fundamentals of a discussion of how things might be otherwise.

Commensuration worked to translate other disciplinary fields of value and worth into economic reason. The legal setting of *forensis* asks the questions of scholarship differently. In part, forensic architecture asks the question what kinds of evidence should have traction in a digital age? How might different forms of data and information, different regimes of value and worth, measure what matters when generating truth that is mediated between sensing objects and sensing subjects? Commensuration philosophically becomes material as much as epistemological; the interdisciplinary domain of the urban a philosophical matrix, materially constituted and rhetorically contested.

This way of thinking might make us configure the interdisciplinary slightly differently. If we ask questions such as 'what constitutes evidence in the disciplines of sociology, anthropology or history as much as in environmental studies, transport studies and engineering', then we might in turn engage in a debate about how regimes of value and worth might be more than justifications of certain genres of knowledge production. We might begin to think differently about when such regimes are commensurable and when their very incommensurability becomes the start of interdisciplinary dialogues rather than the teleological end point of interdisciplinary synthesis.

NOTE

1. With thanks to William Davies, Keith Jacobs and Cathy Mcilwaine for helpful comments on this chapter. This article was completed with support from the PEAK Urban programme, funded by UKRI's Global Challenge Research Fund, Grant Ref: ES/P011055/1. All mistakes are, of course, the author's alone.

Chapter 16

Multiplying Resistance

The Power of the Urban in the Age of National Revanchism

Asma Mehan and Ugo Rossi

In his book *The Rebirth of History*, Alain Badiou has written that in the uprisings of the Arab world in 2011 one can discern echoes of the revolutions of 1848 in Europe. For Badiou (2012), the uprisings of the early 2010s herald a worldwide resurgence in the liberating forces of the masses. In popular uprisings, the act of rebellion originates from widespread willingness to resist injustice and extend power to the masses. In this context, urban space provides the platform, the living infrastructure for liberating the political potential of mass uprisings. As Erik Syngedouw puts it: 'the emergence of political space [. . .] unfolds through a political act that stages collectively the presumption of equality and affirms the ability of "the People" to self-manage and organise its affairs' (2014, 131). Swyngedouw uses the phrase 'Every revolution has its square' to make sense of the revolutionary value of urban space for recent social movements across the world (Swyngedouw 2011). From this perspective, there is no restoration of national sovereignty that can be invoked in response to the crisis of Western-dominated globalization, since the nation-state with its hierarchical organization does not offer room for a radical transformation of society.

The proliferation of urban insurgencies since 2011 is rather a sign of the return to a street politics of emancipation showing the continued relevance, even the centrality, of urban public space in political terms. What is specific of urban public space that leads us to postulate its primary importance? French writer Érik Orsenna once wrote a dystopian story of an island city where a dictator prohibited his people from climbing the surrounding hills, fearing that once the inhabitants could view the world beyond they would begin to question the king's absolute power (Orsenna 2004). In other words, once the people view the world, their encounters lead them to rebel against the dictator. In this sense, it can be assumed that urban public space has the

233

power to propitiate unplanned encounters and, in doing so, to offer unexpected possibilities for a communal life.

Moreover, revolutionary situations that emerge in urban settings 'naturally' tend to mobilize people from all levels of society. Historically, this propulsive force of the urban has shown itself vital in organizing and carrying out large-scale change. In his book *Life as Politics*, Asef Bayat has described what he calls the 'epidemic potential' of protesting on the street, this latter being understood as a 'space of movement and flow', in bringing together the 'invitees' and the 'casual passersby' (2010, 13). Bayat goes on to describe the location of Revolution Street—a site of many protests during the Revolution in Tehran—as 'a unique juncture of the rich and the poor, the elite and the ordinary, the intellectual and the lay-person, the urban and the rural'. In this interpretation, Bayat conceives of 'Street Revolution' as the prevalent phenomenon that happened in Tehran, Cairo and Istanbul where the crowd can easily gather (161–70). In this definition, the political 'community' is always in a process of becoming: never stable, always open to the future, always resisting the forces that repress and impede 'the whole of freedom' (Deleuze 1966, 112–18). So to achieve a 'new community whose members are capable of a belief in themselves, in the world and in becoming', we need both 'creativity' and 'the people' (Deleuze 1995, 176).

In this sense, what is customarily defined—in the US context—'the resistance' to Trump's chauvinistic populism (Cobb 2018) needs to be grounded in the street-level experience of urban public space, of its established order as well as of its possibilities for a 'reversal of perspective', as Raoul Vaneigem (2001) would put it, aimed at a reappropriation of life. In the global occupy movement and in the protests that swept across the Middle East in the early 2010s, street politics became the proverbial 'center stage' upon which people voiced their discontent with the current political situation and demanded democracy (Mehan 2017a, 167).

In this chapter, we evaluate the politically generative dynamic of urban space. Notably, we put forward the notion of the 'multiplier effect' of the urban, referring to its ingrained tendency to multiply resistance to oppression and violence being exerted against subaltern groups and minorities and, in doing so, to turn this multiplied resistance into an active force of social change. We therefore look at the twofold valence of 'resistance': negative and affirmative. Resistance initially takes form as a defensive response to oppression and violence. When this happens, the urban becomes the living platform for a multiplying dynamic of encounter and, potentially, of intergroup solidarity, thus laying the foundations for a cooperative—rather than competitive, as in neoliberal rationality, or inimical, as in national-populist reason—way of 'being together'. After having developed this argument against the backdrop of the women's movement in Tehran and the urban disobedience to anti-immigration policy in Italy, our chapter concludes by reflecting on the multiplier effect of urban resistance within the current context of national revanchism.

THE MULTIPLIER EFFECT
OF RESISTANCE IN URBAN SPACE

In an inspired foreword to the English-language edition of the *Anti-Oedipus*, Deleuze and Guattari's first joint work, Michel Foucault argued that their book could be conceived as an 'Introduction to the Non-Fascist Life' under-stood—he explained—as an 'art of living counter to all forms of fascism, whether already present or impending' (1983, xiii). In order to achieve a 'non-fascist life', Foucault identified 'a number of essential principles' ca-pable of orienting action that he had acquired from Deleuze and Guattari's book, including the following two that look particularly remarkable from the perspective of this text:

> Withdraw allegiance from the old categories of the Negative (law, limit, castra-tion, lack, lacuna) [. . .] Prefer what is positive and multiple, difference over uniformity, flows over unities, mobile arrangements over systems. Believe that what is productive is not sedentary but nomadic.
> [. . .] Do not demand of politics that it restore the "rights" of the individual, as philosophy has defined them. The individual is the product of power. What is needed is to "de-individualize" by means of multiplication and displacement, diverse combinations. (xiii)

In this commentary, Foucault looks radically different from the kind of neo-Weberian theorist, analysing power relationships as an infallible iron cage, subtly seduced by aspects of liberal and even neoliberal thought that in recent times revisionist scholarship has associated with him (Zamora and Behrent 2016). On the contrary, his work along with that of Gilles Deleuze and Felix Guattari, as well as of other critics of capitalist modernization of that time, such as situationist theorist Raoul Vaneigem (see below in this section), provides us with essential insights into the conceptualization of resistance. These authors enable us to understand resistance simultaneously as a refusal of the negative (fascism in the form of today's authoritarian populism) and as an opportunity to experiment with a different use of life aimed at recreating a shared sense of 'we' (Virno 2015).

What does 'nonfascist life' mean today? With the political ascent of Donald Trump after his unexpected election in 2016, the idea of a return of fascism has become increasingly recurrent within public debates in the United States and elsewhere. What kind of fascism are we talking about? As Foucault underlines, by fascism it is not meant a repetition of the historical fascism of the 1930s, but the 'fascism in us all, in our heads and in our everyday behavior, the fascism that causes us to love power, to desire the very thing that dominates and exploits us' (Ibid.). Resistance to new forms of fascism, therefore, has to be found in the realm of everyday life, where the negative can be reversed into an affirmative reappropriation of a communal usage of life. Becoming a resistant, in this perspective, is a process that is not confined to the embrace of an ethical stance, represented for instance by an atomized act of indignation (Invisible Committee 2015), but requires a collective praxis that at the same time arises from and engages with our daily life through connection with others (Ahmed 2017).

Deleuze and Guattari's *Anti-Oedipus* as well as their sequel on 'Capitalism and Schizofrenia', *Thousand Plateaus*, can be used as a primer for collectively resisting the fascistization of the public sphere that we are observing in today's national-populist era. A central notion in their conceptual framework is that of multiplicity. This notion allows an understanding of the different ways in which the multiplication of resistance that we associate with urban space can transform oppression and violence against ethnic minorities and subaltern groups into a life politics of emancipation. In the introduction to this text, our starting point has been that emancipatory politics primarily originates in urban settings as urban public space serves as the key theater of contentions. In fact, as Asef Bayat argues: 'conflict originates from the active use of public space by subjects who, in the modern states, are allowed to use it only passively—through walking, driving, watching—or in other ways that the state dictates' (2010, 11). It is urban street politics that can give rise to what Raoul Vaneigem defined 'a reversal of perspective': a subjective gesture that enables the oppressed becoming a resistant to detect 'the positivity of negation' (2001, 185). In Vaneigem's view, a reversal of perspective arises from the desire to reappropriate everyday life in its entirety: 'in the sights of my insatiable desire to live, the whole of Power is merely one target in a wider horizon', Vaneigem contends (188).

The question is now: how can a subjective 'desire to live' be turned into a larger emancipatory project? In this vein, this chapter aims to assess the political potential in the multiplier effect of the urban, namely how this multiplier effect can lead to a lasting project of emancipation in which cities become major sites of resistance to today's national-populist revanchism. There is no unitary pathway to emancipation, however, within a multiplicity-oriented understanding of radical politics. Pursuing multiplicity through street politics aspires to move beyond both the monism and the pluralism of standard political theory with their universalizing assumptions, as regards the identification of the revolutionary 'subject' in political-ontological terms (Žižek 1999) or that of the decision-making process enabling conflicting organizations to conform to the general interest (Dahl 1978), respectively. In *Thousand Plateaus*, the sequel to *Anti-Oedipus*, Deleuze and Guattari refined their understanding of multiplicity in a social-productive fashion by putting forward their famous notion of rhizome, as opposed to the Freudian sense of unity and identity symbolized by a 'tree or root, which plots a point, fixes an order' (Deleuze and Guattari 1987, 7). Deleuze and Guattari believe in a processual understanding of rhizomatic multiplicity: 'the multiple must be made, not by always adding a higher dimension, but rather in the simplest of ways, by dint of sobriety, with the number of dimensions one already has available—always n - 1 (the only way the one belongs to the multiple: always subtracted). Subtract the unique from the multiplicity to be constituted; write at n - 1 dimensions. A system of this kind could be called a rhizome' (6). This leads them to define 'the principle of multiplicity' as follows: 'it is only when the multiple is effectively treated as a substantive, "multiplicity", that it ceases to have any relation to the One as subject or object, natural or spiritual reality, image and world. Multiplicities are rhizomatic, and expose arborescent pseudo-multiplicities for what they are. There is no unity to serve as a pivot in the object, or to divide in the subject' (8).

The next two sections of this chapter will provide illustrative evidence of some ways in which the process of cities becoming multiplicities through resistance can take place. As anticipated, we will look at the resurgence of the women's movement in the MENA (Middle East and North Africa) region, focusing especially on the insurgence of Iranian women in Tehran, and at the urban disobedience to anti-immigration policy in Italy.

WOMEN'S LIVES MATTER:
Girls of Revolution Street

In 2017, the day after US president Donald Trump's inauguration, the civil rights movement and the LGBTQ movement—a very diverse group of women—organized the Women's March on Washington and hundreds of sister marches across the country and around the globe that brought millions to the streets for a historic day of protest (Schnall 2017). The Women's March had the momentum to build a resistance across the United States. Following from that, in January, protesters flooded US airports by the thousands in the chaos that followed President Trump's first executive order, which banned citizens from seven Muslim-majority countries from entering the United States, as well as indefinitely halting the entry of Syrian refugees.[1] As the Women's March drives the resistance against the Trump administration, the #MeToo and #TimesUp movements have reached an unprecedented level of collective engagement against the commodification and victimization of women as sexual objects and the gendered power differentials that persist in ways that gravely constrain the lives of girls and women everywhere.

In the MENA region, and especially in most Muslim-majority republics in the Caucasus and Central Asia of the Soviet and post-Soviet times (such as Azerbaijan and Uzbekistan), the women's movement has been intertwined with patriarchal and patrimonial patterns. Except for Tunisia, Turkey and to some extent Morocco, egalitarian reforms in family law, whether by revising and reinterpreting sharia law or by replacing it with secular law, have been painfully slow (Tohidi 2016, 78). Here, it is important to note that the type of collective actions practiced mostly in the democratic settings, which have come to dominate our conceptual universe as the women's movements, may not deliver under nondemocratic/authoritarian conditions (Bayat 2007, 160). In many authoritarian Middle Eastern states, such as Egypt, Sudan, Saudi Arabia or the Islamic Republic of Iran, where conservative Islamic laws are in place, the state's gender ideology is grounded in the culture of patriarchy (which is entrenched in religious authoritarian polity), and justified by the patriarchal interpretation of Islam's holy sources (Barlow and Akbarzadeh 2008, 23). In an authoritarian and repressive context, 'collective activities of a large number of women organised under strong leadership, with effective networks of solidarity, procedures of membership, mechanisms of framing, and communication and publicity—the types of movements that are associated with images of marches, banners, organisations, lobbying, and the like', are not feasible (Bayat 1997, 162).

Focusing on the discourse of solidarity, social movements can be defined as the 'organised set(s) of constitutes pursuing a common political agenda of change through collective action' (Batliwala 2012, 3; Mehan 2017b). In this interpretation, women's movements aim to bring women into political activities, empower women to challenge the roles they serve and create networks among women that heighten women's ability to recognize gender relations that are in dire need of change (Ferree and McClurg Muller 2004, 577). In March 2018, thousands of Turkish women flocked to Istanbul's iconic and pedestrianized İstiklal (or Independence) Avenue, for this year's International Women's Day demonstration to demand greater rights and denounce violence. Women chanted slogans including 'We are not silent, we are not scared, we are not obeying' and 'Women are strong together'. In the following weeks, women's rallies were also held in Ankara and the southeastern province of Diyarbakır.[2] In a similar way, across the Arab-speaking world, the popular uprisings in 2011 showed Arab women in countries like Tunisia and Jordan that they could push for legislative advances through cross-border solidarity. In the Middle East, while Saudi Arabia lifted its ban on women driving, women have been at the forefront of pushing for change in Iran. Feminist Bettina Aptheker has discussed the significance of the 'dailyness' or 'ordinariness' of women's resistance (Aptheker 1989).

Deploying the 'power of presence' over the past three decades, Iranian women have refused to be pushed out of the public domain. In Iran, as the result of a social media campaign which was initially called My Stealthy Freedom (which was a Facebook campaign back to 2014), by using the hashtag #whitewednesdays, every Wednesday, images of Iranian women, hair uncovered and hijabs held aloft, pop up in social media.[3]

As we said in the previous section, in popular uprisings resistance starts as a response to oppression and violence, setting in motion a larger process of insubordination that can lead to life emancipation. In this context, we have assumed that the urban acts as a multiplier, possibly turning single acts of rebellion into larger uprisings. Women's antisystemic movement in Iran is illustrative of the multiplying dynamic of resistance that is only possible in an urban context. Dense urban environments of metropolises like Tehran possess unique junctions in the form of parks, streets and squares where the encounter between different inhabitants of the city—what in the introduction we defined as 'invitees' and 'casual passersby'—can turn small protests into insurrections. Tehran expanded its spatiality of revolutions and discontents through recent protests—specifically, the Islamic Revolution of 1979 and the Green Movement of 2009. The recent women's movement highlighted the sociopolitical importance of the Revolution (in Persian: *Enghelab*) Street and Freedom (in Persian: *Azadi*) Square in building and representing spaces of protests in modern Tehran. This venue in the heart of current Tehran provides accessibility in people's everyday life. However, its unique centrality, accessibility and distinctive value for national political memory have transformed this place into one of the most important venues for political gatherings in Iranian modern history.

In today's new wave of women's activism in Iran, bareheaded Iranian women climb on platforms and benches in public spaces to protest daily against their lack of bodily autonomy and compulsory veiling (hijab).[4] These protests were originally inspired by an Iranian woman known for standing out on the utility box in the Enghelab (Revolution Street) in Tehran on 28 December 2017. The young protesters—known as 'daughters of the revolution'—tied their white scarves to the end of poles and waved their hijab flag to protest. According to Homa Hoodfar, 'the struggle is not about a piece of cloth on a woman's head, it is about the gender politics that cloth symbolises, and its use to silently and broadly communicate a rejection of state control over women's bodies' (Hoodfar 2018). After that act of insubordination, the women reenacted her protest (and posted photos of their actions), being branded as the 'Girls of Revolution Street' on social media.

In this respect, the solidarity-action frame became dominant because of the activists' push for equality among all women involved in the fight for freedom. This led activists to build inclusive alliances with one another because of their collective desire for equality. As Fielding-Smith well noted, when the revolution came, no one asked about anyone's background, religious affiliation, political affiliation, regional affiliation and ethnicity (2011). The imagery of rhizomes in which centerless assemblages formed by members who engage in horizontal and nonhierarchical relations describes these revolutionary dynamics. Such organ-less bodies are all made up of a multitude of individuals that can act quite effectively as a mass without any centralized leadership. From this perspective, in order to demand democracy under authoritarian conditions, 'becoming a resistant' is prerequisite. This process of becoming involves 'people to come' who are missing or lacking in the actual world and who 'have a chance to invent themselves' by resisting what is intolerable in the present (Deleuze and Guattari 1994, 110). In this interpretation, if we consider urban society and democracy as elements that are struggling to emerge, resistance movements can be viewed as essential manifestations of the constitutive dimension of politics (Elkin 1985). In this sense, subaltern groups and minorities who experience oppression and violence are not mobilizing in order to pursue defined ends, but are mobilizing primarily in order to assert the power of their presence in the public sphere (Phillips 1998), the ends being the assertion of themselves as a 'willful subjectivity', obstinately speaking out against injustices (Ahmed 2017). This vocal politics of presence is at the heart of street-level resistance turning small-scale insubordination into larger insurrections against authoritarian power.

MIGRANT LIVES MATTER:
Cities Against and Beyond
the National Fetish

In the current context of nationalist revanchism endangering liberal democracies, cities and their social environments are increasingly viewed as bastions of resistance nurtured by an everyday, cross-sectional politics of solidarity. In Europe, as well as in North America, after the economic recession of the late 2000s and the early 2010s, with its impact on urban societies in terms of job losses and public-budget cutbacks, recent years have seen a reenergized localist politics in the form of a radical municipalism, or 'communalism'. The experience of Barcelona, where the previous leader of the anti-eviction movement was elected mayor with the support of a grassroots coalition named 'Barcelona en comù', is exemplary in this respect. The pro-immigrant 'sanctuary cities' movement, which has intensified after the election of Donald Trump in 2016, as well as the Black Lives Matter mobilizations that started in 2013 in response to the killings of unarmed African Americans in different US cities, are other key manifestations of the political vitality of cities and urban social movements.

On a theoretical level, municipalism draws inspiration from the work of ecological anarchist Murray Bookchin (1992), which is now continued by contemporary radical theorists, such as Michael Hardt and Antonio Negri (2017). Today's idea of 'new municipalism' invites to get rid of any nostalgia for the nation-state and to resume the local scale as 'the space of the common', of solidarity and resistance to neoliberal austerity, through a decentered network (refusing centralized leadership) of community-based assemblies and councils. While liberal advocates of city-based empowerment place at the centre of their localist project the role of political and economic leaders in taking the lead in civic coalitions and public-private partnerships (Barber 2013; Katz and Nowak 2017), municipalists look at leaderless alliances comprising both social movements and city administrators who share a belief in an intersectional politics of solidarity among subaltern minorities. Undocumented migrants, ethnic and racial minorities and a revitalized women's movement are at the heart of this politics of solidarity in today's reactionary moment in which a male-dominated ethnic-majority revanchism has become politically prevalent in a growing number of countries across the globe.

The political potential of neomunicipalism associated with what we define here as the 'multiplier effect' of the urban can be appreciated by taking a closer look at the current political situation in Italy. In this country, the general election of March 2018 resulted in a political impasse that lasted two months and was resolved through a coalition government formed in June 2018 by the League and the Five Star Movement, two parties variously associated with the new populist tide. The former is a regionalist-devolutionist party that has recently embraced a sovereign-nationalist, more explicitly right-leaning position; the latter is an online-based, post-ideological political movement characterized by fierce antiestablishment propaganda but also for engagement in environmentalist campaigns at the local level against ecologically disruptive infrastructure projects. The leader of the League—Matteo Salvini, an ambitious politician known for his xenophobic positions, as well as his intensive use of social media—was appointed minister of the interior, pledging to adopt a muscular approach to vexed questions of crime, security and irregular immigration in Italy. From the very start, Salvini's main target has been the humanitarian organizations operating migrant rescue ships in the Mediterranean. Previously, also Luigi Di Maio—the young leader of the Five Star Movement and currently deputy head of government along with Salvini—openly stigmatized NGOs, accusing them of speculating over 'the immigration business' and colluding with people smugglers in the southern Mediterranean (Rossi 2018), even though he subsequently softened his position. Social movements and pro-migrant activists responded to these claims, denouncing anti-NGO discourse as a 'criminalisation of solidarity' (Collettivo Euronomade 2018). Once appointed as interior minister in June 2018, Salvini immediately refused port access to migrant rescue ships, blaming the so-called Dublin Regulation on asylum seekers for overburdening Italy and other countries at EU's external frontiers with a disproportionate number of migrants and refugees.

The historical defeat in the general election deeply weakened the parliamentary left in Italy, which remained almost silent about Salvini's obsessive anti-immigrant discourse. On 10 June 2018, after having rescued about six hundred migrants, the *Aquarius*—a rescue ship operated by SOS Méditerranée and Médecins Sans Frontières (MSF)—was turned away by Italian authorities, struggling for many days to find another port of arrival. At the peak of the humanitarian emergency, the mayor of Naples—Luigi de Magistris—publicly declared that he would have disobeyed the government's decision to refuse port access to the *Aquarius*. De Magistris proudly announced that migrants would be always welcome in the city of Naples. His stance was widely endorsed on social media where the hashtags #umanitàperta (open humanity), #apriteiporti (keep ports open), and #Aquarius became highly popular in response to Salvini's #chiudiamoiporti (keep ports shut). The resulting enthusiasm induced local politicians across the country to embrace de Magistris's position: mayors of major port cities such as Palermo, Messina, Reggio Calabria, Taranto, Cagliari, but even of small towns like Sapri in the southern Campania region sided with Naples' mayor despite their different political affiliations (De Magistris is left-oriented but politically independent). Even the Five Star mayor of the port city of Livorno initially joined the campaign, but had to hastily withdraw his support due to pressures from his party. The multiplier effect of the urban, therefore, unfolded at an interurban level, setting in motion a multiplying dynamic that involved mayors and other local administrators in different cities. Two days later, left-leaning parties, movements and unions finally broke the silence, calling for demonstrations in several Italian cities to protest against the xenophobic drift in Italy: an indefinite number of cities comprising Milan, Naples, Trento, Genoa, Turin, Como,

Pisa, Florence, Brescia, La Spezia, Modena, Ferrara, Parma, Ancona, Lucca and Venice witnessed public gatherings of various sizes. Cities that took part in the protest were many and uncoordinated but altogether they formed a sparse, still embryonic multiplicity of dissenting voices collectively resonating on social media through the #apriteiporti (keep ports open) hashtag.

The mayors' disobedience and the subsequent wave of mobilizations, therefore, brought to the fore the multiplier effect of city-based resistance, thanks also to the amplifying power of social media, in opposing the exclusionary politics of national revanchism. However, one should not attribute the merits for this crucial role of cities in resisting xenophobic discourse and anti-immigration policies (only) to a narrow circle of enlightened mayors and city managers. As spaces of transit, temporary refuge or settlement at the same time, cities and urban environments boast unique institutional thickness in terms of agglomeration and diversity: local welfare services and a myriad of associations, social movements, independent activists and volunteers, as well as countless socially minded singularities. The political potential of cities lies in the contagious vitality of these 'ecosystems of solidarity' grounded in urban everyday life, providing what can be defined 'ius domicilii' urban citizenship in contrast to the exclusionary character of national citizenship (Rossi and Vanolo 2012). In this sense, the value of cities and urban environments largely exceeds the sphere of local government, offering so far unspoilt possibilities for a refounding from below of democracy and community beyond the national fetish.

CONCLUSION

This chapter has theorized the multiplier effect of the urban in instigating a multiplication of resistance processes within the contemporary context of national revanchism and authoritarian populism. In the social sciences, the notion of 'multiplier effect' is customarily associated with the work of economists dealing with economic development issues, especially under conditions of recession or so-called underdevelopment. Writing in the aftermath of the 'great crash' of 1929, Richard Kahn detailed the Keynes-inspired idea of the multiplier, which he understood as an effect of an increase of 'home investment' (typically an increase in government spending) on aggregate demand (1931). In the 1960s, industrial economist François Perroux applied the notion of the multiplier to his theory of growth poles, arguing that investment in new industry has multiplier and accelerator effects on other sectors of the same regional economy (1966). In recent years, writing after the 'great contraction' of 2008/2009, Enrico Moretti has amended Perroux's position, showing how the multiplier effect is more significant in sectors based on high-skill jobs (2010).

Economic theorizations of the multiplier effect are conceived as counter-cyclical policies tackling conditions of economic slowdown and insufficient demand in structurally depressed areas. Keynes's statement that is usually summarized as 'The government should pay people to dig holes in the ground and then fill them up'[5] is illustrative of this idea of the economy that thrives through activity, which means subordinating public interest to the imperative of economic recovery. Within today's 'reactionary cycle' characterized by national revanchism and the crisis of liberal democracies in the West and across the world, an unconditional pursuit of resistance is vital to the recovery of democracy and even to its expansion, which occurs when small-scale or individual resistance unexpectedly gives rise to larger uprisings, as we have seen. To paraphrase Keynes, it can be concluded that in the current political context progressive political forces and social movements should experiment with small-scale resistance that can lead to the happy event of mass uprisings reclaiming democracy and justice. Under these circumstances, the urban has the distinctive capacity to multiply the effects of resistance on politics and society, turning it into an active force of social and political change.

NOTES

1. See CNN Politics: https://edition.cnn.com/interactive/2018/politics/women-who-march-the-movement/.

2. See Hürriyet Daily News: http://www.hurriyetdailynews.com/turkish-women-flock-to-istanbuls-center-to-demand-greater-rights-denounce-violence-128484.

3. See Global News: https://globalnews.ca/news/4014971/iran-hijab-whitewednesdays-girls-of-revolution-street-protest/.

4. In 1936, Reza Shah, the founder of Pahlavi dynasty, issued a decree known as Kashf-e hijab (Unveiling) banning all Islamic veils. However, a few months after the establishment of the Islamic Republic in 1979, a law forcing women to not only cover their heads, but also wear loose clothing to hide their figures, came into effect.

5. Keynes's full sentence reads as follows: 'If the Treasury were to fill old bottles with banknotes, bury them at suitable depths in disused coalmines which are then filled up to the surface with town rubbish, and leave it to private enterprise on well-tried principles of laissez-faire to dig the notes up again' (1964, 129).

Chapter 17

Urban Futures and
The Dark Enlightenment
A Brief Guide for the Perplexed

Roger Burrows

In 2014 the urbanist Anna Greenspan published a book titled *Shanghai Future: Modernity Remade* (2014). Ostensibly concerned with analysing forms of retro-futurism in contemporary Shanghai, it offers an engaging guide to the city informed by a pell-mell of literatures deriving from continental philosophy, cultural studies, planning, science fiction, the social sciences and elsewhere. For those attracted to interdisciplinary approaches to the study of cities it has much to recommend it. However, there is also something slightly awry with the book; despite initial impressions, it slowly becomes apparent that it is not a straightforwardly scholastic volume.[1] As well as drawing upon literatures with which many students of urban studies will be familiar, it also relies heavily upon material—most of it originating online—written by 'Shanghai-based philosopher Nick Land' (3). Greenspan quickly makes it clear that 'Nick Land is my partner. I quote him extensively, since we developed much of the thinking that went into this book together' (xiii, n6). Of course, this could be read as a simple acknowledgement of a common intellectual endeavour, and indeed this may well be the case. However, the nature of the endeavour is what concerns us here.

What follows is an attempt to summarize a number of recent analyses of the life and times of this 'Shanghai-based philosopher' with the aim of providing a brief guide to colleagues working in urban studies, who might otherwise be unfamiliar with his work and political influence. It is a perplexing tale that begins in the crazily inventive atmosphere of the Department of Philosophy at the University of Warwick in the United Kingdom in the 1990s but which, via various complex routes, leads us to the fever swamp of alt-right culture wars (Nagle 2017, 12) and the antidemocratic urban imaginaries of billionaire libertarian investors in technology in the United States (Goldhill 2017; Haider 2017).

Having left the UK academy some two decades ago—he was a lecturer in continental philosophy at the University of Warwick between 1987 and 1998—Nick Land has recently reemerged as a central figure in the promulgation of what have come to be termed *neoreactionary* (NRx) and *right-accelerationist* philosophies (Beckett 2017). These are philosophical positions that, so it is claimed, not only provide a basis for much alt-right political activity (MacDougald 2015), but are also supported by right-wing political strategists such as Steve Bannon (Gray 2017) and, crucially, multibillionaire libertarian technology investors such as Peter Thiel. Thiel has invested heavily in a range of projects concerned with, *inter alia*, 'seasteading' (Byrne 2017), the development of Urbit,[2] a piece of 'homesteading' software, and various 'deep learning' artificial intelligence (AI) systems (Haider 2017). As we will discuss later, not only are these investments all about 'smart cities' technologies designed to bring into being urban futures envisioned by NRx, they are also all led by men deeply implicated in the philosophical development of NRx itself. With this realization in mind, a different—more symptomatic—reading of *Shanghai Futures* becomes possible; one altogether darker.

That we can find significant elements of Landian philosophy in his partner's book about urban China comes as no surprise. It is just another instance of a strategy of what some have seen as 'Pynchonian cyber-scattering' in which readers interested in what Land has to say are forced to become 'momentary data-archaeologists, raking through the datacombs in the hope of finding a measly piece to this chaotic assemblage'. That this quote comes from a blog[3] rather than a journal article, chapter or a book is indicative of the domains that Land now tends to occupy—the culturally and politically darker recesses of the Internet (Nagle 2017). Others have also invoked Thomas Pynchonesque conspiracy theories to make sense of the contemporary reemergence of Land's 'philosophy-fiction' (MacDougald 2016a), describing him as 'the sort of strange, half-forgotten figure that might turn up in an Adam Curtis documentary ten years from now' (MacDougald 2015). If his 'early work'—the writings between 1987 and 2007 (Land 2011)—has been subject to a detailed codification by his erstwhile acolytes—the same, at the moment, cannot be said about his more recent NRx interventions; they exist, purposively or otherwise, strewn and uncurated across myriad, and often obscure, online blogs, journals, magazines, videos, radio recordings and so on. Whether there is any analytic or political continuity between the early Land and his more recent NRx phase is a moot point. For Land himself, however, there seems to have been a fundamental rupture. In the account offered by his publisher at *Urbanomic*, Robin Mackay (2012), for example, we learn that 'According to the present-day Nick Land, the person who wrote the [. . .] [early] [. . .] texts no longer exists'.

However, amidst this scattering, there does exist one online long-form piece, some twenty-eight thousand words, that Land (2012) titled *The Dark Enlightenment*.[4] It has come to be viewed as one of the clearest systematizations of NRx philosophy available and has become widely read. It is, in essence, a collection of *excursuses on* the work of a blogger and Bay Area programmer who goes by the online moniker of Mencius Moldbug. Moldbug, real name Curtis Yarvin, the founder of the aforementioned software start-up, Urbit, is the author of a series of long blogs such as *An Open Letter to Open-Minded Progressives* and *A Gentle Introduction to Unqualified Reservations*, posted from 2007 through to 2016.[5] Although Yarvin is viewed by many as the 'founder' of NRx (Gray 2017; Haider 2017; MacDougald 2016a; 2016b), the manner in which Land takes his material and rearticulates it using discursive strategies more akin to those of (what we will later see called) 'French philosophical cyberneticists Gilles Deleuze and Félix Guattari' (Land 2017) has opened up NRx thinking to audiences who would otherwise probably never engage with, what for some (Goldhill 2017; Haider 2017), tends towards neofascist modes of thought.[6]

One can only agree with MacDougald (2015) that it is 'hard to talk seriously about something with a silly name'—and even more difficult when, on 'first glance, it appears little more than a fever swamp of feudal misogynists, racist programmers and "fascist teenage dungeon masters," gathering on subreddits to await the collapse of Western civilization'. For MacDougald (2015) Land's *Dark Enlightenment* manages to mesh together 'all the awful things you always suspected about libertarianism with odds and ends from PUA culture, Victorian Social Darwinism, and an only semi-ironic attachment to absolutism'.[7] The political project is essentially 'anti-egalitarian' and argues that 'democracy is bust; rule by the people doesn't work, and doesn't lead to good governance' (Gray 2017). The aim of NRx seems to be to dissolve nation-states into 'competing authoritarian seasteads on the model of Singapore' (MacDougald 2015); this is a philosophy that argues that 'society should break into tiny states, each effectively governed by a CEO' (Goldhill 2017). As Land himself puts it: 'The one thing I explicitly and strategically would want to impose is fragmentation' (Bauer and Tomažin 2017).

We will flesh out some of the key elements of NRx philosophy, to the extent that it impinges upon debates about urban futures, in what follows. However, given the brief summary just provided, the interested reader is likely wondering why they should concern themselves with what, on the face of it, is a marginal, likely fascist, 'post-libertarian futurism' (MacDougald 2016b) existing outwith the domain assumptions of most academic protocols. There are, perhaps, at least three reasons why it might be worth persevering. First, the intellectual and political trajectory that Land has taken is a remarkable one; he is widely viewed as being a key figure in the development of contemporary philosophy and his presence continues to find a resonance—even when it is forcibly objected to—in the work of a number of otherwise progressive thinkers. Second, and relatedly, the manner in which Land uses the work of some continental philosophers—Deleuze and Guattari, Lyotard and Manuel DeLanda in particular—offers an insight into the immense conceptual and political flexibility that such influential analytic approaches seem to be able to tolerate.[8] Third, and most importantly, whatever the analytic worth(lessness) of NRx philosophy, it is important to recognize its ideological function (Goldhill 2017; Gray 2017) and the powerful actors supporting its propagation; not least those investing in myriad technologies in Silicon Valley who have seemingly been convinced by Land's idea of *hyperstition*—the creation of fictional entities that can make themselves real. As Haider (2017) puts it: 'If the builders of technology are transmitting their values into machinery this makes the culture of Silicon Valley a matter of more widespread consequence'. The potential instantiation of NRx into urban technologies thus makes a critical engagement with such ideologies an urgent matter for anyone interested in the future of our cities.

THE 'RENEGADE ACADEMY'

The life and times of Nick Land at the University of Warwick have been well documented elsewhere (see, *inter alia*, Beckett 2017; Blincoe 2017; and, especially, Reynolds 2009). Born in 1962, Land studied philosophy at Sussex and then gained a PhD on Heidegger from Essex, before being appointed as a lecturer in continental philosophy at Warwick in 1987, teaching a course titled Current French Philosophy. In 1992, he published his only book, *The Thirst for Annihilation: Georges Bataille and Virulent Nihilism* (Land 1992). Always a thinker keen to push things to the limit, he was also someone who 'produced supporters' (Critchley et al. 2011).[9] Land and these supporters began to organize a series of events, the first of which was in 1994, concerned with *Virtual Futures*.[10] In 1995 Land was joined at Warwick by Sadie Plant, who had previously worked for a brief period at what remained of the Centre for Contemporary Cultural Studies (CCCS) at the University of Birmingham, and who had published *The Most Radical Gesture: The Situationist International in a Postmodern Age* (Plant 1992). Land and Plant struck up a strong intellectual and personal relationship and together established the Cybernetic Culture Research Unit (CCRU), affiliated in some form or another (Beckett 2017; Reynolds 2009)—there are competing accounts—with the Department of Philosophy at Warwick. It was within this context that ideas and practices that would later come to be known as *accelerationism* began to take shape.[11] Described, brilliantly, by MacDougald (2015) as 'a heady cocktail of nihilism, cybernetic Marxism, complexity theory, numerology, jungle music, and the dystopian sci-fi of William Gibson and *Blade Runner*', it is perhaps understandable how, in the dark days following Thatcherism, such a melange had such an appeal to cultural theorists (Featherstone and Burrows 1995),[12] urbanists (Burrows 1997) and many others seeking a form of intellectual and political excitement that was otherwise mostly lacking. Indeed, in an oft-quoted piece by the late Mark Fisher (2011), the extent of his influence is made clear:

'Is Nick Land the most important British philosopher of the last 20 years?' asks Kodwo Eshun [. . .] Eshun's question makes sense because [Land's] small canon of texts [. . .] have had an enormous, but until now, subterranean influence. Their impact was first of all felt beyond philosophy—in music [. . .] in art [. . .] in inhuman feminism [. . .] in theory-fiction [. . .]. Land's influence is also now infesting the philosophy departments which tended to scorn it in the rare cases they were aware of it. Some of the philosophers at the forefront of the most exciting movement in current philosophy, 'speculative realism' [. . .] studied with Land, and their work is still marked by that encounter.[13]

We will briefly discuss the different routes that accelerationist thinking has taken in the last few decades in what follows. However, the intensity of its birth within the CCRU in the mid-1990s was such that Plant decided to exit the academy in 1997, leaving Land to take over the 'running' of the CCRU. As Reynolds (2009) details, the activities of the CCRU were, by this time, such that the unit had to relocate off-campus, ending up in a small office above The Body Shop in Leamington Spa. All manner of creative craziness ensued, involving drugs of various types, sonic experiments, the production of ever more chaotic diagrams and the emergence of modes of communication that were becoming increasingly opaque. As Overy (2015, 16), politely, expresses it:

In a short period of time Land's theory-praxis moved from [. . .] unorthodox yet comprehensible sci-fi dystopianism [. . .] to [. . .] textual chaos [. . .] By this point Land's articles contained little that can be reconciled with the mores of traditional academic practice; though still loaded with references to philosophers and critical theorists, nothing in them approaches a traditionally structured argument. Land was therefore a philosopher determined to exit academic convention not only on a personal level, but also on a theoretical level.

Mackay (2012) is less circumspect: 'In any normative, clinical, or social sense of the word, very simply, Land did "go mad"'.[14] In 1998 he left the academy following various disagreements with the Warwick authorities. The period of the 'renegade academy' was over. Land, who had long written about 'neo-China', relocated first to Taiwan and then, in 2002, to Shanghai. Greenspan, who had completed her PhD at Warwick on 'Capitalism's Transcendental Time Machine', joined him and they have subsequently parented two children. They also set up two presses: Urbanatomy and Spiral Time Press.[15] They also published *Urbanatomy: Shanghai 2008*, a lavishly illustrated six-hundred-page guide to the city, and *The Shanghai World Expo Guide 2010*. Land also began to blog extensively, initially at Urban Futures,[16] and later, and in addition, at Outside In.[17] Originally the Urban Futures blog was largely focused on accelerationist thinking and, as such, showed some continuity with the CCRU work. The Outside In blog, on the other hand, was largely devoted to the development of NRx philosophy. However, over time, this distinction has begun to dissolve and both blogs have become elements of the wider scattering of materials we have already noted. The accelerationist Land and the NRx Land now seem to have very similar concerns, and *right-accelerationism* is a label that some have used to describe this realignment (MacDougald 2016b).

So what are some of the defining characteristics of accelerationist thinking that originated during this period? A number of excellent accounts are now available: Beckett (2017) provides a long-form journalistic description; Mackay and Avanessian (2014) collect together key papers[18]; Noys (2014) provides a critical philosophical treatment; and even Land (2017) himself has offered up a brief critical reflection on the origins of the position. There even exists a video extract of Land, talking in 1994, giving a pithy introduction to the overarching position[19] in which he argues that:

> There is a very similar pattern that you find in the structure of societies, in the structure of companies, and in the structure of computers, and all three are moving in the same direction, that is, away from a top-down structure of a central command system, giving the system instructions on how to behave, towards a system that is parallel, that is flat, which is a web in which change moves from the bottom up [. . .] and this is going to happen across all institutions and technical devices, it's the way they work.

At the time, of course, the language of accelerationism was not being used, but the ideas were firmly couched in the conceptual language of Deleuze, especially the reading of his work offered by Manuel DeLanda; which viewed him not so much as a philosopher but as an 'engineer of the future'.[20] Members of the CCRU were much taken with DeLanda (1991) and he was an early presence at the initial Virtual Futures events. His keynote from the 1994 event, originally published as DeLanda (1993), still provides a remarkably fresh articulation of what later would became known as the 'new materialism'. What is striking now, in retrospect, is the manner in which Land, drawing upon DeLanda, was able to articulate a position drawing on the supposedly radical argot of Deleuze and Guattari, and the cultural aesthetics of Gibsonian cyberpunk (Featherstone and Burrows 1995) that was, even at the time, for all intents and purposes, a reformulation of the extreme free-market discourse of Hayek and Von Mises (Gane 2014) filtered through the cybernetics of Norbert Wiener (1961). Although written more recently, and now explicitly using the language of accelerationism,[21] the account of the position provided by Land (2017) himself illustrates this with a remarkable clarity and, as such, is worth quoting at length:

> For accelerationism the crucial lesson was this: A negative feedback circuit—such as a steam-engine 'governor' or a thermostat—functions to keep some state of a system in the same place. Its product, in the language formulated by French philosophical cyberneticists Gilles Deleuze and Félix Guattari, is *territorialization*. Negative feedback stabilizes a process, by correcting drift, and thus inhibiting departure beyond a limited range. Dynamics are placed in the service of fixity—a higher-level stasis, or state. All equilibrium models of complex systems and processes are like this. To capture the contrary trend, characterized by self-reinforcing errancy, flight, or escape, D&G [*sic*] coin the inelegant but influential term *deterritorialization* [. . .] In socio-historical terms, the line of deterritorialization corresponds to uncompensated capitalism. The basic [. . .] schema is a positive feedback circuit, within which commercialization and industrialization mutually excite each other in a runaway process, from which modernity draws its gradient [. . .] As the circuit is incrementally closed, or intensified, it exhibits ever greater autonomy, or automation. It becomes more tightly auto-productive [. . .] Because it appeals to nothing beyond itself, it is inherently nihilistic. It has no conceivable meaning beside self-amplification. It grows in order to grow. Mankind is its temporary host, not its master. Its only purpose is itself [. . .] The point of an analysis of capitalism, or of nihilism, is to do more of it. The *process* is not to be critiqued. The process *is* the critique, feeding back into itself, as it escalates. The only way forward is through, which means further in. (emphasis in the original)

There is, of course, a probably more well-known variant of 'left-accelerationism', popularized by the journalist Paul Mason (2015) but also present in the work of Srnicek and Williams (2016) and Mackay and Avanessian (2014). However, this is mostly concerned with the possibility of the:

> 'repurposing' of capitalist infrastructures [in order to] attend to the so-called 'socialist calculation' problem [. . .] A viable post-capitalism must [. . .] beat neoliberalism at its own game—that is, push the development of mechanisms

of information capture, algorithmic modelling, and conceptual analysis to the nth-degree, but in a manner that allows for [. . .] 'collective self-mastery', rather than private enrichment at the expense of the common. (Gardiner 2017, 34–35)

Another key aspect of prefigurative CCRU thinking about accelerationism was their obsession with the philosophical analysis of time. The oft-quoted maxim by William Gibson that 'The future is already here—it's just not evenly distributed'[22] gives an indication of their concerns. For Land, time, like much else, is nonlinear, and thus relations between cause and effect are complex. For Land, futurity is in the here and now in the sense that it is not something that just happens to us; it is something we *create*. On occasion portended urban imaginaries—designs, diagrams, dreams, fictions, maps, movies, plans, philosophies, prototypes, theories and more—are plainly *generative* of the future; it is as if the tentacles of future entities reach back through time in order to bring into being the elements necessary for their own materialization. As Haider (2017) explains, there does not exist a simple 'word for this cause-and-effect relationship in ordinary English, but, in the mid-nineties Land coined one: *hyperstition*, that which is "equipoised be-tween fiction and technology"'. For Land:

Hyperstition is a positive feedback circuit including culture as a component. It can be defined as the experimental (techno-) science of self-fulfilling prophe-cies. Superstitions are merely false beliefs, but hyperstitions—by their very existence as ideas—function causally to bring about their own reality. Capitalist economics is extremely sensitive to hyperstition, where confidence acts as an effective tonic, and inversely. The (fictional) idea of Cyberspace contributed to the influx of investment that rapidly converted it into a technosocial reality.[23]

The fictional urban imaginaries offered up by *Metropolis*, *Blade Runner*, *Neuromancer*, *Snow Crash* and many other cultural products are clearly ex-amples of hyperstition; but so too perhaps are broader discursive assemblages that come to function as *ideologies*—imagined dis/utopias—socialism, com-munism, neoliberalism, ethno-nationalism, transhumanism, NRx and so on. Land's 'theory-fiction' was perhaps never innocent? His role in the creation of fictional entities that then struggle to make themselves real should not be underestimated. As Haider (2017) again notes—in what is a wonderfully con-structed essay—'If [. . .] Reagan and [. . .] Thatcher had served up an all-you-can-eat shit buffet [. . .] promoting the free market [Land] responded by taking laissez-faire economics to a perverse extreme'. As we have seen, Land had come to view 'capital itself as the protagonist of history, with humans as grist for the mill'. But even as far back as 1993, for Land (479) the notion of hyper-stition was conjoined with (prefigurative) accelerationism; the hitherto history of capitalism was, for Land, simply 'an invasion from the future of an artificial intelligent space that must assemble itself [. . .] from its enemy's resources'. A quarter of a century on, and that future is now pretty much upon us.

SHANGHAI TIMES[24]

How it was that Land, in 2012, holed up with his family in Shanghai, writing travel guides, horror fiction and occasional blog posts, should come across the online meanderings of Mencius Moldbug, and then take them seriously enough to produce *The Dark Enlightenment* and the texts that have followed, is hard to fathom. As we have already mentioned, Moldbug, real name Curtis Yarvin, is a software engineer, supported by Peter Thiel, and is, seemingly, also a voracious reader of all manner of political theory and philosophy. It was the posts made on Moldbug's Unqualified Reservations blog that Land seemed to find so enticing. Moldbug offers up turgid idiosyncratic prose that meanders all over the place. He combines elements of the work of Thomas Carlyle, Ludwig Von Mises and various strains of individualist libertarianism to offer a long view of history, which concludes that Prussian cameralism, in which a state is conceptualized as a business that *owns* a country, offers a viable ideological model for a future twenty-first-century politics. Originally called 'neocameralism', his position soon became known as 'neoreactionary' philosophy (NRx) and then, once rearticulated by Land, *The Dark Enlightenment*. As Haider (2017) points out, Land seems to have gone from accelerationist *prophet* to NRx *apostle*.

The Dark Enlightenment itself might be best thought of as the application of Land's accelerationist framework to Moldbug's neocameralism. It is a difficult and provocative read, purposively designed to unsettle the dominant sensibilities of progressives; members of what NRx terms the Cathedral. Space precludes a detailed exegesis here, but we might attempt an ideal typical characterization of the position under five broad headings: an opposition to democratic forms of governance; an attempt to construct a new patchwork of (city-) state forms in which 'exit' is the only 'human right'; an attack on discourses that foreground notions of human equality; a (welcoming) belief in the inevitability of an approaching *singularity* in which AI and biotechnologies begin to meld with the human form; and, for now, the necessity to undermine actors who promulgate ideologies of democracy, equality or who advocate for the regulation of science and technology—members of the aforementioned Cathedral.

Both Moldbug and Land point toward the essay by Thiel (2009) in *Cato Unbound* in which he declares that 'I no longer believe that freedom and democracy are compatible'. Land (2012) goes further, suggesting that 'democracy is not merely doomed, it is doom itself'. In this model democratic forms of governance are viewed as the primary dampeners of deterritorialization processes. For Land (2012), 'Democracy consumes progress [. . .] the appropriate mode of analysis for studying the democratic phenomenon is general parasitology'. For Land (2012), democratic political forms involve:

> Cropping out all high-frequency feedback mechanisms (such as market signals), and replacing them with sluggish, infra-red loops that pass through a centralized forum of 'general will', a radically democratized society insulates parasitism from what it does, transforming local, painfully dysfunctional, intolerable, and thus urgently corrected behavior patterns into global, numbed, and chronic socio-political pathologies.

The NRx alternative seems to be to first 'Retire All Government Employees' (RAGE) in order to 'reboot' the economy,[25] and second, replace democratic institutions with a CEO (or even a monarch!). The resulting 'gov-corp'—'a society run as a business'—can then be regulated not via the *voice* of its citizenry—there will be no democracy—but via their ability to *exit* as consumers in a free market for states. Land has become obsessed with the ideas contained in the classic treatise of Albert Hirschman (1970) on the distinction between *Exit, Voice, and Loyalty*. For Land, democratic voice and the irrational 'warm' solidarities of loyalty must be opposed, as they will, as we saw above, cut 'out all high-frequency feedback mechanisms'. Architectures of exit thus become of paramount importance[26]; indeed for Land (2012), quoting Patri Friedman (the grandson of arch neoliberal Milton Friedman), 'free exit is so important that [. . .] it [is] the only Universal Human Right'. Friedman, another NRx entrepreneur-cum-philosopher backed by Thiel's dollars, leads the Seasteading Institute,[27] an organization busy designing permanent (almost Lovecraftian) cities at sea—seasteads—prefigurative gov-corps outside the territory claimed by democratic governments. They are just one example of the NRx envisioning of the emergence of a complex patchwork of small, and competing, gov-corps[28]—autonomous gated communities, city-states, even 'off-world' communities (think Elon Musk)—much as described in the hyperstitious *Snow Crash* by Neil Stephenson as far back as 1992.

The antidemocratic impulse of NRx sits alongside its profound disavowal of any discourses advocating for socioeconomic equality. *The Dark Enlightenment* is, at its core, a eugenic philosophy of what Land (2014) has termed 'hyper-racism'. In Land's schema, the consumers 'exiting' from competing gov-corps quickly form themselves into, often racially based, microstates. Capitalist deterritorialization combines with ongoing genetic separation between global elites and the rest of the population (what Land terms the 'refuse') resulting in complex new forms of 'Human Bio-diversity' (HBD). In Land's apocalyptic argot (2014), the key issue is the rise in assortative mating organized by socio-economic status differences, which:

> tends to genetic diversification. This is neither the preserved diversity of ordinary racism, still less the idealized genetic pooling of the anti-racists, but a class-structured mechanism for population diremption, on a vector towards neo-speciation. It implies the disintegration of the human species, along largely unprecedented lines, with intrinsic hierarchical consequence [. . .] The genetically self-filtering elite is not merely different—and becoming ever more different—it is explicitly superior according to the established criteria that allocate social status [. . .] Neo-eugenic genomic manipulation capabilities, which will also be unevenly distributed [. . .] will [. . .] intensify the trend to speciation, rather than ameliorating it.

This reads like an accelerationist version of *The Bell Curve* (Herrnstein and Murray 1994)—a source upon which Land (2012) does indeed draw. But it is more than that, because it is not just neoeugenic technologies that Land views as pushing us towards neospeciation. These technologies are part of a far greater assemblage directing us towards the singularity and a posthuman future:

> As blockchains, drone logistics, nanotechnology, quantum computing, computational genomics, and virtual reality flood in, drenched in ever-higher densities of artificial intelligence, accelerationism won't be going anywhere, unless ever deeper into itself. (Land 2017)

Hong Kong, Singapore and, of course, Shanghai, all prefigure NRx urban futures. Land has long been interested in 'neo-China' imaginaries, and it is little wonder that he has located himself where he has in order to produce the texts and interventions that he has; ever hopeful, one imagines, of their potential hyperstitious potentialities.

Of course, such hyperneoliberal, libertarian, technologically deterministic, antidemocratic, antiegalitarian, proeugenicist, racist and, likely, fascist ideas have proven to be very unpopular within the academy, and among progressive liberals and metropolitan elites more generally. For Land and Moldbug the ideology of this group, and the various practices that it informs, is at the very heart of all that that is wrong in the world. They have come to think of the universities, the civil service and the media—the old Althusserian ISAs (as we noted above)—with its orthodoxy of egalitarianism, democracy and social constructionism, as the Cathedral; a quasi-religious structure—a descendent perhaps of the Puritan church—that functions hegemonically to suppress dissent. This recognition of the inverted hegemonic functioning of the ISAs in order to stymy accelerationist uncompensated capitalism thus requires, within NRx philosophy, attempts to construct counterhegemonic ideological strategies of the sort described by Nagle (2017). As ideological battles have moved online and away from the traditional institutions of the Cathedral, the likes of Milo Yiannopoulos, Steve Bannon, Thiel and Freidman (all informed by NRx thinking) have invested in their own form of alt-right Gramscian politics. This is the discourse of, *inter alia*, 'post-truth' politics, the critique of expertise and online culture wars of various sorts. These 'Gramscians of the alt-light' as Nagle (53) calls them, have 'been successful beyond any predictions'. Ironically it has been 'those heeding the ideas of the left most closely, from Chomsky's idea of manufacturing consent to Gramsci's theory of hegemony and counter-hegemony', who have been politically the most successful; and that has been the alt-right. For NRx thinkers then the Cathedral must be dissolved; and suddenly all of the often-tedious debates about political correctness, identity politics, 'no-platforming' and suchlike take on a much greater political significance than perhaps many of us still with a seat in the Cathedral have hitherto realized. This is an ideological struggle over articulating principles, but it is one that many in urban studies have perhaps only recently become cognizant of?

The Dark Enlightenment is a profoundly depressing text, envisioning nihilistic, machinic, unequal (in terms of age, class, gender, race and more), antidemocratic urban futures in which human subjects are simply bearers of unfettered capitalist processes. It is a philosophical model that, one would hope, few would encourage. However, it is important that we at least come to know about it; hence this chapter. In a world where Silicon Valley (white male) billionaires attracted to the ideologies of Ayn Rand curate the rise of the alt-right, the new populism, and the mainstreaming of, *inter alia*, misogynist, racist and fascist discourses, those interested in urban futures would do well to look up—if only for an hour or so—from the often comfortable domain assumptions of *their* Deleuzian inflected urban studies, to see what else has been done with that body of work.

NOTES

1. It is produced by a reputable academic publisher and has dustcover endorsements from the likes of Fulong Wu, Bartlett Professor of Planning at UCL.

2. 'If Bitcoin is money and Ethereum is law, Urbit is land' says the blurb on https://urbit.org/. The message is clear.

3. See https://www.meta-nomad.net/nick-land-accelerationism-neoreaction-over view-guide/. As will become apparent, much of the material discussed in this chapter

does not derive from traditional 'academic' sources. Indeed, as we shall discuss later, NRx views itself as fundamentally opposed to what it conceptualizes as the Cathedral—probably best thought of as a crazily inverted ideological state apparatus (ISA) (Althusser 1971)—in which the norms, values and outputs of academics, professionals and liberal metropolitan elites are conceptualized as being designed to fetter NRx thought.

4. It can be read here: http://www.thedarkenlightenment.com/the-dark-enlightenment-by-nick-land/. However, even here, there is complexity. The supposed anonymous NRx originator of the site makes it clear that it has 'become little more than an oft-linked placeholder for three seminal NRx documents—two by Mencius Moldbug, and one by Nick Land'. They continue: 'I'll take this opportunity to make very clear that neither Nick Land nor Curtis Yarvin have ever had any involvement with this site. I have never met or communicated with Curtis Yarvin, and have had only extremely brief, and very occasional, social-media contact with Nick Land'. As we will discuss shortly, Moldbug and Yarvin are one and the same person, and 'both' are critical characters in what follows.

5. All of his work is collected together at https://www.unqualified-reservations org/.

6. Land (2016) himself writes ambiguously about his relationship to fascism, albeit selecting to do so in a right-wing 'news' outlet.

7. PUA refers to 'pickup artist'—members of what have come to be known as 'seduction communities' (O'Neill 2015), who draw upon notions derived from sociobiology and evolutionary psychology in order to 'game' sexual relationships.

8. Even early on, Land's work was sometimes characterized as a form of 'Deleuzian Thatcherism'. See for example the interview with Benjamin Noys carried out by Alexander Galloway here: http://www.3ammagazine.com/3am/crash-and-burn-debating-accelerationism/.

9. Critchley et al. reflect how 'You'd go and give a talk at Warwick and be denounced by people with the same saliva-dribbling verbal tics as Nick and wearing similar jumpers'.

10. All of the events have been curated at http://www.virtualfutures.co.uk/.

11. The term was first coined, critically, by Noys (2010) and subsequently elaborated upon in Noys (2014).

12. This collection contained essays by both Plant (1995) and Land (1995).

13. We have already noted his influence on Sadie Plant and his current partner Anna Greenspan, and it is obvious that both Mark Fisher and Kodwo Eshun have been deeply affected by his work. Others who worked with him and/or have been influenced by his thinking include cultural theorists Matt Fuller and Luciana Parisi; philosophers Roy Brassier, Iain Hamilton Grant and Reza Negarestani; artists Jake and Dinos Chapman (who provided the artwork for the cover of *Fanged Noumena*) and Maggie Roberts (part of the digital art collective 0[rphan]d[rift>]); the musician Steve Goodman (Kode9, responsible for hyperdub); the novelists Hari Kunzru and Nick Blincoe; and the publisher Robin Mackay.

14. Martyn Amos, now a Professor of Novel Computation, but at the time a PhD student at Warwick, recalls in his comment on Reynolds (2009): 'One of the last

times I saw Nick was in the Coop [*sic*] on Earlsdon High Street; in his basket were about six Pot Noodles, and a cabbage ("because I don't want to get scurvy")'.

15. The details of both of which can be found here: https://timespiralpress.net/urbanatomy/.

16. See http://www.ufblog.net/. The most recent manifestation of this is *Urban Futures (2.1): Views from the Decopunk Delta*. On the associated Twitter account Land is @UF-blog.

17. See http://www.xenosystems.net/. On the associated Twitter account Land is @outsideness.

18. See also the excellent reviews of this collection offered by O'Sullivan (2014) and Gardiner (2017).

19. See https://www.youtube.com/watch?v=GMdPLxbuc8Q.

20. See the details in his biography at http://egs.edu/faculty/manuel-de-landa. Or as Land (1993, 474) himself put it: '*Anti-Oedipus* is less a philosophy book than an engineering manual; a package of software implements for hacking into the machinic unconscious, opening invasion channels'.

21. The notion originally comes, of course, from a fragment of *Anti-Oedipus* (Deleuze and Guattari 1972, 239–40), which is widely cited in the extant literature:

> Which is the revolutionary path? Is there one?—To withdraw from the world market [. . .] Or might it be to go in the opposite direction? To go still further, that is, in the movement of the market, of decoding and deterritorialization? For perhaps the flows are not yet deterritorialized enough, not decoded enough, from the viewpoint of a theory and a practice of a highly schizophrenic character. Not to withdraw from the process, but to go further, to 'accelerate the process', as Nietzsche put it: in this matter, the truth is that we haven't seen anything yet.

22. Gibson himself seems unsure when he first used the phrase, but it seems to have been in 1999 or possibly even earlier—see https://medium.com/not-evenly-distributed/the-future-has-arrived-fed56cec3266. However, it has been a major theme of his fiction from *Neuromancer*, in 1984, through to his most recent novel (at the time of writing), *The Peripheral*, (2014).

23. See '"Hyperstition: An Introduction"—Delphi Carstens interviews Nick Land' at http://merliquify.com/blog/articles/hyperstition-an-introduction/#.Wig6vbSFii5.

24. This was the title of the first Urbanatomy Urban Futures Pamphlet that Land produced.

25. In a rare video appearance, Moldbug/Yarvin makes this case; see https://www.youtube.com/watch?v=ZluMysK2B1E.

26. See 'Nick Land's Response to Tech Secessionism', part of the *Ultimate Exit: The Architecture and Urbanism of Tech-Secessionism* event run by the Finnish Cultural Institute in New York: https://www.youtube.com/watch?v=yJMlaupGHTM.

27. See https://www.seasteading.org/.

28. See, in particular, Moldbug (2017), which is a book-length Kindle version of postings originally made on the Unqualified Reservations blog in 2008.

Bibliography

ABC (Australian Broadcasting Commission). 2017. 'Crown Melbourne to Build Australia's Tallest Tower at Southbank'. 9 February. http://www.abc.net.au/news/2017-02-09/crown-melbourne-to-build-90-storey-luxury-hotel-building/8254480. Accessed 24 October 2017.

Abidin, C. 2016. 'Visibility Labour: Engaging with Influencers' Fashion Brands and #OOTD Advertorial Campaigns on Instagram'. *Media International Australia* 161 (1): 86–100.

Ackerman, J. 1990. *The Villa: Form and Ideology of Country Houses*. Princeton, NJ: Princeton University Press.

Acton, H. 1973. *The Villas of Tuscany*. London: Thames and Hudson.

Adkins, L., and C. Lury, eds. 2012. 'Special Measures: Introduction'. *Sociological Review* 59 (2): 5–23.

Agathangelou, A. M. 2018. 'The Time of and Temporal (Un)Civility of the City: MENA Urban Insurgencies and Revolutions'. In *The Sage Handbook of Urban Sociology: New Approaches to the Twenty-First Century City*. Edited by R. Burdett and S. Hall. London: Sage: 349–75.

Ahmed, S. 2017. *Living a Feminist Life*. Durham, NC: Duke University Press.

Ali, D., and E. J. Flatt, eds. 2012. *Garden and Landscape Practices in Precolonial India: Histories from the Deccan*. New Delhi/Oxford: Routledge.

Althusser, L. 1971. 'Ideology and Ideological State Apparatuses'. *Lenin and Philosophy and Other Essays*. Translated by B. Brewster. New York: Monthly Review Press.

Amin, A. 2006. 'The Good City'. *Urban Studies* 43 (5/6): 1009–23.

Andrews, D. 2017. 'Seventh Heaven for the World's Most Liveable City'. Media release issued 16 August by Hon. Daniel Andrews, Premier. State Government of Victoria, Melbourne.

Aptheker, B. 1989. *Tapestries of Life: Women's Work, Women's Consciousness, and the Meaning of Daily Life*. Amherst: University of Massachusetts Press.

Aragon, L. 1994. *Paris Peasant*. Translated by S. W. Taylor. Paris and New York: Exact Change.

Arden, E. 1954. 'The Evil City in American Fiction'. *New York History* 35 (3): 259–79.

Arendt, H. 1967. *The Origins of Totalitarianism*. London: George Allen and Unwin.

———. 1968. 'On Humanity in Dark Times'. In *Men in Dark Times*. New York: Harcourt: 3–31.

Aristotle. 1992. *The Politics*. Translated by T. A. Sinclair. Revised by T. J. Saunders. London: Penguin.

———. 1976. *Nichomachean Ethics.* Translated by J. A. K. Thomson. Revised by Hugh Tredennick. Harmondsworth: Penguin.

Arthur, Christopher J. 2001. 'The Spectral Ontology of Value'. *Radical Philosophy* 107 (May/June): 32–42.

———. 2004. *The New Dialectic and Marx's* Capital. Leiden and Boston: Brill.

Atkinson, R. 2017. 'London, Whose City?' *Monde Diplomatique*. http://mondediplo.com/2017/07/06london. Accessed 24 October 2017.

Aureli, P. V. 2011. *The Possibility of an Absolute Architecture*. Cambridge, MA: MIT Press.

———. 2013. *Less Is Enough: On Architecture and Asceticism*. Moscow: Strelka Press.

Badcock, B. 1994. '"Stressed-Out" Communities: "Out-of-Sight, Out-of-Mind"?' *Urban Policy and Research* 12 (3): 191–97.

———. 2000. 'Home Ownership and the Illusion of Egalitarianism'. In *A History of European Housing in Australia*. Edited by P. Troy. Cambridge: Cambridge University Press.

Badiou, A. 2005. *Metapolitics*. Translated by J. Barker. London: Verso.

———. 2007. 'The Event in Deleuze'. *Parrhesia* 2: 37–44.

———. 2012. *The Rebirth of History: Times of Riots and Uprisings.* London: Verso.

———. 2013. 'On Theatre and Philosophy'. *Lana Turner Journal*, 9 December. http://lanaturnerjournal.com/7/alain-badiou-on-theatre-and-philosophy. Accessed 28 August 2017.

Banks, L. 2018. 'How to Plan an Instagram-Worthy Wedding'. *Vogue Australia*, online, 30 May. https://www.vogue.com.au/brides/trends/the-rise-of-the-instawedding/image-gallery/fd6d40499df921e2f1eb80ba8cff34c9?pos=1. Accessed 7 June 2018.

Barber, B. 2013. *If Mayors Ruled the World: Dysfunctional Nations, Rising Cities*. New Haven, CT: Yale University Press.

Barlow, R., and S. Akbarzadeh. 2008. 'Prospects for Feminism in the Islamic Republic of Iran'. *Human Rights Quarterly* 30 (1): 21–40.

Bataille, G. 1985. 'Rotten Sun'. In *Visions of Excess: Selected Writings, 1927–1939*. Edited and translated by A. Stoekl. Minneapolis: University of Minnesota Press: 57–58.

Batliwala, S. 2012. *Changing Their World: Concepts and Practices of Women's Movement*. Association for Women's Rights in Development.

Bauer, M., and A. Tomažin. 2017. 'The Only Thing I Would Impose Is Fragmentation'. Interview with Nick Land. *Synthetic Zerø*, 19 June. https://syntheticzero.net/2017/06/19/the-only-thing-i-would-impose-is-fragmentation-an-interview-with-nick-land/.

Baum, S. 2008. 'Suburban Scars: Australian Cities and Socio-Economic Deprivation'. Research paper no. 15. Griffith University Urban Research Program, Brisbane.

Bauman, Z. 2000. *Liquid Modernity*. Cambridge, Oxford and Malden: Polity Press.

Bayat, A. 1997. *Street Politics: Poor People's Movements in Iran*. New York: Columbia University Press.

———. 2007. 'A Women's Non-Movement: What It Means to Be a Woman Activist in an Islamic State'. *Comparative Studies of South Asia, Africa and the Middle East* 27 (1): 160–72.

———. 2010. *Life as Politics: How Ordinary People Change the Middle East*. Stanford, CA: Stanford University Press.

Beck, U. 1992. *Risk Society: Towards a New Modernity*. London: Sage.

———. 2005. *Power in the Global Age*. Cambridge: Polity Press.

Beckert, J., and P. Aspers, eds. 2011. *The Worth of Goods: Valuation and Pricing in the Economy*. Oxford: Oxford University Press.

Beckett, A. 2017. 'Accelerationism: How a Fringe Philosophy Predicted the Future We Live In'. *Guardian*, 11 May. https://www.theguardian.com/world/2017/may/11/accelerationism-how-a-fringe-philosophy-predicted-the-future-we-live-in.

Bellofiore, R., and T. R. Riva. 2015. '*The Neue-Marx Lektüre*: Putting the Critique of Political Economy Back into the Critique of Society'. *Radical Philosophy* 189 (January/February): 24–36.

Benjamin, A. 2010. *Place, Commonality and Judgment: Continental Philosophy and the Ancient Greeks*. London: Continuum.

Benjamin, W. 1973. *Charles Baudelaire: A Lyric Poet in the Era of High Capitalism*. London: New Left Books.

———. 1983. *Charles Baudelaire: A Lyric Poet in the Era of High Capitalism*. London: Verso.

———. 1998. *The Origin of German Tragic Drama*. Translated by P. Osborne. London: Verso.

———. 1999a. *The Arcades Project*. Edited by R. Tiedemann. Cambridge, MA and London: Harvard University Press.

———. 1999b. *Walter Benjamin: Selected Writings*, vol. 2, Pt. II, *1931–1934*. Edited by M. W. Jennings, H. Eiland and G. Smith. Cambridge, MA and London: Belknap Press of Harvard University Press.

———. 2003. *Walter Benjamin: Selected Writings*, vol. 4, *1938–1940*. Edited by H. Eiland and M. W. Jennings. Cambridge, MA and London: Belknap Press of Harvard University Press.

Berman, M. 1982. *All That Is Solid Melts into Air: The Experience of Modernity*. 2010 edition London and New York: Verso.

Bernardo, F., J. Almeido and C. Martins. 2017. 'Urban Identity and Tourism: Different Looks, One Single Place'. *Proceedings of the Institution of Civil Engineers—Urban Design and Planning* 170 (5): 205–16.

Bettencourt, L. M. A., J. Lobo, D. Helbing, C. Kühnert and G. B. West. 2007. 'Growth, Innovation, Scaling, and the Pace of Life in Cities'. *Proceedings of the National Academy of Sciences of the United States of America* 104 (17): 7301–306.

Bevan, R. 2006. *The Destruction of Memory: Architecture at War*. London: Reaktion Books.

Blair, T. 2010. *A Journey.* London: Random House.

Bleby, M. 2018. 'Australian Cities Give States Too Much Power over Planning'. *Australian Financial Review*, online, 21 May. https://www.afr.com/real-estate/fractured-governance-australian-cities-give-states-too-much-power-over-planning-20180521-h10cci. Accessed 8 June 2018.

Blincoe, N. 2017. 'Nick Land: Alt-Writer'. *Prospect Magazine*, 18 May. https://www.prospectmagazine.co.uk/philosophy/nick-land-the-alt-writer.

Blumenfeld, H. 1969. 'Criteria for Judging the Quality of the Urban Environment'. In *The Quality of Urban Life*, vol. 3. Edited by H. J. Schmandt and W. Bloomberg. Thousand Oaks, CA: Sage: 137–63.

Boccaccio, G. 1972. *The Decameron.* Translated by G. H. McWilliam. London: Penguin.

Boland, P. 2013. 'Sexing Up the City in the International Beauty Contest: The Performative Nature of Spatial Planning and the Fictive Spectacle of Place Branding'. *Town Planning Review* 84 (2): 251–74.

Boltanski, L., and L. Thevenot. 2006. *On Justification: Economies of Worth.* Princeton, NJ: Princeton University.

Bookchin, M. 1992. *Urbanization without Cities: The Rise and Decline of Citizenship.* New York: Black Rose Books.

Bowen, A. 2015. 'How to Make Your Life Look Like Your Instagram Feed'. *Chicago Tribune*, online, 8 September. http://www.chicagotribune.com/lifestyles/sc-fam-0915-my-instagram-life-2-20150908-story.html. Accessed 7 June 2018.

Bowsky, W. M. 1981. *The Mediaeval Italian Commune: Siena Under the Nine, 1287–1355.* Berkeley, Los Angeles, London: University of California Press.

———. 1962. 'The Buon Governo of Siena (1287–1355): A Mediaeval Italian Oligarchy'. *Speculum* 37 (3): 368–81.

Boym, S. 2017. *The Off-Modern.* New York and London: Bloomsbury Academic.

Brenner, N., ed. 2014. *Implosions/Explosions: Towards a Study of Planetary Urbanization.* Berlin: Jovis Verlag.

———. 2015. 'Is "Tactical Urbanism" an Alternative to Neoliberal Urbanism?' *Museum of Modern Art 'Post'.* 24 March. http://post.at.moma.org/content_items/587-is-tactical-urbanism-an-alternative-to-neoliberal-urbanism. Accessed 16 March 2018.

Brenner, N., and C. Schmid. 2013. *Towards a Theory of Extended Urbanization.* Havard and Zurich: Urban Theory Lab.

———. 2014. 'The "Urban Age" in Question'. *International Journal of Urban and Regional Research* 38 (3): 731–55.

Brittlebank, K. 2011. 'Accessing the Unseen Realm: The Historical and Textual Contexts of Tipu Sultan's Dream Register'. *Journal of the Royal Asiatic Society* 21 (2): 159–75.

Brockway, L. 1983. 'Plant Imperialism'. *History Today* 33 (7): 31–36.

Brown, G. 2017. *My Life, Our Times.* London: Random House.

Buck-Morss, S. 1989. *The Dialectics of Seeing: Walter Benjamin and the Arcades Project, Studies in Contemporary German Social Thought.* Cambridge, MA: The MIT Press.

Burrows, R. 1997. 'Cyberpunk as Social Theory: William Gibson and the Sociological Imagination'. In *Imagining Cities: Scripts, Signs, Memory*. Edited by S. Westwood and J. Williams. London: Routledge: 235–48.

Buxton, M. 2016. 'Melbourne's Planning Mess: We're on a High Rise to Hell'. *The Age*, 10 December. http://www.theage.com.au/comment/melbournes-planning-mess-were-on-a-high-rise-to-hell-20161209-gt7k31.html. Accessed 24 October 2017.

Buxton, M., and G. Tieman. 2005. 'Patterns of Urban Consolidation in Melbourne: Planning Policy and the Growth of Medium Density Housing'. *Urban Policy and Research* 23 (2): 137–57.

Buxton, M., R. Goodman and A. March. 2012. 'Planning Systems, Urban Form and Housing'. In *Australia's Unintended Cities: The Impact of Housing on Urban Development*. Edited by R. Tomlinson. Melbourne: CSIRO: 103–15.

Buxton, M., R. Goodman and S. Moloney. 2016. *Planning Melbourne: Lessons for a Sustainable City*. Melbourne: CSIRO.

Byrne, B. 2017. 'Never Get off the Boat: The "Seavangelist" Scam'. *The Baffler*, 20 December. https://thebaffler.com/latest/never-get-off-the-boat-byrne.

Byrne, M. 2016. '"Asset Price Urbanism" and Financialization after the Crisis: Ireland's National Asset Management Agency'. *International Journal of Urban and Regional Research* 40 (1): 31–45.

Cacciari, M. 1993. *Architecture and Nihilism: On the Philosophy of Modern Architecture*. Translated by S. Sartarelli. New Haven, CT: Yale University Press.

Çalışkan, K., and M. Callon. 2009. 'Economization, Part 1: Shifting Attention from the Economy towards Processes of Economization'. *Economy and Society* 38 (3): 369–98.

Callon, M., and F. Muniesa. 2005. 'Economic Markets as Calculative Collective Devices'. *Organization Studies* 26 (8): 1229–50.

Carl, P. 2000. 'Were Cities Built as Images?' *Cambridge Archaeological Journal* 10 (2): 327–65.

Carpentier, N., and E. Spinoy, eds. 2008. *Discourse Theory and Cultural Analysis: Media, Arts and Literature*. Creskill, NJ: Hampton Press.

Casey, E. 1997. *The Fate of Place: A Philosophical History*. Oakland: University of California Press.

Cassidy, J. 2013. 'Ronald Coase and the Misuse of Economics'. *New Yorker*, 3 September. https://www.newyorker.com/news/john-cassidy/ronald-coase-and-the-misuse-of-economics. Accessed July 2018.

Castells, M. 1979. 'The Wild City'. *The Urban Scene: Myths and Realities*. Edited by J. Feagin. Kingsport: Random House: 42–75.

Chalkley-Rhoden, S. 2017. 'World's Most Liveable City: Melbourne Takes Top Spot for Seventh Year Running'. *ABC News*, online, 16 August. http://www.abc.net.au/news/2017-08-16/melbourne-named-worlds-most-liveable-city-for-seventh-year/8812196. Accessed 7 June 2018.

Chayka, K. 2016. 'Welcome to Airspace: How Silicon Valley Helps Spread the Same Sterile Aesthetic Across the World'. *The Verge*, 3 August. https://www.theverge.com/2016/8/3/12325104/airbnb-aesthetic-global-minimalism-startup-gentrification. Accessed 16 June 2018.

Chisolm, D. 2001. 'The City of Collective Memory'. *GLQ: A Journal of Lesbian and Gay Studies* 7 (2): 195–243.

Chroscicki, J. 1998. 'Ceremonial Space'. In *Iconography, Propaganda, and Legitimation*. Edited by A. Ellenius. Oxford and New York: Clarendon Press: 194–216.

Clark, G., and T. Moonen. 2018. 'Creating Great Australian Cities'. Report to the Property Council by The Business of Cities. Property Council of Australia, Sydney.

Clark, N. 2000. 'Botanizing on the Asphalt? The Complex Life of Cosmopolitan Bodies'. *Body and Society* 6 (3/4): 12–33.

Cleghorn, H. 1865. *The Forests and Gardens of South India*. London: W. H. Allen.

Coase, R. 1960. 'The Problem of Social Cost'. *Journal of Law and Economics* 3 (October): 1–44.

Cobb, J. 2018. 'State of the Resistance'. *New Yorker*, 12 and 19 February. https://www.newyorker.com/magazine/2018/02/12/state-of-the-resistance.

Coleman, R., S. Tombs and D. Whyte. 2005. 'Capital, Crime Control and Statecraft in the Entrepreneurial City'. *Urban Studies* 42 (13): 2511–30.

Collettivo Euronomade. 2018. 'Criminalisation of Solidarity, Right to Escape, Solidarity Cities'. http://www.euronomade.info/?p=10517.

Condon, T. 2018. 'Tough Times Tipped for Our Clean, Green Cities'. *Australian*, 22 May: 2.

Conlon, J. 1999. 'Cities and the Place of Philosophy'. *Philosophy in the Contemporary World* 6: 43–49.

Connell, R. 1997. 'Why Is Classical Theory Classical?' *American Journal of Sociology* 102 (6): 1511–57.

———. 2007. *Southern Theory: The Global Dynamics of Knowledge in Social Science*. Sydney: Allen and Unwin.

Costello, L. 2005. 'From Prisons to Penthouses: The Changing Images of High-rise Living in Melbourne'. *Housing Studies* 20 (1): 49–62.

Cover, R. M. 1982. 'Forward: *Nomos* and Narrative'. *Harvard Law Review* 97.1 (4): 4–68.

Critchley, S., N. Power and T. Vermeulen. 2011. 'Theoretically Speaking'. *Freize*, 1 September. http://web.archive.org/web/20120201142518/http://www.frieze.com/issue/print_article/theoretically-speaking.

Cunningham, D. 2005. 'The Concept of Metropolis: Philosophy and Urban Form'. *Radical Philosophy* 133 (September/October): 13–25.

———. 2008. 'Spacing Abstraction: Capitalism, Law and the Metropolis'. *Griffith Law Review* 17 (2): 454–69.

———. 2009. 'Thinking the Urban: On Recent Writings on Philosophy and the City'. *CITY* 13 (4) (December): 517–30.

Dahl, R. A. 1978. 'Pluralism Revisited'. *Comparative Politics* 10 (2): 191–213.

Dalton, T. 1988. 'Architects, Engineers and Rent Collectors: An Organisational History of the Commission'. In *New Houses for Old. Fifty Years of Public Housing in Victoria*. Edited by R. Howe. Melbourne: Ministry of Housing and Construction.

Data Team. 2017. 'Global Liveability Has Improved for the First Time in a Decade: Melbourne Is the World's Most Liveable City for the Seventh Year Running'. *Economist*, online, 16 August. https://www.economist.com/graphic-detail/

2017/08/16/global-liveability-has-improved-for-the-first-time-in-a-decade. Accessed 7 June 2018.

Davies, W. 2014. *The Limits of Neoliberalism: Authority, Sovereignty and the Logic of Competition.* London: Sage.

Davis, M. 1990. *City of Quartz: Excavating the Future in Los Angeles.* London and New York: Verso.

Davis, M. 2005. *Planet of Slums.* London: Verso.

De Man, P. 1979. 'Autobiography as De-Facement'. *MLN* 94 (5): 919–30.

———. 1982. *Allegories of Reading: Figural Language in Rousseau, Nietzsche, Rilke and Proust.* New Haven, CT: Yale University Press.

De Pierrefeu, F., and Le Corbusier. 1942. *La Maison des Hommes.* Paris: Plon.

Dear, M. 1992. 'Understanding and Overcoming the NIMBY Syndrome'. *Journal of the American Planning Association* 58 (3): 288–300.

Debord, G. 1981. 'Theory of the Dérive'. *Situationist International Anthology.* Edited by Ken Knabb. Berkeley, CA: Bureau of Public Secrets.

DeLanda, M. 1991. *War in the Age of Intelligent Machines.* New York: Zone Books.

———. 1993. 'Virtual Environments and the Rise of Synthetic Reason'. In *Flame Wars.* Edited by M. Dery. Durham, NC: Duke University Press.

Deleuze, G. 1966. *Le Bergsonisme.* Paris: Presses Universitaries de France.

———. 1995. *Negotiations.* New York: Colombia University Press.

———. 1992. 'What Is the Event?' In *The Fold, Leibniz and the Baroque.* Translated by T. Conley. Minneapolis: Minnesota University Press: 76–81.

Deleuze, G., and F. Guattari. 1972. *Anti-Oedipus.* Minneapolis: Minnesota University Press.

———. 1987. *A Thousand Plateaus.* Minneapolis: University of Minnesota Press.

———. 1994. *What Is Philosophy?* New York: Columbia University Press.

DELWP (Department of Environment, Land, Water and Planning). 2015. *Better Apartments: A Discussion Paper.* Victorian Government Melbourne. http://delwp .vic.gov.au/__data/assets/pdf_le/0015/301542/Better-Apartments-Discussion -Paper-FINAL-ONLINE-version.pdf. Accessed 19 June 2015.

Derbyshire, A. 1996. 'Fifties Education: Architecture from a Former Student's Point of View'. 'AA 50/90' Symposium, Architectural Association. London, 16 November.

Derrida, J. 1974. 'White Mythology'. Translated by F. C. T. Moore. *New Literary History* 6 (1) (Autumn): 5–74.

———. 1981. 'Dissemination'. In *Dissemination.* Translated by B. Johnson. Chicago: University of Chicago Press: 317–401.

Desorisières, A. 1998. *The Politics of Large Numbers: A History of Statistical Reasoning.* Translated by C. Naish. Cambridge, MA: Harvard University Press.

Dickinson, L. A. 2003. 'The Promise of Hybrid Courts'. *American Journal of International Law* 97 (2): 295–310.

Dodson, J. 2012. 'Transforming Australia's "Housing Solution": How We Can Better Plan Suburbia to Meet Our Future Challenges'. In *Australia's Unintended Cities: The Impact of Housing On Urban Development.* Edited by R. Tomlinson. Melbourne: CSIRO: 19–34.

——. 2016. 'Suburbia in Australian Urban Policy'. *Built Environment* 42 (1): 23–36.

Donlan, V. n.d. *Living in the Country (Living in the City)*. ABC Music Publishing c/o Mushroom Music, n.p.

Donohoe, J. 2014. *Remembering Places*. Lanham, MD: Lexington Books.

——. 2017. 'Genetic Phenomenology and the Erasure of Place'. In *Place and Phenomenology*. Edited by J. Donohoe. London: Rowman & Littlefield International: 265–79.

Douglas, G. 2018. *The Help-Yourself City: Legitimacy and Inequality in DIY Urbanism*. Oxford: Oxford University Press.

Douglas, M. A., and A. Wildavsky. 1982. *Risk and Culture: An Essay on the Selection of Technological and Environmental Dangers*. Berkeley, CA: University of California Press.

Duncan, P. 2007. 'Drug User Grips Café Strip'. *Mercury*, 16 July: 5.

Dyer, G. 2008. *Climate Wars*. Melbourne: Scribe.

Elkin, S. L. 1985. 'Economic and Political Rationality'. *Polity* 18 (2): 253–71.

Elrick, J. W. 2017. 'Visionary Politics: Technologies of Government in the Capital of Innovation'. *Society & Natural Resources* 30 (7): 860–76.

Engels, F. 1968. *The Condition of the Working Class in England*. Translated and edited by W. O. Henderson and W. H. Chaloner. Stanford, CA: Stanford University Press.

Espeland, W., and M. Stevens. 1999. 'Commensuration as a Social Process'. *Annual Review of Sociology* 24: 313–43.

Fainstein, S. 2011. *The Just City*. Ithaca, NY: Cornell University Press.

Featherstone, M., and R. Burrows, eds. 1995. *Cyberspace/Cyberbodies/Cyberpunk: Cultures of Technological Embodiment*. London: Sage.

Fennell, C. 2015. *Last Project Standing: Civics and Sympathy in Post-Welfare Chicago*. Minneapolis: University of Minnesota Press.

Ferree, M. M., and C. McClurg Muller. 2004. 'Feminism and the Women's Movement: A Global Perspective'. In *The Blackwell Companion to Social Movements*. Edited by D. A. Snow, S. A. Soule and H. Kriesi. Oxford: Blackwell Publishing: 576–607.

Fielding-Smith, A. 2011. 'The Face of Freedom: Stories'. *Financial Times*, 9 December.

Filion, P., and Keil, R. 2017. 'Contested Infrastructures: Tension, Inequity and Innovation in The Global Suburb'. *Urban Policy and Research* 35 (1): 7–19.

Fincher, R., and L. Costello. 2005. 'Narratives of High-Rise Housing: Placing the Ethnicized Newcomer in Inner Melbourne'. *Social & Cultural Geography* 6 (2): 201–17.

Fine, M. D. 2007. *A Caring Society? Care and the Dilemmas of Human Service in the 21st Century*. Basingstoke: Palgrave Macmillan.

Fisher, M. 2011. 'Nick Land: Mind Games'. *Dazed and Confused*, 1 June. http://www.dazeddigital.com/artsandculture/article/10459/1/nick-land-mind-games.

Flanagan, K. 2015a. 'A Genealogy of Public Housing Production: Practice, Knowledge and the Broadacre Housing Estate'. *Housing, Theory and Society* 32 (4): 407–28.

——. 2015b. 'Ordinary Things: An Archaeology of Public Housing'. PhD thesis. School of Social Sciences, University of Tasmania, Hobart.

Florence, M. 1998 [c. 1980]. 'Foucault'. In *Michel Foucault: Aesthetic, Method, and Epistemology*, vol. 2. Edited by J. Faubion and translated by R. Hurley. New York: The New Press: 459–63.

Flores, S. 2013. 'The Roles of Solon in Plato's Dialogues'. PhD diss., Graduate School of The Ohio State University. https://etd.ohiolink.edu/pg_10?0::NO:10:P10_ETD_SUBID:5454. Accessed 17 January 2018.

Florida, R. 2012. 'America's Most Powerful Global Cities: Sizing Up the Global Clout of US Cities'. *CityLab*, 9 May. https://www.citylab.com/life/2012/05/americas-most-powerful-global-cities/1904/. Accessed 16 June 2018.

——. 2015. 'Sorry London: New York Is the World's Most Economically Powerful City'. *CityLab*, 3 March. https://www.citylab.com/life/2015/03/sorry-london-new-york-is-the-worlds-most-economically-powerful-city/386315/. Accessed 7 June 2018.

Florida, R., T. Gulden and C. Mellander. 2008. 'The Rise of the Mega-Region'. *Cambridge Journal of Regions Economy and Society* 1 (3): 459–76.

Forrest, T. 2007. *The Politics of Imagination. Benjamin, Kracauer, Kluge*. Bielefeld: Transcript Verlag.

Forster, C. 2006. 'The Challenge of Change: Australian Cities and Urban Planning in the New Millennium'. *Geographical Research* 44 (2): 173–82.

Foster, J. B. 2013. 'Marx and the Rift in the Universal Metabolism of Nature'. *Monthly Review* 65 (7). http://monthlyreview.org/2013/12/0/marx-rift-universal-metabolism-nature/. Accessed 10 September 2017.

Foth, M., P. Mitchell and C. Estrada-Grajales. 2018. 'Today's Internet for Tomorrow's Cities: On Algorithmic Culture and Urban Imaginaries'. In *Second International Handbook of Internet Research*. Edited by J. Hunsinger, L. Klastrup and A. M. Dordrecht: Springer.

Foucault, M. 1981 [1970]. 'The Order of Discourse'. In *Untying the Text: A Post-Structuralist Reader*. Edited by R. Young and translated by I. McLeod. London and New York: Routledge and Kegan Paul: 48–78.

——. 1983. 'Preface'. In *Anti-Oedipus: Capitalism and Schizophrenia*. Edited by G. Deleuze and F. Guattari. Minneapolis: University of Minnesota Press: xi–xiii.

——. 1991 [1980]. 'Questions of Method'. Translated by C. Gordon. In *The Foucault Effect: Studies in Governmentality: Two Lectures by and an Interview with Michel Foucault*. Edited by G. Burchell, C. Gordon and P. Miller and translated by C. Gordon. Harvester Wheatsheaf, Hemel Hempstead, UK: 73–86.

——. 2002 [1972]. *The Archaeology of Knowledge*. Translated by A. M. Sheridan Smith. London and New York: Routledge.

Franklin, A. 2010. *City Life*. London: Sage.

Freudenburg, W. R., and S. K. Pastor. 1992. 'NIMBYs and LULUs: Stalking the Syndromes'. *Journal of Social Issues* 48 (4): 39–61.

Friedmann, J. 2000. 'The Good City: In Defense of Utopian Thinking'. *International Journal of Urban and Regional Research* 24 (2): 460–72.

Frisby, D. 1985. *Fragments of Modernity: Theories of Modernity in the Work of Simmel, Kracauer and Benjamin*, 2013 edition. Abingdon: Routledge.

——. 2001. *Cityscapes of Modernity*. Cambridge: Polity.

Frugoni, C. 1991. *A Distant City: Images of Urban Experience in the Medieval World*. Translated by W. McQuaig. Princeton, NJ: Princeton University Press.

Fry, T. 2009. *Design Futuring*. Oxford: Berg.

———. 2012. *Becoming Human by Design*. London: Berg.

———. 2017. *Remaking Cities*. London: Bloomsbury.

Fryer-Smith, S. 2000. 'Safe Backyards? Freehold Land and Native Title'. *Legal Issues in Business* 2: 35–41.

Gadamer, H. G. 1986. *The Idea of the Good in Platonic-Aristotelian Philosophy*. New Haven, CT: Yale University Press.

Gandy, M. 2005. 'Learning from Lagos'. *New Left Review* 33 (May/June): 36–52.

Gane, N. 2014. 'The Emergence of Neoliberalism: Thinking through and beyond Michel Foucault's Lectures on Biopolitics'. *Theory, Culture and Society* 31 (4): 3–27.

Gardiner, M. 2017. 'Critique of Accelerationism'. *Theory, Culture & Society* 34 (1): 29–52.

Gavin, W. 2008. 'The Urban and the Aesthetic'. In *Philosophy and the City*. Edited by S. Meagher. Albany, NY: SUNY Press: 140–42.

Gehl Architects. 2010. *Hobart 2010: Public Spaces and Public Life*. Report to Hobart City Council. Gehl Architects, Copenhagen.

Gerrar, M. B. 1994. 'The Victims of NIMBY'. *Fordham Urban Law Journal* 21 (3): 495–522.

Giannetto, R. 2008. *Medici Gardens: From Making to Design*. Philadelphia: University of Pennsylvania Press.

Giddens, A. 1991. *Modernity and Self-Identity: Self and Society in the Late Modern Age*. Stanford, CA: Stanford University Press.

———. 1996. *The Consequences of Modernity*. Stanford, CA: Stanford University Press.

———. 1999. 'Risk and Responsibility'. *Modern Law Review* 62 (1): 1–10.

———. 2009. *Sociology*, sixth edition. Cambridge: Polity Press.

Gilloch, G. 1996. *Myth and Metropolis: Walter Benjamin and the City*. Cambridge, UK: Polity Press.

Ginsberg, R. 2004. *The Aesthetics of Ruins*. Amsterdam and New York: Rodopi.

Glaeser, E. L. 2011. *The Triumph of the City*. London: Macmillan.

Gleeson, B. 2010. *Lifeboat Cities*. Sydney: UNSW Press.

———. 2012. '"Make No Little Plans": Anatomy of Planning Ambition and Prospect'. *Geographical Research* 50 (3): 242–55.

Gleeson, B. J., and P. A. Memon. 1994. 'The NIMBY Syndrome and Community Care Facilities: A Research Agenda for Planning'. *Planning Practice and Research* 9 (2): 105–18.

Glynos, J. 2001. 'The Grip of Ideology: A Lacanian Approach to the Theory of Ideology'. *Journal of Political Ideologies* 6 (2): 191–214.

Glynos, J., and D. Howarth. 2007. *Logics of Critical Explanation in Social and Political Theory*. London: Routledge.

Goldhill, O. 2017. 'The Neo-Fascist Philosophy That Underpins Both the Alt-Right and Silicon Valley Technophiles'. *Quartz,* 18 June. https://qz.com/1007144/the-neo-fascist-philosophy-that-underpins-both-the-alt-right-and-silicon-valley-techno philes/.

Goodman, R., M. Buxton and S. Moloney. 2016. *Planning Melbourne: Lessons for a Sustainable City*. Melbourne: CSIRO.

Graham, S. 2016. *Vertical: The City from Satellites to Bunkers*. Verso: London.

Graham, S., and L. Hewitt. 2012. 'Getting Off the Ground: On the Politics of Urban Verticality'. *Progress in Human Geography* 37 (1): 72–92.

Gray, R. 2017. 'Behind the Internet's Anti-Democracy Movement'. *The Atlantic*, 10 February. https://www.theatlantic.com/politics/archive/2017/02/behind-the-inter nets-dark-anti-democracy-movement/516243/.

Greenspan, A. 2014. *Shanghai Future: Modernity Remade*. London: Hurst & Company.

Gunder, M. 2003. 'Passionate Planning for the Others' Desire: An Agonistic Response to the Dark Side of Planning'. *Progress in Planning* 60 (2003): 235–319.

Gunder, M., and J. Hillier. 2009. *Planning in Ten Words or Less: A Lacanian Entanglement with Spatial Planning*. Farnham: Ashgate.

Guyer, J. I. 2007. 'Prophecy and the Near Future: Thoughts on Macroeconomic, Evangelical, and Punctuated Time'. *American Ethnologist* 34 (3): 409–21.

H.M. Treasury. 2007. *Independent Reviews*, online list, http://webarchive.national archives.gov.uk/20071204130205/http://www.hm-treasury.gov.uk/Independent_ Reviews/independent_reviews_index.cfm. Accessed 2 November 2017.

Haacke, P. 2011. 'The Vertical Turn: Topographies of Metropolitan Modernism'. PhD diss., University of California, Berkeley.

Hague Justice Portal. (n.d.). www.haguejusticeportal.net/index.php?id=305. Accessed 4 September 2018.

Haider, S. 2017. 'The Darkness at the End of the Tunnel: Artificial Intelligence and Neoreaction'. *Viewpoint Magazine*, 28 March. https://www.viewpointmag.com/ 2017/03/28/the-darkness-at-the-end-of-the-tunnel-artificial-intelligence-and -neoreaction/.

Hale, J. R. 1977. *Florence and the Medici*. London: Thames and Hudson.

Hamilton, C., and R. Denniss. 2005. *Affluenza: When Too Much Is Never Enough*. Crows Nest, NSW: Allen and Unwin.

Hampton, P. 2009. 'Marxism, Metabolism and Ecology'. *Workers Liberty* (July): 20–27.

Hanna, B. 1991. 'Utopia and Dystopia: Modernity, Public Housing and Australian Architectural History'. PhD diss., University of Sydney.

Hanssen, B. 2006. *Walter Benjamin and the Arcades Project*. New York: Continuum.

Hardt, M., and A. Negri. 2017. *Assembly*. New York: Oxford University Press.

Harris, A. 2015. 'Vertical Urbanisms: Opening Up Geographies of the Three-Dimensional City'. *Progress in Human Geography* 39 (5): 601–20.

Hartmann, T. 2004. *The Last Hours of Ancient Sunlight: The Fate of the World and What We Can Do Before It's Too Late*. New York: Harmony.

Harvey, D. 1973. *Social Justice and the City*. Baltimore: Johns Hopkins University Press.

———. 2003. 'The Right to the City'. *International Journal of Urban and Regional Research*. 27 (4): 939–41.

——. 2012. *Rebel Cities*. London: Verso.

——. 2014. "Cities or Urbanization?" In *Implosions/Explosions: Towards a Study of Planetary Urbanization*. Edited by N. Brenner. Berlin: Jovis Verlag: 52–66.

Hasan, M. 1971. *History of Tipu Sultan*. Second revised and enlarged edition. Delhi: Aakar Books.

Hatherley, O. 2009. *Militant Modernism*. Hampshire: OBooks.

Hawkes, J., and A. Shimada, eds. 2009. *Buddhist Stupas in South Asia*. Delhi: Oxford University Press.

Hayward, D. 1996. 'The Reluctant Landlords? A History of Public Housing in Australia'. *Urban Policy and Research* 14 (1): 5–31.

Healy, S. 2004. 'A "Post-Foundational" Interpretation of Risk: Risk as "Performance"'. *Journal of Risk Research* 7 (3): 227–96.

Heidegger, M. 1962. *Being and Time*. Translated by J. Macquarrie and E. Robinson. London: Blackwell.

——. 1999. *Contributions to Philosophy (From Enowning)*. Translated by P. Emad and K. Maly. Bloomington: Indiana University Press.

——. 2013. *The Event*. Translated by R. Rojcewitz. Bloomington: Indiana University Press.

Heitzman, J. 2008. *The City in South Asia*. New York: Routledge.

Hell, J. 2008. 'Imperial Ruin Gazers, or Why Did Scipio Weep?' In *Ruins of Modernity*. Edited by J. Hell and A. Schönle. Durham, NC: Duke University Press.

Hell, J., and A. Schönle. 2008. *Ruins of Modernity*. Durham, NC: Duke University Press.

Herrnstein, R., and C. Murray. 1994. *The Bell Curve: Intelligence and Class Structure in American Life*. New York: Free Press.

Hetherington, K. and A. M. Cronin, eds. 2008. *Consuming the Entrepreneurial City: Image, Memory, Spectacle*. New York and London: Routledge.

Heynen, N., M. Kaika and E. Swyngedouw, eds. 2006. *In the Nature of Cities: Urban Political Ecology and the Politics of Urban Metabolism*. New York: Routledge.

Hinchliffe, S., M. Kearnes, M. Degen and S. Whatmore. 2005. 'Urban Wild Things: A Cosmopolitical Experiment'. *Environment and Planning D: Society and Space* 23: 643–58.

Hirschman, A. 1970. *Exit, Voice, and Loyalty: Responses to Decline in Firms, Organizations, and States*. Cambridge, MA: Harvard University Press.

——. 2005. *Bury the Chains: The British Struggle to Abolish Slavery*. London: Macmillan.

Hogan, B. 2010. 'The Presentation of Self in the Age of Social Media: Distinguishing Performances and Exhibitions Online'. *Bulletin of Science, Technology and Society* 30 (6): 377–86.

Hoodfar, H. 2018. 'Daughters of the Revolution: The Iranian Women Who Risk Arrest for Protesting against Hijab Laws and Demanding Equal Rights'. *The Conversation*. http://theconversation.com/iranian-women-risk-arrest-daughters-of-the-revolution-92880.

Hoogenboom, M., and R. Ossewaarde. 2005. 'From Iron Cage to Pigeon House: The Birth of Reflexive Authority'. *Organizational Studies* 26 (4): 601–19.

Hubbert, M. K. 1949. 'Energy from Fossil Fuels'. *Science* 109: 103–9.

Hughes, R. 1996. *The Fatal Shore: A History of the Transportation of Convicts to Australia, 1787–1868.* Harvill, London.

Huyssen, A. 2008. 'Authentic Ruins: Products of Modernity'. In *Ruins of Modernity.* Edited by J. Hell and A. Schönle. Durham: Duke University Press.

Invest Victoria. 2018. 'World's Most Liveable City, Seven Years Running'. 30 May. Department for Economic Development, Jobs, Transport and Resources, Melbourne. http://www.invest.vic.gov.au/why-melbourne/the-worlds-most-liveable -city?card=2386. Accessed 7 June 2018.

Invisible Committee. 2009. *The Coming Insurrection.* Los Angeles: Semiotext(e).

———. 2015. *To Our Friends.* Los Angeles: Semiotext(e).

Isin, E. F. 1992. *Cities without Citizens. The Modernity of the City as a Corporation.* Montreal and New York: Black Rose.

———. 2002. *Being Political. Geneologies of Citizenship.* Minneapolis and London: University of Minnesota Press.

Jabareen, Y. 2015. *The Risk City: Cities Countering Climate Change: Emerging Planning Theories and Practices around the World.* London: Springer.

Jabareen, Y., and N. Carmon. 2010. 'Community of Trust: A Socio-Cultural Approach for Community Planning and the Case of Gaza'. *Habitat International* 34 (4): 446–53.

Jabareen, Y., E. Eizenberg and O. Zilberman. 2017. 'Conceptualizing Urban Ontological Security: "Being-in-the-City" and Its Social and Spatial Dimensions'. *Cities* 68: 1–7.

Jacobs, J. 1972 [1961]. *The Death and Life of Great American Cities.* London and Melbourne: Penguin Books.

Jacobs, K., and K. Flanagan. 2018. 'Shun Profit Motive in Housing Fix'. *The Mercury*, 23 March: 20.

Jameson, F. 1991. *Postmodernism, or, The Cultural Logic of Late Capitalism.* Durham, NC: Duke University Press.

———. 2005. *Archaeologies of the Future: The Desire Called Utopia and Other Science Fictions.* London: Verso.

Jasanoff, S. 1986. *Risk Management and Political Culture: A Comparative Study of Science in the Policy Context.* New York: Russell Sage Foundation.

———. 1999. 'The Songlines of Risk'. *Environmental Values* 8 (2): 135–52.

Jinarajadasa, C. 2005. *A Divine Vision of Man, Nature, and God.* Adyar: Theosophical Publishing House.

———. 2006. *Flowers and Gardens.* Adyar: Theosophical Publishing House.

———. 2007. *In His Name.* Adyar: Theosophical Publishing House.

———. 2008. *How We Remember Our Past Lives.* Adyar: Theosophical Publishing House.

Jones, M. A. 1972. *Housing and Poverty in Australia.* Melbourne: Melbourne University.

Jurkevics, A. 2017. 'Hannah Arendt Reads Carl Schmitt's *The Nomos of the Earth*: A Dialogue on Law and Geopolitics from the Margins'. *European Journal of Political Theory* 16 (3): 345–66.

Kahn, R. 1931. 'The Relation of Home Investment to Unemployment'. *Economic Journal* 41 (162): 173–98.

Kaldor, M. 2006. *New and Old Wars*. Cambridge, MA: Polity Press.

Kallergis, K. 2016. 'Miami Faces $3.5T Loss, Highest Risk of Sea-Level Rise Among All Coastal Cities'. *The Real Deal*, 16 August. https://therealdeal.com/miami/2016/08/16/miami-faces-3-5t-loss-highest-risk-of-sea-level-rise-among-all-coastal-cities-report/. Accessed 11 January 2018.

Kapferer, J-N., and V. Bastien. 2009. 'The Specificity of Luxury Management: Turning Marketing Upside Down'. *Journal of Brand Management* 16 (5/6): 311–22.

Kasinitz, P., ed. 1995. *Metropolis: Center and Symbol of Our Times, Main Trends of the Modern World*. New York: New York University Press.

Katsilidis, F. 2017. 'Australia 108'. www.australia108.com.au. Accessed 24 October 2017.

Katz, B., and J. Nowak. 2017. *The New Localism: How Cities Can Thrive in the Age of Populism*. Washington, DC: Brookings Institution.

Keith, M. 2014. 'Arrivals between Bildungsroman and the City Commons'. In *Migration: A COMPAS Anthology*. Edited by B. Anderson and M. Keith. Oxford: COMPAS.

Keith, M., S. Lash, J. Arnoldi and T. Rooker. 2013. *China Constructing Capitalism: Economic Life and Urban Change*. London and New York: Routledge.

Keller, E. F. 2008. 'Organisms, Machines, and Thunderstorms: A History of Self-Organisation, Part One'. *Historical Studies in the Natural Sciences* 38 (1): 45–75.

———. 2009. 'Organisms, Machines, and Thunderstorms: A History of Self-Organisation, Part Two'. *Historical Studies in the Natural Sciences* 39 (1): 1–31.

———. 2016. 'Open Letter to SF Mayor Ed Lee and Greg Suhr (Police Chief)'. 15 February. https://justink.svbtle.com/open-letter-to-mayor-ed-lee-and-greg-suhr-police-chief. Accessed 16 March 2018.

Kelly, K. 1994. *Out of Control: The New Biology of Machines, Social Systems and the Economic World*. New York: Basic Books.

Keynes, J. M. 1964. *The General Theory of Employment, Interest, and Money*, London: Harvest/HBJ Book.

Klein, N. 2001. *No Logo*. London: Flamingo.

———. 2014. *This Changes Everything: Capitalism vs. the Climate*. London: Allen Lane.

Koch, E. 1991. *Mughal Architecture: An Outline of Its History and Development (1526–1858)*. Munich: Prestel-Verlag.

Koh, S. Y., B. Wissink and R. Forrest. 2016. 'Reconsidering the Super-Rich: Variations, Structural Conditions and Urban Consequences'. In *Handbook on Wealth and the Super-Rich*. Edited by I. Hay and J. Beaverstock. Cheltenham: Edward Elgar: 18–40.

Kojève, A. 1980 [1947]. *Introduction à la lecture de Hegel*. Paris: Gallimard.

Kolbert, E. 2014. *The Sixth Extinction*. New York: Henry Holy.

Koolhaas, R., and Harvard Project on the City. 2001. 'Lagos'. *Mutations.* Barcelona: Actar: 651–719.

Krivý, M. 2018. 'Towards a Critique of Cybernetic Urbanism: The Smart City and the Society of Control'. *Planning Theory* 17 (1): 8–30.

Lacan, J. 1988. *The Seminar, Book I: Freud's Papers on Technique* (1953–1954), Cambridge: Cambridge University Press.

———. 2006. *Écrits*. New York: W. W. Norton.

Laclau, E. 1990. *New Reflections on the Revolution of Our Time*. London: Verso.

———. 2005. *On Populist Reason*. London: Verso.

Laclau, E., and C. Mouffe. 1985. *Hegemony and Socialist Strategy: Towards a Radical Democratic Politics*. London: Verso.

Laing, R. D. 1969. *Self and Others*. London: Tavistock Publications.

———. 1973. *The Divided Self*. Harmondsworth: Penguin Books.

Lake, R. W. 1993. 'Rethinking NIMBY'. *Journal of the American Planning Association* 59 (1): 87–93.

Lamont, M. 2012. 'Toward a Comparative Sociology of Valuation and Evaluation'. *Annual Review of Sociology* 38: 201–21.

Land, N. 1992. *Thirst for Annihilation: Georges Bataille and Virulent Nihilism*. London: Routledge.

———. 1993. 'Machinic Desire'. *Textual Practice* 7 (3): 471–82.

———. 1995. 'Meat (or How to Kill Oedipus in Cyberspace)'. In *Cyberspace/Cyberbodies/Cyberpunk: Cultures of Technological Embodiment*. Edited by M. Featherstone and R. Burrows. London: Sage: 191–204.

———. 2011. *Fanged Noumena: Collected Writings 1987–2007*. Edited by R. Brassier and R. Mackay. Falmouth: Urbanomic.

———. 2012. 'The Dark Enlightenment'. http://www.thedarkenlightenment.com/the-dark-enlightenment-by-nick-land/.

———. 2014. 'Hyper-Racism'. https://alternative-right.blogspot.com/2014/10/hyper-racism.html.

———. 2016. 'The F-Word'. *The Daily Caller*, 17 October. http://dailycaller.com/2016/10/17/the-f-word/.

———. 2017. 'A Quick-and-Dirty Introduction to Accelerationism'. *Jacobite*, 25 May. https://jacobitemag.com/2017/05/25/a-quick-and-dirty-introduction-to-accelerationism/.

Lapavitsas, C. 2013. *Profiting without Producing: How Finance Exploits Us All*. London: Verso.

Latour, B. 1998. 'To Modernize or Ecologise? That Is the Question'. In *Remaking Reality: Nature at the Millennium*. Edited by B. Braun and N. Castree. London: Routledge: 221–42.

———. 1999. *Pandora's Hope: Essays on the Reality of Science Studies*. Cambridge, MA: Harvard University Press.

———. 2008. 'A Cautious Prometheus ? A Few Steps Toward a Philosophy of Design (with Special Attention to Peter Sloterdijk)'. In *Proceedings of the 2008 Annual International Conference of the Design History Society*. Cornwall, UK: Universal Publishers: 2–10.

Laugier, M. 1756. *An Essay on the Study and Practice of Architecture*. London: Stanley Crowder and Henry Woodgate.

Laurier, E., A. Whyte and K. Buckner. 2001. 'An Ethnography of a Neighbourhood Café: Informality, Table Arrangements and Background Noise'. *Journal of Mundane Behaviour* 2 (2): 195–232.

Le Corbusier. 1925. *Urbanisme.* Paris: Editions Crès.

———. 1941. *Destin de Paris.* Paris and Clermont-Ferrand: F. Sorlot.

———. 1947. *The Four Routes.* Translated by D. Todd. London: Dennis Dobson.

———. 1985. *Towards a New Architecture.* Translated by F. Etchells. New York: Dover.

———. 1989. *The City of To-Morrow and Its Planning.* New York: Dover.

Lefebvre, Henri. 1971. *Everyday Life in the Modern World.* Translated by S. Rabnovitch. Harmondsworth: Allen Lane.

———. 1991. *The Production of Space.* Translated by D. Nicholson-Smith. Oxford: Blackwell.

———. 1996. *Writings on Cities.* Translated by E. Kofman and E. Lebas. Cambridge, MA: Wiley Blackwell.

———. 2003. *The Urban Revolution.* Translated by R. Bononno. Minneapolis: University of Minnesota Press.

———. 2014. "Dissolving City, Planetary Metamorphosis." In *Implosions/Explosions: Towards a Study of Planetary Urbanization.* Edited by N. Brenner. Translated by L. Corroyer, M. Potvin and N. Brenner. Berlin: Jovis Verlag: 566–70.

———. 2016a. *Metaphilosophy.* Translated by D. Fernbach. London and New York: Verso.

———. 2016b. *Marxist Thought and the City.* Translated by R. Bononno. Minneapolis: University of Minnesota Press.

Leontidou, L. 1996. 'Alternatives to Modernism in (Southern) Urban Theory: Exploring In-Between Spaces'. *International Journal of Urban and Regional Research* 20 (2): 178–95.

Levey, M. 1996. *Florence: A Portrait.* London: Random House.

Levinas, E. 1969. *Totality and Infinity.* Translated by A. Lingis. Pittsburgh, PA: Duquesne University Press.

Lewis, R. W. B. 1996. *The City of Florence.* New York: Henry Holt.

Lidskog, R., and I. Elander. 1992. 'Reinterpreting Locational Conflicts: NIMBY and Nuclear Waste Management in Sweden'. *Policy and Politics* 20 (4): 249–64.

Live in Melbourne. 2017. 'Melbourne Is Still the World's Most Liveable City'. 16 August. Department of Economic Development, Jobs, Transport and Resources, Melbourne. https://liveinmelbourne.vic.gov.au/news-events/news/2017/melbourne-is-still-the-worlds-most-liveable-city. Accessed 7 June 2018.

Livesey, G. 2010. 'Deleuze, Whitehead, the Event, and the Contemporary City'. https://whiteheadresearch.org/occasions/conferences/event-and-decision/papers/Graham%20Livesey_Final%20Draft.pfd.

The Local. 2017. 'Stuttgart Is the Least Stressful City in the World, Study Finds'. *The Local,* 13 September. https://www.thelocal.de/20170913/stuttgart-rated-least-stressful-city-in-the-world. Accessed 7 June 2018.

Lury, C., L. Parisi and T. Terranova, eds. 2012. 'The Becoming Topological of Culture: Introduction'. *Theory, Culture and Society* 29 (4/5): 3–35.

Luxenburg, A. 1998. 'Creating Desastres: Andrieu's Photographs of Urban Ruins in the Paris of 1871'. *The Art Bulletin* 80 (1):113–37.

Lydon, M., D. Bartman, R. Woudstra and A. Khawarzad. 2011. *Tactical Urbanism: Short Term Action, Long Term Change*, vol. 1. https://issuu.com/streetplanscollaborative/docs/tactical_urbanism_vol.1.

Macaulay, R. 1950. *The World My Wilderness*. London: Virago Press.

MacDougald, P. 2015. 'The Darkness Before the Right'. *The Awl*, 28 September. https://www.theawl.com/2015/09/the-darkness-before-the-right/.

———. 2016a. 'Why Peter Thiel Wants to Topple Gawker and Elect Donald Trump'. *New York Magazine*, 14 June. http://nymag.com/selectall/2016/06/peter-thiel.html.

———. 2016b. 'Accelerationism, Left and Right', 14 May. https://pmacdougald.word press.com/2016/04/14/accelerationism-left-and-right/.

Mackay, R. 2012. 'Nick Land—An Experiment in Inhumanism'. *Umělec Magazine*, January. http://divus.cc/london/en/article/nick-land-ein-experiment-im-inhumanismus.

Mackay, R., and A. Avanessian. 2014. *#ACCELERATE: The Accelerationist Reader*. Falmouth: Urbanomic.

MacKenzie, D., F. Muniesa and L. Siu, eds. 2007. *Do Economists Make Markets? On the Performativity of Economics*. Princeton, NJ: Princeton University Press.

Malpas, J. 2009. 'Cosmopolitanism, Branding and the Public Realm'. In *Branding Cities: Cosmopolitanism, Parochialism and Social Change*. Edited by S. H. Donald, E. Kofman and C. Kevin. New York: Routledge: 189–97.

———. 2012. *Heidegger and the Thinking of Place*. Cambridge, MA: MIT Press.

———. 2018. *Place and Experience: A Philosophical Topography*. Abingdon: Routledge, 2nd edition.

———. 2002. 'Urban Form and Globalization After September 11th: The View from New York'. *International Journal of Urban and Regional Research* 26 (3): 596–606.

Marcuse, P., and D. Madden. 2016. *In Defense of Housing: The Politics of Crisis*. London: Verso.

Marcuse, P., J. Connolly, J. Novy, I. Olivo, C. Potter and J. Steil, eds. 2009. *Searching for the Just City: Debates in Urban Theory and Practice*. London and New York: Routledge.

Marx, K. 1957. *Capital: A Critique of Political Economy*, vol. 1. Translated by S. Moore and E. Aveling. London: Lawrence and Wishart.

———. 1967. *Writings of the Young Marx on Philosophy and Society*. New York: Doubleday.

———. 1973. *Grundrisse*. Translated by M. Nicholaus. Harmondsworth: Penguin.

Marx, K., and F. Engels. 1967. *The Communist Manifesto*. Translated by S. Moore. Harmondsworth: Penguin.

Mason, P. 2015. *Postcapitalism: A Guide to Our Future*. London: Allen Lane.

May, J., J. Wills, K. Datta, Y. Evans, J. Herbert and C. McIlwaine. 2007. 'Keeping London Working: Global Cities, The British State and London's New Migrant Division of Labour'. *Transactions of the Institute of British Geographers* 32 (2): 151–67.

Mazzini, D. A. 2004. *Villa Medici, Fiesole: Leon Battista Alberti and the Prototype of the Renaissance Villa*. Translated by C. Howard. Florence: Centro Di della Edifimi.

McNeill, D. 2005. 'Skyscraper Geography'. *Progress in Human Geography* 29 (1): 41–55.

Mearsheimer, J. 2001. *The Tragedy of Great Power Politics.* New York: W.W. Norton.

Mehan, A. 2017a. *The Empty Locus of Power: Production of Political Urbanism in Modern Tehran.* Unpublished PhD diss. Politecnico di Torino.

———. 2017b. Review of 'The Empty Place: Democracy and Public Space' by Teresa Hoskyns. *ID: International Dialogue, A Multidisciplinary Journal of World Affairs*, 7, 86–90.

Melhuish, C., M. Degen and G. Rose. 2014. 'Architectural Atmospheres: Affect and Agency of Mobile Digital Images in the Material Transformation of the Urban Landscape in Doha'. *Tasmeem* 4. Accessed 1 March 2017.

Merrifield, A. 2013. *The Politics of the Encounter: Urban Theory and Protest Under Planetary Urbanization.* Athens: University of Georgia Press.

Mirowski, P. 2014. *Never Let a Serious Crisis Go to Waste: How Neoliberalism Survived the Financial Meltdown.* London: Verso.

Mitchell, D. 2014. *The Right to the City. Social Justice and the Fight for Public Space.* New York: Guilford Press.

Mitchell, T. 2002. *Rule of Experts: Egypt, Techno-Politics, Modernity.* Princeton, NJ: Princeton University Press.

Moldbug, M. 2017. *Patchwork: A Political System for the 21st Century.* https://www.unqualified-reservations.org/.

Moreno, L. 2014. 'The Urban Process Under Financialised Capitalism'. *City* 18 (3): 244–68.

Moretti, E. 2010. 'Local Multipliers'. *American Economic Review* 100 (2): 373–77.

Mugerauer, R. 1994. *Interpretations on Behalf of Place.* Albany, NY: SUNY Press.

Mulcahy, L. 2007. 'Architects of Justice: The Politics of Courtroom Design'. *Social & Legal Studies* 16 (3): 383–403.

Mumford, L. 1989. *The City in History.* Orlando: Harcourt.

Muniesa, F. 2012. 'A Flank Movement in the Understanding of Valuation'. *Sociological Review* 59 (s2): 24–38.

Muniesa, F. 2017. 'On the Political Vernaculars of Value Creation'. *Science as Culture* 26 (4): 445–54.

Nagle, A. 2017. *Kill All Normies: Online Culture Wars from 4hgan and Tumblr to Trump and the Alt-Right.* Winchester: Zero Books.

Nancy, J. L. 2007. *The Creation of the World, or Globalization.* Translated by F. Raffoul and D. Pettigrew. Albany: State University of New York Press.

Nethercote, M. forthcoming. 'Melbourne's Vertical Expansion and the Political Economies of High-Rise Residential Development, Urban Studies'.

———. 2018. 'Theorising Vertical Urbanisation'. *City* (November): 1–28. DOI: 10.1080/13604813.2018.1549832.

No author. 1975. 'Trees and Plants at Adyar'. *The Theosophist, C. Jinarajadasa Centenary 1875–1975*, 97 (3): 148–50.

Norwich, J. 2001. 'The Religion of Empire'. Review of *Venice Lion City*, by Gerry Wills. *Los Angeles Times Book Review*, 30 September.

Noys, B. 2010. *The Persistence of the Negative: A Critique of Contemporary Continental Theory*. Edinburgh: Edinburgh University Press.

———. 2014. *Malign Velocities: Accelerationism and Capitalism*. London: Zero Books.

Nussbaum, M. 2000. *Women and Human Development*. Cambridge: Cambridge University Press.

———. 2004. 'Beyond the Social Contract: Capabilities and Global Justice'. *Oxford Development Studies* 32 (1): 3–18.

———. 2006. *Frontiers of Justice: Disability, Nationality and Species Membership*. Boston: Harvard University Press.

Obenga, T. 2004. African Philosophy: The Pharaonic Period, 2780–330 BC. Popenguine, Senegal: Per Ankh.

O'Hanlon, S. 1998. 'Modernism and Prefabrication in Postwar Melbourne'. *Journal of Australian Studies* 22 (57): 108–18.

O'Neill, P. 2017. 'Managing the Private Financing of Urban Infrastructure'. *Urban Policy and Research* 35 (1): 32–43.

———. 2015. 'The Work of Seduction: Intimacy and Subjectivity in the London "Seduction Community"'. *Sociological Research Online* 20 (4). http://journals .sagepub.com/doi/abs/10.5153/sro.3744.

O'Sullivan, S. 2014. 'The Missing Subject of Accelerationism'. *Mute*, 12 September. http://www.metamute.org/editorial/articles/missing-subject-accelera tionism.

Ooi, C-S. 2011. 'Paradoxes of City Branding and Societal Changes'. In *City Branding: Theory and Cases*. Edited by K. Dinnie. Basingstoke, UK: Palgrave Macmillan: 54–61.

Orsenna, É. 2004. *Les Chavaliers du Subjonctif.* Paris: Stock.

Osborne, P. 2004. 'The Reproach of Abstraction'. *Radical Philosophy* 127 (September/October): 21–28.

Overy, S. 2015. 'The Genealogy of Nick Land's Anti-Anthropocentric Philosophy: A Psychoanalytic Conception of Machinic Desire'. PhD diss., Newcastle University. https://theses.ncl.ac.uk/dspace/bitstream/10443/3350/1/Overy%2c%20S.%20 2016.pdf.

Paganoni, M. C. 2012. 'City Branding and Social Inclusion in the Global City'. *Mobilities* 7 (1): 13–31.

Pawson, H. 2017. 'One in 10 Australian Dwellings Are Empty—and a Vacancy Tax Won't Solve the Problem'. *The Conversation*, 17 July. http://www.abc.net .au/news/2017-07-17/vacancy-tax-wont-solve-australias-empty-housing-prob lem/8709184. Accessed 24 October 2017.

Peck, J., E. Siemiatycki and E. Wyly. 2014. 'Vancouver's Suburban Involution'. *City* 18 (4/5): 386–415.

Pensky, M. 2001. *Melancholy Dialectics: Walter Benjamin and the Play of Mourning*. Pbk. ed., *Critical Perspectives on Modern Culture*. Amherst: University of Massachusetts Press.

Perroux, F. 1966. Le multiplicateur d'investissement dans les pays sous-développés. *Revue Tiers Monde* 7 (27): 511–32.

Petty, J. 2016. 'The London Spikes Controversy: Homelessness, Urban Securitisa-
tion and The Question of "Hostile Architecture"'. *International Journal for Crime,
Justice and Social Democracy* 5 (1): 67–81.

Phillips, A. 1998. *The Politics of Presence*. Oxford: Oxford University Press.

Pinceti, C. S., and P. Bunje. 2012. 'The Study of Urban Metabolism and its Application to Urban Planning and Design'. *Environmental Pollution* 167: 184–85.

Pinkney, D. H. 1958. *Napoleon III and the Rebuilding of Paris*. Princeton, NJ: Princeton University Press.

Plant, S. 1992. *The Most Radical Gesture: The Situationist International in a
Postmodern Age*. London: Routledge.

———. 1995. 'The Future Looms: Weaving Women and Cybernetics'. In *Cyber-
space/Cyberbodies/Cyberpunk: Cultures of Technological Embodiment*. Edited by
M. Featherstone and R. Burrows. London: Sage: 45–64.

Polzer, J. 2002. 'Ambrogio Lorenzetti's "War and Peace" Murals Revisited: Contributions to the Meaning of the "Good Government Allegory"'. *Artibus et Historiae*
23 (45): 63–105.

Poovey, M. 1998. *A History of the Modern Fact: Problems in the Knowledge of the
Sciences of Wealth and Society*. Chicago: the University of Chicago Press.

Postone, M. 1993. *Time, Labor and Social Domination: A Reinterpretation of Marx's
Critical Theory*. Cambridge: Cambridge University Press.

Pradeau, J-F. 2002. *Plato and the City: A New Introduction to Plato's Political
Thought*. Translated by J. Lloyd. Exeter: Exeter University Press.

Pryor, S. 2018. 'Canberra "Better Than the Brand", Says British Urbanist'. *Canberra Times*, online, 23 May. https://www.canberratimes.com.au/canberra-news/
canberra-better-than-the-brand-says-british-urbanist-20180523-p4zh3k.html. Accessed 8 June 2018.

Przyblyski, J. M. 1995. 'Moving Pictures: Photography, Narrative, and the Paris
Commune of 1871'. In *Cinema and The Invention of Modern Life*. Edited by V. R.
Schwartz and L. Charney. Berkeley: University of California Press.

Puchner, M. 2009. 'The Theatre of Alain Badiou'. *Theatre Research International*
34 (3): 256.

Raabus, C. 2010. 'From New York to Hobart; Making Cities "People Friendly"'. ABC
Hobart, 2 December. http://www.abc.net.au/local/stories/2010/12/02/3082960.htm.
Accessed 8 June 2018.

Rawls, J. 1999. *A Theory of Justice*. Cambridge, MA: Harvard University Press.

———. 2001. *Justice as Fairness. A Restatement*. Cambridge, MA: Harvard University Press.

RBA (Reserve Bank of Australia). 2017. 'Houses and Apartments in Australia, with
Tom Rosewall and Michael Shoory'. https://www.rba.gov.au/publications/bulle
tin/2017/jun/pdf/bu-0617-1-houses-and-apartments-in-australia.pdf. Accessed 25
October 2017.

Reader, J. 2005. *Cities*. London: Vintage.

Rebar Architects. 2016. 'Interview with Rebar'. *The Agent* 3 (Fall): n.p.

Reckwitz, A. 2002. 'Toward a Theory of Social Practices: A Development in Cultur-
alist Theorizing'. *European Journal of Social Theory* 5 (2): 243–63.

Rentschler, R., K. Lehman and I. Fillis. 2018. 'A Private Entrepreneur and His Art Museum: How MONA Took Tasmania to the World'. In *Creative Industries and Entrepreneurship: Paradigms in Transition from a Global Perspective*. Edited by L. Lazzeretti and M. Vecco. Cheltenham, UK: Edward Elgar Publishing, 136–55.

Reynolds, H. 2006. *The Other Side of the Frontier: Aboriginal Resistance to the European Invasion of Australia*, rev. ed. Sydney: University of New South Wales Press.

Reynolds, J. A. 1907. *Fifteen Discourses Delivered in the Royal Academy*. London: J.M. Dent.

Reynolds, S. 2009. '*Renegade Academia*: The Cybernetic Culture Research Unit'. http://energyflashbysimonreynolds.blogspot.co.uk/2009/11/renegade-academia-cybernetic-culture.html.

Rhys Davids, T. W., Translated 2000. *Buddhist Suttas*. Translated from Pali. Escondido, CA: Book Tree.

Richards, S. 2003. *Le Corbusier and the Concept of Self*. New Haven, CT: Yale University Press.

———. 2007. 'The Antisocial Urbanism of Le Corbusier'. *Common Knowledge* 13 (1): 50–66.

Ricoeur, P. 1991. 'Narrative Identity'. *Philosophy Today* (Spring): 73–80.

———. 2000. *The Just*. Translated by D. Pellauer. Chicago and London: University of Chicago Press.

———. 2004. *Memory, History, Forgetting*. Translated by K. Blamey and D. Pellauer. Chicago: University of Chicago Press.

Rittel, H. W. J., and M. M. Webber. 1973. 'Dilemmas in a General Theory of Planning'. *Policy Sciences* 4 (2): 155–69.

Ritzer, G., and N. Jurgenson. 2010. 'Production, Consumption, Prosumption: The Nature of Capitalism in the Age of the Digital "Prosumer"'. *Journal of Consumer Culture* 10 (1): 13–36.

Robinson, J. 2013. 'The Urban Now: Theorising Cities Beyond the New'. *European Journal of Cultural Studies* 16 (6): 659–77.

Rogers, D. 2017. *The Geopolitics of Real Estate: Reconfiguring Property, Capital and Rights*. London: Rowman & Littlefield International.

Rogers, D., C. Lee and D. Yan. 2015. 'The Politics of Foreign Investment in Australian Housing: Chinese Investors, Translocal Sales Agents and Local Resistance'. *Housing Studies* 30 (5): 730–48.

Rogers, R., and R. Brown. 2017. *A Place for All People: Life, Architecture and Social Responsibility*. London: Canongate.

Rohrmann, B. 2006. 'Cross-Cultural Comparison of Risk Perceptions: Research, Results, Relevance'. Presented at the ACERA/SRA Conference. http://www.acera.unimelb.edu.au.

Rose, N., and T. Osborne. 1999. 'Governing Cities: Notes of the Spatialisation of Virtue'. *Environment and Planning D: Society and Space* 17 (6): 737–60.

Ross, J. 1910. *Lives of the Early Medici*. London: Chatto and Windus.

Rossi, U. 2018. 'The Populist Eruption and the Urban Question'. *Urban Geography* 39 (9): 1425–30.

Rossi, U., and A. Vanolo. 2012. *Urban Political Geographies. A Global Perspective*. London: Sage.

Rothschild, E. 2002. *Economic Sentiments: Adam Smith, Condorcet and the Enlightenment*. Boston: Harvard University Press.

Royall, I. 2017. 'Family to Love the High Life At 100-Storey Australia 108 Residential Tower at Southbank'. *Herald Sun.* http://www.heraldsun.com.au/news/victoria/family-to-love-the-high-life-at-100storey-australia-108-residential-tower-at-south bank/news-story/e4b00f01691e301825eab9e20e77f4f1. Accessed 24 October 2017.

Rubinstein, N. 1958. 'Political Ideas in Sienese Art: The Frescoes by A. Lorenzetti and T. di Bartolo in the Palazzo Pubblico'. *Journal of the Warburg and Courtauld Institutes* 21 (3/4): 179–207.

Ruddick, S. 2015. 'Situating the Anthropocene: Planetary Urbanization and the Anthropological Machine'. *Urban Geography* 36 (8): 1113–30.

Ruming, K. 2013. 'Social Mix Discourse and Local Resistance to Social Housing: The Case of the Nation Building Economic Stimulus Plan, Australia'. *Urban Policy and Research* 32 (2): 163–83.

Ruming, K., and R. Goodman. 2016. 'Planning System Reform and Economic Development: Unpacking Policy Rhetoric and Trajectories in Victoria and New South Wales'. *Built Environment* 42 (1): 72–89.

Sandel, M. 2013. *What Money Can't Buy: The Moral Limits of Markets.* London: Penguin.

Sandercock, L. 1997. 'From Main Street to Fortress: The Future of Malls as Public Spaces—OR—"Shut Up and Shop"'. *Just Policy* 9: 27–34.

Sassen, S. 1996. 'New Employment Regimes in Cities: The Impact on Immigrant Workers'. *Journal of Ethnic and Migration Studies* 22 (4): 579–94.

———. 1999. *Guests and Aliens*. New York: New Press.

———. 2002. 'Global Cities and Survival Circuits'. In *Global Woman: Nannies, Maids, and Sex Workers in the New Economy*. Edited by B. Ehrenreich and A. R. Hochschild. New York: Henry Holt and Company: 254–74.

———. 2008. *Territory, Authority, Rights: From Medieval to Global Assemblages*.

———. 2010. 'When the City Itself Becomes a Technology of War'. *Theory, Culture & Society* 27 (6): 33–50.

———. 2013. 'Does the City Have Speech?' *Public Culture* 25 (2): 209–21.

Schama, S. 1996. *Landscape and Memory*. New York: Vintage Books.

Schnall, M. 2017. '2018 Will Be the Year of Women', 14 December. online. https://www.cnn.com/2017/12/14/opinions/2018-will-be-the-year-of-women-schnall/in dex.html.

Schönle, A. 2006. 'Ruins and History: Observations on Russian Approaches to Destruction and Decay'. *Slavic Review* 65 (4): 649–69.

Scott, H. 1933. *Introduction to Technocracy.* New York: John Day.

Scott, J. C. 1998. *Seeing Like a State: How Certain Schemes to Improve the Human Condition Have Failed.* New Haven, CT and London: Yale University Press.

Seaford, R. 2004. *Money and the Early Greek Mind: Homer, Philosophy, Tragedy.* Cambridge: Cambridge University Press.

Sen, A. 1979. *Equality of What? The Tanner Lecture on Human Values.* Delivered at Stanford University. 22 May.

——. 1999. *Development as Freedom.* Oxford: Oxford University Press.

——. 2009. *The Idea of Justice.* London: Penguin.

Sennett, R. 2017. *The Foreigner: Two Essays on Exile.* London: Notting Hill Editions.

Seth, S. 2009. 'Putting Knowledge in its Place: Science, Colonialism, and the Postcolonial'. *Postcolonial Studies* 12 (4): 373–88.

Sheen, V. 2013. 'The Precariat Is Recruiting: Youth, Please Apply'. *The Conversation,* 10 January. https://theconversation.com/the-precariat-is-recruiting-youth -please-apply-10550. Accessed 14 June 2018.

Shimada, A. 2012. 'The Use of Garden Imagery in Early Indian Buddhism'. In *Garden and Landscape Practices in Pre-Colonial India: Histories from the Deccan.* Edited by D. Ali and E. J. Flatt. New Delhi: Routledge: 18–38.

Sica, G. 2007. *The Florentine Villa: Architecture, History, Society.* Translated by U. Creigh. Abingdon: Routledge.

Simmel, G. 1959 (1911). 'The Ruin'. In *Georg Simmel, 1858-1918.* Edited by K. H. Wolff. Columbus: Ohio State University Press.

——. 1990. *The Philosophy of Money.* Translated by T. Bottomore and D. Frisby. London: Routledge.

——. 1997. "The Metropolis and Mental Life." In *Simmel on Culture: Selected Writings.* Translated by H. Gerth. London, Thousand Oaks, CA, and New Delhi: Sage: 174–85.

Simmel, G. 2002 (1903). 'The Metropolois and Mental Life'. In *The Blackwell City Reader.* Edited by G. Bridge and S. Watson. Oxford and Malden, MA: Wiley-Blackwell: 11–19.

Skinner, Q. 1999. 'Ambrogio Lorenzetti's Buon Governo Frescoes: Two Old Questions, Two New Answers'. *Journal of the Warburg and Courtauld Institutes* 62: 1–28.

Sloterdijk, P. 2013. *In the World Interior of Capital.* Translated by W. Hoban. Cambridge: Polity.

Smith, N. 1996. *The New Urban Frontier.* London: Routledge.

——. 2002. 'New Globalism, New Urbanism: Gentrification as Global Urban Strategy'. *Antipode* 34 (3): 427–50.

Snary, C. 2004. 'Understanding Risk: The Planning Officers' Perspective'. *Urban Studies* 41 (1): 33–55.

Sohn-Rethel, A. 1978. *Intellectual and Manual Labor: A Critique of Epistemology.* Translated by M. Sohn-Rethel. Atlantic Highlands, NJ: Humanities Press.

Soja, E. W., and J. M. Kanai. 2014. "The Urbanization of the World." In *Implosions/ Explosions: Towards a Study of Planetary Urbanization.* Edited by N. Brenner. Berlin: Jovis Verlag: 142–59.

Soja, E. W. 2010. *Seeking Spatial Justice.* Minneapolis: University of Minnesota Press.

Sommerfield, J., M. S. Kouyate and R. Sauerborn. 2002. 'Perceptions of Risk, Vulnerability, and Disease Prevention in Rural Burkina Faso: Implications for Community-Based Healthcare and Insurance'. *Human Organization* 2: 139–46.

Sontag, S. 2002. 'Looking at War'. *New Yorker*, 9 December: 82–98.

Spaulding, N. W. 2012. 'The Enclosure of Justice: Courthouse Architecture, Due Process, and the Dead Metaphor of Trial'. *Yale Journal of Law & the Humanities* 24 (1): 311–43.

Spiller, M. 2013. 'Social Justice and the Centralisation of Governance in the Australian Metropolis: A Case Study of Melbourne'. *Urban Policy and Research* 32 (3): 361–80.

Srinivas, S. 2001. *Landscapes of Urban Memory: The Sacred and the Civic in India's High-Tech City*. Minneapolis: University of Minnesota Press.

———. 2015. *A Place for Utopia: Urban Designs from South Asia*. Seattle: University of Washington Press/Hyderabad: Orient Blackswan.

Srnicek, N., and A. Williams. 2016. *Inventing the Future: Postcapitalism and a World without Work*. London: Verso.

Standing, G. 2014. *The Precariat: The New Dangerous Class*, revised edition. London and New York: Bloomsbury Academic.

Stark, D. 2011a. 'What's Valuable?' In *The Worth of Goods: Valuation and Pricing in the Economy*. Edited by J. Beckert and P. Aspers. Oxford: Oxford University Press.

———. 2011b. *The Sense of Dissonance: Accounts of Worth in Economic Life*. Princeton, NJ: Princeton University Press.

Stavrakakis, Y. 1999. *Lacan and the Political*. London: Routledge.

———. 2007. *The Lacanian Left*. Edinburgh: Edinburgh University Press.

Stavrakakis, Y., and N. Chrysoloras. 2006. '(I Can't Get No) Enjoyment: Lacanian Theory and the Analysis of Nationalism'. *Psychoanalysis, Culture and Society* 11 (2): 144–63.

Steadman-Jones, G. 2012. *Masters of the Universe: Hayek, Friedman and the Birth of Neoliberal Politics*. Princeton, NJ: Princeton University Press.

Steele, W., K. Hussey and S. Dovers. 2017. 'What's Critical About Critical Infrastructure?' *Urban Policy and Research* 35 (1): 74–86.

Stephens, S. 2016. 'Plato's Egyptian Republic'. In *Greco-Egyptian Interactions*. Edited by I. Rutherford. Oxford: Oxford University Press: 41–59.

Stoekl, A. 1990. 'Truman's Apotheosis: Bataille, "Planisme", and Headlessness'. *Yale French Studies* 78: 181–205.

Stoler, A. L. 2008. "Imperial Debris: A Reflection on Ruins and Ruination." *Cultural Anthropology* 23 (2): 191–219.

———. 2013. *Imperial Debris: On Ruins and Ruination*. Durham, NC: Duke University Press.

Stringer, C. 2011. *The Origin of Our Species*. New York: Allen Lane.

Sultan, T., and M. Husain. 1900. *The Dreams of Tipu Sultan*. Karachi: Times Press.

Sundara Rao, B. N. 1985. *Bengalurina Ithihasa [A History of Bangalore]*. Bangalore: Vasanta Sahitya Granthamala.

Swyngedouw, E. 2006. 'Circulations and Metabolisms: (Hybrid) Natures and (Cyborg) Cities'. *Science as Culture* 15 (2): 105–21.

———. 2011. 'Every Revolution Has Its Squares': Politicising the Post-Political City. In *Urban Constellations*. Edited by M. Gandy. Berlin: Jovis: 22–25.

———. 2014. 'Where Is the Political? Insurgent Mobilisations and the Incipient "Return of the Political"'. *Space and Polity* 18 (2): 122–36.

Tafuri, M. 1976. *Architecture and Utopia: Design and Capitalist Development*. Cambridge, MA: MIT Press.

Takahashi, L. M., and M. J. Dear. 1997. 'The Changing Dynamics of Community Opposition to Human Service Facilities'. *Journal of the American Planning Association* 63 (1): 79–93.

Talty, A. 2017. 'Bangkok Named Most Popular City for International Tourists in 2017'. *Forbes*, 26 September. https://www.forbes.com/sites/alexan dratalty/2017/09/26/bangkok-named-most-popular-city-for-international-tourists -in-2017/#4e729cc025a2. Accessed 7 June 2018.

Tanke, J. J. 2011. *Jacques Rancière: An Introduction*. London, New York: Continuum.

Taylor, P. J., P. Ni, B. Derudder, M. Hoyler, J. Huang, F. Lu, K. Pain, F. Witlox, X. Yang, D. Bassens and W. Shen. 2009. 'Measuring the World City Network: New Results and Developments'. *GaWC Research Bulletin* 300. Loughborough, UK: Globalization and World Cities Research Network.

Thiel, P. 2009. 'The Education of a Libertarian'. *Cato Unbound: A Journal of Debate*, 13 April. https://www.cato-unbound.org/2009/04/13/peter-thiel/education-libertarian.

Thukral, N. 2016. 'As Asia's Rice Crop Shrivels, Food Security Fears Resurface'. *Reuters*, 2 May. https://www.reuters.com/article/us-asia-rice/as-asias-rice-crop-shriv els-food-security-fears-resurface-idUSKCN0XS1NG. Accessed 20 January 2018.

Tibbits, G. 1988. 'The Enemy within Our Gates: Slum Clearance and High-Rise Flats'. In *New Houses for Old. Fifty Years of Public Housing in Victoria*. Edited by R. Howe. Melbourne: Ministry of Housing and Construction.

Tohidi, N. 2016. 'Women's Rights and Feminist Movements in Iran'. *SUR 24* 13 (24): 75–89.

Trexler, R. C. 1991. *Public Life in Renaissance Florence*. Ithaca, NY: Cornell University Press.

Trimble, M. 2017. 'The World's 10 Most Elegant Cities: France Is Home to the World's Most Elegant City'. *US News*, 27 October. https://www.usnews.com/ news/best-countries/articles/2017-10-27/the-10-most-elegant-cities-around-the -world. Accessed 7 June 2018.

Turku, H. 2017. *The Destruction of Cultural Property as a Weapon of War*. Washington, DC: Palgrave.

Turok, I., J. Budlender and J. Visagie. 2017. 'The Role of Informal Urban Settlement in Upward Mobility'. *World Bank DPRU Working Paper*, February. https://www .africaportal.org/documents/16716/DPRU_WP201701.pdf. Accessed 21 January 2018.

United Nations Department of Economic and Social Affairs, 2018. '68% of theW Population Projected to Live in Urban Areas by 2050, Says UN', New York, 16 May, https://www.un.org/development/desa/en/news/population/2018-revision-of -world-urbanization-prospects.html.

United Nations High Commissioner for Refugees (UNJCR). 2018. *Global Trends Report 2017*. Geneva: UNHCR. https://www.unhcr.org/5b27be547.pdf. Accessed 13 December 2018.

Urry, J., T. Birtchnell, J. Caletrio and S. Pollastri. 2014. *Living in the City*. Department of Business, Innovation and Skills Future Cities Foresight.

Vance, J. 1990. *The Continuing City: Urban Morphology in Western Civilization*. Baltimore: Johns Hopkins University Press.

van der Haak, B. 2002. *Lagos/Koolhaas*. Film. Directed by B. van der Haak. New York: First Run/Icarus Films.

van der Veer, P. 2001. *Imperial Encounters: Religion and Modernity in India and Britain*. Princeton, NJ and Oxford: Princeton University Press.

———. 2009. 'Spirituality in Modern Society'. *Social Research* 76 (4): 1097–120.

Vaneigem, R. 2001. *The Revolution of Everyday Life*. London: Rebel Press.

Vasari, G. 1987. *Lives of the Artists*, vol. 2. Translated by G. Bull. London: Penguin.

Verdouw, J. J. 2016. 'The Subject Who Thinks Economically? Comparative Money Subjectivities in Neoliberal Context'. *Journal of Sociology* 53 (3): 523–40.

Vidler, A. 2010. 'Air War and Architecture'. In *Ruins of Modernity*. Edited by J. Hell and A. Schönle. Durham, NC: Duke University Press.

Virilio, P. 2005. *City of Panic*. Translated by J. Rose. Oxford: Berg.

Virno, P. 2015. 'L'usage de la vie'. *Multitudes* 58: 143–58.

Vogl, J. 2015. *The Specter of Capital*. Translated by J. Redner and R. Savage. Stanford, CA: Stanford University Press.

Wall-E. 2008. Directed by A. Stanton. Burbank, CA: Walt Disney Home Entertainment.

Walzer, M. 1983. *Spheres of Justice: A Defense of Pluralism and Equality*. New York: Basic Books.

Watson, C. 1993. 'Trends in World Urbanisation'. In *Proceedings of the First International Conference on Urban Pests*. Edited by K. B. Wildey and W. H. Robinson. Cambridge: Cambridge University Press: 1–8.

Weber, M. 1958. *The City*. Translated and edited by D. Martindale and G. Neuwirth. Glencoe: The Free Press.

Weitz, R. 2008. 'Who's Afraid of The Big Bad Bus? Nimbyism and Popular Images of Public Transit'. *Journal of Urbanism* 1 (2): 157–72.

Weizman, E. 2014. *Forensis: The Architecture of Public Truth*. Berlin: Sternberg Press.

Welsh, I. 1993. 'The NIMBY Syndrome: Its Significance in the History of the Nuclear Debate in Britain'. *British Journal for the History of Science* 26: 15–32.

Welter, V. 2003. *Biopolis: Patrick Geddes and the City of Life*. Cambridge, MA: MIT Press.

Westacott, J. 2017. 'Trade Opens Up Economy to a Wealth of Ideas'. *Australian*, 28 January. https://www.theaustralian.com.au/news/inquirer/trade-opens-up-economy -to-a-wealth-of-ideas/news-story/b3f6e9f7065346319cb06d5afbde58d1. Accessed 7 June 2018.

Westcoat, J., and J. Wolschke-Bulmahn, eds. 1996. *Mughal Gardens: Sources, Places, Representations*. Washington, DC: Dumbarton Oaks.

Wexler, M. N. 1996. 'A Sociological Framing of the NIMBY (Not-In-My-Backyard) Syndrome'. *International Review of Modern Sociology* 26 (1): 91–110.

Whatmore, S., and S. Hinchliffe. 2003. 'Living Cities: Making Space for Urban Nature'. *Soundings a Journal of Politics and Culture* 22: 137–50.

Whitehead, A. N. 1978. *Process and Reality*. New York: Free Press.

Wiener, N. 1961. *Cybernetics or Control and Communication in the Animal and the Machine*. Cambridge, MA: MIT Press.

Williams, D. R. 2002. 'Leisure Identities, Globalization, and the Politics of Place'. *Journal of Leisure Research* 34 (4): 351–67.

WIPO: World Intellectual Property Organization. 2013. *Customary Law, Traditional Knowledge and Intellectual Property: An Outline of the Issues*; www.wipo.int/export/sites/www/tk/en/resources/pdf/overview_customary_law.pdf.

Wirth, L. 1938. 'Urbanism as a Way of Life'. *American Journal of Sociology* 44 (1): 1–24.

Wolman, A. 1965. 'The Metabolism of Cities'. *Scientific American* 213 (3): 179–90.

Wolsink, M. 2006. 'Invalid Theory Impedes Our Understanding: A Critique on the Persistence of the Language of NIMBY'. *Transactions of the Institute of British Geographers* NS 31 (1): 85–91.

Woodward, C. 2002. *In Ruins*. London: Vintage.

Zamora, D., and M. Behrent, eds. 2016. *Foucault and Neoliberalism*. Cambridge: Polity.

Zhao, X., N. Salehi, S. Naranjit, S. Alwaalan, S. Voida and D. Cosley. 2013. 'The Many Faces of Facebook: Experiencing Social Media as Performance, Exhibition, and Personal Archive'. Paper to Conference on Human Factors in Computing Systems, 27 April–2 May, Paris.

Zipp, S. 2012. 'The Roots and Routes of Urban Renewal'. *Journal of Urban History* 39 (3): 366–91.

Žižek, S. 1991. *Looking Awry: An Introduction to Jacques Lacan through Popular Culture*. Cambridge, MA: MIT Press.

———. 1993. *Tarrying with the Negative*. Durham, NC: Duke University Press.

———. 1999. *The Ticklish Subject. The Absent Centre of Political Ontology*. London: Verso.

Zukin, S. 1991. *Landscapes of Power: From Detroit to Disney World*. Berkeley: University of California Press.

Index

About the Contributors

Roger Burrows is Professor of Cities, Global Urban Research Unit, School of Architecture, Planning and Landscape at Newcastle University in the UK. Burrows is a social scientist who has published on housing and urban studies, the history of research methods, social media, health, illness and the body and various other topics. His most recent research has been concerned with the impact of transnational wealth elites on neighbourhoods in London and the history of spatial classification technologies. His most recent book is the coauthored *The Predictive Postcode* (2018). Before working at Newcastle, he was employed by Goldsmiths, University of London, and the University of York before that.

Katie Campbell is a writer and garden historian. She lectures widely and has taught at Birkbeck, Bristol and Buckingham universities. She writes for various publications and leads art and garden tours for such companies as Martin Randall, Artsturs, Italian Journeys and Penny Howard. Her most recent book, *British Gardens in Time*, accompanied by the BBC television series. Her penultimate book, *Paradise of Exiles*, explores the eccentric Anglo-American garden makers in late-nineteenth-century Florence. Earlier garden books include *Icons of Twentieth Century Landscape Design and Policies* and *Pleasances, A Guide to Scotland's Gardens*. She is currently working on a book about how the Medici villas reflect the changing ideas of the Renaissance.

David Cunningham is Deputy Director of the Institute for Modern and Contemporary Culture at the University of Westminster in the UK. He is a long-standing editor of the journal *Radical Philosophy* and has published widely on philosophy, architecture and urban theory, including in the journals *CITY,*

Journal of Architecture and *Journal of Visual Culture*. He is currently working on a book on the epic and the theory of the novel.

Janet Donohoe is Dean of the Honors College and Professor of Philosophy at the University of West Georgia. She is the author of several articles on phenomenology and place, as well as a book on Husserlian ethics and a book titled *Remembering Places* (2014). She recently edited the volume *Place and Phenomenology* (2017).

Efrat Eizenberg is an environmental psychologist and Assistant Professor at the Faculty of Architecture and Town Planning at The Technion in Israel. Her research topics include urban regeneration, urban struggles and the politics of space, urban nature, landscape perception and planning with communities. She is the author of *From the Ground Up: Community Gardens in New York City and the Politics of Spatial Transformation* (2013).

Kathleen Flanagan is Deputy Director of the Housing and Community Research Unit, at the University of Tasmania. Flanagan previously worked in research, policy and advocacy roles in the Tasmanian community sector. She was awarded her PhD in 2015 for research that used Foucauldian archaeology to understand and problematize the history of the Tasmanian public housing system. A monograph based on the PhD titled *Housing, Neoliberalism and the Archive: Reinterpreting the Rise and Fall of Public Housing* will be published in 2019. Flanagan's work is concerned with questioning the 'taken-for-granted' of contemporary housing policy. She is interested in the ways in which housing, especially social housing and its tenants, is thought about and acted upon by policymakers and in the different ways of thinking and acting that might be possible.

Emma Fraser is Lecturer in Media and Cultural Studies at the University of Lancaster in the UK. Fraser recently completed her PhD on urban ruins and video games at the University of Manchester. Her work is concerned with urban ruins and decay, the work of Walter Benjamin and the fundamentally fragmented nature of digital media. Fraser has researched ruins in Paris, Berlin, London, Detroit, Chernobyl, Sydney and elsewhere, and written on the Apple Watch, urban play, the games *The Last of Us* and *Fallout 3*, urban exploration, and ruin tourism.

Tony Fry is a design and cultural theorist, an award-winning designer, writer and educator. He is Adjunct Professor at the Creative Exchange Institute University of Tasmania in Australia, and Visiting Professor at the University of Ibagué in Colombia. Fry was formerly Professor of Design at the Griffith University in Queensland, and Director of the EcoDesign Foundation Sydney. He is the author of twelve books, including most recently *City Futures in the Age of a Changing Climate* (2015) and *Remaking Cities: An Introduction to Metrofitting* (2017). Fry's current research centres on postconflict urban environments, technology and the rise of the 'design in the Global South' movement.

Yosef Jabareen focuses on the nexus between planning theory and practices in two realms: sustainability and climate change, as well as justice and urban rights. His recent book, *The Risk City*, presents a new theory regarding contemporary city plans and the evolving risk and uncertainties.

Keith Jacobs is Professor of Sociology at the University of Tasmania in Australia. He has published widely on housing and urban policy issues and is the author of *Neoliberal Housing Policy: An International Perspective* to be published in 2019.

Michael Keith is Director of the Centre on Migration, Policy and Society (COMPAS) and holds a personal chair in the Department of Anthropology at the University of Oxford. His research interests focus on the interface between culture, urbanism and migration. His current work looks at the dynamics of urbanism, the study of cultural difference and the impact of migration on structures and processes of governance. His recent books include *Constructing Capitalism in China, London and New York* (2013) and *Power, Identity and Representation: Race, Governance and Mobilisation in British Society*.

Jeff Malpas is Distinguished Professor at the University of Tasmania and Visiting Distinguished Professor at Latrobe University. He has published across a number of disciplines, including philosophy, but also architecture, geography and the arts. A new and revised edition of *Place and Experience* was published in 2018.

Asma Mehan is Postdoctoral Research Fellow at the Future Urban Legacy Lab (FULL) and China Room at Politecnico di Torino in Italy. Mehan earned her PhD from the Department of Architecture and Design (DAD) at Politecnico di Torino in 2017. She was previously visiting Research Fellow at EPFL University in Lausanne, Switzerland, and the Alfred Deakin Institute (ADI) at Deakin University, in Melbourne, Australia. Mehan's work engages critically with the past and present culture of cities in relation to the politics, philosophy, social studies and planning transfers in the Global South focusing especially on Muslim-majority countries in Southeast Asian and Middle Eastern contexts.

Megan Nethercote is a Vice Chancellor's Post-Doctoral Research Fellow at the Centre for Urban Research at RMIT University, Australia. Megan has research interests in urban studies and housing and is currently researching the regulation, design and lived experience of higher-density urban development.

Wendy Pullan is Professor of Architecture and Urban Studies at the University of Cambridge where she is Director of the Centre for Urban Conflicts Research. She was Principal Investigator for 'Conflict in Cities and the Contested State', an international and multidisciplinary research project funded by the Large Grants Programme of the Economic and Social Research Council of the United Kingdom, for which she received the Royal Institute of British Architects' President's Award for Research. Pullan has published widely on European and Middle Eastern architecture and cities, examining the processes of urban heritage, conflict and change, both historical and contemporary. She has done advisory work on issues to do with divided cities, urban uncertainty and Middle Eastern conflicts, especially Jerusalem, including reports and briefing papers for Chatham House, the UN, ICOMOS and various NGOs. Her recent publications include *Locating Urban Conflicts* (2013), *The Struggle for Jerusalem's Holy Places* (2013) and *Violent Infrastructures, Places of Conflict* (2018). She is a Fellow of Clare College, Cambridge.

Ugo Rossi is Associate Professor of Economic and Political Geography at the University of Turin, Italy, and editor of the *Dialogues in Human Geography* journal. He is an urban geographer interested in the critical analysis of urban economies as well as in the appraisal of the political potential of urban environments from a progressive viewpoint. He is author of *Cities in Global Capitalism* (2017), coauthor of *Urban Political Geographies: A Global Perspective* (2012) and coeditor of *The Urban Political: Ambivalent Spaces of Late Neoliberalism* (2018). As part of his political engagement, he is an active member of Euronomade, a collective of researchers and activists engaged in antiracist, feminist and neomunicipalist struggles and in campaigns for a postwork society.

Simon Sadler teaches the history and theory of architecture, design and urbanism at the University of California, Davis, where he is Professor in the Department of Design. Sadler's publications include *Archigram: Archi-*

tecture without Architecture; *Non-Plan: Essays on Freedom, Participation and Change in Modern Architecture and Urbanism*, with coeditor Jonathan Hughes; and *The Situationist City*.

Saskia Sassen is the Robert S. Lynd Professor of Sociology and Member of the Committee on Global Thought at Columbia University (www.saskiasassen.com). Her latest book is *Expulsions: Brutality and Complexity in the Global Economy* (2014), which is available in eighteen languages. She is the recipient of diverse awards, including multiple doctor honoris causa and the Principe de Asturias 2013 Prize in the Social Sciences. She was made a Foreign Member of the Royal Academy of the Sciences of the Netherlands.

Smriti Srinivas, Professor in the Department of Anthropology at the University of California, Davis, has worked extensively on the intersections between embodiment, religiosity and spatiality. Her books include: *A Place for Utopia: Urban Designs from South Asia* (2015); *In the Presence of Sai Baba: Body, City, and Memory in a Global Religious Movement* (2008); *Landscapes of Urban Memory: The Sacred and the Civic in India's High-Tech City* (2001/2004); and *The Mouths of People, the Voice of God: Buddhists and Muslims in a Frontier Community of Ladakh* (1998). She has received numerous grants for her work from institutions such as the Mellon Foundation, the Rockefeller Foundation, the National Endowment for the Humanities, the American Academy of Religion, the Atlanta History Center, India Foundation for the Arts and others. She has led many collaborative projects and faculty-graduate initiatives: most recently, a University of California Humanities Network Working Group (2012–2013) and Multi-Campus Research Group (2013–2015) on religion, place-making and cities; and a Mellon Research Initiative on 'Reimagining Indian Ocean Worlds (2015–2018)'.

Wendy Steele is Associate Professor in Sustainability and Urban Planning, colocated in the School of Global, Urban and Social Studies (GUSS) and the Centre for Urban Research (CUR) at RMIT University, Melbourne, Australia. Her research focuses on wild cities in a climate of change.

Allan Stoekl is Professor Emeritus of French and Comparative Literature at Penn State University and is currently a Visiting Scholar in the Design and Architecture Department at the University of Pennsylvania. He is the author of, among other works, *Bataille's Peak: Energy, Religion, Post-Sustainability* (2007). He is currently working on a book analysing the various implications of the word, and concept, of 'sustainability', from a historical and philosophical perspective.

CPSIA information can be obtained
at www.ICGtesting.com
Printed in the USA
LVHW021701161219
640676LV00002B/162/P